GLOBAL DOWNTOWNS

THE CITY IN THE TWENTY-FIRST CENTURY

Eugenie L. Birch and Susan M. Wachter, Series Editors

A complete list of books in the series
is available from the publisher.

GLOBAL DOWNTOWNS

Edited by

Marina Peterson

and Gary W. McDonogh

UNIVERSITY OF PENNSYLVANIA PRESS

PHILADELPHIA

Published by
University of Pennsylvania Press
Philadelphia, Pennsylvania 19104-4112
www.upenn.edu/pennpress

Printed in the United States of America
on acid-free paper
10 9 8 7 6 5 4 3 2 1

Library of Congress Cataloging-in-Publication Data
Global downtowns / edited by Marina Peterson and Gary
McDonogh. — 1st ed.
p.   cm. — (The city in the twenty-first century)
Includes bibliographical references and index.
ISBN 978-0-8122-4384-0 (hardcover : alk. paper)
1. City Planning—20th century.   2. Central business
districts.   3. Urban anthropology.   4. Culture and
globalization.   I. McDonogh, Gary W.   II. Peterson,
Marina.   III. Series: The city in the twenty-first century.
HT166.G577   2011
307.3'4209—dc23   2011024487

CONTENTS

Introduction: Globalizing Downtown

Gary W. McDonogh and Marina Peterson

"DOWNTOWN!" The word itself, like its myriad global cognates including *el centro*, *wasat al-madina*, *centre ville*, and *zhongwan*, evokes intensities at the core of urban life, space, and capital: "Bright lights, surging crowds, tall buildings, big money, power politics." To speak of *global* downtowns demands careful analysis of the particularities of place and people as well as examination of shared processes connecting and transforming cities worldwide as dense, active sites of encounter, competition, celebration, and conflict. In this volume, we look at widespread processes, knowledge, and mediations underpinning the formations of such central spaces. We consider the global elements of individual cases, the civic consciousness and elite strategies that connect downtowns around the world, and the points of conflict and transformation that spill out into streets and spaces from Barcelona to Los Angeles, Beirut to Mumbai. We listen to and interpret competitive politicians, multinational corporations, cosmopolitan planners, and itinerant tourists while recognizing local citizens, associations, artistic vanguards, and excluded voices in the day-to-day reconstitution of space and image. As crucibles of international flows, downtowns offer unique vantage points on globalization, which we illuminate in this volume through comparative urban ethnography. The concept of "global downtowns" thus captures the ways in which downtowns around the world increasingly share common features, serve as models for the transformation of old city centers and the emergence of new ones, and become sites for the convergence of diverse global processes.

What is a downtown? Our interrogation begins at the urban center, marked in many older cities by monumental statements of hierarchy and power, ritual and administration. Over time, ancient palace and temple precincts have expanded and contracted, giving way to the divergent presence and meanings of city halls, opera houses, stock exchanges, corporate offices, skyscrapers, museums, department stores, sports complexes, hotels, apartments, parks, and promenades that constitute heterogeneous downtowns today. Some downtowns are clearly bounded, some diffuse, and some parts of polycentric networks of activities. Deeply enmeshed with other parts of a metropolitan region, downtowns distill the economic, political, and cultural life of the city as a whole through periods of decline and abandonment as well as florescence—identities evoked by competing terms of spatial reference such as "Main Street," "inner city," and "central business district (CBD)." As our studies show, downtowns are continually in the process of being remade as symbols and sites of human interactions in counterpoint to other metropolitan spaces and functions.

In social and cultural terms, downtowns are embodiments of hegemonic (and competing) elites at the same time that they have enabled public expression of the needs of other groups and interests defined by race, class, mobility, gender, age, and sexuality. Hence, they have been locales for transient publics, divided between day and night, often writ as "civic virtue" and "vice." At the same time, downtowns worldwide are now increasingly defined by new residential populations—young, wealthy, sociable, creative—who challenge this temporality and movement. Yet the lifestyles of such new downtowners may conflict with established institutions and their employees, with world tourists, and even with homeless people who have found niches at the heart of the city.

Downtowns incorporate the past, but they often prove to be even stronger representations of the present and future. As multiple contributions to this volume make clear, downtowns around the world have taken shape through imagined forms and meanings that have global currency: consumption, monumentality, mobility, modernity, gentrification. Yet they are equally inflected with more problematic global dynamics such as stark divisions of capital and class, issues of immigration and assimilation, and problems of inequality and exclusion. Power, memory, creativity, and protest coalesce in downtown as flows of people, capital, and images constitute human spaces of connection and distinction, making and remaking the global in the form of immigration and investment, arts and touristic branding.

Understanding downtowns as centers of human activity and imagination through the investigation of multiscalar intersections of economic, political, and cultural trends enacted and lived therein thus contributes to a richer understanding of global city formation and the theorization of globalization as process.

Still, downtowns remain ambiguous. Meanings converge and compete, as contradictory visions and actions shape them. Downtowns stand for democracy and witness its denial. Theaters and museums embody high culture, scandalize publics, and allow interstices for new creativity. Commerce invites and manipulates some global consumers while excluding others. Burgeoning office buildings host millionaires, managers, and clerks by day and poor immigrant janitors or huddled homeless by night. Public spaces may crystallize the conscience of a nation in protest or be patrolled into emptiness. Downtowns, while places of deep local meaning, have become commoditized for global sightseers who transform museums, cathedrals, markets, and citizens into heritage destinations, exotic experiences, and disposable souvenirs. Many a Center City, selling a dazzling new opportunity for lifestyle choices among late capitalist elites, encloses its promises of downtown for a new and exclusive cohort, challenging its relations to the urban poor, to families in surrounding neighborhoods, and even to commuters from outlying suburbs.

The varied features of the transformation of downtowns have long interested historians, economists, geographers, and planners as well as urban bureaucrats and entrepreneurs (see, among others, Birch 2005, 2009; Fogelson 2001; Ford 2003; Gratz and Mintz 1998; Isenberg 2005; Jacobs 1957, 1961; Loukaitou-Sideris and Banerjee 1998). Drawing on contemporary anthropological theory and practice that combine an investigation of social dimensions with a critical awareness of built form, political economic processes, planning models, and mass media imagery, we insist on the contributions that urban anthropology has to make to discussions at the heart of the city. In examining specific dynamics of urban planning and development, for example, we are committed to understanding advocacy and order, as well as the uneven application and iterations of plans and the ways in which multiple forces both facilitate and hinder developments. While many scholars have focused on local stories as narratives of decline or regeneration, our analyses reflect our commitment to comparative global ethnographies from diverse positions, incorporating social historical processes and multiple levels of cultural understandings of place and people. We employ approaches that examine both material culture and social construction, linking discourses of planning and social sciences. In particular, we insist on the breadth of anthropological subjects, speaking to planners, civic elites, and other academics while showing that plans, politics, the built environment, ideologies, mass media, and myriad texts all provide anthropological material, situated alongside thick ethnographic description of lived experiences of those affected by, rather than shaping, urban development. Thus, through contributions by anthropologists and sociologists, we emphasize the import of qualitative ethnographic work for considering these processes and dynamics, and as such, the potential for an urban anthropology of downtown image, planning, and action.

In bringing together a collection examining global downtowns through the methods and theories of contemporary ethnography, we seek to enhance both interdisciplinary and transnational discussion by underscoring themes and processes that recur among compelling cases. The discourse of downtowns already has strong roots in North American development. Visions of decaying cities and sprawling suburbs after World War II, in fact, fostered an active turn toward preservation, revitalization, and growth that has augmented previous economic, political, and cultural command functions with a new evaluation of downtown lifestyle, with rationales ranging from gentrification to improved environmental planning. In other cities worldwide, histories and changes have varied; central spaces have survived—or been altered by—wars, colonialism, and tourism, while transformations have been wrought through global investments as well as localized competition that sometimes self-consciously focuses on a downtown model. An ethnographic approach offers unique potential for comparison, as careful attention to social dynamics of planning and living in and near downtowns reveals similarities between places and cases that may otherwise be overlooked. In fact, we hope to cast a new light on features of downtowns that long have concerned planners and other urbanists, including but not limited to land use, zoning, cultural programming, mobility, and quality of life (Abbott 1993; Ford 2003; Robertson 1995; Loukaitou-Sideris and Banerjee 1998; Nevarez 2003; see Brash, this volume). In focusing on the social dynamics in and of these features, we weigh their consequences and effects, considering local responses as a way of understanding how large-scale planning measures are implemented unevenly in any given case. At the same time, we understand that urban life is not an even playing field and maintain that the social conditions that shape downtown and its possibilities should also be addressed.

After decades of jeremiads about their decline and danger, American downtowns are "hot" once again. Understanding and analyzing these dynamics in relation to wider, global processes allow multiscalar connections to be drawn that suggest how downtowns around the world are implicated with one another through shared features, imaginings, and aspirations. In this collection, we speak both to our fellow social scientists and to planners, bureaucrats, and citizens whose experiences may be more circumscribed, even as we recognize that the contemporary re-creators of downtowns look to each other as they grapple with conditions of globalization. We examine the specificities of particular aspects of planning, development, and everyday life in order to understand how generalities are realized in practice— how, for instance, Business Improvement Districts in American downtowns use demographics to bolster efforts of homeless removal while promoting corporate interests, how personal memories of downtown residents, commuters, artists, and planners support aspirations for walkable urbanism, and how Beijing looks to Soho and Nashville to Dubai. In fleshing out a longer and wider view of downtown (Birch 2002) through careful reading of spaces, images, contexts, people, and changes, we illuminate important ramifications of what downtowns are worldwide, how they fit into wider global categories, and how these constructions, in turn, draw on and refract centrality, display, congregation, and exclusion, all illuminated by bright lights, tall buildings, and the roar—or absence—of crowds.

Downtowns over Time: Spaces of Local Identity and Global Connection

Current experiences of downtown development worldwide often raise the question of what is new in the processes we are witnessing and in what ways they draw on older structures and formations. Whether rebuilt on the sites of prior centers or constructed anew like the greenfield downtowns of a burgeoning China, today's downtowns draw on the built environments, social dynamics, and myths of the past to support global/local projects. Hence, the impact of mid-twentieth-century modernist plans that emphasized a totalizing view of urban form (Rannells 1956) or envisioned streamlined futures (Hoyt 1933; Knowles 2009) intersect with the imagined memories of those who would evoke the flâneurs of Paris (Harvey 2001), the landscaped visions of Frederick Law Olmsted, or even borrowings from recent suburban successes, like enclosed downtown malls (Schuyler 2002), to refigure central districts. Both old and new city centers, meanwhile, are imbued with global capital, which transforms them into sites of consumption and spectacle, immigration and exclusion.

As many authors in this volume show, while civic centers have been intensely global for millennia, the nature of global connections and flows has changed over time. Some cities became global over cycles of expansion and conquest, whether Qing Beijing at the center of a Middle Kingdom or Barcelona over centuries of global reconfigurations of the Iberian peninsula from Roman times to the European Union. Indeed, the transformations of centrality, form, and meaning of central spaces as part of global dynamics incorporate continuities and changes over centuries. Rome's crossroads, temples, and fora that embodied the unity of its empire evolved through subsequent contests of secular and religious power in cities of the Old World, including Iberian cities and temples claimed by both Christians and Muslims. Later, the 1578 Ordinances of Philip II imagined the central plaza and monuments of authority as a statement of power for the extension of the early modern Iberian empire, although they were scarcely present in Old World cities of the Habsburg imperium. These laws provided a unifying model of space, governance, and commerce in Spanish colonies, meshing with earlier urban forms in the Caribbean and Mexico and extending the city as a medium into a new world. Prescribed locations for a central church, ports, fortifications, government, and merchants tucked under porticos relegated others to the margins of power and the city, reifying divisions of race, class, and gender (Estrada 1999; LeJeune 2003; Low 2000; McDonogh 2008; Rama 1996; see Hill, this volume). These urban cores offered multilayered statements about power, as captured in the splendid critical reading of the intersection of urban plans, built space, and lived experience provided by the Uruguayan critic Angel Rama:

> from the time of their foundations the imperial cities of Latin America had to lead double lives: on the one hand, a material life inescapably subject to the flux of construction and destruction, the contrary impulses of restoration and renovation, and the circumstantial intervention of human agency; on the other hand, a symbolic life, subject only to rules governing the order of signs, which enjoy a stability impervious to the accidents of the physical world. Before becoming a material reality of houses, streets and plazas, which could be constructed

only gradually over decades or centuries, Latin American cities sprang forth in signs and plans, already complete, in the documents that laid their statutory foundations and in the charts and plans that established their ideal designs. (1996: 8–9)

Over centuries, this legacy has experienced further changes and accrued wider, contesting readings. The historical center of Havana has been refigured by the development of an independent Cuba, North American interventions, a socialist revolution, local planners, UNESCO's definitions of world heritage, and contemporary tourism. In its form, history, and meaning, it thus diverges from its shared legacy with the Plaza de Mayo in Buenos Aires, marked worldwide by the silent protest marches of mothers of those who disappeared under Argentine dictatorships. Or the touristic Olvera Street that runs off the Plaza, the first city center of Los Angeles, which now bumps up against Chinatown, itself re-created with props from a movie set (see Estrada 2008; M. Peterson 2010; Rama 1996; see Hill, this volume; McDonogh and Wong, this volume). The family resemblances that constitute global layers of meaning in Havana, Los Angeles, and Buenos Aires at the same time speak to division and change in other colonial and postcolonial cases such as Hong Kong, Zanzibar, and Mumbai.

Industrialization, transportation, and communication further altered the form and meaning of downtowns worldwide in the past two centuries. Consider the pervasive globalizations that have constituted North American downtowns as a "type specimen." Plans, streetscapes, and buildings show the imagination, if not imitation, of European models—imposing a more ordered grid and logical centering than the organic contested spaces of the Old World, whether William Penn's utopian plan for Philadelphia or the sweeping vistas of Pierre L'Enfant's Washington, as well as the heritage of Spanish imperial city building in Santa Fe and Los Angeles. The primary institutions that constituted the center have roots elsewhere, in political and ecclesiastical monuments, markets, squares, counting houses, and memorials of history and high culture. These places and institutions emerged in nineteenth-century America within a framework of global co-evolution. The bright centers and foul slums of New York or Philadelphia, for example, would be legible to those who map industrial Manchester through the eyes of Friedrich Engels (1958) or the emerging Paris of Georges-Eugène Haussmann (Harvey 2001). Richard Dennis underscores the transatlantic transformations of Victorian urban spaces through institutional and commercial edifices: "skyscrapers were built to impress as much out of economic necessity; prestigious buildings were particularly favored by institutions like banks, insurance companies and newspapers that wanted to make a public statement of their virtues and most buildings owned by or named after major institutions were actually occupied by a wide variety of tenants. On both sides of the Atlantic developers attempted to assemble sites large enough to permit substantial buildings" (2008: 278).

Dennis's vision of a nineteenth-century dynamic lays the foundation for transformations that characterize twentieth-century North American downtowns' forms and functions (Fogelson 2001; Ford 2003; Gratz and Mintz 1998; Hoyt 1933; Isenberg 2005; Loukaitou-Sideris and Banerjee 1998;) as well as dynamics shaping Dubai, Mumbai, Beijing, and Barcelona. While North American cities have been especially marked by decades of expansion followed by decline in the face of suburban sprawl and related social and cultural divisions, in recent decades city governance and public-private enterprises have become enmeshed in the construction of signature buildings, public spaces, and events that have revitalized downtowns, reminding us of the observation that "downtowns are more than just an enterprise; they can indeed be seen as an industry" (Loukaitou-Sideris and Banerjee 1998: xix, drawing on Frieden and Sagalyn 1989; see G. Williams 2003 on the postindustrial revitalization of downtown Manchester). Such collective enterprises have had consequences for social relations, structuring both conviviality and divisions along lines of gender, race, and class that persist through preservation, reuse, and consumption of space and goods. As Henri Lefebvre observed for the Paris of the 1960s and 1970s, "Businesses densify in the centre, and attract expensive shops, luxury foodstuffs and products. The establishment of this centrality is partial to the old cores, the spaces appropriated during the course of a previous history. It cannot go without it. In these privileged sites, the consumer also comes to consume space; the collection of objects in the windows of boutiques becomes the reason and the pretext for the gathering of people. They look, they see, they talk and talk with each other" (1996: 170).

In addition to the stark divisions of class emphasized from Engels to David Harvey (2001), observers such as Elaine Abelson (1989), Alison Isenberg (2005), and Richard Dennis (2008) have addressed the ambivalent centrality of women for downtowns. Through institutions such as department stores, nineteenth-century men and women recast the meanings of class, gender, and consumption, as captured by Émile Zola in his *Au bonheur des dames* (1883):

For Zola the great success of the *grands magasins*, their seduction of middle-class masses and their turning of consumption into a way of life were all part of the poetry of modern activity. He too was dazzled by the new emporia, and he wrote most powerfully of the spectacle of their displays and the flow of their crowds, reflecting constantly a personal fascination with the size and scope of their vast operations. Yet the portrait that emerged in *Au Bonheur des dames* encompassed another, less alluring, side to the department store world. To the stores' fashionable shoppers was added "la foule," the masses of women whose identity was captive to the goods they could buy. To the magnificence of displays was added the decline in standards. (Miller 1991: 190)

Although women were generally seen as users rather than owners of downtowns, Isenberg (2005) underscores women's roles as workers and reformers as well as consumers, struggling against male control of downtown spaces and fighting to ameliorate some of the negative consequences of capital.

This example is telling, moreover, since department stores as one of the defining institutions of the global center emerged from widespread connections of commerce and transportation far beyond Paris, New York, Chicago, and Berlin. Lane Crawford opened its doors in colonial Hong Kong in 1850 before growing into a department store, while Harrod's of London extended its reach to Buenos Aires and Philadelphia's Wanamaker's opened branches in Paris and Tokyo. In Tokyo, the seventeenth-century kimono store Matusuzakaya became a department store in the early twentieth century alongside modern competitors like Mitsokushi and Kyoto's Takashimaya, which would open branches in New York and Paris. The crowds of women whom Zola envisioned in Paris found their own ways to Macy's, Harrod's, Marshall Field's, and Mitsukoshi. Moreover, these emporia became nodes through which worlds of goods and capital moved through American and other global downtowns, orienting their varied citizenry to new desires and connections through transportation and mass media (Abelson 1989; Benjamin 1978; Harvey 2005; Schivelbusch 1977). These institutions, images, and publics of the mid-nineteenth century foreshadow connections and competitions across downtowns that are today forged through film, televisual media, and global electronic connections (McQuire 2008). At the same time, they remind us of the pressures of consumption and development on downtowns, as department stores have moved from former central monuments to competing suburban malls and online sales.

The sheer mobility of people adds further layers of history to globalization seen through urban capital and social formations. Downtowns became hubs for new technologies of transportation that included streetcar, subway, bus, and highway, as well as serving as points of connection for rails and harbors (with airports providing a striking counterpoint, Kasarda and Lindsay 2011). These transportation systems have brought new populations to the center while also promoting centripetal growth. In this regard, North American downtowns—including Toronto, Havana, and Mexico City as well as New York, Philadelphia, and Chicago—again differ somewhat from other nineteenth- and early twentieth-century centers in the intense globalization of peoples present from their very origins. Across the Americas, Europeans urbanized space, exiled Native Americans, and brought in African slaves. Colonialism was refracted not only in the heritage of the center but also in postcolonial constructions of race and ethnicity as American cities constructed downtowns of inclusion and exclusion around waves of European immigration, highly controlled Chinese entry, Latinos caught up in an expanding nation-state, gawkers from rural homesteads, and the desires of free African American populations—themselves rooted in global commoditization. All of these brought varied faces and demands to American downtowns by the turn of the twentieth century. The business and administrative functions of many centers, combined with palatial elite residences (sometimes coupled with alternate secondary residences outside the city), contrasted with the humble spaces of African Americans and poor immigrants who faced structured exclusions from public centers like department stores or museums (Isenberg 2005) or clustered in their own, segregated downtowns (McDonogh 1993; see Burgess 1925; Rotenberg, this volume; McDonogh and Wong, this volume). These diverse crowds nevertheless eventually imposed a democratizing stamp on North American downtowns, where patrons of museums of European art and opera houses rubbed shoulders with consumers of immigrant-filled nickelodeons amid the exuberant life of the downtown sidewalks.

In the twentieth century, economic transformations, suburbanization, new technologies, and changing patterns of social mobility, land use, inclusion, and exchange reshaped the spaces and activities of the center. Isenberg, for example, offers a synthetic litany of transformations that have characterized American downtowns: "the emergence of an inspiring new Main Street ideal during the progressive era, the challenges posed by 1920s metropolitan growth, the collapse of real estate values during the depression, the melodrama of urban renewal, civil rights demonstrations, riots and the tantalizing breakthrough of nostalgic marketplaces or Main Street preservation by the 1980s" (2005: 11). By the middle of the century, broad plans for renewal ranged from drastic erasure and reconstruction to imitations of other metropolitan forms, in cities large and small. This is evident in David Schuyler's reading of planner Clifton Rodgers's vision for the small city of Lancaster, Pennsylvania:

> Rodgers explained that the proposed new downtown would be a visually exciting, economically attractive area that had successfully deflected the challenge of suburban retailing. Ironically, in determining how to resurrect downtown Rodgers applied the principles of planning that had become standard in the design of suburban malls everywhere: everything from peripheral parking, arcaded pedestrian ways, street furniture, signage and such amenities as cafés, theaters and plazas. There was apparently no attempt to understand why downtowns had developed as retail centers, what features other than convenience of access had made them dominant commercial areas for generations. For planners of the postwar generation, there was no usable past. (Schuyler 2002: 67)

The mixtures, strategies, and problems of polyglot North American cities must be compared carefully with emergent movements and downtown encounters worldwide. In multicultural Paris and Barcelona, Roma, Arabs, Africans, and Latin Americans may still feel unwelcome in the stores—and imaginaries—of the central core. Meanwhile, internal migrants from poorer areas of the nation-states of Africa, Asia, and Latin America to their cities have threatened glamorous downtowns with squatters and slums as well as political protests, with responses ranging from "cities of walls" to newly deserted downtown areas (Caldeira 2000; Vladislavić 2009). Other cities have maintained their cores, albeit with added polycentricity through the creation of multiple stratified centers, as exemplified by Paris's suburban Grands Ensembles and Ville Nouvelles or Hong Kong's dense public New Towns. Here, the metropolitan dialectics of downtown invert North American patterns: where a generation of American suburbanites learned to fear the "inner city"—and then to gentrify it—unemployed immigrant youth of the

Parisian *banlieue* (suburbs) have borrowed "inner city" rap imagery to explore their own displacement. Reform and neglect, riots and renewal, inclusions and displacement constitute continuing dialectics of global downtowns.

Even in closely related settings, divergent trajectories must be explored to understand downtowns as global laboratories. In their work on Mexican border cities, for example, Daniel Arreola and James Curtis delineated differences between these centers and the values of activity and consumption that would come to shape the evolution of many multicultural American downtowns as residential and leisure spaces:

> Even though the centro may lack the glitz of the tourist district or the modernity of the new strip developments, it is a vibrant quarter with a boisterous street life that is inactive from early morning until late night. Its bustling public life is a marked contrast to the North American downtown, which has evolved into a largely financial, legal and governmental complex with only limited retail and residential functions. It has been widely criticized for its sterility and near-abandonment after normal business hours and on weekends. In el centro, where people live as well as work, the streets and sidewalks are crowded with residents who are drawn to the area's restaurants, entertainment facilities, public spaces, and stores, which stay open well into the evening. The presence of many large neon signs and the sounds of music played on radios and stereos in stores contribute to its lively and evocative nocturnal character. The sidewalks and curbside host a variety of individual businesses, including shoe shine stands, bookstalls, lottery outlets, and especially food and drink vendors. . . . Perhaps as well as any single element, these street vendors suggest that many differences between the North American central business district and the Mexican border-city are not only visually apparent but also culturally meaningful. (1992: 225–26)

As we write, these vibrant Mexican centers are nevertheless among those most scarred by a new globalization of drugs and violence that has challenged civic life. Meanwhile, cities to the north have sought to enhance downtown retail, residential, and street life as antidotes to stodgy stability.

Contemporary downtown transformations worldwide, as we show in this volume, continue to conceal as well as reveal the power structures that shape them. The once visible urban hierarchies of empire and religion have largely receded, replaced by museums and antiquities. For many, global corporations and touristic consumption coexist with public spaces and public works transmuted into projects for downtown revitalization, connection, and competition. Through these changes, elites continue to jockey for power and position. Planners and experts work with investors in neoliberal formations of mutual facilitation and constraint, dynamics that help us read neoliberalism as process rather than explanation. Nonprofit institutions—universities, hospitals, philanthropies, and other associations—have become anchors and landlords in urban regeneration. Global corporations take on new roles, offering neither factories nor warehouses but iconic headquarters complete with spaces of consumption while acquiring neon naming rights for downtown stadia or sponsoring cultural institutions (Hackworth 2006; Harvey 2007; Leitner et al. 2007; J. Mitchell 2001; Strom 2008). And images of downtown spread globally through websites, tourist literature, and public documents to audiences far beyond the metropolitan region.

At the turn of the twenty-first century, a widespread move from a downtown of administration, business, and entertainment to one with multiple residential populations has created different structures, values of land, and claims of ownership and agendas. In fact, the rebirth of today's downtowns demands reexamination of the mid-twentieth century as a moment of intense negotiation over the terms of downtown—and urban—development. We can see many residues of the debates of midcentury American planners and urban sociologists in current transformations. Jane Jacobs's call for understanding how people use downtown and for mixed-use urbanism (1957), for example, has informed current trends such as New Urbanism, walkable cities, and slow food (Leinberger 2005). Investigations into the relation between land value, commerce, and the city center reveal shifting preferences for residential location alongside persistent differences between cities and citizens (Alonso 1964; Firey 1947; Hoyt 1933; Rapkin and Grimsby 1960). At the same time, downtown regeneration is not a generic or neutral process, but rather entails key arenas of power brokering that shape downtowns in and through social dynamics of ownership, wealth, and control (Brash, this volume). Hence, we acknowledge salient critiques discussed by planning and policy theorist Susan Fainstein in her work on the just city:

> Beginning in the 1960s, scholars of urban politics have criticized urban decision makers for imposing policies that exacerbated the disadvantages suffered by low-income, female, gay and minority residents. In

particular, they have condemned policies that favor downtown businesses while ignoring neighborhood needs and giving priority to tourist facilities and stadiums over schools and labor-intensive industries. These critiques have implied a model of the just city—that is, a city in which public investment and regulation would produce equitable outcomes rather than support those already well off. (2010: 3)

As we look backwards, we must also look forward. The emergence of retiree populations, gayborhoods, the creative class, and part-time dwellers as specific users and audiences of downtowns; the ecologies of urban spaces as crucibles for new visions of sustainability; the evolving relationship of center cities, near-central areas, and older suburbs marked by ethnicity and class; the meaning of wireless and virtual connections for centralization; and even the relationship of downtowns with creativity, the arts, and sports all raise questions that planners, citizens, and analysts alike are now exploring and that resonate with the global discussion we present in this volume (Fainstein 2010; Florida 2004; Lloyd 2010; McQuire 2008; Newman and Jennings 2008). We recognize, rather humbly, that downtowns are changing faster than we can describe them, even as we outline key shared and divergent patterns, trajectories, and problems within this rapid evolution.

Global Downtowns

Recognizing multiple flows and impacts over millennia, we understand the "global" today as something that is both presumed and produced, taking shape in and through neoliberal capital and its effects, international legal frameworks, and the circulation of people, things, and ideas—processes in which cities play especially prominent roles (Appadurai 1996; Grosfoguel and Cervantes-Rodríguez 2002; Hopkins 2002; Inda and Rosaldo 2008; Knox and Taylor 1995; Marcuse and van Kempen 2000; Mignolo 2000; Sassen 2001; Smith 2001; Taylor et al. 2007). The ethnographic approaches in this volume capture multiple modes of scaling, indicating how the global is enacted through specific social practices and how local dynamics are shaped by and support recognizably global processes. Through ethnographic, historical, and processual study, we posit an understanding of globalization that emphasizes the imbrication of global processes with practices of everyday life. As these case studies further suggest, the global can simultaneously be taken for granted, motivate individual and collective decisions and investments, imbue the quotidian, and be deployed for strategic political ends.

At the same time, in assessing global downtowns, we interrogate that which is taken as distinctly "local" and "global." In recent decades, a network of global cities, cosmopolitan civic awareness, and scholarship has influenced many of the projects, choices, and outlooks of downtown development around the world. While particular historical, political-economic, social, cultural, and architectural features appear—or are made to appear as—distinctly local, these spaces host itinerant researchers, capital planners, and communications nodes that link cities instantaneously. These trends include centralizing processes and reinvestment in historic downtowns that mark a mediated specificity, a clear image in a hypermediated world. Downtowns around the world share new signature architecture projects designed by "starchitects" (star architects) such as Norman Foster, Frank Gehry, and Zaha Hadid (Kanna, this volume). Governments and citizens cast their gazes toward other cities to shape and understand their own showcase centers. The language of global downtowns has gained a shared vocabulary we know too well—recreational ports and waterfronts, Olympic and professional sports complexes, designer architects for designer brands, cutting-edge cultural centers and museums, and the electronic mediation of news, cinema, and websites. To enliven dialogues, downtown Dubai is advertised on Manhattan's gentrified Lower East Side and Olympic Beijing glances at Olympic Barcelona (and vice versa).

While globalization of the image seems to be a concern and product of contemporary mass media, awareness of architecture and global imagery has deeper roots, as illustrated by heritages as diverse as Iberian colonial planning, the multicity career of Daniel Burnham (Rotenberg, this volume), and the long-mediated images of New York and Los Angeles (Ethington 2008). Yet all these innovations have come with costs and exclusions that we analyze as well, speaking to planners' interests in a downtown that is not only attractive and cosmopolitan, but inclusive and fair (Fainstein 2010).

Though global cities literature discusses the kinds of social and cultural processes addressed in this volume, little of it seems to engage with downtowns per se as distinct and significant social spaces (see Abrahamson 2004; Brenner and Keil 2006; Durrschmidt 2001; Eade 1996; Keil 1998; Sassen 1992, 2001; Short 2004; M. Smith 2001). Globalization in the context of downtowns and the role of downtown in global city formation has been examined largely in relation to structurations of mobile capital that constitute centrality via nodes of power and command (Abu-Lughod 1999; Sassen 2000; see Ren, this volume). In this context, downtowns—and other urban spaces—become symbols of the centralization of capital, power, and people rather than lived and transforming spaces.

We argue instead that downtowns' centrality—whether geographic or symbolic—is especially significant for its complex social construction within local contexts, even as downtowns serve as economic, social, political, and imagined centers for cities, regions, states, and the world. The current significance of downtown is especially apparent as cities and their central business districts have become sites of dramatic international reinvestment worldwide. On the urban and regional level, downtowns, often long disinvested, provide new markets for capital and foci for governance and development within their regions. As sites of global consumption, mobility, and competition for both local and nonlocal tourists (Judd and Fainstein 1999; Urry 1991; Bissell, this volume; Hourani, this volume), cross-cultural flows of investment, tourism, migration, and capital also change the global meaning and location of centers. Hence, we pay attention to critiques of neoliberal strategies around the world while reading them in relation to wider conjunctions of downtowns' diverse social activity and the multilayered intermeshings of different peoples, institutions, and spaces with global processes.

Our analysis of global downtowns refracts and interrogates some of the dominant perspectives in the global cities literature. As we show, global downtowns, like global cities, are not all the same. A central strain in global cities literature has been a preoccupation in rankings of cities, identifying those that are most global in political economic control or diversity or size or connections (Friedman 2000; Knox and Taylor 1995; Sassen 2001). Certainly, some cities selected as case studies in this volume are recognized avatars of globalization, celebrated in large projects like the Global Cities exhibit at Tate Modern in 2007 (Burnett and Sudjic 2008) or the University of Loughborough's Globalization and World Cities project (http://www.lboro.ac.uk/gawc). Los Angeles and New York, for example, reappear consistently "atop" lists of global metropoles. Other cities have a more ambivalent status, where claims to global recognition by events, iconicity, or culture complement more political economic criteria—Barcelona, Dubai, Mumbai, and Chicago have all advanced strategic claims about their status as world cities. Some cities—Beirut, Beijing, and Havana—are also capitals of nation-states, while others, like New York, Mumbai, and Barcelona, have been central in the formation of national economies and identities. Finally, we also have been careful to look beyond these cases to smaller, diverse conurbations and related meanings of globalization, as experienced in cities such as Zanzibar, Lima, and Nashville.

We are especially critical of models that offer globalization as an explanation rather than a process. This use of globalization has been particularly prevalent in popular debates over what is the "most global city," which tout Tokyo, London, or New York as nodes dominating multiple realms of politics, economics, culture, information, and style. In this regard, it is important that while elites of Barcelona, Chicago, and Dubai have all become engaged in urban strategies to reinforce their international visibility as "models" for national and global cities, London, Tokyo, Paris, and New York have also been among recent candidates to host the iconic Olympiads. In fact, our cases underscore voices of critics who also see a conscious framework of manipulation of criteria of globalism by self-aware urban elites that underpins what geographer Neil Smith has identified as a "global gentrification" (2002, 2003) with concomitant social and cultural dislocations. As other researchers have noted, "most local decision makers never appear to question the need for deregulation, privatization or structural adjustment in the continuous quest for city competitiveness. In this regard, powerful, global, neoliberal economic agents are increasingly successful at creating real change in cities around the world, as well as in creating and maintaining an enabling discursive space among global and local economic . . . and political agents" (Amen, Archer, and Bosman 2006: 204–5).

A critical ethnographic reading of globalization has allowed us to scrutinize how *visible* "exceptionalisms" figure in ideologizing the histories of downtowns. In each of our urban settings, administrators, planners, and poets celebrate the special attractions of "their" center, evoking an exceptionalism that is especially apparent in the rich historical literature on the American downtown as place and concept (for example, Banerjee and Loukaitou-Sideris 1992; Burgess 1925; Davis 1992; Florida 2004; Ford 2003; Hall and Hubbard 1998; Isenberg 2005; Keil 1998; Logan and Molotch 2007; see Rotenberg, this volume). Today, despite varied histories, powerful images of renaissance and rebirth at the center have become part of competition for consumers and investors on national, regional, and global scales. This process of branding a city as unique by means of shared global features has concerned scholars of cities, architecture, and mass media (Aaker and Joachimsthaler 2000; Greenberg 2008; Klingmann 2007). Such branding represents an awareness of globalization by elites, citizens, and mobile agents that recurs throughout our analyses.

Themes of global architecture, events, knowledge, and human flows, as we show, are shared by cities large and small, national and regional, underscoring the importance of downtown as a frame through which to read multiple dimensions and figurations of globalization (Guggenheim and Söderström 2009; Koolhaas 1978, 2009; McNeill 2009; Turtinen 2000). Again, as ethnographers, we complicate this picture with flows and actions of people and knowledge, including the mobility of ideas and images as well as diverse interpretations of space and power. Here, we engage with discussions of intense mobilities of peoples, ideas, and communication that suggest how movement within, into, and across cities actively transforms categories and experiences of space and time, public and private, materialities and socialities (Breese 1949; Sheller and Urry 2003; Thrift 2004; Urry 2007). Histories, monuments, conflicts, and vivid images of contemporary global downtowns recur across our essays—Chinatowns with neon signs and late-night commerce; centers with vibrant music; immigrant vendors hawking street food, crafts, and pirate goods in Barcelona, Los Angeles, New York, and other central business districts worldwide; and above all the crowds, life, and sheer vitality of downtowns. In downtowns worldwide, elite visions continually meet diverse, everyday popular imaginings and global flows find local meanings. Metropolitan citizens "go" downtown for museums, diversions, government tasks, or exotic meals. Apartment dwellers move there for work or social life. Tourists seek out Manhattan's Times Square, Barcelona's Rambles, Old Havana, or Tokyo's Ginza with many agendas. In downtowns, diverse peoples meet each other as well as encounter the monuments and bureaucracies of cities, states, businesses, and institutions, the service personnel who keep downtowns alive, and others who survive by licit or illicit means. The noise, the bustle, the rhythms, the clashes, and the excitement of downtowns define global and local experiences of growth and protest, vision and exclusion that we seek to bring to the foreground in the essays that follow.

Our detailed case studies should spark comparative and theoretical discussion of how current transformations of urban downtowns reflect and support global city formation. These cases raise issues of form and planning, investment, tourism, and imagery, along with conflict and exclusion that have made city centers contested zones; each article addresses a different constellation of features and processes while speaking to the central issue of downtown. The strengths of the volume consist not only in these individual studies but also in bridges that illuminate multiple human dimensions of downtown's global meanings and take them into account for future plans, conflicts, and creativities.

Framing Comparison

As this volume argues, the intersections of global downtowns around social and cultural developments and transnational connections are complex. Drawing from ethnographic material about what people see, do, and invoke in these centers, we have framed comparison by themes rather than applied typologies, understanding reading as a process that creates connections between downtowns. Three sections, titled "Imagination," "Consumption," and "Conflict," organize the numerous ways in which downtowns are global and the multifaceted nature of global downtowns. Most of the cases included speak to more than one of these themes. In organizing the chapters by their relative emphasis, we trust that readers will make their own connections regarding how these and other themes play out across downtowns.

Part I of this volume focuses on "Imagination," including both visions and histories of downtown, speaking to planners and historians in an anthropological voice. Imagination includes both local development and the ways in which downtowns look to each other—and to an abstraction of "downtown" that is drawn from particular aspects of given places—as they are made or remade as city centers. Imagination encompasses urban theories, planning visions, and the creative action of groups of citizens over time—brought to life in theoretical models of Chicago, commercial districts of Beijing, revitalized port projects in Barcelona, and twenty-first-century visionary starchitecture of the Persian Gulf. Yet, in each case, imagination has been tempered by histories of local context and global competition. The work of planners plays a key role in providing general forms that might be implemented in particular ways, and for studies of specific downtowns that are deployed as models. Meanwhile, connectivity between urban centers becomes tangible in downtown as a site of consumption and in contestations over the implementation of planning and development schemes.

Part I begins with Robert Rotenberg's "Toward a Genealogy of Downtowns," which anchors some of the primary conceptual and historical material of the volume as a whole. Rotenberg provides a critical analysis of theoretical imaginations about centrality and downtown, from Ernest Burgess and the Chicago School and Burnham's planning to the present. Working through the dominance of Central Place Theory in urban anthropology and geography, Rotenberg ends with contemporary implications of Richard Florida's *Cities and the Creative Class* (2004; see Lloyd and Christens, this volume; Peterson, this volume). At the same time, Rotenberg shows how the lived city of Chicago "becomes" global through its role as an urban model, providing a touchstone city to which several essays will return (Ren, this volume; Peterson, this volume; see also Madigan 2004).

Xuefei Ren provides an important long-term sense of place, history, and power in her chapter, "From Peking to Beijing: Production of Centrality in the Global Age." This essay traces the changes in the location, function, and meaning of downtown Beijing in four periods—the Imperial phase (1400s–1911), the Republican era (1911–1937), the Socialist regime (1949–1978), and the global phase (1978–present). Ren explicates the larger forces of planning and policy at work in competing elite aspirations and political and economic forces that constructed and reconstituted what has been identified as the downtown throughout the city's history. Shanghai is often taken as "the Global City" of modern China because of its international contacts (Chen 2009), and Hong Kong and the Pearl River Delta embody development to the south (McDonogh and Wong 2005). Yet Peking/Beijing claims a unique power over history as well as the future, as seen in the transformations discussed by Ren as well as its successful bid for the 2008 Olympics.

Turning to planning and imaginations in Europe, Francesc Magrinyà and Gaspar Maza, in "Simulations of Barcelona: Urban Projects in Port Spaces (1981–2002)," offer a careful examination of projects—and failures—of urban planners and the creation of recreational public spaces in the industrial port that has flanked and supported central urban areas. Here again, Barcelona's planning and governing elites have sold the transformations of the city as a model for other cities worldwide, making a close reading of specific processes even more important (Bohigas, Buchanan, and Lampugnani 1991; Borja, Nello, and Valles 1998; Busquets 1992; Capel Sáez 2005; McDonogh 1999). While the port of Barcelona has been a key element of global urban growth adjacent to the city's central business district and administrative core for millennia, tensions have become acute around the transformation of that postindustrial district into an attraction for changing urban/global populations. Magrinyà and Maza's article underscores internal contradictions in the development process and imagination of downtown futures that invoke comparisons with chapters by Liza Weinstein, Ahmed Kanna, Julian Brash, Marina Peterson, and Richard Lloyd and Brian D. Christens.

Finally, turning to even more futuristic visions of downtowns, Ahmed Kanna's "Urbanist Ideology and the Production of Space in the United Arab Emirates: An Anthropological Critique" uses two cases from the contemporary United Arab Emirates—Ras al-Khayma and Dubai—to argue that in the context of the neoliberal global south, urbanist projects simultaneously present themselves as timeless and purely technical phenomena, while always being shaped by and situated in complex and multiform ideological and cultural contexts. Kanna asks how these imaginative projects relate to the interests and everyday intellectual and cultural experiences of such classes and formations. The author further considers how and under what conditions existing urban histories and urbanities are selectively drawn upon or erased—themes that resonate with history and change in Barcelona, Havana, and Beijing. Dubai, in turn, becomes a model for American downtowns, as shown in the chapter by Lloyd and Christens.

In Part II, we turn to "Consumption" as a central theme defining global downtowns in their history and revitalizations since the days of marketplaces and department stores. We also recognize that consumption now transcends goods and services to include the consumption of downtown itself as place, real estate, and lifestyle. In Part II, we highlight local experiences framed around markets, housing, and varied arts of downtown— architecture, performing arts, film, and food—that now attract global visitors, immigrants, new residents, and investors. Looking at the redesign of Nashville in the shadow of Dubai, the neoliberal reinterpretation of the central souq in Beirut, the revitalization of Old Havana, and the transformative power of a film festival in Zanzibar, the authors of Part II reiterate the extent to which consumption in the modern global city is inextricably linked to cosmopolitan consumption of the city as global brand. Crafting downtowns as sites of consumption—whether as things to be consumed in themselves or as places where one may go to consume through shopping and cultural experience—is also a way of imagining downtown in a particular form, organizing development around heritage as structured by UNESCO or utilizing local market forms as the basis for new shopping areas, while connecting to themes of New Urbanism, walkable cities, ecological and social sustainability, and visions of the creative class, among other globalized concerns.

In the first chapter in Part II, "Reaching for Dubai: Nashville Dreams of a Twenty-First-Century Skyline," Richard Lloyd and Brian D. Christens link the starchitecture of the Middle East that Kanna has presented to an American city not often read as a center of globalization—Nashville, Tennessee. Drawing on a counterpoint of Nashville and Dubai presented by a local developer, the authors trace both the features that threatened many American downtowns after World War II and the patterns of contemporary revival that have turned downtowns into new and elite residential "neighborhoods" to be consumed as part of the construction of urban imaginary. In this city of the American South, culture, music, history, and recreation all come into play as elements of urban consumption.

Najib Hourani, in "From National Utopia to Elite Enclave: 'Economic Realities' and Resistance in the Reconstruction of Beirut," explores the dialectic of a central place of consumption—the souq of Beirut—caught between a prewar past and a global future, while making concrete an alternative reading of the Middle Eastern city. Hourani carefully reads the reconstruction of the Lebanese capital between 1990 and 2009 within the framework of neoliberalism and global capital, as the preserve not of state institutions but of private real estate holding companies. His focus on the provision of new global services in a space identified with a local tradition of the marketplace explores intersecting dynamics of New Urbanism, transnational architects, created meanings, and conflictive interests as well as resistance embedded in local and regional experiences of an even longer, mythic past.

William Cunningham Bissell's "When the Film Festival Comes to (Down) Town: Transnational Circuits, Tourism, and the Urban Economy of Images" refracts similar questions through an examination of development plans and programs that have centered on refiguring a section of Zanzibar, Mji Mkongwe (Stone Town), as local and world cultural heritage. Here, the Zanzibar International Film Festival embodies the central role in "reviving" urban spaces and fortunes organized around selective narratives of the city's history while reminding us of the cinematic visions through which so many downtowns are read. This chapter and the following consider how UNESCO has taken on a determining role in shaping city centers around the world through heritage, indicating, at the same time, how both global forces and local politics are selective and partial.

Selling in downtown becomes global selling *of* downtown with the historic center of Havana, as examined by Matthew J. Hill in "The Future of the Past: World Heritage, National Identity, and Urban Centrality in Late Socialist

Cuba." This essay covers a broad timespan from the late 1400s to the present, allowing Hill to bring together the local, national, and transnational social practices that "articulate" the processes of producing downtowns and the power differentials and differently scaled identities that emerge in relationship to these processes. Hill's essay develops an analytical frame to examine contemporary historic preservation of downtowns as a translocal process that is respatializing the old colonial urban core in Havana, Cuba, while showing that ethnographically grounded case studies of heritage-driven revitalization can illuminate underlying issues of representation, agency, and spatial politics that are foreclosed by globalization's structuralist master narratives.

In casting an ethnographic eye on such global efforts, we see as well how models are implemented unevenly in any given case, relating not only to particularities of culture but to power dynamics and social inequalities. Hence, these efforts and images are often contested, whether by the poor who are displaced or by struggles between new and old elites, making downtowns sites of local and global conflict. Thus, we conclude this volume with essays that revisit globalization and downtowns through the lens of division and conflict (although divisions of rights, groups, ownership, and use underpin all these studies). The essays in Part III, "Conflict," crystallize spaces of difference and contestation within a range of contemporary cities, at times throwing planners and governments into relief as antagonists as well as agents of development. Here, the conflicts between bourgeois pioneers staking out a new residential/leisure downtown for Los Angeles and the immigrants and homeless people who live there resonate with the macro-conflicts of massive slum redevelopment projects in contemporary Mumbai. A chapter on New York City highlights the conflicts among elites—politicians, businessmen, planners—that have surfaced in analyses of Beijing, Dubai, Barcelona, and Beirut, while the closing chapter uses Chinese globalization as an alternative prism through which to read evolving divisions in central areas of Chicago, Philadelphia, Paris, Los Angeles, and Lima.

Beginning with a premier global American city that has often been accused of lacking a downtown, Marina Peterson, in "Utopia/Dystopia: Art and Downtown Development in Los Angeles," explores agendas behind urban redevelopment organized around the arts. Globalizing downtown Los Angeles through neoliberal capital investment, gentrification, and an invocation of cities with clear downtowns as a model for urban development, these processes also reflect the flip side of neoliberal globalization, as each element of the creative economy draws a painful class divide between the new residents and existing homeless and immigrant populations. Responding to these pressures, a Skid Row theater group presents work that critically engages the terms of these dynamics and their consequences for the poor and homeless living downtown.

In Mumbai, slums have become the new site for "downtown" development, as developers build high-rises and housing for slum residents. Considering the growth of "downtown" development in areas removed, both physically and socially, from the city's traditional center, Liza Weinstein, in "'Slum-Free Mumbai' and Other Entrepreneurial Strategies in the Making of Mumbai's Global Downtown," explains the ways that global land speculation and the transnational dispersal of economic activity are reconfiguring Mumbai's geography of centrality. Once again, the role of planners and consultants in shaping the terms and forms of urban development recasts a theme apparent in many of the preceding articles and opens a space for dialogue.

Julian Brash brings elite division in historical concerns of urban regimes and downtowns into perspective with his essay on a changing New York and its neoliberal agenda, "Downtown as Brand, Downtown as Land: Urban Elites and Neoliberal Development in Contemporary New York City." Using interviews with planners and bureaucrats as well as critical readings of planning projects, Brash explores tensions between an older family-based elite that sees the central business district as land and a newer competing elite, including Mayor Bloomberg and his Olympic dreams, that perceive New York as a brand in a global marketplace. Brash's and Weinstein's essays resonate particularly well, showing the use of neoliberal and entrepreneurial governance strategies on opposite sides of the globe.

The volume concludes with an essay by Gary W. McDonogh and Cindy Hing-Yuk Wong, "Beside Downtown: Global Chinatowns." Rather than focusing on any one downtown, it follows a diasporic population through different downtown contexts worldwide. The authors use Chinese globalization, grassroots and elite, as an alternative position through which to compare widespread processes of urban centrality, conflict, and change. Chinatowns worldwide emerged near central industrial-commercial areas but have been altered repeatedly by demands of politicians, planners, and local civic imaginaries. Chinatowns, meanwhile, also exist as part of multilayered Chinese globalizations, where they provide alternative downtowns for multiethnic populations, connect widespread suburban Chinese, and participate in global networks of immigration, media, investment, and governance. And new

Chinatowns, like the re-creation of Dubai, suggest further dreams of reinventing downtown in the twenty-first century.

Individually and comparatively, these chapters read and refract multiple
themes of centrality and globalization as authors explore their models,
interests, and parameters in particular cases while contributing to a wider
discussion. In this Introduction, we have suggested a framework, drawn connections, and teased out implications that we as ethnographic social scientists hope global readers might draw from this discussion, especially with
regard to the need for recognition of human complexity and change in such
an emblematic urban creation. These are not comprehensive views of downtowns so much as complements to the work and theories of historians, planners, politicians, and citizens with whom we work. We hope to open a space
for further research and exploration, with the aim that our readers might go
beyond these materials and suggestions to reconsider downtowns in their
own experience, as places, problems, and opportunities—and to learn from
the questions asked in and around other central areas worldwide.

PART I

Imagination

1

Toward a Genealogy of Downtowns

Robert Rotenberg

How do we sense a city? Is it a matter of directing our gaze from building to street to traffic to neon signs and back to the building again, accumulating impressions of line, scale, enclosure, mass, and spectacle, just as we do when viewing a painting of a landscape? No, the immediacy of our body's movement through the city requires a different kind of gaze, one that filters and edits our impressions according to preestablished systems of knowledge. For those cities where we consider ourselves at home, the knowledge is different from what it is for cities where we are visiting for the first time. At home, we enjoy exquisitely detailed knowledge of streets, buildings, traffic, and neon, as well as the memory of past experiences in these locations. This familiar knowledge of places and practices employs the city as a canvas on which we live our lives. First-time visitors, in contrast, see the city initially as a mirror of received knowledge: the city as icon of a region, the city as site of history, the city as filled with identifiable monuments, the city as outlet for enjoying regional foods and drink, and so on. Each of these represents an artifact to be collected, consumed by the senses, and made material through postcards and bric-a-brac that can be exhibited to the folks at home as evidence of the transforming effects of travel. After spending some time among the locals, the visitor begins to see the city as a possibility for living a life beyond a hotel room and suitcase, a more difficult-to-communicate series of impressions that tend to fade rapidly. Of course, even visitors are rarely without some previous experience in cities.

The global downtown, the focus of the chapters assembled in this volume, is a globalized, neoliberal variety of the new downtown. The new downtown is a redesign of the urban center, often sponsored and financed by corporate, rather than municipal, interests and employing design principles that simulate the features of cities without people. In this way, it is a refashioning of the morality of the urban community. It enters the experience of the knowers of the city as their bodies move through a city's built environment. Redesigns of the urban center are not particular to the last forty years. They have a history that stretches back over 180 years. The whole concept of downtown qua downtown may be bound up with the process of redesign. My goal here is not to write that history, but to excavate the layers of that experience. I hope to lay bare the artifacts that contribute to the experience of redesigned downtowns, so that what have been called the "new downtowns" can be seen in sharper relief.

In describing the genealogy that has led us to these new downtowns, I want to explore the common experiences of all who enter the downtown, regardless of their place of habitation. Such a project is possible even while acknowledging that people with different histories will experience some aspects of the city differently. All ages, classes, genders, ethnicities, and races experience the organized waiting that is a traffic jam, and its opposite, the joy of free-flowing circulation through city streets. How one expresses the waiting or the joy may vary from person to person, perhaps even group to group, but the ways in which the city inhibits movement and then releases it again levels social distinction. It is therefore appropriate to begin with movement.

Latrocinium, with Apologies to Italo Calvino

Recently, I reread Italo Calvino's *Invisible Cities* (Calvino 1978). The book describes fantastic cities framed by an extended conversation between a narrator named Marco Polo and an interlocutor in the person of the aging emperor Kublai Khan. In that book, the narrator constructs and deconstructs fifty-five different ways of life in cities, each more fanciful than the next, all to the delight of the reader. I want to begin this unwrapping of the term *downtown* by imagining a city that Calvino did not describe. I call that city Latrocinium.

Kublai Khan asks Marco Polo what cities lie just beyond the borders of his empire. "Highness," begins Marco Polo, "there is a most famous city entirely devoid of any buildings, walls, gardens, or towers. That city is called Latrocinium, the capital of the Esconian Empire. One approaches Latrocinium on a five-lane highway through a desert. As one moves toward the city, the highway becomes increasingly crowded with vehicles of all sorts: wagons, chariots, dog carts, sport utility vehicles, semi tractor trailers, circus wagons, rag top convertibles, and motor scooters. As one nears the actual city limits the traffic appears to stop. This is, in fact, an illusion. You are definitely moving, but only very slowly. The pace is so slow, that you feel as if you are at a dead stop. You have truly entered Latrocinium.

The people of Latrocinium spend their days moving down this highway. It takes so much time to move around the city that they take pains to speak to each from their vehicles. To not do so would deprive them of one of the few opportunities for human contact. In this way, they form the same sorts of bonds one finds in the other cities I have described to you. However, in Latrocinium these bonds last only as long as the parallel lines of traffic progress at the same speed. In one of my visits, the line I was in suddenly accelerated, leaving behind a philosopher in the vehicle on my left with whom I was engaged in a conversation about the agency of the word, and a woman on my right with whom I was shamelessly flirting. Several minutes later, I found myself in an entirely different neighborhood of Latrocinium, as the people in the vehicles around me were now strangers.

[In the interests of space, I will exclude from the account several paragraphs where Marco Polo tells Kublai Khan how children are schooled in Latrocinium, how people provision themselves without abandoning their vehicles, and how the people of Latrocinium bury their dead.]

After several months of moving down the road in this fashion, your vehicle suddenly begins to pick up speed. The vehicles around you are moving, too, but at different paces. Then, spaces begin to grow between the vehicles. It seems as if there is more road available. You accelerate. You are now leaving Latrocinium. You are among the few who chose the road that actually leads somewhere else.

This new Invisible Cities story raises the sort of questions that have troubled intellectuals working in cities since Vitruvius, the fourth-century Roman architect and planner. Are cities one social organization or many? Are cities primarily territorial entities of mortar and brick, steel and glass, inhabited by people, or are they constructs of the imagination that people then give material form?

I have found the culture concept a useful analytic for parsing such questions, especially when dealing with the unambiguously large, internally complex versions of urban settlements, the metropolises of the world. As an analytic, the culture concept directs our attention toward "the socially acquired patterns within which people think, feel, and do, not the people themselves" (Brumann 1999: S23). Making generalizations about specific features within an aggregate is a different analysis task and a different rhetoric than making generalizations about the distinct-ness and qualities of an aggregate as a whole. (i.e., the culture of the city). The former approach "does not require physical proximity or a specific type of Gemeinschaft ties, only social interaction, however (mass-) mediated and casual this may be—just seeing, hearing or reading of one another may suffice for mutual imitation" (Brumann 1999: S23). As ethnographers of Latrocinium culture, we can say nothing at all about the city as a city. However, we can say a great deal about the practice of making and breaking social relationships as the traffic speeds up and slows down. We might even be able to generalize about specific features of this interior relational practice. What goes for Latrocinium also goes for all those other social organizations in the contemporary world in which the flow of people, goods, ideas, and energy is the primary organizational feature shaping people's lives.

The Barest Essentials: The Isolated City

If one were to strip away the asphalt, cement, bricks, and mortar of cities, what would be left of urban life? The first principles of the urban are to be found in what is known as primitive trade. First identified by Karl Polanyi (1975) and elaborated by Conrad M. Arensberg, Harry W. Pearson (Polanyi, Arensberg, and Pearson 1957), and Marshall Sahlins (1972), primitive trade is balanced reciprocity between strangers where the goal of the exchange is the satisfaction of want, rather than the maintenance of social relations. This form of trade is contrasted with social exchanges of "gifts" where the ongoing social relations dwarf the values of the object exchanged. In trade, surpluses of goods and services in one location are exchanged to meet desires that cannot be satisfied adequately through production in another location. Because it takes place between relative strangers, that is, people who do not have sustained ties with each other, such trade is conducted in places outside the settlements of the actors involved. The resulting markets, fairs, and bazaars can be temporary, periodic, seasonal, or permanent. The longer they exist in the same place, the more often ancillary and opportunistic activities will co-occur in that place. This intersection of exchange among strangers in specific times and places is the one activity that is consistent across all urban experiences. Whatever co-occurs, such as ritual, administration, military, transportation, or production, gives this intersection its uniqueness, what Calvino might call its visibility. However, it is the exchange activity that gives rise to the phenomenon of the central place.

Central place is the name of the location where strangers assemble to trade. People's use of land was shown by Johan Heinrich Thünen in 1826 to be a function of the exchange value for agricultural surplus production and the distance to the place of exchange, thereby establishing the importance of the calculation of marginal cost in people's lives (1966). For producers in a region where places of exchange compete with each other, the desire to reduce this marginal cost and enjoy higher prices in exchange is a strong one. This must compete with population growth, which forces people to move away from each other and toward unused space to meet their basic needs. Over time, new places of exchange and transportation links are established. As the region fills with central places, people in the different locations begin to compete with each other to provide more specialized exchanges, the ones people desire most but exchange less often and are therefore willing to spend more time, effort, and treasure to attain. Every good, every service has a threshold where consumers will no longer move to exchange for it (Stine 1962). Out of this, Walter Christaller noted in 1933, a hierarchical system of central places develops, each level of the hierarchy marked by increases in specialization in the goods and services available for trade (1966; Lösch 1954). These principles apply to periodic markets (Skinner 1964), although some reflect these locational effects less clearly than others (Bromley 1974), as well as to towns and cities. Important exceptions to the hierarchy of central places are observable in cities and towns that follow the rank-size rule: the higher the center is in the hierarchy, the larger its size. This rule was elaborated by Brian J. L. Berry in 1971 to show that growth actually trickles

down through the hierarchy from central city to suburb except when political processes intervene to distort this hierarchy (Berry 1971). Distorted hierarchies and uneven growth are more the norm than what he expected when
he attempted to test the rank-size principle in real regions. The very highest
nodes in the hierarchy are also places of great economic and political power.
This power is used to restrict the growth of secondary and tertiary places to
ensure that the metropolis, or primate city, will receive the greatest share of
growth, wealth, and cultural prominence (Mera 1973; Rotenberg 1979).

William Cronon identifies the river as the natural feature that promoted
Chicago as a central place. It provided a sheltered harbor for canoes, and
later sailing ships, a passage from the lake to the interior prairie, and a boundary between open and flowing waters. With the Calumet portage a few miles
to the south, the river was a gateway to the Mississippi watershed and trade
routes throughout North America. This feature reduced marginal costs for
every commodity that passed through it. It was this favorable transportation position that grabbed the attention of the market agents after 1833.
They convinced investors that this site was a unique candidate for a central
place that would quickly ascend the regional hierarchy, bringing the value of
property along with it. Even after the first speculative boom collapsed in
1837, the site's transportation advantages sustained market development
disproportionate to all but a few other central places in all of North America
(Cronon 1991: 23–41).

Stripped of its streets and buildings, the urban place is a central place, a
place of exchange. As we add back the built features through which we identify cities, we are still seeing a place of exchange. Where, when, and whom to
include and exclude from the exchange practices are the reason for the city
to exist. Without that place of exchange, the very absence of which makes
Latrocinium so disconcerting, the city cannot be seen.

Enter the Downtown: The Legacy of Burnham and Burgess

Neither Daniel Burnham, author of the plan for Chicago, nor Ernest Burgess, author of the seminal chapter of urban growth and development in
Robert E. Park, Burgess, and Roderick Duncan McKenzie's canonical Chicago School text, *The City* (1967), invented the idea of the downtown, the
central business district. The continued popularity of this book contributed
to distributing the idea among several generations of designers and planners.

The liminality of the center, the *axis mundi*, is an idea as old as settled communities. However, both Burnham and Burgess gave it shape in ways that permitted powerful institutions to focus on it as a place of control. Nor were they operating in an intellectual vacuum. European urban restructuring of the downtown had been ongoing since the 1830s. What these fin de siècle modernists did was to brand the center for the planners and designers who followed them. The two were of different generations and never met, though they walked the same streets and were inspired by the lake-river city of Chicago for many years.

At the time when Burnham was developing his plans, the discourse on shaping the downtown to serve the powerful was dominated by two nineteenth-century planning regimes: the archaic school championed by Camillo Sitte, which designs a downtown as a holistic aesthetic with far-reaching sensory and psychological effects, and the modern school championed by Otto Wagner, which plans the downtown as an engineering problem of moving people and goods safely, hygienically, and without risk of fire (Rotenberg 1995: 161–66). Burnham's plan for Chicago chose to privilege traffic flows over psychological comfort, remaining firmly within the modernist regime. It demanded a center to the web of streets, though the actual shape of that center itself can vary from a rectilinear to the radial grid. Paris (rectilinear) and Vienna (radial) provided two different models of how the center of established cities could be reconfigured for modern traffic flows, retail trade, and commercial real estate markets.

Burnham took the traditions of the nineteenth-century urban design visionaries and the Beaux Arts neoclassical design aesthetics of that school and produced a master plan for Chicago. That plan, published in 1909, allowed for almost infinite growth while retaining the City Beautiful Movement's sense of grandeur and metropolitan self-consciousness that previously has been enjoyed only by the imperial metropoles of Europe. In sumptuous watercolor renderings, Burnham portrayed a city as if in the civil twilight of a new dawn. The shining beacon of light is located in an arbitrary place on the grid, near the river and the lakefront. This privileged place would become known as the downtown. The influences were readily apparent: Baron Haussmann for the radiating boulevards, Ebenezer Howard for the outer ring, Frederick Law Olmsted for the integrated park system, Charles McKim and Louis Sullivan for the water elements and the neoclassical simplicity in the sightlines, and Maxfield Parrish for the color palette. Yet of all the features, the system of circles radiating from a center of a rectilinear grid, like a stone tossed in a placid lake, is the prominent feature of the plan. These increasingly brighter circles are not evident in Burnham's plan for San Francisco. There are more "circles on squares" in his plan for Manila, completed one year earlier. Starting with Manila and Chicago, Burnham would employ the style of illuminating the center of his cities with this bright light of color. This modern regime unfolded globally. It is first enacted in the metropol and later in the colonial capitals.[1]

These "circles on squares" are important in leading Burgess to think about the growth and social development of Chicago. Written in 1925 (fifteen years after the publication of Burnham's plan and its wide dissemination under the patronage of the Commercial Club of Chicago), Burgess's chapter is local in its vision, global in its impact. Park, McKenzie, and Louis Wirth, the other three authors of the book's chapters, were more directly concerned with the social organization of specific groupings in the city. It was Burgess who focused on the space and its places. Even his metaphor for urban growth, urban ecology, was taken from nineteenth-century notions of the spatialization of animal and plant communities in nature. He was not putting the people of Chicago into Burnham's plan. He was putting Burnham's plan on the people of Chicago.

For Burgess the boundary between any two circles was both cultural (native vs. newly arrived) and class-based (roomers vs. workingmen's residences), both of which were the sources of social pathologies. Both Burgess and Park believed that the morality of communities depended upon the emergence of a set of communal rules of belief and conduct that bind individual behaviors. Social pathologies result from the breakdown of those sets of beliefs because of residential instability, low wages, and disease, with the personal and property crimes that attend to these conditions. When the rules are not in place to blunt competitive and individualist instincts, urban life is dangerous and ugly. As one moves from the center to the edge of the city, according to Burgess, each zone in space represents a distinct zone of increasing moral order, the highest of which are the residential and commuter zones. The city is a matrix of different moral communities, each identified by its class standing, relative nativity, and economic stability. The downtown was where all the communities mix. It was a place made simultaneously visible and invisible. It is made visible by the surveillance of governmental authority to insure against the outbreaks of lawlessness from the culture clashes of contrasting neighborhoods immediately surrounding it.

The writings of the Chicago School (officially known as the Local Community Research Committee) were not the idle jottings of philosophers speaking and listening only to themselves. This was an academic enterprise whose proponents populated the government offices and academic departments throughout North America, inventing several traditions for imagining, naming, and evaluating the twentieth-century urban experience throughout the world. The most durable of these traditions would prove to be the imaginary of the downtown.

The missing element in Burgess is the economic basis for the regional role of newly emergent urban forms. Sociogenic forces such as class and ethnicity will distort Christaller's regular system of central places for a time, but these forces cannot prevail in the long run. The practice of seeking lower marginal costs in exchanges will always produce some place as the most complex node in a system of market nodes in the region. By complex market node, I mean the location where the provision of goods and services includes frequently accessed outlets, less frequently accessed outlets, and rarely accessed outlets, all in one place—in other words, a location where a pharmacy, a green grocer, a bank, a stationery store, a store selling fur coats, a store catering to coin collectors, and a boutique in which the least expensive frock is $3,000 all occupy the same block. This highest node must always exist in a region as a statistical artifact, if not as a well-defined spatial brand. Burgess focused on the branding of the place, not on the practical reason that led to its existence.

Simulacrum: Florida and Ford

The transportation revolution, which for North America began in the period after the American Civil War, is primarily responsible for the creation of a downtown population that changes its composition between day and night. The alternating rhythm of the use of space is entirely modern in its origins. The European tradition of municipal lock laws ensured that their downtowns would be deserted after the theaters let out. We take for granted the idea that work and home should be separated today, but this was not the case before the second half of the nineteenth century. Such a separation would have been impossible without cheap and available transportation. The location of the wage job is no different from the location of any other exchange. As long as the marginal cost is too high, one will forgo the job in the central business district in favor of one closer to home. When transportation technology lowers that cost, greater distances can separate families and their wage employments. The choice of where to work and where to live can be separated much more easily than was ever the case historically; adding ease of transportation onto the modernist design regime results in a flow of people back and forth from the center of the grid to its outskirts every workday. The downtown benefits by becoming a transportation node equal in importance to its role in the central place hierarchy. The population of wage earners mixes with shoppers during the day, while at night people who live in or near the central business district stroll these same boulevards.

Who, then, can be said to inhabit the downtown? Who are indigenous to the district? The quick answer is both the commuters and the nearby residents. Richard Florida has recently offered a more complex answer to this question. Instead of the orthogenetic growth of urban regions that I have emphasized in the discussion of Burgess's locational practices, Florida takes a heterogenetic approach: the development of an open, tolerant cultural environment combines with the locational decisions based on marginal costs to boost some nodes in a region to greater growth. Florida is writing in the tradition of the human capital school of regional growth. Robert E. Lucas sums up the core principle of this school as follows:

> If we postulate only the usual list of economic forces, cities should fly apart. The theory of production contains nothing to hold a city together. A city is simply a collection of factors of production—capital, people, land—and land is always far cheaper outside cities than inside . . . It seems to me that the *force* we need to postulate to account for the central role of cities in economic life is of exactly the same character as the external human capital. . . . What can people be paying Manhattan or downtown Chicago rents for, if not for being near other people. (Lucas 1988: 38–39, cited in Florida 2004: 32 with ellipsis)

Edward L. Glaeser has shown that agglomeration, a feature of the older orthogenetic locational economics that accounts for the clustering of firms to take advantage of networks of suppliers or customers, is actually better explained by the advantages of locating around a common labor pool (1998). Florida expands on this view, showing that labor itself clusters because of the co-availability of technology (such as transportation, but also technological innovations), talent (such as his Bohemian Index, measuring the density of artists), and tolerance (such as his Melting Pot Index, measuring density of foreign-born, and his Gay Index, measuring the density of gay couples) (Florida 2004).

Burgess was not oblivious to the argument Florida wants to make, though Burgess does so through his bourgeois lens. He locates a group he calls "Bohemians" just outside the central business district as part of an urban "underworld." If one lays Burgess's schematic on a real map of Chicago, the part of the city under the term *underworld* falls directly over the River North location of the Tree Studios, less than one mile north of the Loop. This was a late nineteenth-century application of Florida's thesis: a half city block of studios built in 1884 by a prominent statesman and judge to retain the artists and sculptors who had contributed to the Columbian Exposition, and thereby to boost the reputation of Chicago as a center of artistic production. Lambert Tree built the studios behind the stables in his own backyard. Having served as U.S. ambassador to France, Tree realized that the presence of working artists gave a city stature. This was not a case of "build it and they will come." Many of the creative class were already in the region. They had come because of the commissions available for this temporary, disposable project of the Columbian World Exposition. They would ordinarily disperse to other projects because there was nothing in the Chicago of the time to hold them there. This was a case of "build it and they will stay." And stay they did. By the 1920s, the area around Tree Studios was a vibrant bohemian colony, the older gentry residences having been leveled to make way for commercial and multifamily buildings. For Burgess, the district was the quintessential underworld, in the older, pre–Elliot Ness sense, a social sphere below the level of ordinary life inhabited by people of questionable respectability. From their location just outside the downtown, the Bohemians were able to set up a counter-world of possibility. Much the same role was played by Greenwich Village in New York City. It was the counter-world to Gotham, the strip between Washington Square Park and Forty-Second Street that through much of the twentieth century was arguably the most diverse, talented, and technologically significant place in North America, if not the world.

The human capital school uses indices that locate the creative class in standard metropolitan statistical areas and census tracks, rather than specific places, like Tree Studios. This is not location in the same sense as Christaller's central places. For this reason, the creative class cannot be associated with the downtown today anymore than it could in Burgess's day. Instead, a high score on the Creativity Index, Florida's composite of the various indices he devised, contributes to the city's brand without really inhabiting a specific district. That visitors to New York City, Boston's Route 128 Corridor, or Silicone Valley will rarely encounter any specific place of creativity is irrelevant to the power of the presence of creative people in a technologically sophisticated and socially tolerant setting, and the products these residents contribute to the market. The formula for integrating the avant garde into the economy has always been Cultural Capital plus Commoditization equals Money.

Florida is convincing when arguing that a strong and vital creative class and the economic growth of a city are correlated. In what way could the first cause the second? Here we enter the realm of symbolic economies, notably the relationship between representations of value and the social exchange matrix in which those representations are currency. The competition among cities for new capital and the enhancement of economic growth that follows is a tournament of value, an auction in which the highest investments are made in locations that offer the most "value." Among the intangible elements that contribute to the evaluation of a location's "value" are the available amenities or symbolic assets that accrue to the investor through the location. Constructing these amenities is shared among artists, performers, and designers, but also among architects, sports franchises, civil engineers, local charitable foundations, and even the Department of Streets and Sanitation. Each has a role to play in the representation of the city that will be in play during the auction for investors.

The city that these investors are "consuming" is a simulacrum, a perfect copy (in their minds) of a city that never existed, except in small, local, and fleeting instances. Yes, there was a moment after World War II, for example, when painters, poets, and musicians found common cause with each other, as well as common residence in Greenwich Village, and in so doing created a Zeitgeist and a durable and saleable image of the New York avant garde. Then, it was gone, commoditized into galleries, bookstores, and music stores. There was a time when Steve Jobs and Steve Wozniak made computers in their garage, instantiating the durable and saleable image of the Nerdopolis (Florida's term) of Silicon Valley. Then, it was gone, commoditized into Apple, Inc. The investors who came later, looking for lightning to strike twice in the same place, were investing in a simulacrum.

Nowhere in the city are the signs that reference this representation denser than in the downtown. To display them in the artists' quarter would be to undermine the signs of decay and seediness that establish the authenticity of the avant garde. Even the corner store selling postcards with the likenesses of the district's most famous residents must be requisitely derelict. No other district will afford as many eyes on the signs as the downtown, its very density supported by the commingling of workers and shoppers. It is the downtown that must carry the symbolic assets of the city, including those of the creative class. That presents a very interesting problem to planners. The downtown already has its preestablished set of symbolic assets. They exist in the local imagination as never quite fulfilling their promise as the city's front room. This is because familiarity and the myth-building powers of simulacra are mutually destructive. The indigenous build resentment toward their downtown, just as the city's economic development office stocks the district to the brim with representations of the "value" the city has to offer.

The locals develop a mythology of their own about the downtown, fueled by the commonsense-producing distributions of newspapers and local media. Larry R. Ford debunks these myths, so I will not do so again. I include his concise list here for the resonances they produce in the discourse on downtowns:

1. Downtowns have become ugly, sterile, and culturally distant. (They used to be beautiful and highly symbolic.)
2. American downtowns are ragged, ever-changing, always under construction. (They were once stable, finished, and orderly.)
3. Downtowns have been privatized into fortress-like spaces that exclude much of the populace. (They were once full of more egalitarian public space.)
4. Downtowns have become superficial, inauthentic, and homogeneous. (They once had a strong sense of place resulting from local economic traditions and architecture.)
5. Downtowns are dangerous, crime-filled places, especially at night. (They used to be safe, law-abiding, and full of nightlife.)
6. Downtowns are physically and psychologically distant—they are poorly served by public transit and parking is expensive and unavailable. (Everyone used to go downtown easily and cheaply on the bus or trolley.)
7. In the age of office parks and malls, downtowns have become so much like suburban developments that there is no point going there. (Downtowns used to be unique; there was nothing like going downtown.)

8. Downtowns rely on the exploitation of low-paid "post-Fordist" labor. (They used to rely on a well-paid and well-trained working class.)
9. No one lives downtown; it is not a twenty-four-hour place. (The downtown once had a large, middle-class residential population.)
10. Downtowns are expensive toys built primarily for tourists and visitors. (They used to better meet the needs of ordinary city residents.)
11. Downtowns are polluted and dirty, especially compared to the green and spacious suburbs. (Downtowns used to be clean and tidy.)
12. Downtowns are crowded and congested compared to the spacious suburbs. (Downtown density was once manageable, but with the advent of cars and trucks, congestion is out of control.) (Ford 2003: 29–43)

One might reasonably assume that the first statement in each of these tropes would be the local view, while the second, parenthetical statement would belong both to the sentimentally nostalgic local resident and to the economic developer. Move each of those second statements to the present or future tense, and they provide the basis for a development campaign aimed at seeking outside investment. The bridging logic between the past, the present, and the future is the existence of a large and vital creative class.

The Invisibility of the New Downtowns

We need to probe deeper into the negativity at the base of this discourse. Why are people willing to believe negative imagery and narratives about downtowns? The reason must lie with people's experience of these districts. The imprecise boundaries of the old downtown, its associations with the cultural devalorization documented by Ford, and the anonymity of the new downtown that replaces it are all retained in the memory of the direct experience of urban space. This experience has not been a particularly satisfying one for reasons that may be surprising.

The urban field is crowded with spaces of various kinds. Scholars have catalogued these for the last half-century, beginning with Maurice Merleau-Ponty (1966) and Henri Lefebvre (1992), and continuing to Michel de Certeau (1984) and Marc Augé (1995). To begin, we experience space differently from place. Place is a location of elements that we find meaningful. It might be an address, a park, a battlefield, an office building where we work, or a beach we go to in our minds when we want a little peace and quiet. Place does not have to be real. In fact, the most satisfying places combine elements of real locations with imaginary ones. Place is difficult to manufacture. It is the stuff of history, memory, and mythology. One experiences place through memory, narrative, and monument. One becomes attached to places emotionally or intellectually through associations that one builds in the mind between memories, narratives, and monuments.

The Greek word *topos*, place, is used as the root to describe various anomalous combinations of real and imaginary places that depart in some way from our ordinary experience of place. *Utopia*, literally "no place," is a literary genre for imagining a society that works in some more satisfying fashion than the writer's own. *Dystopia*, on the other hand, is a "sick place" where things work in a far less satisfying way. *Heterotopia*, a term coined by Michel Foucault, refers to places that take on very special meanings for people, especially if those meanings are associated with powerful institutions, relationships, or cosmologies (Foucault 1986; Rotenberg 1995). Augé, following an analysis by de Certeau, has recently described a fourth anomaly, the nonplace, or what I shall call the *atopia*. An atopia designates two complementary but distinct realities: spaces formed in relation to certain specific urban activities, usually transport, transit, commerce, and leisure, and the relations that individuals have with these spaces (Augé 1995: 94). We cannot call a public transit bus a place in any meaningful way. One bus is very much like another. Something meaningful can happen to a person on a bus that might be the basis for place making, but that particular bus, its number, its peculiarities among other buses, will not be part of the memory. As for the other people on the bus, their relationship to each other is the same as their relationship to the activity they are engaged in. They are solitary and anonymous. The bus is an urban atopia, a nonplace.

Space is experienced through the movement of body. Space is produced as one moves from place to place. One frequents a space, intersects with other moving bodies, and transforms space into lived experience. Take a street, any street. The street is there because someone decided it would be a good place to build a street. It probably is not a mere paving of an old cow path, as many residents of older cities might believe. It is a place in the mind of planners, engineers, residents, and merchants. Only when people move through the street does it become a space.

A bus has the characteristics of a space. One moves on a bus, even as the bus moves through the streets from place to place (bus stop to bus stop). In his analysis of this movement, Augé notes that the stops of the Paris metro inevitably reference monuments and historic districts of one sort or another, in other words, places. This is one of the features of atopias that make them interesting to think about. They have the same role as ordinary places in the production of urban space even though they are devoid of the embedded social relations of places. They are nonplaces because the only relationship possible is a contractual one (you bought a ticket, right?) focused on the activity at hand.

The specific urban activities that are likely to engender atopic spaces are transport (airports, train stations, intercity bus terminals), transit (taxis, automobiles, buses, subways, escalators), commerce (of the chain store, franchise restaurant, mall outlet variety), and leisure (the theme park, urban attraction, "must see" vista, or staged festival). These have their parallels in ordinary spaces: the shared ride using the personal autos of each rider in rotation, the corner "mom and pop" grocery where names and greetings are exchanged with each transaction, and the regular Saturday morning chess game in the park with the same three people for the last five years, weather permitting. Not only are the former contractual and solitary, while the latter are consensual and social; the scales of the atopic spaces are large enough to accommodate many more people.

The new downtown, the subject of the analyses in this book, is a collection of atopic spaces. These districts will always be a palimpsest, a reconstruction of a space scraped of its previous buildings, associations with memory, and human relations. The erasure is never complete. Augé describes the echo of the lost places as follows:

> The town center is an active place. At regular weekly intervals, on Sunday or Market Day, the center "comes to life." The new towns produced by technicist and voluntarist urbanization projects have often been criticized for failing to offer "places for living", equivalent to those produced by an older, slower history: where individual itineraries can intersect and mingle, where a few words are exchanged and solitudes momentarily forgotten, on church steps, in front of the town hall, at the café counter or in a baker's doorway: the rather lazy rhythm and talkative mood that still characterizes Sunday mornings in contemporary provincial France (Augé 1995: 66).

The old district remains in the memories, histories, and narratives of the residents; the new one is unable to complete itself because the place it occupies is never fully emptied of its former relations. Instead, like a bus, the new center succeeds only as solitary, contractual atopia.

To frequent space, de Certeau writes, is "to repeat the gleeful and silent experience of infancy: to be other, to go over to the other, in a place" (Certeau 1984: 164). This is not possible in the new downtowns. As we move through the space that connects nonplaces, we catch glimpses of a landscape whose features are so homogeneous that we lose track of what city we are in. We feel we ought to look at something, even if it is the one variation in the architecture that is not consistent with every other outlet or franchise of this corporation all over the world. There is nothing to see. Yet, we are forced to take a position toward the landscape, a point of view, or lose any possibility of pleasure.

The new downtown is invoked through words, or more precisely, through clichés, rather than through sights. We are offered texts, rather than memories. We are guided with instructions, rather than relationships. Spaces offer messages that inform us about the permissible activities that each is prepared to contain. In ordinary spaces, we read the semiotics of the space by observing the people who are already in the space. The messages of atopia are written on the walls. There is no response possible, no conversation. One remains alone walking in the space because one need not interact to know how to use the space. Information, prescriptions, and prohibitions are well signed and paths are clearly lighted: "enter here," "place order here," "pay here," and "validate ticket before returning to vehicle."

Ordinary spaces are formed out of people relating to other people through the construction and negotiation social identities. Even strangers passing on the street, whether they indicate each other's presence or not, read each other and form a silent, momentary relationship. Where multiple interactions are commonplace, the algorithms of conversation and references to shared experience combine to produce more individualized identities. In atopic spaces, each has the same identity: passenger, cashier, customer, driver. This temporary anonymity has its positive side. It can be felt as liberating. The judgments of role performance are suspended. One need only be told where to go, how to get there, and what to avoid. In the atopia, one is alone, but so is everyone else. The only aspect of the experience that connects one to the other is that each has made the same contract: holding the ticket, queuing for the bus, waiting to be seated, or staking out blanket space at the free concert. The old bonds that attach people to their social selves are relieved. In their place, one experiences what Augé calls "the passive joys of identity-loss, and the more active pleasure of role playing. . . . What he is confronted with, finally, is an image of himself, but in truth it is a pretty strange image. The only face to be seen, the only voice to be heard, in the silent dialogue he holds with the landscape-text addressed to him along with others, are his own: the face and voice of a solitude made all the more baffling by the fact that it echoes millions of others" (1995: 103). Whenever one goes to look at a new downtown, one finds oneself. It is in this sense, then, that the center is rendered invisible. We have entered Latrocinium.

Toward a Genealogy

A genealogy is warranted whenever we feel ourselves lacking a history. The genealogy is not a search for origins. Nor is it the narration of a constructed sequence. Instead, according to Foucault, it reveals the traces of a plural and sometimes contradictory past through which power has influenced truth (1977). In the preceding discussion I have tried to uncover the artifacts that contribute to our experience of downtowns to put the new downtowns in sharper relief. In particular, I explored the common experiences of all who experience the downtown, regardless of their place of habitation.

The earliest layer of the common experiences is the movement of body through the space that will eventually be filled with places. The first of these places to be established is the one that locates the practice of trade among strangers. Its spatial outcome is the central place. This central place is the first instance of what will eventually be called the downtown. The downtown was where different moral communities, each identified by its class standing, relative nativity, and economic stability, mix. The surveillance by governmental authority mitigates conflicts from the clashes among these communities, a surveillance that is acutely felt in the downtown where high-end retail outlets, often the targets of thieves, are concentrated. It is simultaneously a transportation hub, disgorging and swallowing workday commuters, tourists, and migrants. They mix with permanent residents who pay premium rents for the opportunity to be with others with similar cultural capital, whether bohemian or bourgeois. And it is the bourgeois who keep the bohemians close, ensuring access to an avant garde market in which commodities carry extraordinary social distinction. Nowhere are the signs

of social distinction denser than in the downtown, culminating in contradictory expectations for downtowns that are never fully realized. For the
city's boosters, the aim is to stock the district to the brim with representations of the "value" the city has to offer. For the residents, an alternative
mythology builds that sees the district as "ugly, sterile and culturally distant."

Conceived by the modernist grandchildren of Burnham, these new
downtowns have become "so much like suburban developments that there is
no point going there." In the popular imaginary, what was once a communal
front parlor filled with memories of family, fraternity, and familiarity has
become alien, anonymous, and atopic. Where once we were conjoined, now
we are isolated. It is an alternative morality, a space in which our movements are anticipated and narrated for us. Indeed, we cannot move off from
the proffered path; entry is not authorized. The old downtown that lies
beneath, the movement of body through space to trade among strangers, is
fully present but now transformed. Rather than being filled with places of
real memory, real experience, and sustained relationships among strangers,
the new downtown constructs its places out of an imagined memory, simulated
experiences, and temporary relationships between strangers. Such downtowns
are truly new. They are also on the verge of collapsing under the weight of
their contradictions. These are not the first experiments in designed spaces.
We can relate them to mid-twentieth-century public housing, itself another
example of spatial truths distorted by power, another designed morality.
Like public housing, new downtowns will eventually be abandoned, torn
down, or transformed into spaces that do respond to real practices. This will
happen when the appeal of the trade in goods they offer no longer attracts
the curious or the affluent. Indeed, it may already have begun.

2

From Peking to Beijing: Production of Centrality in the Global Age

Xuefei Ren

On August 7, 2008, one day before the opening ceremony of the Beijing Olympics, Qianmen Avenue reopened to the public and tourists after several months of extensive renovation. Qianmen (meaning "front gate" in Chinese) is adjacent to Tiananmen Square, the geographic and symbolic center of Beijing, and it was once the major marketplace in the late Qing period. The area declined after the demise of the Qing dynasty in 1911 and was replaced by newer marketplaces that emerged in other parts of the city. By the early 2000s, it had become a dilapidated inner-city neighborhood crowded with lower-income households, migrants, street vendors, and shoppers looking for cheap bargains. Right before the Beijing Olympics, the city government included Qianmen on its extensive list of "bad corners" that needed to be renewed to make "New Beijing."[1] The relocation of businesses and households in the Qianmen area was costly because of the high residential density and land value, so the city government solicited financial help from private developers to take part in the renewal project. SOHO China, a trendy real estate firm that has built dozens of high-profile projects in the central business district (CBD) in the eastern part of Beijing, was chosen as the main partner. After 46 million RMB[2] were poured into the neighborhood for demolishing old houses, relocating residents, and upgrading infrastructures, the once dilapidated Qianmen area was turned into a Disneyfied historical downtown, equipped with newly paved pedestrians-only streets, brand shops, street lamps, and cable cars resembling the cityscapes of republican Beijing (1910s–1930s). The makeover of Qianmen is just one example, among many others, showcasing how new centers are made and remade with state power and private capital in rapidly globalizing Beijing.

The changing spatial organization of Beijing in the past and present is illuminating for reconceptualizing the meaning of downtown, and urban centrality more generally, in a global and comparative perspective. In this chapter, by tracing the changes in the location, function, and meaning of central places in Beijing from the imperial period to the present, I argue that we need to pay close attention to the shifting and contingent relationships between places—instead of taking a categorical approach by viewing centers, subcenters, and off-centers as geographically fixed entities engaging in a zero-sum game for residents and investments, we need to adopt a processual approach by examining the local and translocal processes in specific historical contexts that make and unmake different types of urban centralities.

Downtown, as exemplified by the Loop in Chicago, is a quintessential American concept (see Rotenberg, this volume), typically referring to an area of a city with high concentrations of business activity. Historically, Beijing never had a downtown in the fashion of Chicago's Loop, primarily because the city was the administrative center of the Chinese empire, and for a long period of time the political sphere dominated the socioeconomic spheres of the city life. In the first part of this chapter, I present a historical analysis examining the broader political and socioeconomic forces at work that have made and unmade the centers in Beijing from the imperial period to the present. In the imperial and socialist periods, as China was relatively isolated from the world economy, the economic center of Beijing was largely defined and shaped in national and regional contexts, suppressed and overshadowed as an inferior commercial space by the political centers of the empire and the communist government, respectively. I argue that the term *downtown* as center for economic activities is inadequate to capture urban centralities in many non-Western contexts in history, as the case of Beijing demonstrates—marketplaces for commerce and business were marginalized and urban centrality resided in the political domain.

Contemporary Beijing, however, has enthusiastically adopted the Western and specifically the American notion of "downtown redevelopment," and in the short period since the 1990s, multiple new downtowns—financial, historical, and cultural centers—have emerged in the city, and they have been competing with one another for tourists, investment, and government subsidies. For financial centers, driven by intense competition among district governments, Beijing has seen the emergence of three financial districts, or CBDs.[3] Historical downtowns have also been revived as local governments and private developers rediscover the economic value of old architecture and neighborhoods. Many historical sites—city walls, gates, temples, and marketplaces—have been repackaged into themed environments drawing large crowds of tourists, such as the aforementioned Qianmen Avenue.[4] Competing with new financial and historical downtowns, cultural centers have also appeared after the mid-2000s. As cultural industries have gained popularity among policy makers, the city government has designated dozens of artist villages on the urban fringe as official "cultural districts" and turned them into new clusters of creative industries.[5] These new nodes of centrality exemplify entrepreneurial practices of urban governance that are prevalent in today's Chinese cities and indicate the transplantation of *downtown*, a term closely associated with American cities and imbued with neoliberal ideologies, into the context of urban China.

In the new financial, historical, and cultural centers in Beijing, we see an interesting fusion of the power of the Chinese state, local, and transnational capital, and globetrotting architects who lend legitimacy and embed symbolic capital in the newly constructed megaprojects. In the second part of the chapter, I shift the analytical focus to contemporary Beijing and examine how China's new urban elites have eagerly pursued prestigious international architects to make new downtowns in the city. The practice of using global architectural and planning professionals is not unique to China (see Weinstein on Mumbai and Kanna on Dubai, this volume). With the recent neoliberal turn of urban governance, similar initiatives of constructing architectural megaprojects with signature design have appeared in different urban and regulatory contexts. However, neoliberal urban policies have always been homegrown and path dependent, and empirical research is needed to identify the similarities and variations of this "actually existing neoliberalism" (Brenner and Theodore 2002; see also Brash, this volume). The specificity of the neoliberal project of global city formation in China, I would argue, lies in the unique mix of power by global architects and the devolved communist party-state, mediated through the private sector of property development. I argue that the rescaled Chinese state—with power, authority, and resources converging in municipal governments—has become a key enabler of transnational architectural production. The case study of building the new CBD in Beijing demonstrates the power of the Chinese local state, private capital, and global architects in reshaping the built environments in Chinese cities today.

Production of Centrality in the Global Age

Centrality is one of the most heavily debated subjects in urban theory. In his classic essay "Growth of the City," Ernest Burgess (1925) describes the tendency of any city to expand from its center or downtown to periphery in a concentric fashion. According to the Chicago School, urban expansion typically takes place through ecological processes such as succession, invasion, and differentiation, as individuals compete with one another in the free market for the best location (see also Rotenberg, this volume; McDonogh and Wong, this volume). Among the criticisms launched against the Chicago School—for example, its free-market assumption and lack of cultural-political analyses—one of the most contested issues is the school's treatment of urban centrality. The Chicago School assumes the dominant power of center/downtown over periphery/hinterland by arguing that large metropolitan systems are organized around an urban core.

Many have questioned such power relations between center and periphery as pictured by the Chicago School. The most polemic critic comes from the Los Angeles School. Michael Dear (2002b) proposes an alternative view of an urban future based on new empirical conditions emerging in Los Angeles and other metropolitan areas in the United States since the 1970s. The Los Angeles School scholars posit that decentralization, suburbanization, and urban sprawl have reordered power relations between center and periphery, and that it is the periphery and hinterland that dominate the center and downtown in the twenty-first century. Dear writes, "it is no longer the center that organizes the urban hinterlands, but the hinterlands that determine what remains of the center" (16). Quoting Joel Garreau, Dear adds, "every American city that is growing, is growing in the fashion of Los Angeles" (6).

However, recent reurbanization trends—redevelopment of downtowns, gentrification in near-centers, and the return of young professionals to inner cities—provide ample evidence of the reinvention of downtowns, and therefore undermine the claim made by the Los Angeles School about the diminishing role of the center. Even in the case of Los Angeles, a city that has been historically lacking a powerful center, we now see new redevelopment initiatives aimed at reinventing downtown, such as the construction of flagship architectural projects, conversion of loft apartments, openings of galleries and art venues, and rapid residential gentrification (see Peterson, this volume). In addition to urban policies attempted to subsidize business and attract investment, art and cultural events have become increasingly used as a tool for downtown regeneration (De Frantz 2005; De Frantz and Keating 2004; Evans 2003; Hall and Hubbard 1998; Harvey 1990). The downtown renaissance taking place in Los Angeles and beyond brings new empirical conditions to the debate on centrality and requires a new conceptualization of the form and meaning of urban centrality that goes beyond the dichotomy of urban core versus periphery.

Rather than viewing the power relation between center and periphery as a zero-sum game, Saskia Sassen (2001, 2007) redefines urban centrality in terms of power and suggests the emergence of flexible new forms of centrality in the age of globalization. She argues that new technologies and organizational structures have altered the spatial form of centrality and there is no longer a simple, straightforward relation between centrality and such geographic entities as downtown and CBD. The center can take the form of a grid made up of nodes of intense business activities expanding in a metropolitan area, a network of powerful global cities as command-and-control centers of the world economy, and a de-territorialized digital network in electronic space, as well as state-of-the-art new financial districts built on former suburban fringes (for example, Docklands in London, La Defense in Paris). By redefining centrality as a function of power, this new conceptualization frees urban centrality from geographic constraints and redirects research attention to the underlying forces and processes that produce new centralities.

By rearticulating centrality in light of a broader conceptualization of power, in the next section I examine how the downtown, or the economic center, of Beijing has been constituted or marginalized by imperial, colonial, socialist state power in different historical periods. Rather than asking which scale—downtown, inner city, urban fringes—predominates over others, I question how centrality comes into being and what larger socioeconomic conditions help produce particular types of centrality. Powerful forces and actors can make nowhere into somewhere, and effective place-making mechanisms change over time. Downtowns are constantly made, unmade, and remade by local and translocal forces when viewed in a longer historical span. The urban fortunes of places—centers, near-centers, and off-centers—largely depend on the work of such forces.

Historical "Downtowns" in Peking

Peking/Beijing is an ancient city that has served as the capital of five imperial dynasties and one modern regime.[6] Here I focus on how the economic center of Beijing has migrated within the city in three historical periods—the imperial (1403–1911), the republican (1911–1937), and the socialist (1949–1978).[7] I use *Peking* to refer to the city before the market reform in 1978, and *Beijing* to refer to the new city rapidly transformed by institutional reforms and economic restructuring after 1978.[8] *Downtown* is used here to explicitly refer to the business and commercial center of a city, that is, the *economic* center of a city. I emphasize the term *economic* because, as we shall see, the political and economic centers were often two separate spheres throughout much of the city's history. Drawing on existing scholarship about the urban and social history of Peking, this section traces how the economic center of the city has migrated and identifies the larger forces accounting for the shifting downtown(s).

Imperial Peking (1400s–1911)

Imperial Peking was the node of government and administration networks of the Chinese empire. The tremendous economic, political, and cultural resources commandeered by the state connected Peking indissolubly to the empire (Naquin 2000). Imperial families and government were the largest employers in the city, and their activities overflowed into many aspects of local urban life. Economic centers were submerged under the shadow of the political center and the imperial domain. The dominance of political spheres over economic spheres left clear imprints on the cityscape.

Ming and Qing Peking consisted of several walled cities nested in concentric rings (Figure 1).[9] The Forbidden City, as the residence of the imperial family, is located in the geographic center. It was the focal point of imperial Peking and a world closed off from residents. The surrounding Imperial City enclosed private gardens, lakes, and workspace exclusively reserved for the

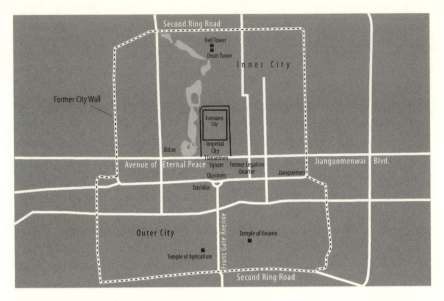

Figure 1. Map of Beijing. Photo by author.

ruling family and high-ranking bureaucrats. The sparsely populated palaces and eunuch-managed Imperial City were off-limits to the public. This inaccessible space occupied a large proportion of the built-up area of the city, and it was both the geographic center of Peking and political heart of the empire. Compartmentalization by walls and gates was fundamental in organizing the society of imperial Peking. The concentric orientations of imposing city walls asserted the centrality of the emperor and played a symbolic role in constructing Peking as the capital of the empire.

The rest of Peking was divided into two distinctive parts—the square-shaped Inner City in the north and the rectangular Outer City in the south. The Outer City was smaller than the Inner City and lacked the majestic imperial center. Because of the presence of the imperial palaces, there were more residences—mostly those of noble families and high-ranking bureaucrats—in the Inner City, and more commerce took place in the Outer City. During the Qing period, as the new ruling Manchu elites ordered all Chinese residents and commercial activities to be relocated to the Outer City, the economic centers of gravity further shifted to the Outer City.[10] Imperial city walls imposed significant barriers to traffic, and therefore city gates became major transportation arteries. The major commercial center of imperial

Peking developed around the central city gate—Qianmen, which connects the Inner City and Outer City. A downtown section appeared near the streets and markets in the densely populated area just outside Qianmen. Here developed a great congestion of merchants, shopkeepers, peasants, workshops, and laborers. Residents were concentrated in the highly commercialized, densely settled lanes and alleys near Qianmen. As the business expanded, reedy swamps were gradually drained, shops appeared outside the walls, and residential neighborhoods multiplied. Although other subcenters also emerged during the Ming and Qing periods,[11] Qianmen occupied the top rank with its large number of permanent shops catering to the demand for luxury goods stemming from the city's officials and aristocrats. As the primary downtown of imperial Peking, the commercial and entertainment quarter at Qianmen attracted sojourners from throughout the empire and beyond.

The location of the downtown in imperial Peking was influenced by the political and economic system of the period and was characterized by an imbalance in the amount and level of business between the Inner City and Outer City (Dong 2003). The imperial presence in the Inner City made the center off limits to commercial activities. The highest-level market, Qianmen, was located in the Outer City, separated by city walls from its main customers. In spite of the bourgeoning economic activities in the downtown Qianmen area, contemporaries of imperial Peking felt that the Outer City could not match the elegance of the palaces and imperial domains in the Inner City. The local urban life in the Outer City was only sketchily represented in visual media before the nineteenth century, as compared to that in the Inner City. According to Naquin (2000), the recommended tourist sights represented in popular guide books in this period were mostly limited to places in the Inner City and the countryside. Downtown as the economic center of Peking was conceived by its contemporaries as an inferior secular space, in sharp contrast with the sacred imperial domain. The physical and symbolic centrality of the imperial domain skewed the locations of markets and defined the meaning of downtown in imperial Peking.

Republican Peking (1911–1937)

The fall of the Qing dynasty in 1911 marked Peking's transition from tradition and imperialism to modernity. The republican period witnessed major changes in the market system and locations of downtowns in Peking, with the Inner City having an upper hand over the Outer City (Dong 2003). Qing's restrictions on Inner City commerce had vanished, and the concentration of wealthy families there provided the clientele for high-end markets. The variety and number of businesses increased, and old and new styles of commercial establishments proliferated. Hosting new styles of specialty shops, department stores, and indoor markets, Wangfujing emerged as the new downtown commercial center. It surpassed Qianmen and became the emblem of new consumerism and cosmopolitan urban life in Peking. The rise of Wangfujing as the new economic center in republican Peking was the result of its geographic proximity to the foreign community. The transnational connections in the semicolonial republican Peking redefined the economic geography and reordered power relations between places in the city.

The history of Wangfujing is the history of Peking's encounter with the West.[12] After its defeat in the Opium War in 1860, China was forced to sign the Treaty of Tianjin which sanctioned the establishment of a permanent international settlement in the city—the Legation Quarter. The arrival of a large number of foreign bureaucrats, diplomats, and politicians in the early 1900s contributed further to the growth of Wangfujing as a cosmopolitan marketplace. Many of the commercial establishments at Wangfujing were owned by foreigners, and almost all of them sold imported goods from Europe, Japan, and America. The economic clout and tastes of foreigners from the Legation Quarter propelled Wangfujing's growth (Broudehoux 2004). The foreign community was the key clientele at Wangfujing's specialty shops and antique dealers. Local Chinese bourgeois and aristocrats rubbed shoulders with foreigners while strolling along the paved and well-lit shopping promenades at Wangfujing.

Wangfujing, Xidan, and Qianmen formed a triangle of commercial centers around which lived the wealthiest residents of Peking (Dong 2003). [13] Among the three centers, Wangfujing was characterized as more Western and modern, while the older Qianmen market appealed to the masses with cheaper and traditional products. Wangfujing was a transnational marketplace formed by and primarily catering to the foreign community. By the 1930s, Wangfujing gathered all the elements of a modern downtown, with theaters, department stores, cafés, and other cultural institutions in place. Replacing the imperial political domain, the new downtown district of Wangfujing became the center of Peking's spatial organization and the focal point of cosmopolitan urbanism.

Socialist Peking (1949–1978)

Chinese communist leaders developed strong animosities toward the conspicuous consumption and lifestyles of the cities in the republican period. The new rulers saw cities as places of vice, corruption, and class exploitation. Although the CCP (Chinese Communist Party) was active in the cities in its early days, after 1927 it was driven into the countryside by the Nationalist Party and had to devise means for mobilizing a rural revolution while watching the Nationalist Party rule the cities (Whyte and Parish 1984). After the CCP came to power in 1949, it initiated a series of reforms to purge urban evils and to transform the pre-1949 consumption cities into socialist production centers. These measures included, for example, the elimination of foreign control and influence, the deportation of all foreign residents, the building of heavy industrial facilities in city centers, the minimization of service sectors, and the end of private property ownership. For the CCP leaders, the ideal city should be a Spartan and productive place with minimal lifestyle differences and without conspicuous consumption.

The anti-urban biases of the communist leadership had a devastating impact on the urban economy. Between the 1950s and the 1970s, Peking and other mainland Chinese cities suffered severe disinvestment, shortages, and poor quality of goods and services. Many stores were closed down, and those open were often stuffed with unfriendly clerks. According to Martin King Whyte and William Parish (1984), Peking had 10,200 restaurants in 1949 when the population was less than 2 million. But by the 1970s, when the total population was almost 5 million, there were only 656 restaurants. The number of shops declined from 70,000 in the early 1950s to 10,000 in 1980. These were the results of the three decades of reform aimed at changing Chinese cities from consumption sites to production centers.

Earlier downtown commercial centers invariably suffered from the anti-urban disinvestment policies. During the socialist period, Wangfujing's cosmopolitan and international character was changed, as foreigners were deported and private shops were replaced with state-owned department stores. Foreign signs and road names were replaced with versions that included Chinese names and strong socialist appeals; for example, the main street at Wangfujing was renamed People's Street (Broudehoux 2004). Most goods were allocated through the local state in the centralized planning system, and state-owned retail establishments lacked incentives to compete for customers. The department stores at Wangfujing failed to update their facilities and continued selling substandard products, and Wangfujing eventually lost its former cosmopolitan glamour and appeal in the socialist years. After a short-lived commercial renaissance in the republican era, in the new socialist production city, downtown Peking became subordinated again to the political domain. The communist leaders set up their administration apparatus inside the compounds of the former Imperial City, and ruled the country from there for nearly three decades until 1978, when the Great Cultural Revolution ended and the market reform began. The inaccessible government complex at the geographic center of the city was also the symbolic center and the political heart that organized the urban society and spatial structure of the socialist Peking.

The Making of the CBD in Global Beijing

The urban structure in socialist Peking was fundamentally altered after 1978 when China initiated neoliberal market reforms. In contrast with functionally mixed districts, post-Mao Beijing has become increasingly specialized. One of the new emerging urban spaces is the CBD. Much of this new development has taken place just beyond the margin of the built-up areas in close proximity to the city center (Gaubatz 1995, 1999, 2005). In Beijing a new CBD was built at the intersection of the East Third Ring Road and the extension of Chang'An Avenue, which is the main west-east axis of the city. The new CBD is a result of targeted state planning and global flows of design expertise, ideas, and capital. Art and architecture are the new tools used for promoting the CBD to domestic and international investors. Using other global downtowns for reference, the local business and political elites articulated a new vision of modernity in the construction of the CBD, a vision that prioritizes the transnational capitalist class and excludes the majority of urban residents.

State Power and Global Design

The plan to build a CBD was first proposed in the *Beijing General City Plan*, which the State Council approved in 1993. It stated that "a modern central

business district with multi-functions of finance, insurance, trade, information, commerce, culture, and entertainment should be built in Beijing."[14] In
1998, the Beijing city government issued the *Specific Controlling Plan* indicating that the CBD would be located in the Chaoyang district in the eastern
part of Beijing.[15] The CBD Administration Committee was established to supervise all development activities. In 1999, the central government appointed
Wang Qishan, the former executive of the China Construction Bank, as the
mayor of Beijing. Since then, one of the primary goals of the new administration has been to build a financial district capable of luring multinational
firms and financial institutions to Beijing. The area allocated for the CBD is
approximately four square kilometers at the crossing of the East Third Ring
Road and Jianguomenwai Boulevard. The site used to be an industrial area
with a number of large manufacturing facilities. Approximately 54,000
households worked and lived in the area.[16] However, the city government
envisioned a new modern business district emerging from there. The existing manufacturing facilities had to be relocated elsewhere, old residential
buildings demolished, and residents evicted.

The first step in turning the area into a modern business district was to
draft a master plan accommodating global business functions. In preparing
a master plan, Beijing followed Shanghai's practice of inviting international
architectural design firms as a promotional tool (Olds 2001). In 2000, the
Chaoyang district government organized the first international design competition for master plan proposals. Eight international firms were selected
and invited to submit designs. Among them were firms from America, Germany, Japan, and Holland. Only two entries among the eight were from
Chinese firms.[17] The participation of international architectural firms was
widely publicized in local and national media. To reflect the "international"
character of the design process, the organizers also put together a jury committee composed of not only Chinese but also international experts in architecture and planning. The committee finally selected the design by Johnson
Fain & Partners (USA) for the first prize. In 2003, the committee held a second
international design competition to select a detailed plan for a smaller core
area of the CBD. The design proposal from Pei Cobb Freed & Partners (USA)
won the competition.

Although two American firms won the international design competitions, neither of their designs was implemented as the final master plan of
the CBD. Beijing Planning and Design Institute, a de facto government-owned
design institute, combined features from different proposals and finalized the

master plan. The participation of international architectural firms in the design competitions was seen as a great success in itself. For local governments, it was not of great importance that the final master plans were eclectic selections from different proposals pieced together by local design institutes. What matters more is that the final master plan resulted from international design competitions, and therefore it is a global product. International design competitions in this case acted as publicity campaigns to promote the new CBD even before it was built.

After the master plan was approved, the Beijing municipal government issued a series of policies designed to entice multinational and Fortune Global 500 companies to establish their regional headquarters in the CBD. These policies aimed to reduce the operation costs for business service firms by providing tax cuts, subsidies, and other benefits. Backed by the strong economic performance of China as a whole, these entrepreneurial policies have had visible effects. Currently a large number of multinational corporations have established branch offices in the new CBD in Beijing.

Architecture as Advertising

Unlike historical downtowns, the CBD is a brand new megaproject undertaken by the local government in an attempt to attract global capital and transform Beijing into a global city. There is little cultural heritage and history associated with the place that can be used for place-marketing. To fill this cultural vacuum, local businesses and political elites invited prestigious international architects to lend legitimacy to the new downtown. Dozens of signature buildings were constructed on the site, including the high-profile China Central Television (CCTV) headquarters designed by Rem Koolhaas and OMA (Office for Metropolitan Architecture). These architectural projects not only provided a state-of-the-art physical infrastructure for the work of globalization to get done but also created the symbolic cultural capital desperately needed by local boosters for place making.

The fusion of power of the local Chinese state and global architects is mediated through the private market of property development. The case of SOHO China, a private real estate firm based in Beijing, offers an excellent example of how architecture has become a strategic tool for capital accumulation in the process of global city formation. SOHO China distinguished itself from other developers with its self-portrait as patrons of avant garde architecture. From the very beginning, the developers intended to build a new landmark in Beijing's CBD with bold architectural design. In October 2000, SOHO China invited Arata Isozaki, Riken Yamamoto, and Rocco Yim to submit design proposals for its project Jianwai SOHO—a mixed development project including two office skyscrapers, seventeen apartment buildings, and more than 300 retail shops located right in the core area of the CBD. The developers were looking for a design that would be modern, non-Chinese-looking, and marketable to wealthy Chinese investors and foreigners alike. Among the three proposals submitted, Isozaki's design was full of Chinese metaphors in abstract forms, integrating features found in traditional animal and mythological figures such as phoenixes, turtles, and cranes. It is ironic that a design full of Chinese references was actually proposed by a foreign architect. However, the developer was looking for a completely modern design and was not impressed by Isozaki's China-inspired proposal. The CEO Pan Shiyi commented, "Chinese elements don't have to be expressed in specific architectural languages."[18] Rocco Yim's design was rejected as well for being too experimental and impractical. Pan Shiyi commented, "This is a very interesting design, but it's too experimental, and nobody would buy a house like this in Beijing." There are limits to the patronage for avant garde architecture—experimentalism has to be practiced within marketability. Finally, Riken Yamamoto's ultramodern design was selected among the three. Yamamoto's design stresses minimalism, with high-tech, modern-looking, and strong visual appeals, all characteristics sought after by the developers. In an interview with the developer Pan Shiyi, Pan explained his preference for foreign over Chinese architects: "Chinese architects tend to think of architectural design only as paper drawings and engineering, and they don't see it also as art. What I want is something different from others, something that will surprise people, and something people will talk about." As the developer expected, Jianwai SOHO did become the most "talked about" project in the CBD.

The sale of office and residential properties at Jianwai SOHO far exceeded that of other projects in the CBD. Pan Shiyi became a Donald Trump–like celebrity and later ventured into other cultural industries such as publishing, television, and movie production. His other projects have also caused a media frenzy and became the most desired properties in the CBD. Signature architecture turned the new CBD from a nowhere into the new center of Beijing.

Imagining Modernity

Both local government officials and private developers use a set of images of global cities as a reference point in their imagination and discursive construction of the new CBD. Most of these references are drawn from the CBDs in the West, especially Manhattan, New York. On the official website of the Beijing CBD, a flashing picture of Manhattan's skyline is prominently displayed. Under the gleaming image reads a slogan: "New York/Manhattan— Beijing/Chaoyang." Another section of the website is devoted to "Foreign CBDs" in Tokyo, London, Paris, Frankfurt, Toronto, and other global cities.[19] Global downtowns and CBDs have thus become part of the official imagination of urban modernity for city builders in Beijing. The imagined modernity is narrowly centered on office skyscrapers, new infrastructures, and the priority of attracting investment. In the documents accompanying the master plan, the city government clearly emphasizes the significance of creating a modern cityscape symbolizing a financial district. A vertical "financescape" with concentrating skyscrapers exceeding 300 meters is seen as the right urban form to symbolize the rise of Beijing as a global city. The new CBD must not be just like another downtown. It has to be bold and it has to impress. The CBD achieves its visual impact because of its dense concentration of dozens of skyscrapers in the narrow area on both sides of major highways cutting across the CBD. In a similar fashion, private developers at SOHO China also invoked other global cities as role models to emulate. Here is a quote from a brochure of Jianwai SOHO: "There are restaurants, shops, offices and people living here at Jianwai SOHO. It is like the center of New York, Paris, and London. . . . Beijing needs this cosmopolitan lifestyle. We hope that Jianwai SOHO can partly meet this need. . . . Beijingers have started to live a lifestyle of that of New Yorkers, Parisians and Londoners in their newly built city" (Pan 2000: 89).

The developers project a new cosmopolitan lifestyle that they believe is attractive to wealthy Chinese and foreigners. They suggest to potential investors that by living and consuming at Jianwai SOHO, people can experience the lifestyle of cosmopolitans in other global cities. Designed by international architects, Jianwai SOHO is a transnational space exclusively reserved for the few who can afford it. Such a vision of modernity has excluded most urban residents. The original residents living on the site were forcibly relocated to suburban living quarters with inadequate infrastructure. Their visions and concerns are largely marginalized in the official discourse and imagination of global CBDs.[20]

Shifting Centers, Shifting Powers

New geographies signify new power relations. By tracing the changing locations, functions, and meaning of downtown Peking/Beijing, I have examined the larger socioeconomic forces at work that defined the downtown space in the city in different periods. The shifting power balance of economic, political, and cultural spheres largely explains the migration of the downtowns. As the commercial and business section of the city, downtown Peking was located in the inferior Outer City, separated from the Inner City by city walls in the imperial period. The power of the empire organized the spatial patterns of the city, with the imperial political domain occupying both the geographic and symbolic center of Peking. Transnational connections in the republican period reordered these power relations, as Wangfujing replaced the old Qianmen as a more cosmopolitan marketplace mainly catering to the foreign community. The short-lived commercial renaissance vanished quickly after communist leaders took power in 1949. Under the austere communist regime, the political power of the Communist Party reorganized the spatial relations in the city. The three decades of urban reforms had a devastating impact on the urban economy. As a result, manufacturing replaced commercial and business activities downtown, and Peking was transformed from a consumption city to a socialist production city. In the post-socialist period, the entrepreneurial city government conducted a grand experiment by planning a new CBD at the former urban fringes. For a city such as Beijing that lacks the infrastructure for advanced economies, the new CBD provides a platform and functions as the nodal point connecting Beijing to other major cities in the global urban network. The imperial palaces and communist government compounds, once perceived as signifiers of power and centrality, have now been replaced by state-of-the-art buildings in the CBD that house the work of globalization.

Rather than viewing center and periphery as geographically fixed entities, in this chapter I have projected a more dynamic relationship between places and focused on the contingent and transitory nature of urban centrality. By identifying changes and continuities of urban processes, the historical analysis in this chapter hopefully can correct some of the biases in the current scholarship on Chinese cities that is largely ahistorical.[21] Comparative studies in the rest of the book further explore the context-specific processes at work for reinventions of other global downtowns, as well as the conflicts and exclusions that characterize the making of urban centralities.

Postscript

The planning of the 2008 Olympics has left clear legacies in the spatial organization of Beijing and reordered the hierarchies of places within the city once again. The main venues such as the Bird's Nest (National Stadium), the Water Cube (National Olympic Swimming Center), and major exhibition and hotel complexes are mostly concentrated in the north side of the city around the new Olympic Park. Property prices are rapidly rising, and this area has become the next most coveted real estate for upscale residential and commercial development.

3

Simulations of Barcelona: Urban Projects in Port Spaces (1981–2002)

Francesc Magrinyà and Gaspar Maza

For a long time, urban port areas have been conflictive zones, spaces of transition, attractive and inhospitable at the same time. Spaces of dubious legality, they are where mysterious overseas exchanges take place, an exchange with what lies beyond. Spaces filled with promises, dreams, and menaces. In the last instance, these spaces carry an ambiguous but intense cargo of meaning and metaphor. Conscious of the importance of this dimension of meaning, often, promoters of this class of operation around the world have played the card of nostalgic simulacrum to the hilt: with port activity eliminated, new installations force themselves to recreate a maritime air to continue to simulate that which they are not and to dissimulate that which they have become.

—Pep Subirós

The large port zone close to central Barcelona has witnessed, in a brief period of time, an important series of urban reforms. This area has been transformed into a new civic space without losing its older condition of *zona franca* (a distinct port authority). The space also now houses new commercial buildings, offices, and cultural centers in the form of museums, an aquarium, and a 3-D IMAX cinema. Thus, it has been labeled by the city as a new area of centrality, in a sense, a new "downtown" near but not connected to either the ritual and political center of the city or its shopping centers (Ajuntament de Barcelona 1991). At the same time that these objectives were achieved, however, they were undercut by urban disorders in the form of ongoing conflict, violent incidents, and rapid changes. Thus, shortly after these new spaces made their debut, there was a need to react to issues there via new projects of reform that altered them. Both the appearance of this new urban centrality and these processes of rapid change led us to our ethnography of this space with the goal of understanding the different projects that have converged there and their lessons for other central spaces, either revitalized downtowns or newly constructed ones.

Our first question is whether the port actually constitutes a space where meaning has been added, a recuperation of public space, or if there simply has been a substitution of businesses and industries. In this sense, it is necessary to investigate whether we are dealing with fictional centralities or if the area will really become a new center of attractions. A second set of questions involves whether these areas have been appropriated or rejected by citizens and how. This leads us to corollary questions: Is this a place for citizens or a place for tourists? Is this a public space, or does it continue to be an autonomous space? And a final question we consider vital: What are the causes of the sequence of urban actions that have reshaped this place?

To respond to this set of questions, we begin with a brief historical review of the reconstruction of the port and its repercussions on the wider city. We then concentrate on what we call the "Reconquest" of public space in the port (1981–2000). Here, from an ethnographic viewpoint, we have identified three principal stages: success, decadence, and reform of the reform. Finally, we analyze the absence of social mechanisms of appropriation in these new spaces and the consequent fragility that has dominated this emergent "non-space" (Augé 1995). To do so, we use an analytic model based on the centrality of networks in the disciplines of geography (Raffestin 1980) and urbanism (Dupuy 1996).

The City and the Sea: Making Sense of a Contradictory Relationship

The first reports of port structures in the area of Barcelona go back to the fifth and fourth centuries B.C.E. At that time, the Iberians used an area near the mouth of the Llobregat River as a port: this lies to the west of Montjüic where the current Zona Franca (primary port) now lies. By the early Middle Ages, Barcelona had become a great maritime power without really having a true port. The Llotja (Stock Exchange) building near the Place of the Palace (Pla del Palau) functioned as a market, built on the shores of the Mediterranean although other centralized functions of government and religion (the Cathedral and Santa Maria del Mar) were further inland. Despite many attempts to construct a breakwater there, the first documented works on the port of Barcelona were not begun until 1439, when Barcelona's maritime and commercial power already had begun to decline.

Any breakwater, in fact, created eddies that, with drainage ditches, caused an accumulation of sand. The space occupied by the present-day Barceloneta came into existence through this process of accumulation of sand around the east breakwater (now Clock Wharf). The Barceloneta itself later was built as a Baroque residential district in 1735 to harbor fishermen and citizens displaced by construction of the massive ciutadela (citadel) that dominated a once-rebellious city (Tatjer 1996). In recent decades, the Barceloneta, too, has become the site of intensive gentrification and tourist-oriented development.

In 1529, on the occasion of a visit by the emperor Charles V, further public works were recommended including a sea wall (Muralla del Mar) to protect the city from pirates and Turks. This wall was finished in 1562 and would define the image of the port of Barcelona well into the eighteenth century. This coincided with the development of the Rambles, a promenade from the sea toward the mountains that soon combined commerce, institutions such as theaters and operas, and fashionable promenades in an incipient downtown district.

Nonetheless, until 1874, and the completion of a project by Mauricio Garrán, the city lacked a modern port, understood as an assembly of technical installations and marine spaces adapted for all operations of loading and unloading. After this initial construction, however, the port continued to grow with the industrializing metropolis. By 1914 it generally had achieved the shape it would maintain until its final remodeling in 2000: an industrial port whose activities "turned their back" on the bourgeois city of the Rambles and more elegant residential districts. Only with the 2000 renovation was the port opened to the city, in a plan characterized by the segregation of uses dividing the space of civic activity and recreation (Port Vell) from a commercial zone and a logistical zone (ZAL), a pattern typical of port renovations of the late twentieth century (Montero 1997).

From a historical perspective, the port has evolved facing the new necessities that the city has generated over time as an instrument to gain space *from* the sea while establishing an intimate alliance between the objectives of the port and those of the city as a whole. As such, it has established a dialectic with central districts of governance, religion, commerce, and society that became increasingly inland spaces until the renovations of the 1992 Olympic city.

At the same time, the port close to the center of the city has evoked changing images and feelings. When the medieval government, the Consell de Cent, discussed the advantages of a solidly constructed port with a dock to protect it, the necessity of improving the city and its entrance was a principal argument: "It is clear that the fervent desire to have a port has arisen from time to time and perhaps precisely when some notable arrives in the city and it is necessary to build an entire bastide so that that person can land on the beach without his feet getting wet or that some men of the shore need to carry them on their back" (Campany 1990: 13).

After 1562, with the construction of a promenade along the wall, the city gained a lookout and the counselors of the city, full of pride, affirmed: "The Passeig de la Marina, which goes from the Gate of the Sea to Drassanes [the medieval shipyards, now a museum] has become a great boon for the city, given how many people, noble and otherwise, as well as outsiders frequent it, whether in summer or winter" (Garcia Espuche 1995).

With the industrial development of Barcelona in the nineteenth century, the port took on connotations of an industrial zone and an area tied to illicit activities: "the port is the open road to all evils and among the evils that are not to be overlooked are naturally sin, marginalization, the low life where all is sold and cheap" (Campany 1990: 48). The port, nevertheless, was also a stronghold of worker pride, as seen in the defiant verses of Joan Salvat-Papasseit, son of a fireman in the Barceloneta who worked on the Transatlantic shipping line. In his *Nocturne for Accordion*, he wrote nostalgically: "You all do not know what it is like to guard wood on the wharf" (Soldevila 1957: 22).

By the twentieth century, the port zone had become an isolated precinct within the city, with access closed by the wharfs that surrounded the pier, by the Barceloneta, and by the wide Paseo de Colon. Urbane leisure was localized on the edge of the port, along the promenade beside the breakwater and in the nearby neighborhood and alternative pleasures of the barrio chino/Raval (McDonogh 1999; McDonogh and Wong, this volume).

The relationship between the city and the sea began to change in the early 1980s, under the first democratic mayors who followed the long regime of Francisco Franco (1939–1976). The reform of the port was seen as an important element for the nearby Ciutat Vella—the historic center that housed government, ecclesiastical centers, museums, and tourist services and a variegated population (although population, big business, and consumption all had shifted westward). Reform would serve the city as a whole. The sea lay behind a wall demanding recovery, as socialist mayor (and geographer) Pascual Maragall signaled: "yesterday I had a dream. . . . I dreamed that Barcelona opened to the sea. And that new beaches, real beaches, appeared in the sites where old industries now lie. I dreamed that I walked down from the Sagrada Familia to the sea in half an hour, with nothing blocking my way" (Mauri and Uría 1998: 208).

In 1986, as Barcelona prepared its candidature for the 1992 Olympic Games, the need for a complete reform of the port and its connection with the new multiservice Olympic City along the coastal highway reemerged. It was in this moment that the document was formalized that would legitimate a discourse of new areas of centrality as priorities for the city. The Port Vell thus joined the four initial areas of the Olympic Games (Montjüic, Vila Olímpica/Olympic City, Vall d'Hebron, and Diagonal-Camp Nou).

This renovation campaign was decisively influenced by a renewal of relations between the port and the city. This began with the baptism of the areas as a new "Port Vell." To support this change, the municipal administration sought to develop pride in the city, offering citizens the opportunity to design a new edge of the city and the sea as well as the invitation to discover this zone, with promises of spaces hitherto inaccessible. All these actions were seen as pathbreaking efforts in disentailment so that civic consensus could be created, using previous urban histories as a justification:

First, in 1888, it was the Ciutadela; then, in 1929, then it was the mountain of Montjüic, and now we have reached the hour of the Port Vell. In a century, Barcelona will have recovered three spaces that history had stripped from its jurisdiction. . . . Recuperation is not just an idea of today. The reencounter of the city and the sea is an objective that could scarcely achieve more social and political consensus. The first step was the disappearance of the port service rail line and the urbanization of the Moll de la Fusta, a space that had become emblematic because of its exceptional status. Later, as a

fundamental piece of the Olympic project came the great opportunity to renovate the maritime frontier of Poble Nou with the construction of the Olympic Port (Vila Olímpica). The disentailment of the
Port Vell is, thus, the task facing us. (Juliana 1988: 80)

Seen in perspective, the Barcelona initiative with regard to its port, in
spite of its supposed originality, paralleled port reforms in Europe (London,
Liverpool, Hamburg, Rotterdam, Lisbon, Genoa), the Americas (San Francisco, Baltimore, Toronto, Buenos Aires), Asia (Osaka, Yokohama, Hong
Kong, Singapore), and Australia (Sydney). While touted as intensely local,
this renovation of the center was also intensely global, even if it was a globalization of imitation and competition.

By contrast, the discourse of the owners of the lands of the Autonomous
Port of Barcelona (PAB) about the recuperation of public space for the city
did not share the same civic feelings. We see this in the first two lines of the
Master Plan of the Port of Barcelona of 1989, which foresee plans "(1) to
arrange the physical growth of the port towards the South and central areas
and (2) to take advantage of the proximity of the city to initiate other activities" (Montero 1997). In general, these clashing visions and strategies show
us distinctive models of production of the center city on the same territory,
a gentrifying sensibility versus an entrepreneurial one. These played out in
specific projects and their histories.

The Postmodern Reconquest of the Port: Four Projects for Public Space

In the case of the Port Vell, we can trace the spatial "Reconquest" of the city
through four major projects: (1) 1981–1987 Moll de la Fusta (Timber Wharf);
(2) 1988–1993 Moll de la Barceloneta (Barceloneta Wharf)/Passeig Joan de
Borbó; (3) 1994–1996 Moll d'Espanya (Spain Wharf)/Maremagnum (Mall);
and (4) 1998–2000 Moll de Barcelona (Barcelona Wharf/World Trade Center).
Within two decades, project followed project in different parts of the port
with a rhythm we will analyze in the next section.

The Moll de la Fusta project constituted the first stage in the reconquest
of the port. The project emphasized recuperation of the past, seen in a mixture of uses envisioned by the architect responsible for the project, Manuel

de Solà-Morales: "I wanted the project to have an intention of permanence that would give the feeling of having been there permanently. It was a project shaped by many diverse conditions that obliged us to mix many things: the idea of public space, a solution to transportation infrastructure, buildings with urban character, etc. This combination of elements is that which sets the project apart and which most attracts the foreign specialists who have visited the Moll" (De Castro 1987).

This reconquest of space began on May 28, 1981, taking advantage of Armed Forces Day. This first event was programmed to prepare what we can consider the "pre-discovery" of the place. After this, the wharf was closed to the public for six years, until Epiphany 1987 and the Barcelona passage of the Paris-Dakar rally on January 4. This second inauguration faced press criticism for its delays, the length of the work, and the money it had cost. Another critical point raised was the persistent difficulty in access to the sea that this project had been planned to eradicate. Nonetheless, Solà-Morales declared: "No one has ever seen the sea from this view point and in any case, Barcelonans will now understand that with this new balcony they have gained a wider vision of the port, although until all parts of the project are opened to the public they will not be able to value this new perspective" (De Castro 1987).

After the inauguration of the Moll de la Fusta, its social life became intertwined with the hypermodern bars built there, such as Gambrinus, Blau Marí (Navy Blue), and Distrito Marítimo (Maritime District). These were extensively publicized in many different guides and periodicals as a new type of bar—selective, distinctive, and with unique seaviews: "Seated in one of the tables on its terrace with views of the port of Barcelona you can see anyone from drag queens to the richest people on the planet. The beautiful people abound in this spot that is impossible to even get into during summer weekends. Music changes according to the DJ who plays that night" (Pomés and Feriche 2001: 80).

To commemorate history, the urban project of the Moll de la Fusta, especially in the zone of the Paseo de Colon, referred to Antoni Gaudí in its serpentine-form seats and the use of broken tiles (*trencadis*) in its decoration. At the same time, this new ludic zone also incorporated references to the Barcelona Football Club through blue and red shields. Other elements of the project that gained international acclaim were many sculptures in different forms, from realism to pop. Busts of Joan Salvat Passapeit (the poet worker referred to above) and Romulo Bosch Alsina (mayor of Barcelona and proponent of its first reforms) are the work of Luxembourg sculptor Robert Krier, brother of urbanist Leon Krier. Meanwhile, Roy Lichtenstein's monumental sculptural *Barcelona Head* represents pop art, again clothed with broken tiles in homage to Gaudí. The most singular element of the area is Javier Mariscal's *La Gamba*, a gigantic shrimp crowning one of the beach bars (*chiringuitos*).

Meanwhile, the streetscape of this proto-downtown maintained the separation of distinctive forms of transportation: highways, trains (underground), and pedestrians near the port, now relegated to pleasure boats. On the Moll de la Fusta, for example, next to the sea, the city constructed a palm grove against a widely separated cobblestone base. This surface actually made pedestrian transit difficult until it was rebuilt in 2001. By then, though, the Moll de la Fusta had already lost steam to the Moll d'Espanya.

The subsequent reform of the Barceloneta Wharf signified a new phase marked by growing experience in urban design. Nevertheless, its development made clear the lack of an overall plan for the port zone and its relation to the city or other centers. The primary thrust of reform in this section was the destruction of existing warehouses and their substitution with a new promenade. This promenade negotiated dual roles as a neighborhood avenue and a port space, without having any clear function of its own. Yet this space also eased the transition in areas closest to residences with trees, opening out visually from this esplanade onto the port.

Only the section known as the Moll del Dipòsit (Deposit Wharf, attributed to the major nineteenth-century architect Elies Rogent) was saved from this destruction as part of the city's patrimony. Rechristened the Palau de Mar (Palace of the Sea), it filled with restaurants, offices, the Museum of History of Catalunya, and the welfare offices of the Catalan government. In the section closest to the sea, some spaces for fishermen and port activities were also constructed.

The rest of the reconquered space became public space, forming part of the Passeig Joan de Borbó, work of architects Jordi Henrich, Olga Tarraso, and Rafael de Cáceres, 1991–1993. Here, two classes of complementary metaphors emerged. Nature became metaphoric through careful placement of varied trees, coordinated even in details such as different seasons when their leaves change, in order to convey the idea of a programmed garden. Another set of elements in the boulevard on the surface of the dock was an installation of lighted skylights by artist Mario Mertz, almost artistic winks that practically disappeared in further reforms in 2002. These sections, however, emphasized open space over the more concentrated downtown energies of initial designs.

Pedestrian circulation moved onto different levels, over surfaces including tiles, stones, and granites. The circulation of vehicles, though, was constrained with pylons shaped like ceramic jars. The bars of this area were much more modest than those of the neighboring Moll de la Fusta. Utilitarian bars that could open and close in minutes took their spot with a maritime style for daylight hours. There were also some nighttime bars, but these were suppressed within a year.

Between 1995 and 1998, however, the dominant social activity of this space became rollerblading, with heavy concentrations of skaters evident on Tuesdays and Thursdays. At its height, this craze even led to a rental shop for skates serving the Passeig. In short, the space was appropriated by people as a space of movement with skates, bicycles, or electric scooters. The city government, meanwhile, countered with official events such as a fair for the elderly, organized by the welfare departments, boat exhibitions to accompany the international boat show, and events related to the citywide patronal festival of Our Lady of Mercy (La Mercè). These imposed the interests of the city as a whole while excluding marginal populations.

In 1994, the reform of port space reached the Spanish Wharf (Moll d'Espanya), facing the Moll de la Fusta. Once the warehouses were torn down, the first intervention there was the creation of a new access from Barcelona's historically central Rambles, an aquatic bridge called the Rambla de Mar (Helio Piñón, Albert Vilaplana). Unlike the Barceloneta project, this space entailed a direct connection to the historic downtown as well as a continuation or competition of its functions. At the end of the Rambla de Mar, for example, a shopping center labeled Maremagnum appeared. Not a large mall like those then emerging around greater Barcelona (similar to global megamalls), this building, whose name evokes the Roman Mediterranean, had a net surface of 16,439 square meters, housing 120 stores and a naval station. There are neither department stores nor large supermarkets. Most telling are the discotheques situated on one side of the first floor and covering the second floor. The naval station, including unused customs facilities, allows the whole establishment to be classified as a maritime station and kept open after closing hours for other city clubs.

A chain of cinemas, an aquarium, and a 3-D IMAX completed the re-urbanization of the zone. They were built with a certain cubist flavor, especially the IMAX, yet they also turned their back on the water, contradicting any idea of recovering the waterfront. The scant separation among these cinemas and the aquarium also produced a sense of massivity that overpowered the space.

Meanwhile, the utilization of decorative elements, commemorations, and witty historical references continued to shape this space as it had its predecessors. The Rambla de Mar referenced the sea through metal waves all along its trajectory. In the Colón section, a great electronic billboard promoted some "downtown" characteristics of the new place like "Maremagnum: a place where things always happen. The most active and most relaxing spot in Barcelona."

Different elements such as an entrance ramp covered with lawn, benches, and a plaza named for the Odyssey conveyed a sense of designed public space. This space had an undulating cratered design, simulating waves like a simple plaza or a small surrealist dream by Salvador Dalí. A series of pergolas saying "Made in Barcelona" rose in front of the aquarium, blocking much of the façade. The most widely used features of the space were seats and benches which, unlike the rest of the city, were wide and not compartmentalized.

An article by Barcelona author Sergi Pamiès, "Sopa de Maremagnum" (Maremagnum Soup), underscores the global centrality that Maremagnum had taken on as well as local alienation:

> The architects hate it because it is ugly. The residents of nearby barrios hate it because of its noise. It is enormous, open every day of the year and it has a parking lot divided into sections that carry the name of animals and that let the driver identify with one beast or another according to the state of his spirit.
>
> Before the midday avalanche, when calm still reigns, the waiters and cooks of the restaurants eat at their own table. They hardly speak. Perhaps because they come from different countries and are there in transit. There are Pakistanis, Filipinos, Ecuadorians, Italians, Koreans, Chinese, Peruvians. They enter and leave through emergency exits and fire doors, pulling stuffed containers while they glance at the boats they see through the windows, carrying on their enviable dance of flags. They wave in the wind: Norwegian, English, Turk, looking for anchorage in this globalized port with tourists on pleasure voyages on the one hand and multiracial service personnel on

the other. Those who wish to know what is happening in this country should pass some time here, in Maremagnum—a territory stolen from the sea, an independent commercial republic. (*El País*, February 4, 2001)

The success of this nonplace, more than an actual public space, has raised many questions. For many tourists it has become one of the central icons of the city, while for many Barcelonans it is a place to visit once and never return.

Finally, between 1998 and 2000, another dramatic transformation took place in the wharf area with the appearance of the World Trade Center (WTC)—invoking yet another global reference and claim to centrality. This was supposed to be a new project for the reconquest of space, but its perspective actually corresponded to that of a private operator developing his own space. The Moll de Barcelona project favored high-quality offices and a luxury hotel. The central element of this reform was the construction of the building itself by Pei Cobb Freed & Partners, whose starchitect firm has taken on iconic projects worldwide; the hotel belongs to an international chain that has another 130 WTC franchise buildings. This project also entailed the replacement of the old maritime station. Thus, the WTC represents a project that was less ludic and public and much more entrepreneurial, with no concessions to public space or play, consecrated to business, hotels, and congresses—a globalization of capital and capitalists for the twenty-first century, rather than an evolution of local history or even recent socialist models of the city.

Mechanisms of Simulacrum: From Innovation to Decadence and Reform

These projects that underpinned divergent constructions of new central spaces shared common functional mechanisms that recurred according to the demands of three principal moments: inauguration-success, decadence, and reform. These processes relied on the complicity of the citizens themselves who participated actively in these new spaces especially in their first moments of success and later let them slide into oblivion and into the hands of foreign publics, especially tourists. The partial appropriation of these spaces that were built principally on the basis of specialized usages (recreation, culture, or nightlife) meant that these activities took on an especially powerful position on the Moll de Fusta and Moll d'Espanya, until the arrival of their own crises and revitalization. In this, the projects not only echo downtown developments elsewhere in this volume but encapsulate rapid and condensed processes of urban change.

Inauguration and Success

Efforts to promote new public spaces focused on the moment of their inauguration. In fact, the debut of these spaces often was planned to coincide with city-wide public festivals and global events. The Moll de la Fusta opened with the arrival of the Paris-Dakar rally in Barcelona and Epiphany 1987 (*El País*, January 2, 1987); one headline even read "The Magi Opened the New Marine Promenade of the Moll de la Fusta Today" (*El País*, January 5, 1987). Passeig Joan de Borbó and Maremagnum opened during the city's patronal Festival of Our Lady of Mercy (1994, 1995) and different activities were associated with the 1992 Olympic Games.

On the Moll de la Fusta, one of the most successful social events occurred in June 1989 with an exposition of works by Javier Mariscal, the designer of the Olympic mascot, which took place on board the ship *Rey Favila*:

> The festival that followed the inauguration was never disappointing. Mariscal closed three of the five small buildings of the Moll de la Fusta to gather his friends. In Gambrinus, crowned with its immense shrimp. In Blau Marí and Distrito Marítimo, enough drinks were served to sate even the thirstiest. The terraces of those establishments brought together Barcelona's modernity—from survivors of the underground to Olympic architects passing through the professions that mingle to give the city a vitality that fit the times to some Valencians who did not want to miss the celebration of their compatriot. Almost everyone, infected by Mariscalian happiness, stayed until late dawn. As if a background to the celebration, the *Rey Favila* basked in the pleasant spring night. Above it floated, in multicolored neon letters, the Mariscalian syllables: Bar–Cel–Ona. And a few meters higher, a balloon with an interior light simulated a captive moon, perpetually enamored of the ship (Moix 1994).

With this event, some political discrepancies were also resolved, including the criticism that the president of the Generalitat, Jordi Pujol, previously had leveled against Javier Mariscal over his dislike of the doglike Olympic mascot. The boom of modernity represented by the party became part of the new constructions of the Moll de la Fusta. These areas became, for a few years, a public space for Barcelona at the same time that they represented a private space for distinguished parties.

By contrast, the inauguration of the Moll of Joan de Borbó, named for the father of the king of Spain, produced another variation. It was a smaller event with a stronger political content. It was covered in the press with much less fervor, including brief but realistic comments like "emotions come to the new Paseo Joan de Borbón" (*La Vanguardia*, September 25, 1993).

With the inauguration of the projects of the Moll d'Espanya, the dynamic of masses and multitudes returned: "Barcelona has gained new public spaces: mass waves in the Rambla de Mar" (*El País*, September 24, 1994). This event invited all Barcelonans as participatory citizens into this new space. The data available on tourism in the city, in its first years of functioning, identified it as one of the most visited sites in the city. The IMAX had 929,052 visitors in 1996; 1,112,316 in 1997; and 1,124,208 in 1998. The aquarium received 1,678,000 visitors in 1996; 1,513,790 in 1997; and 1,557,185 in 1998. By comparison, other traditional urban monuments including Gaudí's Sagrada Familia scarcely reached a million visitors in 1997; neither the Picasso Museum nor the Museum of the Barcelona Football Club reached that. The director of the port, Joaquin Tosas, claimed that 15 million visitors arrived in the wharf area in 1999 and the newspaper *Expansión* cited 17 million people in 2000 (July 6, 2000). Yet a period of decline soon followed, first in the Moll de la Fusta and then in the Moll d'Espanya.

Decadence

One of the most singular characteristics of the projects for public space in the port of Barcelona was the rapidity with which they moved from success to decay. In some cases, four or five years were enough to precipitate a crisis. This speed speaks to a fragility that is one of the most characteristic peculiarities of postmodern spaces designed around activities and specialized publics, an important contrast with traditional central business districts whether the religious-administrative center of Plaça Sant Jordi, the centurial

Rambles, or newer commercial cores. Under their apparent success, these postmodern simulacra conceal important paradoxes. Even an initial success, for example, created the need for perpetual new efforts to maintain, augment, or reinvent success so as to avoid decline.

One of the first indications of a problem in a part of the new port spaces came in the falling number of visitors. We can appreciate this through data on visits to the Moll d'Espanya/Maremagnum complex, which peaked at 18 million visitors but then dropped each year to 15 million visitors in 2003. While visitors were numerous, the continuing decline created a sense of failure, implying that the place had not been taken to heart by Barcelona once its day of fashion had passed. This decay hit the Moll de la Fusta first, with the closure of its *chiringuitos* in May 2000. The flight of "beautiful people" from this space filled the mass media with generalizations like "The novelty has worn off," "A shipwreck of ideas," "The degradation of nocturnal modernity," "The end of the oasis of design," "Impossible to reconcile vehicles and pedestrians," and "Cirrhosis closed the wharf." Criticisms of this space focused on problems like the lack of bathrooms in the bars or the insecurity of the parking lot below the bars themselves. On the ruins of the project, after administrative closure, the buildings were actually occupied by young immigrants who had previously lived in the street: "The Barcelona City Hall sent various brigades yesterday to empty, clean and seal the five bars of the Moll de la Fusta that have been used for the last few weeks by twenty or so Maghrebi minors, protagonists of thefts and robberies with violence in the [nearby] Gòtic Sur" ("Los magrebíes del Moll de la Fusta se enfrentan a las administraciones," *El Periódico*, December 15, 2000).

Writer Quim Monzó offered an eloquent synthesis of this rise and fall:

In the '80s, the authorities insisted in presenting us with the Moll de la Fusta as a symbol of the Barcelona which was believed to be the Mecca of cocktails and what we then called design. They gave us the Moll as the ultimate night spot, the obligatory place to meet that no one with any pedigree could afford to miss. But, as often happens, those who create nightlife are not good with following orders and began to look askance at the Moll, or openly laughed at it. Those bars with the undulating roof, those waiters who looked down their nose, the Moll de la Fusta never caught on—not as a zone for restaurants nor as a place to have some drinks and let down your hair. (Monzó 2002)

Nonetheless, the city continued to use the Moll de la Fusta as it agonized about wide-ranging activities that could not be enclosed in smaller zones— the Festival of Diversity, the Festival of Wine, and others. Yet, even worse problems followed, embodying both global flows and polarization of global populations.

Violence and Racism in Maremagnum

The Moll d'Espanya zone faced crises that emerged from a much more free-wheeling and popular social night life. By day, the wharf survived through the inertia of the social life created by the commercial center, the aquarium, and the 3-D IMAX cinema. At night, this zone attracted a mélange of foreign tourists, school groups on vacation, and youths from Barcelona and nearby cities. The successful nightlife of this site, situated in such a geographically central place, ultimately produced problems directly related to the massive nighttime disco scene there. These erupted in the form of fights, violence, racial incidents, and many differences when it came to interpreting rights of entry.

In the first six months of 2000, some fifty news items appeared talking about problems in the zone. Talking about the shopping center, sensational headlines appeared like "Maremoto en el Maremagnum [Seaquake in Mare-magnum]: The Wave of Incidents in the Port Zone Preoccupies the City" (*La Vanguardia*, January 1, 2000). Despite numerous incidents, however, only eleven were actually discussed in the press:

1. Beating of two Cuban women in a musical bar (one newspaper located the incident in the Maremagnum although it actually occurred in a bar of the Vila Olímpica)
2. Bouncer attacks a client, January 14, 2000
3. Raid in which 35 minors "without papers" are taken, January 23, 2000
4. Fight between youths and security guards, February 20, 2000
5. Two youths fall from the second floor to the ground, March 28, 2000
6. Bouncers have incident with two architects, April 5, 2000

7. Fight among three youths, April 26, 2000
8. Four Kosovar citizens attack two policemen, May 7, 2000
9. Youth hurt by a knife, July 14, 2000
10. English tourist killed by a knife, July 28, 2000
11. Person hurt by a doorman, August 17, 2000
    (*El País*, June 6, 2000).

More serious problems were still to come. In July 2002, Wilson Pacheco, a citizen of Ecuadorian origin, was beaten by bouncers in a discotheque and thrown into the water, where he died. At this moment, the image of the commercial center reached its nadir. These different events ended with accusations against the manager of the port, Odissea 2000, by organizations like SOS Racisme. This group ended up denouncing any incidents tied to persons of immigrant origins, criticizing "bars that had given instructions to keep immigrants out [like] the bars of the Port Vell where racial discrimination was practiced" (*El País*, June 6, 2002) Thus, the Moll d'Espanya changed from a welcoming center for daytime global/local visitors to a dangerous nighttime zone dominated by discotheques that made space ever more fragile and exclusionary.

The Reform of the Reform

By 2001–2002, those responsible for the Port Vell projects accepted the excesses of any claims for centrality for this area and its emergence as a "nonplace." As a consequence, they sought to transform the port into a more familiar space, to reduce the number of foreigners, to control ludic activities, and to implement new projects in other areas of the port. These new objectives began a new stage of reforms in the renovated port.

The reform of the reform in the case of the Moll d'Espanya was oriented toward the destruction of the cinemas to make the Odyssey plaza larger and to create better views from the aquarium, with the criterion that this improved access to the sea: "The port authority will tear down its movies and replace them next to Maremagnun. The project the Municipality has approved will begin in 2002 and last three years. This demolition will make it possible to enlarge the central plaza and improve its views of the sea. A spokesman for Port 2000, the enterprise that runs the Port Vell, explained that this reform intends to improve the quality of leisure, now concentrated at night, and attract a family friendly daytime crowd" (*El Periódico*, August 12, 2001). At some points, there was even discussion of building a hotel in the port, but this plan was finally rejected in order to preclude an excessive focus on nighttime activities and the generation of further incidents.

In practice, as of 2000, other kinds of events began to take place in this area, such as free movie screenings in the Maremagnum on Sunday morning, ballroom dancing in the center, and theatrical representations for children. The future became one of urban cultural dynamism tinged with new historical references, as in the headline from *El País*: "The Port of Barcelona Turns the Port Vell into a Cultural Center" (November 21, 2001). The article noted: "The creation of the Blue Axis was foreseen in a plan to make the zone more dynamic as early as 1999. This plan also foresaw reconstruction of the historic port from the end of the 19th century and beginning of the 20th. This reconstruction will be placed at the end of the Moll de la Fusta, near the Royal Yacht Club and will include the anchorage of several historical boats. It is ready to begin between February and March of 2003" (*El Pais*, May 1, 2002). New spaces and more sedate local culture closed the era of parties and problems in the Moll d'Espanya.

The Moll de la Fusta also faced a reform of reforms with a 2002 project that consisted in a change of pavements and heights in the promenade zone, as well as renewed maintenance for the famous *chiringuitos*. This reform eliminated their role as bars by making them sculptured places, producing a curious hybrid of walkways and skeletons of bars.

The reform initiated in the Barcelona Wharf with the construction of the WTC also constituted a prelude for new objectives. The project was given to private operators and there was no further discussion of its public character, perhaps as a reaction to previous experiences. With this action, the port became oriented toward what it always was despite the presence of earlier simulacra: a space of business instead of an inclusive urban space that would be closer to global models and practices of downtown. No one walks there or seeks the sea or even produces elements of social decadence.

In 2002, the last project of new spaces for the port received a green light. This reform meant the localization of a new entrance for the port along the breakwater. On land reclaimed from the sea, construction began on a new esplanade that would hold an edifice in the shape of a giant sail, from local starchitect Ricard Bofill and, paradoxically, would offer a new recreation center with definitive sea views. This project has spurred opposition because of its projected height (120 meters, later reduced) as well as the possible consequences including destruction of access to the port from the Passeig Joan de Borbó and collapse of the Barceloneta neighborhood. (See *El Mundo*, November 8, 2001.)

The Fragilities of New Spaces: The Port and the Privatizing Gentrification of the Business of Culture

Throughout these diverse processes, we also see some wider process of place and urban process that have converged in the repeated failure of the Port Vell projects as new centers or public spaces. These include the ambiguities of control, the absence of traditional forms of appropriation or access to spaces, the displacement of activities connecting the city and sea to new areas, and divergences between traditional models of public spaces that evolve over time with multiple users and the demands of a consumer economy. An analysis of networks (physical networks of transportation, logistical networks, and personal networks) explains the mechanisms leading from success to decadence. This urbanist perspective underscores that connections of transportation and telecommunication have radically changed uses of new spaces. Moreover, shopping centers form new elements of the organization of consumption in contrast to traditional neighborhood stores. At the same time, they have changed personal relations and interactions in public spaces.

Confusion of Control

A space becomes a territory when it is appropriated for an institution or for citizens through the use they make of it. The primary question we raise in the case of port zones we have analyzed is who exercises control and who appropriates a space that traditionally has been a frontier zone with regard to the city in a quest for centrality and new meaning. The struggle for control of this type of spaces is scarcely new but emerged in different historical episodes like that of the ancient walls surrounding the center of the city, the Park of the Ciutadela, or Montjüic. The first were claimed by both City Hall and the Ministry of Defense. One result was the Plaça de Catalunya, whose indefinite trapezoidal form reflects competition over a frontier space destined to be a central space, an ambiguous anchor or connector for downtown zones (see Magrinyà y Gimeno 1994). The latter two became sites on which to mount major global expositions that sought to alter the world status of the city in 1888 and 1929 (as well as the 1992 Olympics).

In 1978, the Port of Barcelona, having obtained its own statute of autonomy, gained the competence to act as both a public entity and a mercantile enterprise governing the port territory according to private law. Thus the port became an ambiguous place where private and public spaces converged, leading to extensive discussions of who held power (Juliana, *La Vanguardia*, September 17, 1995). From the standpoint of the municipality, principal competitor for port authority, the port had been a frontier for the city, the limit that had to be broken. The response of the Port Authority to this claim was to relinquish the space of the Port Vell but to maintain control. The Port Authority reserved for itself fundamental rights such as the decision about new activities in the zone, the choice of projects to pursue, or the hour of closure of the businesses: "the port authority based its claims on the closing hour for Maremagnum precisely on the fact that this recreational complex lay within a maritime station" (*La Vanguardia*, February 12, 2002). In practice, this meant that rather than a disinterested handover or a conquest of land by the municipality, in the end there was a transformation of activities in which warehouses were traded for boutiques, discotheques, and restaurants, but with no loss of autonomy.

Another consequence of this territorial ambiguity was the problem of security. Port police took primary responsibility until they were overwhelmed by the incidents in the Maremagnum in 2001 and 2002. Within private spaces, security was handled by private companies that became completely disorganized. At moments, as many as sixteen different security firms worked in the Maremagnum. To this confusion we must add the conflicts over legitimate power among the port police, the civil guard, the national police, the Catalan police, and the city police. The traditional legitimacy of the port police had been limited to guarding merchandise, sometimes with customs obligations. But with a change of functions, from commerce to leisure, this mission became obsolete, and they confronted conflicts with citizens for which they were unprepared. Moreover, the important influx of global immigrants to clubs focused on entertainment produced confused reactions. Thus, any type of incident became classified as racism, whatever the underlying issues and actions. The Port Vell and especially the Mare-magnum and its environs were tainted by this ambiguity.

Disappearing Connections

We also need to consider the remodeling of the port from an urbanistic standpoint. An urbanism of imagery dominated the first phase (1981–1993), as it did in other projects across the city. Between 1981 and 1987, the trans-formation of the Moll de la Fusta was planned, but not that of the Moll de la Barceloneta, where maintenance of the warehouses was still envisioned. The Moll de la Fusta was seen as a balcony for the central city, as it had been in past times of the promenade on the Maritime Wall. At this time, there were no plans for the Moll d'Espanya, either, which figured in the project as an isolated island without any commercial function.

From 1988 to 1993, the municipality negotiated the Moll de la Barcelo-neta for the city but in return ceded the Maremagnum complex to the Port Authority. This period was dominated by a design of urban furniture and other projects shaped by the urbane projects of the wider city rather than this specific area. After the hangover from the Olympic Games (1994–1996), a new series of projects began on a new urban scale embracing outlying areas and massive urban development (Diagonal Mar as a central urban bou-levard, new urban malls at the La Maquinista factory site, and La Sagrera). The construction of Maremagnum in the Moll d'Espanya embodied this new type of project with wider social and commercial impact. Up to this point, orthodox urbanism had not accepted the possibility of a commercial center in the center of the city. This concept changed with the activities of prestige architects in malls around the city.

The process of reform was changing substantially in a short time without any clear planning. It evolved from an urbanism on a small scale in the 1980s (Moll de la Fusta) to a 1990s urbanism focused on style and solutions of branding Barcelona (Moll de la Barceloneta) that coexisted with a large-scale urban transformation based on commercial centers and offices (from Mare-magnum to the WTC). At the same time, the classical ideal of public space in which the municipality had taken the lead gave way to a scenario in which private operators and special institutions were the primary protagonists.

The discourse of the Barcelona model in the 1990s had focused on the production of quality public space. But in new areas of centrality, beyond the construction of decors using urban furnishings of quality, it was not clear that the designed spaces would have any clear mechanisms of appropriation.

Based on our analysis of the predominant relations in the Port Vell, in fact, the physical relations of city and sea were substantially altered with the renovation of the entire coastal zone (Olympic Port, Mar Bella). Between 1981 and 2002, there was a transformation in which access to the sea focused on portside streets on a northern line through the Olympic Port to the site of Barcelona's 2004 Universal Forum of World Cultures. Looking at pedestrian flows and movements through the Port Vell, we can also see that the streets around the former seaside areas became more difficult to get to and lost their status as an urban promenade. Access to the sea (not the port) from the Ramblas became peripheral, while access to the sea focused on the beaches of the Barceloneta and the north, reached via metro stations.

Nor were urban projects between the Moll de la Fusta and the Moll de la Barceloneta well connected among themselves or with their context. No axis from the Ramblas to the Maritime Passage had existed, since the *chiringuitos* broke any connection. No real connections existed among the wharfs. The poor linkage of the port to the city's historical center relied on two badly placed bridges that did not connect to major urban streets. Finally, the sheer noise level of the underground Coastal Highway made the Moll de la Fusta an unpleasant space destined for self-enclosed activities such as fairs or other special events that turned their back to the street. Thus the older center city lost an opportunity to connect to the sea, opting instead for a bridge to ephemeral leisure consumption.

In addition to the poor resolution of relations between the city and the sea, these new spaces also had problems of sheer urban character. If a space lacks a minimal articulation of relations and mobility among people, its meaning becomes fragile (Magrinyà 2003). In these new areas of centrality, the only spaces that established any ties of proximity were the Maritime Club, the Nautical Club, the fishermen's area, and the movies. The first two are private clubs. The fishing zone was marginal to the city and its economy. And the movies failed without any regular clientele from surrounding areas. This contrasts with other port areas such as Rotterdam and Baltimore, where housing was also included in the renovation of the port area, which never occurred in the Port Vell. Nor were there activities central to public life, such as a library or a film center.

Instead, if we look closely at these spaces, we see that in their claims to a new centrality, people who value familiar spaces were thrown together with those who lacked this same rootedness. People who tended to relate among homogeneous groups (for example, families) encountered those who clustered around unknown counterparts (for example, university students). This confusion of relations and mobilities produced a recurrent fragmentation of space and flow that precluded any authentic appropriation of space unless it was determined hierarchically. Maremagnum, for example, as a principal space, lacked known features of public space such as a street and those of a collective space associated with a mall (themselves complex and fragmented). This ambiguity of public and collective space led to confusion and confrontations, producing, in the end, a nonplace.

The question is how we make sense of a space that offers so many confusing characteristics that it eventually becomes a nonplace, in the sense that Marc Augé applied this concept to airports, stations, and other spaces of transition. We take Augé's definition as fundamental. "If a place can define itself as a place of identity in relations and history, then a non-place must be undefined as a space of identity, either in relational or historical terms" (Augé 1995). In the Port Vell, those elements that are missing are precisely those that offer the possibility of historical continuity in the newly reformed areas. For example, activities such as the sale of fish near the docking of the boats, the operations of entry and departure for cruise lines, and the everyday activities of residents in the vicinity all will need time to take root in this new area. Meanwhile, an element as historical as the Wharf of the Clock, the oldest part of the port, has been hidden, while the Fisherman's Wharf has been spatially marginalized and cut out of the public image of the port.

The image of the port as a destination for cruise ships has also been fragmented. There are some functions on the Barcelona wharf, but the large ships go to a nearby dock because there is no space in the interior zone. Hence the maritime station in the Moll d'Espanya becomes a pure simulacrum that is never used. Meanwhile, the traditions of the areas as an urban seaside passage have been displaced toward the Olympic Port and Mar Bella. If the warehouses had not been destroyed, they might have anchored some of these functions as well as serving as key symbols for the port. But all these circumstances shattered the historical continuity of the space and made it lose identity, adding to the fragility of the space and the elements that crystallize it as a nonplace.

The economies of spaces of collective consumption pose other challenges. The Moll d'Espanya, as we have seen, became dominated by bars and discotheques. But these spaces also rely on novelty for success, and businessmen know that they must invest a great deal of initial capital to renovate such a spot and convert it into a fashionable destination. With this, they can attract crowds and recoup their investment and convert it into a real business. Yet, knowing that fame is fleeting, owners are also thinking about their next investment. This cycle does not coincide with that of traditional public spaces, which layer their activities and construct an identity slowly over time, with a scale that permits continuity and avoids the fragility of new leisure spaces. Ultimately, this creates a perverse imbalance in which urban projects become fragile and the characteristics that defined a nonspace reproduce it as such.

Conclusion: "Nothing Is What It Seems"

The maritime station within Maremagnum remains a key element in the simulacrum of public space that is the Port Vell. This station was situated on the second floor of the commercial center, below one of the largest discos. It has a small embarkation ramp to connect it to the ocean that no ship has ever used. Nor has anyone ever departed from it. Despite this failure, it has remained furnished and even offers signs for nonexistent passengers: a ghost of a station, almost always closed. Without staff, without passengers, without information about arrivals and departures, it remains in a state both phantasmagoric and disquieting. It is also the best distillation of the simulacrum of the site itself: a place constructed and never used for its original function that nonetheless justifies other ends such as the hours for bars that differ from those of the rest of the city (*La Vanguardia*, December 2, 2002).

Yet, as we have seen, it is not the only simulacrum at the port but is one that participates in a much longer chain of simulacra. The Port Vell, in the period we analyze, was presented as an original space, a product of the Barcelona Model (even if London and other cities had inaugurated similar renovations beforehand). It was presented as a model of urban reform even if the document explaining the reconversion of the Port Vell was not approved until 1989, eight years after work was begun on the Moll de la Fusta. It was presented as a center for urban crowds, a new central space to be appropriated by Barcelonans, but the majority of its visitors are actually foreigners. Urbanistically, it was a reconquest of space for the city, but the authority to do so was never clarified. It was presented as a public space and instead became a space of collective consumption. It was organized as a leisure space for a new city but its uses never became clear. In this, development of the Port Vell embodies and comments on many themes of global downtowns in this volume—questions of iconography, of ownership, of authority and use—even as it has competed with and become disconnected from the shifting spaces of centrality in the city.

The Moll de la Fusta and subsequently the Moll d'Espanya-Maremagnum, with their respective crises, represent the postmodern odyssey of spaces built on purely spatial simulacra, spaces that claim so many meanings that they finally lose them all: "The result is certainly a radical negation of the sea, practically invisible from most of the public spaces of the complex, and of any traditional port ambience. But neither is the result a new piece of a real city: only a simulacrum. The ambiguous and metaphoric charge of the port city has given way to a closed and imposed model, that reduces the complexity of space and urban relations to the city understood unilaterally as a center for commerce and leisure, reducing the citizen to the category of spectator-consumer" (Subirós 1996).

The nonplaces we have analyzed here appear to be public space but are not. Like many other postmodern spaces, they result from an urbanism that has been excessively visionary and even pretends to be anthropological, but in the end lacks any soul. Tearing away train lines, factories, or warehouses is a constructive action that modern cities need to reconstitute functions. But to build social life in a public space involves other processes that cannot be created by urban projects read as décor alone.

Certainly we can see from this case that a first major element in constructing new central areas must be the decision as to whether it is a public space controlled by municipal authorities or a part of a collective space controlled by private operators. In either case, it is also important to see what activities will link this space to its neighbors or to citizens who will help build the space as a public space, with all its meanings. Second, it is important to analyze spatial, social, and cultural elements. This can allow a continuity of history in the place and the articulation of new functions with old in order to shape an identity that will define the character of the place. A third element we see here is the need to control activities that demand rapid substitution by new activities. These promoted the process of inauguration-decadence-reform that ultimately converted these projects not into a new center, a parallel downtown, but a nonplace.

The new spaces of the port that we analyzed in their different stages both as urban projects and in their internal contradictions suggest that similar planning might occur in other areas, including renovations of downtown areas seen in this volume. This is especially true if public space is constructed on the basis of a scenography of space without connections to its environs or people around it. This process of the production of space corresponds to a process of gentrification that demands the support of ideological constructions so strong that they must be based in manipulation of the very sentiments of citizens. As a consequence, these spaces demand new projects to keep going or hold on to their status as fashionable destinations. They must reinvent themselves so as not to lose publics—especially those coming from abroad.

Such new urban public spaces, once the edges of the city, after such rapid transformations, risk becoming nonplaces in the city, zones of conflict or social fragmentation rather than a real area of urban centrality—a non-downtown. With this analysis, we hope to highlight some clues about the problems in creating such nonplaces instead of central spaces, understanding the conditions that create them, sustain them, and reproduce them. And perhaps to share these lessons with other cities as well as future imaginers of Barcelona who will pay attention to social as well as formal characteristics, formations of publics and public spaces rather than simulacra.

4

Urbanist Ideology and the Production of Space in the United Arab Emirates: An Anthropological Critique

Ahmed Kanna

Ever since its origins, the State expressed itself through the void: empty space, broad avenues, plazas of gigantic proportions open to spectacular processions.

—Henri Lefebvre, *The Urban Revolution*

Every place has its own identity, and we have to create . . . a beautiful identity for Ras al-Khaimah. Naturally, environmentally friendly.

—Khater Masaad

Along with China, the contemporary Arabian Gulf is undergoing an urbanization of massive proportions. Possessing 40 percent of the world's proven oil reserves and flush with profits from recent spikes in global oil prices, the six countries of the Gulf Cooperation Council were devoting trillions of dollars to construction projects before the 2008 economic crisis (Brown 2008).[1] Architects view the Gulf, whose member states are run by tiny elites disposing of immense wealth and nearly nonexistent labor and environmental regulation, as a liberating place in which to work. (There are parallels here to architects' views of China). No Gulf country has been as aggressive in advancing top-down, large-scale, institutional urbanism (Lefebvre 2003: 79) as the United Arab Emirates (UAE).

The UAE consists of seven principalities, or emirates, each of which enjoys loose sovereignty in a federated system. Each of the emirates is ruled by one family, with one of these, the Al Nahyan, ruling both the administrative capital of Abu Dhabi and the entire federation. Of the seven states of the UAE, three—Abu Dhabi, Dubai, and Ras al-Khayma—have embarked upon enormous development projects ranging from highly iconic skyscrapers to mixed-use entertainment developments to so-called sustainable cities. In the last case, entire conurbations are designed by architects and master planners and intended for realization outside the existing cities to which they would be nominally connected. The rhetoric of local government officials, architects, and the media—what Henri Lefebvre might call "urbanists" (Lefebvre 2003: 156–60)—avails itself of various discourses of progress and architectural radicalism to justify such projects. These discourses, and the ways in which they help to articulate global architectural practice with local institutions and discourses of urban power, are the subject of this chapter.

Before the 2008 world economic crisis, individual emirates of the UAE, especially the wealthiest two, Abu Dhabi and Dubai, tapped so-called starchitects in a large project of urban entrepreneurialism (Broudehoux 2007; see also Weinstein, this volume, which provides an excellent literature review on the topic).[2] The list of the famous firms that were "rushing" (Brown 2008) to participate in the UAE's architectural "Xanadu" (Fattah 2007) was a who's who of global north starchitecture: Tadao Ando, Norman Foster, Frank Gehry, Zaha Hadid, Rem Koolhaas/OMA, Jean Nouvel, Skidmore Owings Merrill (already a veteran on the UAE scene), and Snøhetta (along with many lesser names). The case of the Waterfront City of Dubai introduces some of the problems of starchitecture, and urbanist ideology more generally, with which I am dealing. The project, designed by the ubiquitous genius of contemporary global urbanism, Rem Koolhaas and his Rotterdam-based Office for Metropolitan Architecture (OMA), was conceived in its rectilinear plan as covering 6.5 square miles on an artificial island off Dubai's coast. Koolhaas claimed that it was an experiment with his "Generic Cities" theory (Koolhaas 1978)—in which cities consist of repetitive buildings centered on an airport housing "a tribe of global nomads with few local loyalties"—by "find(ing) optimism in the inevitable" condition of commodification (Ouroussof 2008).

Figure 2. A new dowtown for Dubai. EMAAR construction site, 2006.
Photo by author.

Starchitects are a new breed of architect whose mere name has become
so enveloped in the mystique of genius that urban elites the world over now
consider the commissioning of a building by one of them to be a municipal
priority, regardless of the aesthetic or design quality of the project, its expense, or the demands it makes on local resources (see McNeill 2009). The
rise of the starchitect as a global player indicates a quantitative if not (arguably) qualitative change in the project of urbanism over the last quarter-
century. Downtowns have become transformed from contexts, primarily,
for functional centrality to centers of symbolic capital (see Figure 2).[3]

With the development both of information and design technologies,
it has become possible to design increasingly radical and flamboyant—
"iconic"—buildings and to disseminate images of this photogenic architecture instantaneously on a global scale. Images of downtowns bristling with
aesthetically fanciful buildings, instantly consumable for their vividness
and superficiality, are now standard implements in the advertising toolkit
of booming towns across the geography of global urbanism. The rise of the

downtown as image, a spatial representation symbolizing ideal neoliberal space over the past couple of decades, is not without its unexpected twists (as Lloyd and Christens, writing on Nashville in this volume, confirm). While cities such as Shanghai, Bombay, and Dubai borrow from the architectural and aesthetic idiom of high modernism and postmodernism, cities in the deindustrializing North in turn borrow from the apparently unrestrained, future-oriented spirit of cities in the Global South.[4] The image of a certain kind of downtown—shared by established and emergent cities north and south—becomes central to twenty-first-century urban politics. Starchitecture, which privileges the role of the architect as aesthete and genius of pure form and elevates a few brand-name architects, investing their names with symbolic power, is well suited to the demands of such urban projects.

The invocation of dialectical theory ("finding optimism in the inevitable") to express the radicalism of Koolhaas's architecture is intriguing. As students of dialectical theory will be aware, arguments about the mobilization of the materials of everyday "mass" culture for projects of radical critique are not new (Adorno 1952/2005; Bloch 1986; Lefebvre 1991). Koolhaas's architecture is a *soi disant* variant of immanent critique, an immanent architecture of late capitalism (Jameson 2003). But some questions remain: in what specific ways are such projects radical? How do they relate to elite power and elitist agendas for urban spatial production? Can such elite projects be reconciled with architectural and urbanist discourses of progress? Do they depart in significant ways from prevailing clichés and stereotypes about urbanism in the local contexts in which they intervene?

This chapter is a discursive and ideological critique of contemporary urban developments in the UAE. As I hope will become clear, however, this critique can be applied more generally to developments elsewhere in neoliberal urban contexts. Urbanism, as Henri Lefebvre saw, is both a political and an imaginative process (Lefebvre 2003; see also Holston 1989; Scott 1998). The production of space is a social process involving the confrontation and negotiation of various practices (architectural, institutional, and quotidian) that is determinate, embedded in concrete relations of power. "Urbanism is, although unwittingly, class urbanism" (Lefebvre 2003: 160). Urbanism is thus an ideology and a set of discourses consisting of representations deployed in specific projects of the imagination of the urban. While the bulk of my analytical attention will seem to focus on starchitects—primarily because this group presents the most complex and contradictory case of urbanism in the UAE—I should emphasize that the term *urbanism* has a much wider application in my critique. Not only architects and planners, but technocrats, bureaucrats, and intellectuals more generally are involved in urbanism (related to what Lefebvre called "urbanist ideology"). In this chapter I follow Lefebvre in applying the terms *urbanism* and *urbanist* specifically to the intersection between local elites (landlords, landlords' development firms, and various official and quasi-official technocrats and intelligentsia who share the landlords' and developers' spatial ideology) and transnational actors such as journalists, academics, and, not least, architects who work in the UAE.

In this chapter, I am particularly interested in the intersection between the uses of "culture" and conceptions of built space. Selective, ideological notions of history and culture are particularly visible, and the recourse to clichés particularly salient, when architects deal with cultures with which they are unfamiliar. A sympathetic reviewer of Koolhaas's Waterfront City proposal, for example, notes that "the plan's geometric grid gives way to an intimate warren of alleyways, like a traditional souk" (Ouroussof 2008). As I show in this chapter, urbanists almost automatically reach for such cultural stereotypes when writing about or imagining spaces in non-Western societies. In the chapter's conclusion, I bring in the voices of some of the marginalized alternatives to elite-starchitectural spaces. If the spaces envisioned by players such as the ruling elites and experts imply a specific politics, so do these alternative voices.

An effect of the dependence by architects and other urbanists on cultural and historical clichés is the erasure of both their own power and that of the local elites with whom they collaborate on urban projects.[5] Unaware of its social and political determinations, urbanist ideology reproduces some of the more elitist traditions in architectural history. Starchitecture, for example, reduces urban practice to pure aesthetic experimentation, in turn cloaking itself in the rhetoric of radicalism while unwittingly playing handmaiden to local hierarchies of power and spatial production. This is ironic, because urbanists talk a lot about cultural sensitivity and a concern with local conditions. In practice, however, they end up replacing these with cultural stereotypes and an almost total erasure of local power relations. Another irony is that urbanism does not overcome the polarization in local urbanist discourses between romantic notions of "authenticity" and "local culture," on the one hand, and "modernity," on the other; rather, starchitecture intensifies this polarity.

Urban Entrepreneurialism: Global and Local Urbanists Collaborate

Anne-Marie Broudehoux argues that recent urbanization in China is dominated by "urban entrepreneurialism" (Broudehoux 2007). Her insights can also be applied, with minor modifications, to the UAE. Broudehoux notes the manipulation of the landscape to transform it into a "cultural resource that can be capitalized upon and repackaged for new rounds of capital accumulation and consumption" (Broudehoux 2007: 383). Moreover, "designer buildings have become essential tools of city marketing. Motivated by what could be called the Bilbao effect, cities around the world have embarked on a competition for global preeminence by building the tallest, most daring, and most technologically advanced buildings" (Broudehoux 2007: 384). Broudehoux discusses the less well-publicized facts—from private-land confiscations by the state to forced internal emigration to public revenue losses—that are the social costs of urban entrepreneurialism.[6] She also points out that this phenomenon has similar results independent of the formal political system in which it takes place (albeit in extreme form in China). This is the broader context of urban entrepreneurialism that contemporary urbanists do not mention.

The urbanist production of depoliticized space connected to an ahistorical notion of culture precedes the arrival of starchitects in the UAE and is today a wider reality (although starchitects and their signature projects have a unique power to give such spatializations an authoritative imprimatur).[7] An early example of global-local urbanist interconnection from Dubai shows well the uses of historical and cultural stereotyping. In 1960, the then ruler of Dubai, Rashid bin Said Al Maktoum, commissioned a master plan for the city by British architect John Harris. A 1971 archived document I was able to access at a Dubai library in 2004, a modification of the 1960 plan, reveals the workings of cultural-representational and spatial logics operative in these plans (Harris 1971).[8] The document is, of course, a description of and a prescription for urban development in Dubai. Less obvious, however, is the fact that it is more than a simple technical exercise. Rather, it makes unwitting assumptions about the culture and history of Dubai that resonate with more recent starchitectural and urbanist representations.

The 1971 modified plan begins with a history of Dubai: how the town was founded as a settlement by an offshoot of the Bani Yas tribe (the rulers of Abu Dhabi), how it became a haven for merchants in the Gulf, how liberal and visionary the rulers were, and so on (Harris 1971: 4–6). To the reader unfamiliar with local history, it is a very bloodless, somewhat optimistic account of elite ingenuity and good policies through the ages. Those familiar with local history will recognize the foundation myth of the ruling Al Maktoum structuring this historical account. For example, there is a frequent conflation between the ruler and "Dubai," which comes to be represented as an extension of the ruler's will and agency. British imperialism is euphemized as "the British presence" and as a consensual relationship between "Dubai" and Britain (Harris 1971: 6). The local political system Harris calls "traditional Arab desert democracy" (Harris 1971: 8). This "grants the leader ultimate authority.... His Highness the Ruler directs and controls all development personally with the help of informal committees and representatives of all the interests concerned in each project" (Harris 1971: 8).

This is quite similar to the tendencies of the starchitects more recently commissioned by Rashid's son and successor Muhammad. The analogy is not perfect, however. According to architecture scholar Yasser Elsheshtawy, who has looked more closely at the relationship between Harris and Rashid Al Maktoum, Harris was a modest and competent practitioner, not a preening "theorist" or self-styled "genius."[9] That Harris was far from a brand-name architect was intentional. Rashid seems to have had someone like him in mind because in the 1960s the Dubai ruler could only afford to hire a relatively unknown architect. Moreover, according to Elsheshtawy, and unlike elsewhere in the Gulf, Rashid and Harris did not want to raze the old town and replace it with a modernist grid. Rashid and Harris wanted instead to integrate the old town with the new infrastructures and developments envisioned for the 1970s and thereafter.[10] Harris, for his part, seems to have been genuinely sympathetic to local people, to local architectural vernaculars, and to Dubai's urban traditions. He was also serious about reconciling urban planning with local lived realities. The Dubai of the 1970s, according to Dubayyans to whom I spoke, had successfully integrated the old urban center with the new modern plan, a testament to Harris's ability.

Nevertheless, we must distinguish the intentions of the author of cultural and spatial representations from the structural forces that constitute the possibility of those representations. There is in the modified plan of 1971 a tendency to assume the naturalness and wisdom of the absolute monarchy, to neatly divide the "traditional" from the "modern," an implicit and at times explicit affirmation of the trajectory undertaken by the family-state, and a culturalization of the "traditional," representing it as intrinsically linked to an almost autochthonous local society. The effect (if only inadvertently) is to affirm one interpretation of local history and culture, the ruling family narrative, as the authentic narrative. In this articulation between apolitical expertise and the family-state, there is a strong resonance between the unassuming Harris and the more recent starchitects.

A more recent and more overt expression of urbanist legitimization of local power comes from the PBS film *The Sand Castle*, which aired in 2007.[11] Though excellent in many ways, the film (about an architectural competition to build a city from scratch in the emirate Ras al-Khaymah) also exhibits the flaws of contemporary urbanism, specifically, the lack of serious interest by urbanists in the ways that power articulates with cultural representation. In the filmmaker's notes section of the website, the director, Eirin Gjørv notes "the Sheikh's (i.e., the ruler of Ras al-Khaymah's) openness" to the presence of the film crew and the film's subjects, architects from the Oslo firm Snøhetta (Wide Angle 2007). Gjørv's account of her experience strongly echoes Harris's from a quarter-century before, emphasizing the ruler's liberalism and entrepreneurialism and euphemizing the global architect–local elite relationship as a meeting of like spirits:

> We had the exclusive opportunity to follow some of the most outstanding architects of our time as they work with the progressive and powerful men of Ras al-Khaimah, working to create change at speed we rarely have seen before. Though the main characters in the film have very different cultural backgrounds, they all share a creative desire that builds bridges despite cultural differences. This joint creativity made it possible for our small team to get close to the characters throughout the year as we documented a process that reflects the entrepreneurship found in this Middle Eastern corner of the world. (Wide Angle 2007)[12]

Other recent intersections between architects and local elites have led to a (perhaps retrograde) redefinition of architecture as well. In the UAE, the starchitect enacts some of the least egalitarian traditions from the history of

modern architecture. The iconic and monumental quality of buildings demanded by urban entrepreneurs has often been noted (Broudehoux 2007;
McNeill 2009; Parker 2005). This is usually (correctly) interpreted as part of
the capitalist transformation of urban space into commodified space. There
are, however, reasons for iconicism and monumentalism that have more to
do with the history of architecture and the formation of architects as self-
styled artists exclusively concerned with aesthetic form than they do with
capitalism in the abstract. In a scathing critique of high modernism, Lewis
Mumford referred to Le Corbusier's urban plans of the 1920s and 1930s (the
so-called Contemporary and Radiant cities) as "pathological," exhibiting a
Victorian obsession with bigness, a Napoleonic dream of centralization, and
a Baroque insensitivity to time and functional flexibility (Fishman 1977: 258–
59). James Holston points to another quality of modernist space by comparing
it to preindustrial space in Brazil: while preindustrial space is characterized
by streets acting as figural voids and buildings as continuous ground, modernist space exhibits the reverse pattern. "In the modernist city, streets appear
as continuous void and buildings as sculptural figures" (Holston 1989: 125).
Holston is here comparing the so-called organic city of premodernism, with
its intimate, winding network of streets, alleys, and courtyards, with the
modernist immensity of Brasilia, its sweeping emptiness criss-crossed by
superhighways and punctuated by the occasional awesomely scaled monument. Both Mumford and Holston suggest that the modernist sculptural
solid–continuous void relationship (of which the monumental iconic building, disconnected from any urban context, is an example) is an architectural
instrument of authoritarian domination of urban space.

Buildings, in this view, must manifest "authority" (Fishman 1977: 237).
They are the expression both of the architect's and of the state's genius
(J. Scott 1998: 56). They represent a "geometric order [that is] most evident,
not at street level, but rather from above and from outside, . . . in short, a
God's-eye view, or the view of an absolute ruler" (J. Scott 1998: 57). Frank
Gehry described the Saadiyat Island project, a large arts and museums en-
clave in Abu Dhabi (for which he is designing Abu Dhabi's branch of the
Guggenheim Museum), in the following way:

"It's like a clean slate in a country full of resources. . . . It's an opportunity for the world of art and culture that is not available anywhere else because you're building a desert enclave without the contextual constraints of
a city" (Fattah 2007).[13] When Gehry talks about a "clean slate," he does not
mean this in the literal sense, because there is at least one source of constraint,

the client. For example, when the Norwegian architecture firm Snøhetta proposed a convention center design to their client, the ruler of the emirate of Ras al-Khayma, it was rejected because it was not iconic enough. As the assistant to the ruler put it as he literally sent the Snøhetta team back to the drawing board: "In the end, you know, if you see [sic] history, the people who built the big places, what they have built, all these crazy kings . . . if we take Ludwig, he built this Neuschwanstein in Germany. It is a crazy place, but today everybody is visiting it. . . . Versailles, everybody is visiting it; Tour Eiffel, everybody . . . it is grandiose, something which impresses people. I think you can create more than this . . . this is a costly structure, with the same cost, you can make something much more grandiose" (Wide Angle Transcript 2007: 12).

The Production of Space as a Clean Slate

Thus, the "clean slate" refers to the wider social world in which architect and client operate. It is a space evacuated of history (as human struggle) and culture (as richly textured everyday practice). Such space in turn becomes the arena for the unlimited creativity of the architect-genius. Henri Lefebvre argues that the elitist collaboration between state, market, and architect is a major obstacle to the breakthrough to the urban revolution, in which space is liberated from "the imperialism of know-how" (Lefebvre 2003: 59). Class urbanism creates inert space, space as nothing more than a container for objects, be they animate or inanimate, and for fetishized "needs." The city, in this view, becomes "a simple spatial effect of a creative act that occurred elsewhere, in the Mind, or the Intellect" (Lefebvre 2003: 28). Most damningly, "ever since its origins, the State expressed itself through the void: empty space, broad avenues, plazas of gigantic proportions open to spectacular processions" (Lefebvre 2003: 109).

The case of Dubai is instructive. Like Los Angeles, it is developing into an extreme version of the multicentric city. Since the early 1970s, when it had a definite center around a natural inlet, the *Khor Dubai* or Dubai Creek, the city has exploded into its present form. The sprawl of Dubai is not a simple product of technical requirements or an innocent canvas for aesthetic experimentation. It enables and consolidates the political power of the Maktoum corporation and major landlords and the class power of wealthier city residents, by whom and for whom this development is made (see the far more detailed discussion in Kanna 2011). This reality is not reflected upon in starchitectural and urbanist discourse. According to the conventional narrative, Rem Koolhaas has over the course of his entire career been prevented from fully realizing his Generic Cities theory. "Now he may get a chance to create his own version (of a Generic City)," writes a reviewer of his Waterfront City, commissioned by Dubai real estate developer Nakheel (Ouroussof 2008). The reviewer continues: "Koolhaas's design proves once again that he is one of the few architects willing to face the crisis of the contemporary city—from its growing superficiality to its deadening sterility—without flinching" (Ouroussof 2008). In this narrative, only Koolhaas and his aesthetic quest are relevant. The local context of the application of this vision—Dubai as a real, concrete city—is replaced by the cliché "the contemporary city" and endowed with abstract qualities: "deadening sterility," "superficiality" (sterile to whom? Superficial by whose standards?) The willful obliviousness of the architect, whose only experience of "the city" is managed by a local urbanist elite, is valorized as "unflinching" and courageous. The architect sacrifices himself and jumps into the void to rescue this "pathological space" (Lefebvre 2003: 157).

This conventional understanding of the architect is shared by other starchitects. For example, Patrik Schumacher of Zaha Hadid Architects describes the UAE in this way: "We are trying things out for the first time which we wanted to try out, but couldn't. . . . We have found an unusual degree of receptiveness to new ideas in the Gulf" (Brown 2008). For Schumacher, "the Gulf provides a research and development lab for the architectural industry" (Brown 2008). PBS's *The Sand Castle* describes the Ras al-Khaymah competition between Snøhetta and Koolhaas's OMA as a race to "invent a city on the sand dunes" of the UAE (Wide Angle 2007). "The coolest thing about building in the desert," says Snøhetta's Kjetil Thorsen in one of the film's opening scenes, "is the desert!" The scene cuts to a meeting at the firm's Oslo office, in which Thorsen dumps a mound of sand on the table, presses a ruler into the mound, and says: "This is a section of the site. . . . This is the hillside. This is the water. And take something like this (i.e., the ruler). And just make an imprint into that landscape. And that's the city" (Wide Angle Transcript 2007: 1).

Once the clean slate is produced, a set of needs can be created. Martin Giesen, the former dean of the College of Architecture, Art and Design at the American University of Sharjah, UAE—one of the Gulf region's top architecture schools—claims that "the experience of the vacuum, of the void" was central to the culture of "the Bedouin" (BBC Radio 3 2004). He reasons that contemporary architecture in the UAE is therefore the culture's attempt to lift itself out of the void, to create a sense of permanence. Emiratis do this by emphasizing the colorful, extraordinary, and decorative in architecture, he argues. A colleague of Giesen's concurs, suggesting that since the mid-1990s, Emiratis have looked to architecture to define their identity (BBC Radio 3 2004).[14]

The Spatial Re-Orientation of the East:
Urbanism's Dubious Anthropology

Urbanist projects in the contemporary Gulf often begin with references to "culture." Contrary to the technocratic myth of architecture fashioned by high modernists (Fishman 1977: 238), "culture" is at the center of urbanist discourse on the UAE. A 2007 Harvard Workshop on sustainable architecture in the Gulf was opened with the following comments by the workshop organizer, in which he connected sustainable architecture to cultural sensitivity. The organizer wanted to distance himself from Miesian modernism, which, he maintained, "eliminates culture, consider[ing] it to endanger the purity of form." Culture, he went on, should be thought of as a passage from childhood to youth to maturity to old age. "Youth is the search for identity"; the UAE is a culture still in its "youth." The mission of architects is therefore to provide this youthful culture with its identity: "we are dealing with societies [those of the Gulf] that need iconography." He then proceeded to a slideshow of a recent project in Qatar, a seventy-story building called "the Intelligent Tower." The tower, he argued, "has a cultural inspiration," bringing back the garden of traditional Arab houses (the tower has roof gardens which, he maintained, have as their referent "traditional" house gardens).[15] The building is also an iconic structure, modeled on the cypress tree or *saar*, which is "a cultural symbol": it is self-fertilizing, incorporating the male and the female as well as personal freedom and longevity or eternity, values that the architect sees as culturally inspired.

This recourse to culture talk (Mamdani 2004) is justified by urbanists as a progressive, positive critique: the architect or expert divines the supposedly authentic core of the society to build in a more organic or humanly responsive way. This is certainly a laudable intention. But in practice, things are more complicated, because most of the time, urbanists end up reifying local culture rather than responding to it, thus creating justifications for their elitist projects.

Instead of perceiving the invented nature of the correlation between national identity and specific cultural icons, such as camels and "traditional sports," dhows (Indian Ocean sailing vessels), desert landscapes, and Gulf national dress (Suleyman Khalaf 1999; Onley 2005; Onley 2007), urbanists usually take these icons at face value, assuming that they are expressions of authentic Emirati culture. One of the seemingly interminable debates through which architectural practice is framed polarizes Emirati culture between "tradition" and "modernity." The former is equated with authenticity, the latter with its opposite. Amr Mustafa, an Arab expatriate who teaches architecture at the American University of Sharjah, maintains that Dubai's architecture is generally inauthentic, aping foreign postmodernist styles, which is in turn a result of the nonparticipatory nature of urban development in the city (Mustafa 2004). Echoing Harris's reference to "Arab democracy," he recommends "the tribal system" of the UAE as the basis for a more participatory public sphere (ignoring the inconvenient fact that "tribalism" is largely an invented identity of the post-1971 or nation-building era).[16] This framing of authentic Emirati culture is ubiquitous among urbanists in the UAE, both local and foreign (BBC Radio 3 2004; Koolhaas 2009). Among other things, it underpins recent programs of so-called heritage revival in various emirates (Suleyman Khalaf 1999). Even those who reject notions of authenticity or vernacular in the Emirati built environment do so, almost exclusively, in the terms set by this tradition-modernity debate, with tradition signifying autochthonous aesthetic forms and cultural values and modernity signifying the rejection of these and the embrace of Western, especially neoliberal, notions of progress (Kanna 2011).

Nader Ardalan, the Boston architect who led the 2007 Harvard seminar, echoes Mustafa's sense of ennui with the region's "modern" architecture and counsels a revival of the "traditional city" as an antidote both to urban anomie and to contemporary Gulf cities' disproportionate ecological impact. "You have to follow in the footsteps of your grandfather," he argues, pointing to "the privacy-seeking, security-seeking world of the courtyard" as a model for future architecture. Sustainable architecture, for Ardalan, manifests a "coincidence between architecture and spiritual beliefs."

Even immensely talented architects such as Tadao Ando and Jean Nouvel—both, like Foster, Gehry, Hadid, and Koolhaas, winners of the Pritzker Prize, the profession's top honor, and the latter the designer of Paris's stunning Institut du Monde Arabe, a building of deep sensitivity both to the local urban context and to the Arab experience—cannot avoid the occasional use of abstract culture talk. Taking the Emirati state's heritage revival project at face value, Ando incorporates the icon of the dhow as a signifier of the Arab authenticity of his Abu Dhabi Maritime Museum (it is notable that this pan–Indian Ocean sailing vessel is converted into an Arab one): "Dhows, Arab sailing vessels with triangular or lateen sails, float over the voids of the interior space and help create an intense visual experience by relating objects to one another and to the museum architecture as a whole. Below ground, there is a second space, a reception hall with an enormous aquarium. A traditional dhow floats over the aquarium and is seen from different perspectives" (Arcspace 2007).

Nouvel's comment on the Saadiyat Island, where his and Ando's projects will be located, points to an urbanist notion of landscape as almost the opposite of urbanscape, landscape as a repository of the primal, the authentic, and the intuitive: "The island offers a harsh landscape, tempered by its meeting with the channel, a striking image of the aridity of the earth versus the fluidity of the waters. These fired the imagination towards unknown cities buried deep into the sands or sunk under water. These dreamy thoughts have merged into a simple plan of an archaeological field revived as a small city, a cluster of nearly one-row buildings along a leisurely promenade" (Arcspace 2007).

As my final example, I return to the PBS film *The Sand Castle*, which recounts the competition to build a new capital for the emirate of Ras al-Khaymah (Wide Angle 2007). The film is in many respects a good example of urbanist ideology as it pertains to developing countries in the early twenty-first century and its perhaps inadvertent loss of critical perception as it encounters the cultural other. Both in form and content, the film tends to romanticize both the figure of the architect and local culture.

The film opens with a shot of the desert. As the audience takes in the landscape, a *mu'azzin* calls the Muslim prayer on the soundtrack. As the *athan* (call to prayer) continues, the scene shifts to a closeup of Kjetil Thorsen, head of the Snøhetta team, kneeling in the sand and sketching an imaginary city as his colleagues look on. After a short vignette (the mound of sand on the conference table in Oslo, described above), the film returns to the UAE to give more atmospherics. A scene from a Bedouin dance, performed for all visiting dignitaries and at heritage museums as an example of authentic Emirati culture, is followed by a scene from a performance of the *rimaya*, "traditional" rifle shooting, another recent invention of the Emirati heritage industry.

The camera then shifts to a position behind the four Snøhetta architects, the film's protagonists. They are depicted walking in the desert. The viewer senses that they are searching for something in vain, something not quite concrete or definable. A close-up of Thorsen's face comes next, indicating a sudden discovery: "Beautiful! Landscape, landscape, landscape, landscape!" (Wide Angle Transcript 2007: 4). To emphasize the centrality of the landscape, the next two shots are, respectively, a mid-shot and a wide shot, again from behind the four architects. The audience follows them as they climb a hill overlooking an immense, empty desert landscape. The last shot in the sequence is reminiscent of Caspar David Friedrich's *Traveling above the Clouded Sea*, with the traveler-architects' figures shrouded in darkness as they gaze out into the distance.

As the architects contemplate the ineffable Emirati *Landschaft*, the narrator intones, "the Snøhetta team is not alone—in delighting in the romance of the desert—*and* bidding for the capital's masterplan" (Wide Angle Transcript 2007: 4, emphasis in the original). This brings Rem Koolhaas into the action. The landscape is also central to his attraction to the UAE: "It's heartbreakingly beautiful" (Wide Angle Transcript 2007: 4). As Koolhaas says this, the camera shoots the landscape through the windshield of the jeep he is riding through the desert. The soundtrack kicks in with Arab flute music. The shot through the windshield continues, again emphasizing the landscape. As the windshield frames the shot, the audience is given the impression that the landscape is divided into four bands: the blue-white layer of the sky above the tan layer of the desert above the silver strip of the car's hood above the black band of the dashboard. A newer interpretation of landscape, perhaps, than the previous, Friedrich-esque reading, but the basic message is the same: the landscape is primal, consisting of simple, bare colors and emptiness. The Koolhaas vignette is completed with a close-up of the architect's face as he sits in an airplane gazing at the urbanscape of Dubai: the architect as a brooding genius attempting to penetrate from above the essence of the landscape in which he will realize his vision.

There are various other representations of the landscape and the figure of the architect, but each advances the unfailing message: the local culture is steeped in "tradition," iconically represented by exotic, aestheticized expressions of identity; the architect and his local elite client are visionaries who will excavate the landscape's hidden potential, transforming it from its intuitive, primal immanence into its concrete final shape. As the film closes, the narrator says, "Ras al-Khaimah today still boasts a pristine Arabian Desert landscape of sand and rock. Soon a new city will stand here, an architectural landmark to attract the world's businesses to this ambitious 21st century kingdom" (Wide Angle Transcript 2007: 21). The final shot has Kjetil Thorsen, standing in an immense desert landscape at dusk, asking Khater Masaad, the ruler's assistant and main handler of the Snøhetta team, "Can you see it already?" (Wide Angel Transcript 2007: 21). "Yeah," says Masaad, "I see it already. Yes" (Wide Angle Transcript 2007: 21).

Conclusion

Rem Koolhaas is, as is often the case with him, an example of the complexities and contradictions of contemporary starchitecture. Celebrated, justifiably, not only for his talent as an architect but also for expanding the profession's definitions of design and even of architecture itself, he has cultivated a persona which he and his admirers situate within modern Western traditions of radical critique. For example, he criticizes the profession for being politically "lobotomized" (Freund 2001), elitist, and out of touch with "the world" and "the other" (Lacayo 2008; Lubow 2000). A main theme of works such as *Delirious New York*, *S, M, L, XL*, and the projects he led on the Pearl River delta, Lagos, and shopping is the embrace and critique from within of the "inevitable" character of the urban condition in the late twentieth and early twenty-first centuries: such aspects of cities as their generic quality and increasing commodification. This idea has a venerable pedigree within radical thought. Ernst Bloch, a founding figure of Western Marxism, argues, for example, that everyday forms of cultural expression can conceal elements of radical critique of the status quo, an idea that would influence the thought of Theodor Adorno and other Western Marxists (Bloch 1986; see also Adorno 2005; Jacoby 2005; Jameson 1974; Jameson 1991). Henri Lefebvre reached similar conclusions in turning Heidegger on his head and composing a Marxist "critique of everyday life" (Lefebvre 1991). Yet Koolhaas's results are, at best, radical in a highly idiosyncratic way, requiring a great deal of interpretation even by Blochian standards to discern their radicalism. One example was the ill-fated Venetian Hotel Guggenheim project in Las Vegas. Intended by OMA as a transformative collision of high art and leisure space, the project has become, less than ten years after its conception, a theater whose main function is the daily staging of the *Phantom of the Opera* (Hawthorne 2008). Another is the collaboration with the Italian fashion designer Prada, which was drawn to Koolhaas as a result of his book on shopping: "Capitalizing on the insight that people spend more money in spaces that are not seen as purely commercial, Koolhaas has designed the Prada store in New York to be adaptable to cultural performances. . . . OMA is reformulating not only the space in which you shop but also the way in which you shop. The office team compiled a list of annoyances in shopping and devised many clever improvements" (Lubow 2000).

Is this radical engagement or merely expertise making the prevailing power relations more efficient in securing their domination? These examples suggest at least that the line between political engagement and political accommodation is a blurry one and that encomia to the inevitability of neoliberalism may be different from immanent critique.

Particularly marred by a facile and dubious reasoning are Koolhaas's invocations of the other, culture, and related themes.[17] Responding to an interviewer's question about the future of architecture, Koolhaas once asserted, "With globalization, we all have more or less the same future, but Asia and Africa feel much more new. I've been doing research on China recently, investigating cities that emerge suddenly, in eight years or so, seemingly out of nothing. These places are much more vigorous and representative of the future. There, building something new is a daily pleasure and a daily occurrence" (Heron 1996).

Singapore, he goes on, has succeeded by "removing any trace of authenticity. . . . And many Asian cities are like this now, seeming to exist of nothing but copies" (Heron 1996). Elsewhere, he tells us that Asian markets and African cities remain spontaneous, alive, and richly social, while in the West these have lost their spontaneity, have become more regimented and cold: "You could say that the shopping project is . . . about nostalgia for a pre-modern condition" (Sigler 2000).

Thus, although Koolhaas argues for an architecture that is more open to the world, his imagination in practice ends up increasing the gulf between architecture and its everyday contexts. Instead of a genuinely worldly architecture, we are presented with a way of conceptualizing space that relies on clichés about culture, urbanism, and globalization. Far from urban space becoming more open-ended and spontaneous, this approach strengthens power's claim over and identification with space.

How does urbanism relate specifically to local politics, to contemporary outcomes of ongoing struggles, and to marginalized alternatives? The Emirati intellectual and political theorist Abdul Khaleq Abdulla, a Dubai native who now writes a regular column for the Sharjah-based *Al-Khaleej* newspaper and whose writings are full of insight into the development of his home city, gives us some clues. In one of his more substantial recent academic publications, Abdulla writes that in Dubai "politics are inconceivable" (Abdulla 2006: 14). This is because, for the ruling family led by Dubai ruler Muhammad Al Maktoum, "there is one and only one priority, and that is trade and nothing but trade . . . the economy and nothing but the economy" (Abdulla 2006: 14). Or, as one of my interlocutors put it during my field research, in Dubai "trade is the religion and the religion is trade (*al-tijara din wa-l-din al-tijara*)." For Abdulla, this is connected to the way in which Dubai has globalized during the past two decades: "There is no difference in the age of globalization between the commodity, the state, merchandising (*al-bida'a*), the city, cultures, and services. All are equivalent, and in the context of competition, the relationship between them becomes ever tighter . . . for in order to remain in the vanguard (*al-muqaddima*), Dubai must prioritize promotion and marketing . . . because appearance is as important as essence, and the surface, in this day and age, is as important as content itself" (Abdulla 2006: 12–13).

This is the contemporary outcome of historical struggles between the official, hegemonic social formation on the one side, and reform movements on the other. How Dubai looks and what kind of city it is today are connected to the encounter between the Arab Gulf and the British Empire, and to the consequent dependency of the UAE on Western protection. As other studies (Abdulla 1984; Davidson 2008; Kanna 2011) have discussed in greater detail, the period between 1930 and 1960 was a time of great volatility and struggle in the UAE, with Dubai, the main Emirati arena where questions of royal legitimacy, nationalism, and anticolonialism were negotiated, being the focal point. The British Political Resident, for example, described with great anxiety a rising reformist movement in the late 1930s as a "democratic wave that aimed at putting more power in the hands of the people" (Davidson 2008: 33). Among other things, these reformers, whose social basis was the nonroyal merchant class, demanded that the ruler share 85 percent of the rent income on oil concessions and an airstrip given to him by the British, as well as the formation of consultative council and oversight of rent expenditures. A Dubai merchant recalled that these events evoked in the British "fears about what they saw as the emergence of progressive tendencies . . . and the establishment of an assembly which was actually representative of the community" (Davidson 2008: 35). "It would be easier," he added, "to keep dealing with traditional tribal structures than the more diffuse, less predictable activities of popular assemblies" (Davidson 2008: 35). By the mid-1950s, inspired by Egypt's Gamal Abd al-Nasser, a more nationalist and overtly anticolonial movement, the so-called Dubai National Front, arose, demanding nationalization of education, popular accountability of the royals, and separation from Britain. The colonial archives once again record the fears of the Political Resident and those of the eventual ruler, Rashid bin Said Al Maktoum (father of the present ruler, Muhammad). The Resident, for example, theorized that education would lead to demands for changes in the "existing patriarchal forms of government" (Davidson 2008: 52), something that must be avoided at all costs and that can be ensured by shoring up Rashid's hold on the throne. This reformist upsurge was echoed in 1979–1980, when the Iranian Revolution inspired another nationalist critique of royal monopolies on Emirati power (Abdulla 1980).

These potential threats to royal domination were averted, in each case, by a recourse to (neo)colonial protection, a process made even more unforgiving with the oil wealth of the post-1970s period (Abdulla 1984: 95). For Britain and the United States, the role of the UAE was simple: "to produce and export crude oil and import goods manufactured in the advanced capitalist countries of the center" (Abdulla 1984: 96–97). Abdulla also describes the ideology of the ruler and his elite merchant allies: "(this group) thinks of itself as the most modernized social segment and empathizes with the Western upper-class consumer life-style" (Abdulla 1984: 176). They identify modernity with consumption of Western luxury goods and espouse a free-trade ideology (Abdulla 1984: 124–25). For Abdulla, this consumerist, free-market absolutism is the flipside of a political system "characterized by an invariable tendency towards an authoritarian and politically marginalizing system, which closes all possible channels of political participation and systematically suppresses opposition movements" (Abdulla 1984: 181–82). The general population, in turn, had little choice but to reconcile itself to a petrodollar and consumer spending–fueled "political deactivation" (Abdulla 1984: 182).[18]

In the UAE, as in many other contemporary developing countries, starchitecture plays a central role in complex local contexts of urbanism. Starchitecture's homogenizing culturalization of local spaces and histories resonates strongly with local elites' class or national agendas for reconfiguring urban spaces or creating them from wholecloth and converting them into spaces of power. To starchitecture, what a city's specific, locally conditioned social and cultural politics are is largely a matter of indifference. Histories of struggle over identity, particular groups' claims to specific spaces, and the social conditions of the actual production of architectural projects are displaced by notions such as "authentic culture," teleological accounts of local history, and celebrations of the ingenuity of local elites for providing seemingly ideal conditions for architectural experimentation. From Shanghai to Dubai, starchitecture and urbanism more generally enter complex political and cultural alignments, oblivious to their real character.

PART II

Consumption

5

Reaching for Dubai: Nashville Dreams of a Twenty-First-Century Skyline

Richard Lloyd and Brian D. Christens

> *We think this building is public art* [emphasis added]. Signature [Tower] is not about maximizing my net worth. It will become a landmark, an icon. We do build buildings that are about making money, but not this one.
>
> —Tony Giarratana

So Nashville developer Tony Giarratana told the *New York Times* in 2006 (Chamberlain 2006), referring to the proposed Signature Tower, a residential high-rise projected to radically transform Nashville's skyline. Given that Giarratana had opted to eschew public subsidy on the project and was still seeking the necessary private financing to realize his grandiose ambitions, the claim that the building was not "about making money" is a stunning and perhaps ill-considered admission. Nevertheless, "build it and they will come" had become a mantra for globally financed, impossibly extravagant architectural projects colonizing unlikely locales, with spectacular if short-lived models of success in Dublin and Dubai. In fact, over lunch, one of Giarratana's employees, a canny, Harvard-educated Nashville native named David, mused that the shock city of the United Arab Emirates, with its artificial island, indoor ski slope, and six (!) star hotels, provided about the best precedent he could think of for the Signature Tower, ludicrously out of scale to the southern city's squat downtown.

Figure 3. Rendering of the proposed Signature Tower in downtown Nashville.
Courtesy of Giarratana Development LLC.

Representing the peak of Nashville's ambitions for a twenty-first-century *cosmopolitan* skyline, Signature Tower was a proposed high-rise condominium building that at its most fanciful was projected to grow to seventy-one floors, with a $7 million ornamental crown that would make it the tallest building in the Southeast, and the tallest residential tower anywhere in the United States. A boutique hotel was to occupy the lower floors, intended principally as an amenity to provide laundry and food service for the permanent residents above. Presale prices listed from $280,000 (for spectacular views of the next-door public library) to $5,000,000 (the penthouse, for spectacular views of, presumably, Atlanta). The exceedingly credulous *Times* article, riddled with inaccuracies, printed as virtually fait accompli this remarkable promise by a private developer to construct a multimillion-dollar work of *public art* in a sprawling midsized city with virtually no history of downtown residential development. Such boosterism of overheated architectural ambition is in fact revealing of the mood of the early twenty-first century. It appeared, as we now know, on the eve of the bill coming due for the mass fantasy in which privately financed seventy-one-story towers are loss-leaders selling city identity.

David's comparison of Nashville to Dubai is overblown, in the sense that *everything* looks modest compared to the Burj Dubai, the world's tallest building. Moreover, though Nashville's downtown residential economy would be shortly pummeled by the financial crisis, it hardly approaches the spectacular collapse in Dubai, or even in Miami. And yet, David was still onto something, as both Nashville and Dubai represent projected or actual injections of a highly leveraged, profoundly symbolic hypermodernism tabula rasa into regions generally understood as reactionary bastions rejecting modernity. Rejecting the spare modernism of the mid-twentieth-century skyscraper, Signature Tower and the Burj are characterized by postmodern ornamental flourishes; further, both Dubai and Nashville model in ambience as much on the desert oasis of Las Vegas as on modern metropolises such as New York and Chicago, dreamscapes of fantasy and consumption rather than monuments of Fordist production.[1] Indeed, as we see in this chapter, the boom in downtown residential development in Nashville corresponds to the ongoing failure of the downtown as an old-fashioned central business district.

The scale of Signature Tower represents discontinuity not only with the modernist skyline of the mid-twentieth century but also with the deconcentrated, deracinated urban environments of the Sun Belt, which are themselves artifacts of postmodern urbanism and globalization, as Los Angeles School theorists have shown. As in Dubai, the absolute epitome of the twenty-first-century financial phantasmagoria,[2] Signature Tower signals the reach for cosmopolitanism via brute verticality and derivative ornament. Giarratana's appeal to public art is apt; far from form following function, this emergent model of the global downtown objectifies and aestheticizes in its own manner the hyper-abstractions of finance capital. There is a tenuous relationship at best between a seventy-one-story work of public art and the "real" economy governed by modern "laws" such as supply and demand; as

financial markets demonstrated a seemingly endless capacity to spin deriva-
tives increasingly removed from the "brick and mortar" base,[3] so the designs of Dubai and the "new" Nashville could be conjured absent precedent
or apparent necessity.

The Burj Dubai actually opened in 2010; nothing like the originally
planned Signature Tower will be built in Nashville in the foreseeable future.
Dubai will inevitably serve as the monument par excellence to a period of
urban extravagance and global finance whose consequences continue to
unfold. Nashville will not. Still, sometimes the best material appears in the
footnotes, and in the midsized, mid-South Music City we can glean the dif-
fusion of a global logic of the downtown development at the dawn of the
twenty-first century, as well as its distinctive structural underpinnings.

When David made his offhand comparison, Signature Tower still appeared a go in its most spectacular manifestation, and numerous more
modest but still significant residential towers were already being erected
throughout the downtown with gaudy presale figures. Dubai, meanwhile,
still appeared a spectacular triumph of vision and unregulated capitalism.
In fact, both local economies were heavily reliant on neoliberal logics: Dubai,
born apparently full-grown as a financial capital and eager host to shell corporations, and Nashville, whose higher-profile music industry is in fact
dwarfed by for-profit health care and corrections. Both Dubai and Nashville,
at admittedly divergent scales, depended on the spectacular liquidity of
finance capital and the intense commitment of local power structures to
lightly regulated private development, and both evinced a commitment to a
kind of brute cosmopolitanism inscribed in the shock skyline. In both the
United States and the emirates, the building boom of the early twenty-first
century relied significantly on immigrant labor (in Dubai, the famously exploited Asian "guest workers"; in the United States, mostly Latinos, often
undocumented), safely quarantined in ghettos and compounds invisible to
the glamour zones they created (Ali 2010; Associated Press 2010; Porter
2007). Both Nashville and Dubai will be shaped in years to come by the legacy of these cosmopolitan ambitions.

On the other hand, Dubai aspired to the very short list of global cities
hosting the uber-rich financial class, along with oil sheiks and Russian oli-
garchs, and developed its amenities accordingly (Krane 2009). Nashville,
conversely, tailored its new culture and design aspirations to a larger and
more modestly compensated artifact of twenty-first-century stratification,
the "creative class" of culture and technology workers.[4] This distinction

means that there are important divergences as well as similarities between logics of development; we will close this analysis with an examination of the so-called creative class and its relationship to new design discourses in the mid-South. Still, even if the targets of development discourse—the fantasy population accompanying the fantasy skyline—differ, extravagant financial elites on the one hand and hipster creatives on the other, both models amp up the attention to cultural amenities and cosmopolitan symbolism.

Globalization and U.S. Cities: Los Angeles, New York, Nashville

Following the urban crisis of the 1970s, theorists have gleaned the reanimation of city landscapes in the United States according to a new logic of globalization, distinct from the national industrial economy that spurred the first great wave of U.S. urban expansion. The logic of urban morphology delineated by University of Chicago sociologists in the first half of the twentieth century is taken to be outdated, respondent as it was to the impetus of industrial production, national economies, and now superseded constraints of communication and transportation technologies. Globalization manifests itself in a variety of forms: the collapse of the urban industrial base in bastions such as Detroit, Chicago, and Philadelphia; the rise of an informational economy and of finance capital (Castells 1996; Sassen 2001); the apparent triumph of neoliberal economic ideology (Hackworth 2006; Harvey 2007); new immigrant populations transforming urban landscapes and promoting a new transnational imaginary, or cosmopolitanism from below (Davis 2001; Nashashibi 2007; R. Smith 2005); the impact of global tourism and the aestheticization of cityspace (Gotham 2007; Lloyd and Clark 2001). By the 1990s, two competing approaches to globalization and the city dominated urban studies, derived from the two largest U.S. cities: the "LA [Los Angeles] School" (Scott and Soja 1996), emphasizing deconcentrated urbanization, and Saskia Sassen's (2001) theory of New York as a "global city," restoring attention to the dense, vertical downtown. Both of these approaches can usefully inform an analysis of downtown Nashville's development patterns in the face of globalization, instructive for both the correspondences and the divergences evinced. But neither is ultimately adequate for understanding the rapid and surprising developments at the dawn of the twenty-first century.

Nashville, located on the northern fringe of the economically and demographically dynamic Sun Belt region, appeared in the late twentieth century to have followed the growth logics exemplified in Los Angeles (and like Los Angeles, its best known if not largest economic sector is in the cultural industries). Coming out of the crisis-ridden 1970s, Los Angeles sped past Chicago as the nation's second city in population, leading the charge of Sun Belt cities as the fastest-growing metro areas in the United States. These cities diverged sharply from the urban styles of the Midwest and Northeast, expanding horizontally rather than vertically, with comparatively weak or nonexistent downtown identities. Against the vertically integrated, bureaucratic imperatives of industrial capitalism, theorists of the Los Angeles School perceived the fragmentary logic of global capitalism inscribed on the deracinated Angelino topography.

By standard measures, Nashville's metropolitan region is among the lowest-density regions in the United States, with rapid population growth accompanied by sprawling, suburban development (Fulton et al. 2001; Lopez and Hynes 2003). The downtown is challenged by various edge city locales (Garreau 1991), especially Cool Springs, in which the horizontal corporate campus trumps the high-rise office tower. In fact, Nashville's downtown, never especially robust, entered an extended period of profound distress beginning in the late 1960s, its most iconic structures abandoned and at times demolished. Downtown morbidity continued even as the metro region boomed in the 1990s behind the impetus of country music, religious publishing, and for-profit health care. The most important of the many corporate relocations to Middle Tennessee exemplifies this trend. Nissan North America moved from Gardena, California, in 2006 to be closer to its southern manufacturing base (with a major Nissan plant in nearby Smyrna, Tennessee), taking temporary residence in downtown's AT&T building pending completion of its Cool Springs custom campus. In fact, even as he was the face of downtown's vertical ambitions, Tony Giarratana was also tapped as the developer of the proposed May Town office, residential, and shopping complex in Davidson County's pristine Bells Bend, meant to compete for the sort of corporate enterprises captured by Nashville's collar counties, and strongly opposed by environmentalists as an impetus to further sprawl (Kreyling 2007). Michael Dear (2002b) is fond of noting that in the late twentieth century, "every city that is growing, is growing in the manner of Los Angeles," and Nashville, with its endless suburbs, embattled urban core, and widely dispersed corporate economy, seemed to prove the case.

On the other hand, as Marina Peterson shows in this volume, even Los Angeles no longer grows only in the manner of Los Angeles, at least not in the manner of the "postmodern urbanism" posited by Los Angeles School stalwarts like Dear (2000) and Soja (1989). The New Los Angeles, like the New Nashville, has distinctively un–Sun Belt–like aspirations for walkable street environments (against Missing Persons' claim that "Nobody Walks in LA"), coherent urban space, and robust downtown identity including a high-end (and midrange) residential population that values public art and cultural performance beyond the canned offerings of the much-vaunted cultural industries of Los Angeles (M. Peterson 2010). Nashville is thus not idiosyncratic in recent aspirations to develop downtown vertically, injecting an oasis of core city density in the sprawling metro region. If anything, it has been a laggard in this regard. Thus, while it would be incorrect to suggest that suburban expansion has been reversed in the South, trends apparent in cities such as Houston, Atlanta, Austin, and Charlotte indicate that the production of a recognizable and economically vital urban core is a central agenda in a new phase of *balanced* Sun Belt urbanism, including substantial modeling on the examples of older, northern core city neighborhoods and vertical downtowns (Lloyd 2011).

Given that New York's skyline has become the absolute symbol of global finance and cosmopolitan modernity not only in the United States but worldwide (a fact not lost on the 9/11 terrorists), we should mine theories of Manhattan for clues to Nashville's downtown ambitions. The most influential and sophisticated theorist of New York's return from the brink of collapse in the 1970s to global capital is Saskia Sassen. While Los Angeles School theorists dismiss the downtown and stress polynucleation, Sassen (2001) sees globalization as generating a dialectic of dispersal and (re)concentration, with prototypical cities such as New York, London, and Tokyo emerging as command and control centers for a radically dispersed system of production and consumption. In this case, large-scale industrial manufacturing deserts older urban locales (though not necessarily the degraded semiformal sweatshop economy, which actually makes a comeback in New York and Los Angeles, tapping new immigrants from the global South; Sassen 1991). In industry's absence, the erstwhile tertiary sector becomes a "postindustrial production site" generating innovations in high-end producer services, especially law and finance.

In contrast to the initial proponents of the "world city hypothesis" (Knox and Taylor 1995), Sassen thus does not see even multinational corporate headquarters as the key to reconcentration; these can, like Nissan North America in Nashville, profitably relocate on the urban periphery. But elite service providers are in many cases not so liberated, requiring the social connectivity of the dense core. Sassen (2000) notes that producer services are also surging in the cities of the second and third tiers, though these are more likely to be articulated to regional rather than global economies and to be subordinated to the global command centers (see also Hodos 2007).

As Susan Fainstein (2001) shows, global restructuring in New York and London is accompanied by a distinctive built environment, including a flurry of upscale residential developments, both imaging the world of global high finance and underwritten by it. Thus, global city labor requirements—which, importantly for Nashville, extend beyond the financial sector to include specialized inputs in media and technology—join with new development strategies emphasizing in-town living in urban citadels (Smithsimon 2010). The new economy's educated and cosmopolitan workers demand a distinct amenity mix unavailable in the suburbs and exurbs (Lloyd and Clark 2001), generating urban glamour zones and a new culture of consumer cosmopolitanism, a modality of city value that is most fully formed in New York's convergence of finance, media, and fashion (Currid 2007), though even sleepy Southern cities can cast a wistful eye in its direction. At the same time, this high-end revaluation of erstwhile "fear city" creates significant complications around the concept and use of public space, as privileged residents encounter the wretched and dispossessed of the neoliberal city (Greenberg 2008; Smithsimon 2006). Similar issues, as we will see below, accompany the injection of high-end residence and a robust entertainment economy into a district that had functioned as Nashville's de facto skid row as recently as the mid-1990s.

Global Nashville

Nashville's embrace of downtown residential development suggests a new turn in Sun Belt development, moving us away from the postulates of the Los Angeles School. In its embrace of urban design trends including high-rise construction, New Urbanist streetscapes, and adaptive reuse, New York becomes the new model for cosmopolitan aspirations in the mid-South. Still, can Sassen's theory of the global city's economic base, concentrated in financial services, explain new developments in Nashville? After all, while Nashville once was a regional center for the kind of financial services that underlie the "command and control" capacities of the classic global city—especially banking and insurance—it has since surrendered Southeastern centrality in finance to Charlotte and Atlanta. Moreover, while New York is the un-American capital of globalization, outré fashion, and modern art, Nashville is the uber-American capital of cornpone culture, spawning Shoney's, Goo-Goo Clusters, and the Grand Ole Opry.

It is true that in the first part of the twentieth century the financial elite aspired to a certain sophistication, if not exactly cosmopolitanism, setting up a genteel and exclusive country club community in the near west suburb of Belle Meade and promoting their city as both the Wall Street of the South and the Athens of the South (the latter both for the robust concentration of educational institutions and for the city's cheesy neoclassical monuments, especially the bizarre replica of the Parthenon in Centennial Park).[5] This conservative upper crust was increasingly dismayed as Nashville instead began to earn a reputation as the "hillbilly capital of the world," hosting tacky nouveau riche stars in the emergent country music industry (Hemphill 1970).

Still, they had no one to blame but themselves. If the Belle Meade bankers and insurance executives imagined themselves as "New South" elite, their client base was largely poor and dispersed throughout a still overwhelmingly rural region. In order to reach these simple folk, National Life and Accident's flagship radio station WSM ("We Shield Millions") began to broadcast the Saturday Night Barn Dance, which would in short order become the Grand Ole Opry, the foundation on which Music City USA was built (Havighurst 2007; R. Peterson 1999). Thus, unlike Chicago, in which regionally articulated futures markets would eventually price currencies and commodities for global exchange, the financial services sector would not prove Nashville's portal into the global economy—that role, to the extent that it has been filled at all, would fall to Belle Meade's bastard child, Music Row.

Music provides Nashville with its brand identity, and the city's musical output has become a global commodity, ironically trading on regional embeddedness for its niche in international markets. Indeed, Nashville's rise as a center for culture industry inputs—which implies a substantial specialized labor force in sound engineering, production, tour management, music publishing, promotions, and other services that support the music industry alongside North America's greatest *concentration* of working musicians—has been spectacular over the past half-century, making it in some ways a peer city to the coastal media Meccas of New York and Los Angeles (Florida and Jackson 2008; Raines and Brown 2006; Rothfield et al. 2007). The corporate headquarters and support services (production facilities, music publishers, entertainment lawyers, management companies, etc.), are quartered just outside the downtown, on the charmingly and misleadingly provincial Music Row, a stretch of real estate so low-key it could easily be mistaken for a residential neighborhood. Despite its roots in rural folk culture, Nashville's now multibillion-dollar music industry helps fuel the imagination of an affluent, culturally sophisticated population of high-rise dwellers, and in fact, teenage megastar Taylor Swift owns the penthouse in Mid-Town's Adelicia, which opened just off Music Row in 2007.

If the Opry originally consolidated folk musicians from a largely rural geographic swath extending from West Virginia to Bakersfield that Peterson refers to as country music's "fertile crescent" (Peterson and Davis 1977), today expert labor and aspiring artists are drawn from all over North America and indeed the world. The industry consolidation in Nashville has especially produced an influx from the coasts, importantly for the marketing rhetoric for the downtown condominium explosion, as these new arrivals are supposed to evince more cosmopolitan consumer preferences than has typically characterized the mid-South (Echegaray 2009). As an owner of a hip, Los Angeles–style bar that served as a "new amenity" beachhead into the downtown Gulch (once a sparse former warehouse district along the railroad tracks, now a hip downtown entertainment zone where the largest completed residential tower, 424-unit ICON, is sited) put it: "You're looking at the younger music professionals, 25–35 with a pretty significant amount of disposable income, that wanna have a big city lifestyle, go to a big city place. A lot of people that have traveled outside and live in Nashville because of the music business, we've been lucky enough to get through the door." In interviews we conducted in 2005–2008, condo developers similarly trumpet this worldly set as a key to their projected markets.

Along with the attraction of elite culture workers, country music's global popularity has increased Nashville's stature as tourist destination for international travelers, who throng the downtown honky-tonks to consume "authentic" American music. Old habits die hard, and some city boosters have a hard time letting go of the idea of the "hillbilly" music industry as an impediment to a more cosmopolitan imaging of Nashville. On the eve of the 2008 presidential election debates held at Nashville's Belmont University, former mayor and current Tennessee governor Phil Bredeson indicated: "A lot of visitors think everybody's going to have bare feet and a guitar slung over their shoulder. And they don't. They see a city where music is important, but they also see a very sophisticated city" (Sledge 2008). More typically, though, the Music City USA designation has been embraced as an integral part of city identity and strategies for downtown resurgence. Thus, the Country Music Hall of Fame has been relocated into palatial digs just off Broadway (where it sits across the street from the recently built Schermerhorn Symphony Hall), and the annual four-day Country Music Association's Festival (Fan-Fair) has been moved from the Tennessee fairgrounds to the downtown riverfront.

In terms of its other leading industries, Nashville cannot be said to evince much in the way of global integration. It is the seat of the Southern Baptist convention and the U.S. leader in religious publishing and recording (culture industries that actually eclipse country music in revenue, but without the international market scope). Otherwise, Nashville's greatest contribution to the national economy has been in cutting-edge neoliberalization in health care and corrections, with the largest operators of both for-profit hospitals (Hospital Corporation of America, or HCA) and prisons (Corrections Corporation of America). Here its innovations have been exceptionally profitable—HCA is the foundation of the Frist family fortune—but not exactly global; even if neoliberalism has become, in Pierre Bourdieu and Loic Wacquant's (2001) words, a "new planetary vulgate," countries outside the United States have still been relatively slow to privatize their hospitals and prisons. The other leading employment sector is government jobs and related lobbying and legal services; Nashville is the state capital.

The global elements in Nashville's downtown skyline, then, owe not to locally based financial services or multinational corporations (Nissan notwithstanding), but rather to the globalization of mortgage markets that was changing building strategies everywhere in the early 2000s (in Nashville more slowly than in many other Sun Belt cities, actually) and to a correspondent isomorphism, of both built form and lifestyle, originating in legitimate global cities such as New York and Los Angeles and advertised through mass-mediated images. "Welcome to the new Nashville skyline," Tracy Moore (2008) writes in *The Nashville Scene*. "It's frighteningly high, undeniably modern and so *money*. It's no Nashville you've ever seen, because it's every bit an image straight out of Miami or Los Angeles—or at least a [TV] show set there."

The real estate bubble that exploded in 2007 produced uneven effects throughout the United States, at least insofar as it impacted the built environment. Among them was the sudden come-to-Jesus moment concerning the desirability of trading split-level suburban homes for high-rise apartments and loft conversions—even in Sun Belt cities like Nashville with relatively little available to convert.[6] Low interest rates, exotic mortgage vehicles, and the shift in underwriting from George Bailey's Building and Loan to deracinated REITs and CMOs all strongly supported the residential bias of speculative excess, and along with this a new way to approach the renewal of perpetually embattled downtown areas (Gotham 2006). It is important to note that such development comes accompanied with cultural scripts, discourses of urban culture, and design that are leveraged to support the new vertical utopia. But in reviewing the history of Nashville's core city decay and development, we should not make the mistake of assuming that the speculative excesses and grand designs of the 2000s represent the first incursion of abstract global forces into the sleepy, provincial mid-South. In fact, though seldom understood as such, the Southeast has long represented a cutting-edge environment in global economic restructuring.

Tabula Rasa: Downtown Decline from the 1940s to the 1990s

Both the sorry state of Nashville's downtown as recently as the mid-1990s and its more recent revival are artifacts of the progression of globalization over the past half-century. Indeed, a persistent bias among scholars maintains an anachronistic notion of the region as isolated, rural, and reactionary, despite the proliferation of "New South" discourses (a perpetual trope since the end of the Civil War) and the economic and population dynamism of the region (Applebome 1997). In fact, the South has evinced a parasitical pattern of rapid urban growth, a magnet for both residents and industries from fading midwestern and northeastern cities (Beauregard 1996). With its negligible union penetration, low taxes, and "pro-business" regulatory climate, the South would preview globalization's race to the bottom as industries from poultry packing to automobile manufacture shifted below the Mason-Dixon. This included a substantial amount of foreign direct investment, as well as substantial immigration of documented and undocumented workers by the end of the twentieth century (Cobb and Stueck 2005). In contrast to northeastern and midwestern industry, Southern industry developed in a new transport and technology era, allowing it to skip over agglomeration in the urban core. Moreover, the impact of the automobile age, urban renewal, suburban housing subsidy, and post–civil rights white flight weakened already underdeveloped downtowns at the expense of sprawling expansion (Bullard, Johnson, and Torres 2000; Lassiter 2006).

Thus, despite being a part of the economically vital Sun Belt, and winning occasional notice from mostly right-wing outlets for its exemplary "pro-business" climate, downtown Nashville has struggled to attract investment and development for the past sixty years. In classic urban renewal fashion, the 1940s to the 1990s saw many historic downtown structures demolished to make way for new development, much of which never materialized. Signature Tower's proposed location, near the geographic center of downtown on the corner of Fifth Avenue and Church Street, is emblematic of this history. Currently one of many surface parking lots punctuating the built environment, it had been the site of the downtown Cain-Sloan department store, the anchor of the old downtown shopping corridor and the venue for one of the first lunch counter sit-in protests during the Civil Rights movement (Doyle 1985; Morris 1984: 205–14).

One block to the east of the Signature site, the Life & Casualty Tower (L & C) still stands at thirty stories. Built in 1957 for $6.5 million, the L & C briefly held the distinction of being the tallest building in the southeastern United States, a fair depiction of the cut-rate quality of southern skylines at midcentury. Signature Tower, of course, aimed to win back that trophy for Middle Tennessee in spectacular fashion. The L & C would remain the tallest building in Tennessee for a decade, a symbol of the time when Nashville was a regional banking and insurance hub, and even today it features prominently in the image of the downtown skyline, which is not surprising given the arrested development of succeeding decades.

Across the street from the L & C, the Maxwell House Hotel stood for ninety-two years before burning to the ground on Christmas Eve in 1961. This landmark hotel hosted many famous visitors, including seven presidents, Thomas Edison, and "Buffalo" Bill Cody. Its eponymous coffee inspired a national brand. A block up north, Giarratana dismayed local preservationists by razing another landmark in 1990, the fifty-year-old Sudekum Tower, an art deco–style, twelve-story building whose ground level housed the Tennessee Theater.[7] The theater had the distinction of hosting the 1973 Grammy Awards ceremonies, the only time the event has ever been held outside New York or Los Angeles.

The 1973 Grammys were a bright spot in an otherwise dim era for downtown Nashville. In a stark symbol of downtown deterioration, the famed

Ryman Auditorium, home to the Grand Ole Opry since 1943, was shuttered in 1974 as the Opry made for the suburbs and a theme park locale, Opryland USA. In the latter half of the twentieth century, Nashville did not attract the level of investment and development that city boosters would have hoped. Yet, it proceeded with plans of urban renewal and infrastructure development, similar to those being deployed by cities that were experiencing significant downtown growth.[8] Old structures were routinely razed, either for new transportation infrastructure or to clear the way for potential future development. In most cases, the spaces cleared for new development sat indefinitely in expectation of the development that had justified the demolitions. In the meantime, the metropolitan Nashville region has developed into the sort of polynucleated, automobile-centered built form commonly seen in highly suburbanized regions.

A 1967 edition of *Nashville* magazine gives voice to the hopes of city boosters, which hinged, at the time, on the construction of a loop of interstate highway that would encircle downtown. Ninety percent of the project was to be federally financed, and the resulting loop would join six interstate highway spokes. "Only eight other cities in the nation will be the focal point for as many as six interstates and only Chicago will gather in seven highways" (Aden 1967: 5). The construction of the downtown loop necessitated the acquisition and demolition of many structures, including numerous businesses along Church and Broad (now Broadway) Streets. The magazine article's author admonished those who saw the construction of the interstate loop as too costly: "Only with the completion of Nashville's loop system will the full meaning of the many sacrifices be understood and appreciated" (Aden 1967: 5).

Interstate traffic would not prove to be the catalyst for urban development that earlier forms of shipping and transportation, such as rivers and railroads, had been. Housing and businesses demolished by the construction of the interstate left lots that were never filled with the gleaming city of the future that some had imagined. Instead, many remain vacant or are occasionally used for special events parking. Most others are filled by automobile-related uses, such as gas stations or tire shops. The northern part of the downtown, around the state capitol, by the 1990s had lost nearly every resident, becoming a bland central business district peppered with nearly equal parts office tower, surface parking lot, and (primarily entertainment-oriented) historic building stock. The southern part of the downtown loop became a repository for sex shops, strip clubs, and the homeless.

By 2000, only three downtown buildings other than the L & C Tower had reached thirty stories or higher, with the AT&T (formerly BellSouth) looming tallest at thirty-two floors (630 feet). Meanwhile, other cities in the region (most comparisons by Nashvillians aspiring to grow the skyline are to Atlanta, Georgia, which is 215 miles away) were erecting fifty-, sixty-, or even seventy-story structures in their downtowns. It is this pattern of stagnant and squat core development, with a negligible residential component and a bleeding market in office space, that lends to the proposed Signature Tower project, and to a lesser extent the numerous more modest high-rises actually built in the 2000s, the Dubai-like quality addressed above.

The Advent of the Downtown Residential Tower

While maintaining a reputation as a destination for country music, downtown Nashville lagged behind its peer cities in terms of office, retail, hotel, and residential construction as cities nationwide made lurching and uneven moves to rebound from the severe crisis of the 1970s, the hinge on which global restructuring turned. The 1980s and 1990s brought a wave of subsidized megaprojects and thematic entertainments designed to entice visitors and investors to revive the ailing downtown, following a pattern of "Disneyfied" development evident in New York's Times Square, Baltimore's Inner Harbor, and Chicago's Navy Pier.[9] Consistent with the criticisms of these development strategies, new projects during this period evinced little interest in the legacy of downtown's historic culture, especially its inherited musical identity. A downtown convention center was ham-fistedly placed between historic structures on lower Broadway; its architectural orientation plainly illustrated the lack of esteem that the city builders had for the country music bars. The walls of the center facing lower Broadway and the Ryman Auditorium[10] are blank, while the entrance to the center faced the appropriately named Commerce Street.

A Planet Hollywood restaurant had a brief tenure on lower Broadway, and Church Street, the former heart of Nashville's shopping district, very briefly was home to a suburban-style indoor shopping mall, dubbed "Church Street Center." The mall's businesses quickly closed as shoppers clearly indicated their preference for malls far away from the parking and panhandling hassles of downtown. A few downtown residential structures were built during the 1980s and 1990s, but the widespread shift in U.S. culture toward desiring "in-town living" was channeled locally into the rapid gentrification of Nashville's first-ring suburbs in south, east, and north Nashville. Neighborhoods in each of these areas were stocked with cheap Victorian-styled houses and bungalows, which were turned over en masse and sold to successive waves of increasingly affluent new residents.

The Metropolitan Development and Housing Agency (MDHA), seeking to redevelop a large tract of city-owned property south of downtown, commissioned a feasibility study by Economic Research Associates. Marking a strategic turning point, the study emphasized the importance of residential construction for the revitalization of Nashville's downtown. This recommendation was in harmony with recent changes in city policy, which had shifted in 2000 from using Tax Increment Financing (TIF) to incentivize downtown retail and office construction toward using TIF exclusively for encouraging residential development. The emerging consensus among city decision-makers was that only attracting residents to downtown Nashville would allow the desired cultural amenities to be successful. The failed earlier attempts at retail development were retrospectively attributed to the lack of downtown residents, and in the initial attempts to recruit new downtown residents, developers and agents assured the "urban pioneers" that retail and other amenities would follow them downtown.

In fact, while Signature Tower impresario Tony Giarratana was credited by the *New York Times* in 2006 with "single-handedly creating a market for residential housing in the central business district" (Chamberlain 2006: 1), the real visionaries seem to have been headquartered in the modest-digs MDHA, whose offices are located, of all places, on the grounds of the city's largest public housing project, James Cayce Homes.[11] Wielding the popular and complicated incentivizing vehicle of TIF (providing public subsidy for private development with the expectation of recouping the money through subsequent increases in property taxes), MDHA encouraged an initially reluctant Giarratana to wade into downtown residential development. Giarratana, whose career had been in commercial real estate, was confronted with a frosty market for downtown office space when he approached MDHA to discuss developing the former Sudekum Tower site:

I said, "I'm not gonna get to develop an office building on this property in the near term. There's just no demand for office, financing's not available for office. What would you like developed on this property?" And [MDHA director Gerald Nicely] didn't hesitate. . . . "I'd like to have apartments developed on that property." I said: "I don't do apartments. What else would you like developed on that property?" He said, "I would like to have apartments developed on that property and I will provide six million dollars in tax increment financing if you'll develop apartments on that property." I said: "I'm your guy. I'll develop apartments" and walked in to a meeting with my advisors and I said, "What the hell is tax increment financing?" I had no idea, but six million dollars is more than I had when I walked in there, so I learned about tax increment financing, I learned about apartments, and we built the Cumberland on that site. You've heard the expression "necessity is the mother of" . . . what is it?

The twenty-four-story Cumberland opened in 1998; it would be another eight years before Viridian came online and Nashville's new age of downtown residential mania would enter full swing, fueled by city money and the new mood of global finance capital. Still, abstract as the financial transactions underwriting the boom may have been, from local TIF money to the leveraged lending of regional banks such as Charlotte-based Wachovia (which "had its name on every shitty project in the city," one developer told us candidly) to the dissipation of mortgages into the ether of global bond markets, few things are in the end as tangible and as rooted as a building, and even in the Sun Belt, few places can exert such a pull on the imagination of lived city identity than its downtown.

The general tenor of mistrust of downtown residence turned rapidly to exuberance after the first genuine high-rise, Giarratana's Viridian, "sold out" nine months prior to its completion in 2006—thirteen years after zoning laws changed to permit such construction. The tenor of the marketing plan was evident in the launch party, held months before the groundbreaking, at the trendy Midtown sushi-fusion restaurant Virago, in which complementary "Viriditinis" (fruity blue-green vodka cocktails in martini glasses) were served to trend-setting prospects. In what would prove an increasingly rare event, Viridian's buyers actually took occupancy as a beachhead for "hip and cool" colonization of the core. On the heels of the 305-unit Viridian, a slew of new projects (see Table 1) began to transform Nashville's downtown into a "crane city," including Velocity (265 units), Encore (333 units), and ICON (424 units).

The more than a thousand new units that would have the poor fortune to come online in 2008 and beyond also showed brisk action on the presale

Table 1 Downtown Residential Multiunit Construction (>100 Units) 1999–2009

Developments:	No. of units	Type	Estimated/actual completion date
Encore	333	new	2008
Griffin Plaza*	150	new/reuse	
ICON	424	new	2008
Rolling Mill Hill (Phase 1)*	175	new/reuse	2009
Signature Tower*	435	new	
Terrazzo	109	new	2009
Velocity	265	new	2009
Viridian Condominiums	305	new	2006

*Projects currently delayed, partially delayed, or canceled.

front, with the largest project, ICON, allegedly selling out in forty-eight hours. But in their cases, "sold out" proved to mean something other than sold out, with relatively modest deposits counted as sales, and a large number of "buyers"—some of whom, it is clear, were pure speculators—ultimately walking away as the market soured in 2007–2008.[12] Thus, today, megaprojects such as Encore and ICON are eerily dark, reminiscent of the vast, empty Overlook Hotel that tortured Jack Nicholson to insanity in *The Shining*. These colossal wrecks, with their Lido decks, onsite fitness facilities, and rec centers, do indeed evoke the feel of a resort hotel, though as Moore (2008) observes, "more like a resort in the offseason."

The Cosmopolitan Life

If we can in retrospect see clearly the structural underpinnings of the new yen for in-town living in the abstractions of financial capital—and it is safe to say that this aspect was not well appreciated by its proponents, especially the triumphalist school of New Urbanists—we must also note that bubbles come complete with cultural scripts, in this case a sudden and dramatic repudiation of suburban cul-de-sacs in favor of cultural diversity and stimulating street environments. The pitch flew in the face of the past half-century of deconcentrated urban growth and in fact of stubborn demographic realities of persistent dispersal alongside the speculative boom in downtown high-rises and near-ring gentrification (Kotkin 2008).

The carriers of the new zeitgeist, as always, are mostly the younger generation—open minded, well educated, and above all, creative. Richard Florida's (2002) best-selling *Rise of the Creative Class* has for several years been the bible for the new downtown imaginary, clutched to the bosoms of political leaders and city planners. In Florida's analysis, regional success depends on nurturing the lifestyle preferences of tech-savvy, highly mobile creative workers, weaned on the Manhattanized visions of urban glamour proffered by *Friends* and *Sex and the City*. The model image of the new, and in Nashville unprecedented, downtown dweller is summed up by *Nashville Scene* writer Tracy Moore (2008): "young, sophisticated, aesthetically blessed and elegantly draped in white linen, a smart cocktail in [a] bronzed, well-moisturized hand . . . wildly successful, well-traveled, and highly cultured."

Cutting edge in skill-sets and consumption preferences, those in this cadre reject the alienation and angst of bohemia, but they like the lively and surprising street environment of Greenwich Village. Single, childless, and apparently subsisting on cappuccinos, cupcakes, and cosmopolitans, the "creative class" cares little for signature suburban amenities such as supermarkets, malls, and good schools (dog parks are another matter), craving instead fitness facilities, cafés, and art galleries. Meanwhile, the baby boomers, loathe to miss out on any major trend, joined the party as "empty-nesters," living, sometimes uncomfortably, cheek to jowl with the postcollegiate crowd (Casselman 2007). Parroting the new conventional wisdom, Giarratana describes these twin demographics as "the hip and the cool" and "the mature professionals." Given the incommensurate financial resources characterizing these two groups, Giarratana's relatively down-market Viridian (including affordable housing set-asides) targeted the former, while the proposed Signature Tower was mature professional all the way.

In 2007, Nashville's District 6 councilman Mike Jameson visited Richard Lloyd's Urban Community course at Vanderbilt to talk about downtown development.[13] Jameson explained to an unusually attentive group of undergraduates (no doubt imagining their own urbane futures) and one rapt professor:

> I was asking a young lady . . . who lives in the Viridian "Why would you move to the city?" She said "What television shows did you grow up watching?" I said, well, the Brady Bunch and Bonanza and so forth. She said "If you think about it, in those shows, it's a suburban lifestyle." When Little Joe wanted to go see Hoss, he got on a horse

and rode across the Ponderosa and twenty minutes later, there was Hoss. When the Brady kids wanted to go see classmates, they got out of their suburb and drove and drove to another suburb. But not her. She said she grew up watching *Friends* and *Seinfeld*, and when Joey wanted to see Ross, he walked across the hallway, and when they wanted to get a cup of coffee, they went downstairs and across the street. When they wanted to go to the store, they went to the building next door. It was sort of that mixed-use but compact and dense lifestyle that she was after. That's why she's in the Viridian.

Unfortunately, as the above history indicates, downtown Nashville is hardly blessed with the rich history and diverse amenity mix of Manhattan, though Giarratana, after polling his Cumberland residents on their biggest complaint (no shopping), allowed an HG Hill Market to open on the ground floor of Viridian virtually rent free. Developers along Fifth Avenue have similarly sold street-front space to art galleries at dramatically submarket rates, loss leaders for the much vaunted Avenue of the Arts. Still, a compact and dense lifestyle is not a traditional Nashville amenity. James Howard Kunstler (2003), the leading contemporary prophet of the new urbanism, wrote after a visit to the city in 2003:

> A walk from the Vanderbilt campus across the river to Five Points in East Nashville [passing through downtown] is comparable in distance to a stroll in central Paris from Gare St-Lazare to the Luxembourg Gardens. The difference is that the journey in Paris is rewarding to the spirit every step of the way, whereas the journey in Nashville takes you through moonscapes of urban desolation, deserts of parking lots, demoralizing walls of submerged and elevated freeway and past desultory one-story industrial and commercial bunkers, for which there is not enough Prozac in the world to mitigate the psycho-spiritual punishment.

Nevertheless, Kunstler was encouraged by the potential for the city to atone for its decades of sprawling sin, especially praising the efforts of the local Civic Design Center, a major proponent of new urbanist principles. As it happens, both creative class guru Florida and new urbanist Kunstler claim as their patron saint the one-time iconoclast Jane Jacobs (1961), whose mid-century defense of the dense working-class neighborhoods against urban renewal has been co-opted into the agendas of neoliberal city governments, high-rise developers and near-ring gentrifiers.

These avatars of new design consensus share a common principle, diversity—in Jacobs's parlance, "mixed primary uses"—featuring a panoply of consumption opportunities and nurturing serendipitous street encounters. But the pop culture images selling the glamour of these environments are distinctly choosy about what does and does not get to count as desirable diversity, and beyond the patent unreality of the Manhattan-dwelling *Friends* actually being able to afford their awesome apartments, a range of diverse elements in the actual city are conveniently suppressed. Nashville city policy in general aims to protect the insularity of the new downtown residential population, making Viridian's population diverse in the same way that, say, MTV's *The Real World* cast is diverse.[14] Thus, while TIF incentives come with strings attached, typically a 20 percent set-aside of new units as affordable housing, these in practice have turned out to be largely subsidies for early-stage "creative class" workers. As Jameson puts it: "[The affordable units] are all filled with 27-year-old kids with $50 haircuts."

Giarratana concedes as much, noting that the affordable units in Viridian allowed sales to younger buyers and goosed the vibe of hipster energy. "Normally, I hate government interference in the market," he explained. "But this helps exactly the people it's supposed to help." When asked about the de facto subsidy of young, educated workers in the emergent condo market, a progressive member of the city council conceded, in line with Florida's creative class argument: "The city needs those people." Interestingly, Jane Jacobs (1961: 39–40) herself doubted the capacity of yuppies to serve as anchors for lively neighborhood environments, suspecting that their transience and self-absorption would make them insufficiently attentive custodians of sidewalk culture.

Meanwhile, the honky-tonk row along Lower Broadway has become an attraction both for tourists from the world over ("I just sold a CD to a family from *Japan*," a local crooner told us one afternoon with appropriate aw-shucks wonderment) and for the fledgling hip and cool crowd. Thus a Saturday night might include sampling the nascent gallery scene on the Fifth Avenue "Avenue of the Arts," hitting the reopened Ryman to catch Belle and Sebastian (where the Scottish art-rockers will wax rhapsodic about playing in the Mother Church of country music), and then dropping into the honky tonks to cap the night. This omnivorous trajectory is consistent with the new urban elite culture, even if some elements are infused with a strong scent of irony: the same entrepreneur who opened the elitist "big city bar" in the Gulch with its velvet rope opened a honky-tonk on Broadway aimed at "20-somethings" and modeled on a trailer park. "I like to get dressed up and drink cosmos with models," he told us. "But I also like to wear a t-shirt and drink beer."

As for the population that until the late 1990s made up a major portion of the downtown street population—the homeless—they have been subject to increasingly punitive social control, shunted from the skid row–turned–tourist trap Lower Broadway into the wasteland of the near south Lafayette district, anchored by the Campus for Human Development and the Rescue Mission, and littered with day labor brokers, liquor stores, and pornography outlets. Though Florida insists upon tolerance as one of the "three Ts" of creative economy development (along with technology and talent), Nashville's noveau-cosmopolitans are, according to Councilman Jameson, extremely "wary" of the unhoused who encroach upon downtown. "The downtown residents—if you were to really talk to them for a long time—will start by talking about [the homeless] in very sensitive terms, but at the end of the conversation you realize the downtown residents just want the vagrants rounded up and shot. That's just about as blatant as it gets."

Despite the evident displacements and social violence evident in the neoliberal remaking of the core, there is still much to like about the aspirations for denser development in Nashville, even if the "vibrant" cosmopolitanism sold is rather different from Jacobs's vision of the lively city. A compact and walkable city, and a coherent core identity, can easily be imagined a resource for diverse populations in the region even if this has not really been the marketing script. There are further environmental advantages that become ever more painfully obvious as the twenty-first century inches along. In fact, the mixed-use development in the Gulch (whose trendy restaurants and vast unfilled condominium towers uneasily abut the Lafayette wasteland) has recently been awarded silver certification through the U.S. Green Building Council's Leadership in Energy and Environmental Design (LEED) (impressively, the development is only the thirteenth neighborhood worldwide to earn LEED certification) (Sisk 2009b: 7B). This was a particular victory for Councilman Jameson, who has made environmental responsibility his signature issue. Ironically, though, this announcement appeared in the local paper the same day that the news that Bristol, developer of the Gulch's massive ICON condominium tower, was preparing to sue its legions of deadbeat depositors.

With the groundbreaking on Signature Tower now infinitely deferred, Nashville's Dubai-like dreams of grandeur, launched like the desert proto- type virtually overnight and fueled by the excesses of global capital, are similarly on hold. The 27-year-olds with $50 haircuts may be finding even their subsidized starter homes more a liability than a gift, given the sud- denly frozen resale market, and may be enjoying a downscaled version of urban glamour for longer than they planned. Nevertheless, while Nashville's reach for Dubai grabbed air, the legacies of the 1990s will shape the local built environment and the local culture for decades to come, much as post- war urban renewal, with its superblock public housing, highway exchanges, and razed neighborhoods, did for decades after its ideological underpin- nings were discredited.

6

From National Utopia to Elite Enclave: "Economic Realities" and Resistance in the Reconstruction of Beirut

Najib Hourani

On October 1, 2009, officials of the Lebanese Company for the Development and Reconstruction of the Beirut Central District (BCD), or *Solidere*, as it is popularly known, offered journalists a guided tour of the company's flag-ship development: the new Beirut Souks.[1] Slated to open to the public the following day, the new Souks embody what the company and its supporters argue is the primary virtue of private sector-led urban redevelopment: the ability to reconcile the imperatives of market-driven globalization with re-spect for and preservation of historically generated urban form and memory.

The product of an international design competition, developed with Western consultants specialized in shopping mall design and management and featuring 163,000 square meters of floorspace, the shopping district will be the largest destination-shopping venue in the country (www.solidere. com/souks2/). Housing dynamic international brands such as Armani, Guess, Tommy Hilfiger, and Timberland, along with a fourteen-screen Cineplex and a food court dominated by international chains, the project will "conse-crate [the] Beirut city center as a global retail district" (Solidere 2009: 4).

At the same time, the company claims, the urban design of this new shopping district pays homage to a unique multisectarian nation of traders; a nation nearly destroyed by fifteen years of civil war (1975–1990). Built on the site of Beirut's most famous nineteenth-century markets, the Souks Project, they argue, is not to be confused with a modern shopping mall. In incorporating the original street grid, archaeological discoveries made during excavation, and the historic *sūq* names such as Ayass, al-Arwam, al-Jamil, al-Tawila, the company presents the Souks project as a respectful embodiment of urban memory. The visitor is channeled through pathways "inspired by medieval city planning, with its gates and meanders." The permeable layout of the district and its intimate architecture are intended to recall the "mood and atmosphere of the old souks" (Solidere 2008: 29). According to the company's website, once Phase Two of the project is completed in 2012, the development will "bring the charm of traditional souks into the 21st century" (Solidere 2009: 5).

It would be easy to dismiss the company's apparent attention to culture and a national urban imaginary as mere rhetoric meant to mask the material realities of market-driven urbanism. It could be argued that the narrative obscures what is in actuality the deepening commodification of culture under late capitalism. Is not the creation of spectacular spaces of consumption, as David Harvey (1990) and Frederic Jameson (1991) point out, a defining feature of such market-driven urbanism rather than a resistance to it?

These arguments capture important dimensions of contemporary urban redevelopment. Yet they are not only scholarly representations of how the urban world operates; they are also productive of it. As J. K. Gibson-Graham (1995), Wendy Larner (2003), Timothy Mitchell (2002), and Helga Leitner et al. (2007) have pointed out, such arguments, based as they are upon an ontological binarism between the economic realm and its superstructural others—the political and the cultural—privilege the economic as a universal realm of the real. In so doing, they reproduce and reinforce the central tenet of neoliberal ideology itself, that in which human freedom is understood as the liberation of a universal economic rationality from the fetters of politics and culture. Indeed, as Solidere's presentation of its flagship project indicates, such oppositions as those between global economic imperatives and local culture or market and nonmarket, played a powerful role in the debates concerning the reconstruction of downtown Beirut. What effects does this privileging of the economic, understood as an all-powerful realm of universal rationality, have on strategies of resistance to neoliberal urbanism? What politico-economic dynamics does this opposition hide from view?

In what follows, I trace the relationship between the currently dominant neoliberal discourse of the market and its perceived "others" through the local debates over the development of the Souks project. On the one side stood those who argued that Solidere, as a real estate venture, was to be the flagship of Lebanon's free-market renaissance. In the name of securing Lebanon's role as a regional and, indeed, global center of finance, tourism, and trade, they argued that the company's priorities should be determined primarily by the economic requirements of Beirut's integration with global markets, and so with a universal trajectory of economic development toward globalization. On the other side were two sets of architects and urban planners who opposed market-driven urbanism and its effects in the reconstruction of the city center. Both argued that the city center was the geographical and cultural heart of the cosmopolitan Lebanese nation—a nation that had nearly been snuffed out by fifteen years of sectarian civil war. Therefore, the reconstruction of the BCD could and should play a special role in the reintegration of a once and future cosmopolitan nation. Accordingly, they argued that Beirut's history and culture, its urban memory, should be preserved in the face of the deterritorializing imperatives of globalization. For each, however, the locus of this history and culture differed, and, accordingly, so too did their strategies for resistance. This chapter asks how each engaged with the discourse of the market and to what effect. It also considers the dynamics that the deployment of debates in these binary terms hid from view.

The Beirut Central District

It is not possible to analyze the Souks project without an understanding of its place within the larger debates concerning the once and future role of the Beirut city center. The development of the BCD around the Beirut port, lifeline of the prewar "Merchant Republic" (Gates 1998), concentrated commercial, touristic, financial, and governmental functions in the area. It also drew together Lebanese from all social classes and sectarian communities, rendering it, for many, not only the commercial heart of the capital, but also the heart of the cosmopolitan nation.[2] As one editorial in the business monthly *Al-'Iqtisaad wal-'Amal* put it, downtown Beirut "is the heart of the capital, and is the heart of all Lebanon." In bringing together people from different sects and regions, it was "the lung through which Beirut and Lebanon breathe economic activity," and represents "the heart that beats day and night, pumping through the veins of the nation the vital flow and constant interaction (Real Estate Agency 1992: 42).

MEDITERRANEAN SEA

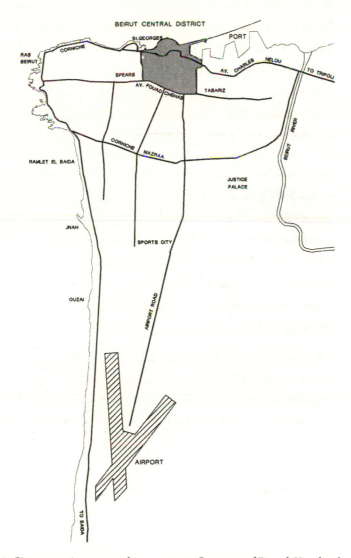

N

BEIRUT CENTRAL DISTRICT

St.GEORGES

PORT

CORNICHE

RAS
BEIRUT

SPEARS

AV. CHARLES HELOU

TO TRIPOLI

AV. FOUAD CHEHAB

TABARIZ

CORNICHE MAZRAA

BEIRUT RIVER

RAMLET EL BAIDA

JUSTICE
PALACE

JNAH

SPORTS CITY

OUZAI

AIRPORT ROAD

AIRPORT

TO SAIDA

Figure 4. City center in metropolitan context. Courtesy of Dar al-Handasah.

For politicians and planners across the political spectrum, the city center was a "strong symbol" of communal coexistence. Its immediate reconstruction, it was argued, would constitute definitive evidence, both at home and abroad, of the war's end. In restoring the center to a city violently divided into sectarian enclaves, reconstruction would call forth the cosmopolitan nation from the ashes of war. In the words of Henri Edde, former minister of Public Works and author of the first postwar master plan, with successful reconstruction, "Beirutism" (*Al-Bayrata*) will replace "Lebanonism" (*Al-Labnana*), which had become synonymous with "internal disorder" (*fitnat dakhiliyyat*) around the world (Ayyash 1991). If not carried out rapidly, warned Al-Fadel Shallaq, president of the governmental Council for Development and Reconstruction (CDR), the city center would continue to "represent a center of chaos" (*haba wa daba*) and remain a "political and social bomb ready to explode at any minute" (Hammoud 1991).

As is the case in other instances in which cities seek to recover from the devastation of war or natural disaster (Boyce 2002; Gunewardena and Schuller 2008), the reconstruction of Beirut brought to the forefront debates over the proper the roles of state and market in the Lebanese economy. On the one side stood institutions such as the World Bank and the IMF, which view postwar reconstruction as an "important window of opportunity" in which to effect not only economic stabilization, but more importantly structural transformations that would, according to neoliberal ideology, underpin future, market-driven growth (World Bank 1998: 46). Indeed, barely a month after the Syrian air force ended the final phase of the civil war on October 13, 1990, the IMF and the World Bank began to pressure for a rigorous program of structural adjustment. Along with the standard package of business-friendly reforms that included, in addition to a freeze on public-sector wages, the end to subsidies on basic foodstuffs and fuel, the IFI demands included the privatization of the reconstruction program ("Economy Continues to Decline" 1991: 4 and World Bank 1993). Without such policies in place, the international financial institutions (IFIs) argued, investor confidence would not return, and Lebanon's recovery would be in jeopardy.

In making reconstruction aid to a fragile postwar government conditional upon the implementation of harsh austerity measures and privatization, the IFIs lent their full weight and ammunition to those among the Lebanese merchant and financial elite who sought a postconflict restoration of the preconflict "free-market" economic order. Gathered around Saudi-

Lebanese billionaire banker Rafiq al-Hariri, the candidate preferred by the United States and Saudi Arabia for Lebanon's prime ministry, they revived the ideology of the "Merchant Republic" and reinforced it with the market triumphalism of the contemporary globalization discourse. According to this ideology, Lebanon, as a small country without natural resources or military might, had no alternative to economic openness. Blessed with ample human capital and a national spirit of entrepreneurialism, Lebanon was uniquely suited to become the regional center for financial services, trade, and tourism. With the post-cold war globalization of markets, these "economic realists" argued, Lebanon had no choice but to adopt policies that would ensure Lebanon's position in the new global order (Baz 1998; Kabbani 1996).

Nowhere were their efforts more determined than in relation to the Beirut city center, which they envisioned as the urban expression of Lebanon's regional and global role. While asserting the national importance of rebuilding the BCD, they combined pragmatic arguments rooted in the particularity of the postconflict environment with neoliberal ideology to advocate for private sector-led reconstruction with minimal government involvement. First, they argued, given the existence of traditional practices of landholding in the city center, relations between the thousands of right-holders were far too complex for the government to handle. The municipal and national administrations that oversaw property relations were in disarray, and, moreover, a large percentage of the property registers had been destroyed during the war. Second, even if the government had the institutional capacity to undertake such a project, the wartime collapse of the treasury rendered it fiscally unable to do so (Saba 1992).

These pragmatic arguments resonated with neoliberal ideology's emphasis on market-driven development. Given the practical challenges and the chaotic political atmosphere of the immediate postwar environment, these "economic realists" argued, resort to the private sector was the only viable choice. Drawing upon the neoliberal opposition between the economic sphere and its noneconomic fetters, they argued that only market rationality could effectively "insulate the reconstruction of the BCD from political polarization and traditional government inefficiencies." Only the private sector, driven by such priorities, could "provide proper leadership and attract funds" and thereby ensure that Beirut rapidly claim its place atop the emerging hierarchy of Arab cities (Kabbani 1996: 66).

Capitalist Placelessness

The initial master plan was presented to the public in the summer of 1991, prior to the promulgation of a plan for the reconstruction of Lebanon as a whole, as debates over the proper institutional balance between state and private sector raged in the media. The "Edde Plan" (so named after its lead engineer, Henri Edde) was produced in the Cairo offices of Dar al-Handasah, one of the region's largest private consultancies, and was bankrolled by Rafiq al-Hariri himself. Accordingly, the plan assumed reconstruction by a private real estate holding company with monopoly powers (Dar al-Handasah 1991: 16).

Just as the IFIs viewed the postconflict environment as ideal for the imposition of painful and unpopular structural adjustment policies, the plan's authors viewed the moment of urban reconstruction as a "unique opportunity to reorient the urban development of the Centre as well as of the Capital." Indeed, they argued, the city center had, even prior to the war, "suffered from an anarchy in no way justified by the vitality it displayed" (Dar al-Handasah 1991: 1). Assuming the BCD would be stripped of its fine-grained, many-layered social fabric, the Edde Plan envisioned a new city center based upon the functional specification, architectural monumentalism, and heavy transport associated with the era of high modernism. The BCD was to be cut off from its surroundings by a high-speed, sunken ring road, and trisected by three large north-south boulevards. This urban enclave connected to an offshore island—home to a new, high-rise financial district—by means of three bridges. The plan called for the reconstruction of two prominent sūq districts—the first just west of the Martyrs Square and housing Sūq Sursock, the Gold Sūq, and Sūq Abu al-Nasr, and the second being the location of Solidere's Beirut Souks project. Only the French Mandate-era fabric, centered on the Place d'Étoile and characterized by colonial neo-Islamic architecture, was retained as a heritage preservation zone.

The high modernism of the urban plan was not limited to questions of transport, design, and architecture. In addition, the plan sought to impose a land use strategy based upon modernism's conceptions of the rationally ordered city. Seven of the area's eleven planning zones were dedicated to single, specific land uses, with a hotel district segregated from a governmental district devoted entirely to public-sector buildings, and another for commercial and office space. Functions associated with the degradation of the prewar city center, such as the small factories, workshops, and warehouses that had constituted much of the prewar urban scene, would be removed (Dar al-Handasah 1991).

Together with marketing materials that depicted huge apartment blocks and office towers arranged according to a rigid, rationalist geometry, Edde's efforts provoked a strong reaction in architectural and planning circles. Critics charged that, rather than re-creating a Beirut recognizable to any Lebanese, such finance-driven modernism would result in a "new Brasilia" (Zakhour 1992). Nabil Beyhum (1992) charged planners with the creation of a city without history, as if arising anew from the open desert, made possible only by the dictatorship of the petro dollar and accessible only to the super-wealthy. Still others criticized the planned incorporation of architectural references to other cities—the twin tower "World Trade Center," the "Champs-Élysées-type layout" and "the mini-Manhattan island"—as profit-driven, postmodern kitsch (Kabbani 1992; Tabet 1993).

The Solidere Narrative: Design-Based Resistance

Objections to the importation of what critics took to be an essentially foreign urban landscape into the heart of the city resonated throughout Beirut, especially with those who saw the city center as the heart not only of the capital but also of the nation. Today Solidere's self-representation credits such criticism with forcing the reconsideration of the Edde Plan. Although the plan was formally accepted by the government in October 1992, attempts to revise it continued for another year under a new team. Headed by Angus Gavin and made up of planners and architects largely trained in the United States and England and at the American University of Beirut, the team produced new master and detailed plans that rejected the terms of Edde's "false start" (Gavin 1998: 218). Leading members of the planning team knew the drawbacks inherent in market-driven redevelopment. "Real estate companies are, by definition, very bad things," said one Solidere planner. Given the dilapidated condition of the state and its finances, however, he drew upon the realists' arguments to claim that there simply was no choice but to rely upon the private sector. "It is an investment-led operation," he explained with resignation. At its heart was the need "to reach a density target that will theoretically create a certain cash flow that will theoretically create the rate of return that you are after. . . . Private investment, in this case, leads the planning." From an urban planning point of view, he recognized the BCD reconstruction was "really stood on its head."[3]

New plans were approved by the government in March 1994. In the planners' view, this represented a victory in what was "a cross-cultural debate" between "a 'top-down', tabula rasa approach that favored the grand gesture" and imposed "new patterns of order on the city in the continental European tradition," on the one hand, and "Anglo-Saxon contextualism" on the other, which sought to restore and rebuild the city from the "bottom up" (Gavin 1998: 219).

While accepting, as Edde had, the need for "widespread demolition and restructuring" of the war-torn city center, the new approach drew upon place-making strategies associated with the New Urbanism and Kevin Lynch's city imaging. Accordingly, the new plan stressed the virtues of human-scale, mixed-use districts and archaeological and architectural heritage preservation in an effort to resist its predecessor's placelessness. More importantly, in planners' eyes, the "community-building" ethos of New Urbanism (Gavin 1998: 220) was uniquely suited to foster the reintegration of a nation divided by civil conflict: "At stake is the rebirth of the center of a capital city after its destruction by war. The pattern of development that it engenders must inform the future and cherish the past. . . . It must provide a social arena and a means to reconnect a once-divided city. *In the quality and example that it sets, and in the value placed on the city's heritage and its archeological treasures, it must also instill a renewed sense of national pride and identity*" (Gavin and Malouf 1996: 13; emphasis added).

In the new master plan, topography and existing transport orient the skeleton of the district. Edde's "mini-Manhattan" was transformed through reclamation of land from the sea to an extension of the city center. Known as the Normandy Remblais, two thirds of the extension would be devoted to high-rise development, while the remainder was set aside to become one of Beirut's largest public parks. The terrain, gently sloping down to the sea, enabled the establishment not of Grand Axes, as in the Edde Plan, but, through the manipulation of building heights, a series of "view corridors," extending northward across the city center.

The plan still broke the area into ten subsectors, each designed to have its own particular character. In replacing Edde's single-use districts with mixed-use districts, the planners hoped to ensure that the city center housed a diversity of functions and activities and remained animated outside of business hours. Archeological parks showcasing the ruins left behind by the successive Phoenician, Roman, and Ottoman civilizations, among others, were incorporated into the plan as significant elements of urban memory. The new plan still retained the Place d'Étoile, with its French Mandate architecture and concentration of churches and mosques. Two older residential neighborhoods, Wadi Abu Jmil and Saifi, were designated "historic preservation zones," in which retained buildings would be interspersed with sympathetic infill development. The inclusion of these neighborhoods together with a number of other architecturally significant buildings increased the total number of preserved structures from 100 to 265 and reconnected the center to its surroundings and to the architectural memory of the city (Dar al-Handasah 1994).

The attention paid to the re-creation of a national cosmopolitanism is reflected not only in the architectural historicism of the area. In keeping with Solidere's understanding of the civil war as primarily a conflict between primordial sectarian communities, the inscription of religious identities—architecturally asserted yet bound together and overcome within the company's national image of the city—reinforced Solidere's self-representation as cosmopolitan nation-builder. Indeed, company representatives often point out the retention of sixteen religious structures, the ownership and responsibility for the restoration of which lies with each sect's religious authorities, and stress the $150,000 restoration subsidy the company has granted each community represented in the city center.[4]

According to Solidere planners, the inscription of a national history and culture into the urban fabric of the BCD did not solely depend upon the presence of physical markers, but also required the unification of these elements into a distinctive and recognizable image. Drawing on Lynchian urban imaging, the plan specifically sought to create unity from the underlying diversity. Architectural monuments such as tall or unique buildings marked each of the gateways into the city center, and announced one's arrival into a distinct space. The view corridors, dependent upon the position of the viewer overlooking the city, converted this distinct space into an image to be viewed from above and outside and grasped as a unified whole. A similar logic was at work in each of the sectors as well. Streetwall and façade controls and regulations governing building heights, landscaping, and even exterior paint ensured that heritage zones such Wadi Abu Jmil and Saifi not only maintain but proclaim a unified historic identity.

The unification of the national "image of the city" was to be experienced in movement as well. For example, the plan called for the connection of the archaeological discoveries with a series of "heritage trails" that would wind through the downtown area. In linking these sites, the plan bound the urban products of diverse societies into a progressive and unified history, what Anderson (1991) calls the "homogenous, empty time" of the nation. It was this imagined progression of "the nation" from antiquity forward that the Solidere motto "Beirut, an Ancient City for the Future" sought to evoke.

There can be little doubt that the new master and detailed plans, with their explicit commitment to context, heritage preservation, and place making, represented an improvement over the placelessness of the modernism embodied in the Edde's original effort. The degree to which the new plans represented a design-based resistance to the market-driven part of the equation, however, is far less certain. In terms Harvey and Jameson would appreciate, the overthrow of the Edde Plan seems to have deepened, rather than tempered, the commodification of space in the Beirut city center. Indeed, the new planners reproduced the dominant ideology of neoliberal urbanism as articulated by the World Bank and their allies among the Lebanese financial mercantile elite, albeit with a critical awareness.

The introduction to the 1994 planning report set out the goals of the project in terms of the opposition between heritage and history and the imperatives of market-driven globalization, and adopted the mythology of the "merchant republic" to reconcile them in the name of the cosmopolitan, entrepreneurial nation. "[T]he main challenge," the authors tell us, "is to integrate what remains of a rich city heritage to the new city fabric," to create a "vibrant city centre" which can "fulfill the aspirations of an enterprising nation" as it strives to "compete and occupy the place it deserves amongst Capital cities in the Middle East region" (Dar al-Handasah 1994: iv). Again, it naturalized this ideological construct: "In view of the predominantly service-oriented nature of the Lebanese economy, and considering the small size of the country," the authors claimed, "the development of a strong and prosperous BCD must benefit from an intense interaction with the outside world" (31).

With the free-market ideology and globalization-driven, interurban competition as founding assumptions, the reconciliation of the opposition between culture and economy was one in which attention to the former existed only in terms of the latter. In their discussion of city fabric and historical memory, the authors made this connection explicit. The incorporation of cultural and heritage features would "create value" in terms of interurban competition.

"In a situation where Beirut will be in competition with other cities in the Middle East and the Eastern Mediterranean for an international role and prominence," the authors argued, "the creation . . . of a unique cultural and historic identity will have special significance" (Dar al-Handasah 1994: 13).

It could be argued that the replanning of the district to add two heritage preservation zones, the incorporation of an additional one hundred architecturally significant buildings, and the reduction in densities required to establish the urban image nonetheless represented successful resistance to market imperatives. This would be so if the transition from placelessness to place making was not, itself, paid for by other changes to the plan to boost profitability. While decreasing densities in heritage preservation zones and areas designated view corridors, the new plan compensated company investors through the transfer of saleable built-up areas in these districts to the highrise district of the new financial center, the most profitable real estate in the Solidere portfolio. In fact, in pursuit of returns to investors of 15 to 16 percent, the new plan increased overall densities in the BCD by roughly a million square meters.[5] In so doing, the planners' design-based resistance itself became central to the deepening of neoliberal urbanism in postwar Beirut. Nowhere was this process more evident than in the planning of the Beirut Souks.

Planning the Beirut Souks

The initial stages of the design process for the Beirut Souks highlighted the company's commitment to global urban planning practices, which included, in addition to heritage preservation and adaptive re-use, the use of juried international competitions to produce designs for signature buildings. In November of 1993, the BOF launched an "International Ideas Competition" and appointed a panel of local architects and urbanists to judge the 350 submissions received from around the world. While the proposals were housed in a public exhibition, the panelists carried out their evaluations in conjunction with foreign consultants. These included the U.S.-based Benjamin Thompson and Associates, known for New York's South Street Seaport and Boston's Faneuil Hall, among others. Participating architectural firms were given a four-volume competition packet detailing the history of the area as well as a general outline of the area's future program. The packet included a photographic survey of Beirut's architecture, recollections of the area provided by well-known writers, poets, and academics, and the larger philosophy of Solidere urbanism: "The theme of this Competition revolves around the notion of the **Souk**, used to mean not only a commercial space, but **an image, a memory, a place that honors tradition. . . .** [T]he new *Souks* should provide a familiar and comforting physical environment, one which reinforces the citizens sense of belonging . . . which breeds tolerance and allows for diversity" (Solidere 1994: vol. I: 1; emphasis in original). Agreement upon what that image should be, whose memory it should embody, and whose traditions should be honored proved impossible. After a number of rounds of deliberations, the company selected four finalists and assembled a master planning team under the direction of Lebanese architect Jad Tabet, charged with drawing the winning proposals into a unified program ("Roundtable Discussion Concerning the Souks Plan in the Beirut Central Commercial District"; hereafter, "Roundtable Discussion" 1998).

The selection of Tabet, a consistent critic of Edde's modernist vision, surprised many. Tabet had attacked not only the placelessness of the Edde Plan, but the insurrection of the image with which Solidere replaced it as well ("Roundtable Discussion" 1998). While architecture and design, he argued, play a significant role in preservation, the key to the restoration of Lebanon's cosmopolitan heart would be found in the people who once populated it and the social organization of their activities. As the Solidere master plan designated the Souks sector a "special planning area" pending the completion of the competition, the sector plan required approval, at the national level, by the Council of Ministers. Therefore, the Tabet team viewed the project as the last chance to ensure the Lebanese middle class, in the form of prewar sūq merchants, a place in the heart of Beirut.

The Souks master plan was completed in late 1995 and integrated much of what the Tabet team felt was valuable and distinctive about the prewar sūqs with consultant recommendations. The plan rejected a stand-alone, enclosed shopping mall. Rather than lifting the space out of its urban context, it sought to maintain a "street-based and permeable" district. The plan envisioned a space, "neither private nor exclusive, neither walled nor elevated from the plane of everyday life." It was to be an urban district that "feels and works like other parts of the BCD" and connects with and extends "the fine grain of the adjacent historic core of the city" (Tabet and Benjamin Thompson & Associates 1995: 14–15). The maintenance of continuity and the plane of everyday life called for an architecture of small spaces and multiple passages to create a seemingly unplanned urban fabric that might have developed over time.

Figure 5. Artist's rendition based on Tabet plan. Courtesy of Solidere.

At the same time, the Tabet team organized the five major program-matic elements within an overall framework dictated by principles of shop-ping mall design as developed in the United States. Specifically, it adapted the classic "dumbbell" pattern mall to fit a dense urban fabric. This pattern calls for large "anchor" tenants at the four corners of a rectangular interior space that houses a mix of medium-sized and smaller shops. The strategic location of the anchor tenants, such as department stores and cinemas that draw customers to the mall, effectively pulls shoppers through the develop-ment, thereby "irrigating" the smaller shops with a steady stream of foot traffic. The Tabet plan called for the northwest anchor to be a major depart-ment store, while the northeast would house a multiscreen cineplex. The southwest corner hosted a small, inner-city supermarket. The southeast an-chor was to be a new jewelry market—a cluster of shops that recalled the famous Suq al-Sagha, once located on Martyrs Square. The fifth element, the main core, consisted of hundreds of small shops along the historic north-south streets and east-west passageways. This hybrid form remains the basis of the Beirut Souks developed by Solidere.

Architecture and design alone, however, were not sufficient to the urban memory of the cosmopolitan nation. The key, Tabet argued, was the return of the sūq traders—the middle class that animated the prewar city center. Throughout the planning process, the team advocated for a regulatory framework that would ensure that these war merchants could occupy the hundreds of small shops of the Souks core. Specifically, the team sought to re-create the commercial organization of the war sūqs by once again grouping merchants according to the merchandise in which they dealt. The proposed "merchandising scheme" clustered, for example, ready-made clothing in one section of Souk Ayyas, and fabric shops in another. Souk Tawileh was to house higher-end fashion, again, in keeping with the prewar pattern. An antique sūq would inhabit the northern stretch of Souk Arwam, while the open square, just to the south, would be home to a bulk-foods souk, where the scents of coffee beans and spices would, once again, provide an aromatic element to the area. Tailors and shirt makers would line the nearby north-south Fakhry Bey Street, so as to reestablish the linkages between traders and small-scale workshops that anchored sūq life in the prewar city center.

For the combination of the merchandising scheme and the small-scale architecture to reproduce the mix of activity and feel of a sūq, they believed a third element was required: a progressive rental policy that would make the return of the small prewar merchants possible. To this end, the team proposed that the company charge higher rents for the anchor locations and those on the periphery of the project, as well as on larger spaces designated for upscale shops and restaurants. These higher rents would subsidize the lower rents asked of the prewar merchants for smaller shops in the core. In short, the company would create partially decommodified spaces that would be managed to ensure a social mixture that, Tabet feared, would be lost should a free market in retail space determine the tenant mix.[6]

The Tabet plan, with its architecture of small spaces linked to surrounding fabric and incorporating archaeological finds unearthed in the area, received considerable support as it moved through the design process. French consultants, who had recommended a closed, standalone shopping mall featuring an enormous hypermarket, were defeated by a coalition including Tabet's team, BTA, Angus Gavin, and the town planning department and a number of sympathetic members of Solidere's board of directors.

The effort to make it possible for the prewar sūq merchants to return to the city center—what Tabet called the "social engineering" dimension—did not fare so well. Despite support from key members of town planning and as many as three members of the Solidere board, following the approval of the Souks master plan, the project began to change.[7] As it moved to the detailed planning stage, the Souks became the concern of those real estate professionals responsible for marketing and leasing. For them, questions of heritage and the return of prewar tenants were of secondary importance at best. More often, such issues were costly distractions from what they argued were the objective bases of urban redevelopment: "market realities."

Economic Realities

Upon completion of the master plan, Tabet and his team disbanded, handing the Souks over to five company-appointed architects, each responsible for a different section of the project. By that time, however, the context within which the company and its planners operated was rapidly changing. The neoliberal framework for the reconstruction, insisted upon by the World Bank and IMF and adopted by the Hariri government, had failed to produce the promised economic renaissance. While the BCD project was privatized under Solidere, the government embarked upon an "ambitious program of public investment" (World Bank 1993). Entitled "Horizon 2000," the national reconstruction plan relied on the private sector to design and develop a host of infrastructure schemes through public-private partnerships. The bulk of the plan, frontloaded both chronologically and financially, was financed through loans and the issuance of debt in the form of high-interest treasury bills, the majority of which were bought up by the local commercial banking sector (Republic of Lebanon 1995).

As is the case in other instances in which neoliberal programs were implemented, the wave of economic development the plan promised did not materialize. Rather than returning Beirut to its imagined prewar status as a center of finance, services, and international trade, the liberalization of the property regime, in combination with infrastructure projects and the government-funded expansion of banking sector liquidity, led to an explosion in speculative real estate development.

Leading the way in new real estate investment, which was estimated to have grown from $2 billion in 1993 to $3 billion in 1995, were luxury apartments, upmarket hotel and tourist developments, and shopping malls, all of which, theoretically, constituted competition to Solidere ("Real Estate Market in Lebanon" 1994: 42–48; Khoury 1996).[8] The upscale neighborhood of

Verdun, for example, quickly became the city's premier retail location, featuring shopping complexes such as the Holiday Inn Dunes Center, the Verdun Plaza I and II, and Verdun 730 and 732, each of which combined luxury apartments and office space with upscale, international brand-driven retail.

Purpose-built shopping malls, too, appeared on the horizon. Attracted by cheaper land serviced by brand new, high-speed transportation routes, the Agora Project, in the southeastern suburb of Hazmiyyeh, promised a "modern shopping and leisure experience." The project, which only recently got underway, is anchored by a 9,000-square-meter department store and a 13,000-square-meter hypermarket in addition to a further 26,000 square meters of retail (Karam Group n.d.; Nash 2009). The new ABC Mall, in the nearby Beirut neighborhood of Achrafieh, boasts 42,000 square meters of retail and restaurants as well as an eight-screen cinema (www.abc.com.lb).

By 1996, it was clear that the Solidere program, which had, in tandem with Harirism, promised to return Beirut to its prewar position as a center of international trade and finance, needed to be reconsidered. During the war, other Arab countries developed their own transport links with Europe, and thus replaced Lebanon as the regional center for entrepôt trade. New communications technologies and improvements in human capital in the Arab world stripped Lebanon of its comparative advantage in financial services and banking. These regional shifts were accompanied by the deepening concentration of "command and control" functions in global cities. In the words of Oussama Kabbani, the idea that the BCD could recapture its role as the regional financial center had become "a lot of crap." The financial capital of the Middle East, he explained, "is not in the Middle East, unfortunately. It's in London."[9]

Moreover, the social costs of Harirism—the direct result of capital-friendly policies that favored financial and real estate speculation over job-producing industry and agriculture—had exacerbated social inequalities to such an extent that by the late 1990s, the number of Lebanese who could afford what Solidere had to offer was severely limited. A department of statistics survey, published in 1996, found that more than a third of the population now lived in poverty, defined as a family of 5.6 persons earning less than $630 per month. According to economist Kamal Hamdan, a full 60 percent lived on less than $800 per month. In contrast, only 7 percent of the population earned more than $2,000 per month (Leenders 1998: 8–9). Even this figure does not adequately reflect the severe concentration of wealth in postwar Lebanon. A study conducted by the Central Bank in

1992—prior to the further concentration of wealth attributable to Harirism—
found that more than 55 percent of the cash and other assets held in the
banking sector were concentrated in the hands of a mere 450 individuals
("Government Fights Attacks from Parliament and Media": 6). The contradiction between Solidere's utopian self-representation and the economic
policies that had enabled its creation had by the late 1990s brought the project to a grinding halt.

Revenge of the Realists: The Tourist Enclave

Free-market ideology, anchored as it is in an imaginary "economic sphere,"
is always able to externalize the reasons for its failures. Political interference,
imperfect implementation, or vaguely specified cultural impediments can
always be deployed to explain the failure of otherwise sound economic policy. Accordingly, Lebanon's "economic realities" did not lead to a reconsideration of the neoliberal bases of the project, but rather provided ammunition
to those within the company who viewed the project as primarily a market-
driven real estate venture. Thus, the board of directors chose a new path:
tourism development. With this new priority, restoration of the onetime
urban heart of the nation was eclipsed by a drive to produce an urban enclave
for international business travelers and the wealthy of the Arab world. Beirut
would no longer be an "Ancient City for the Future." Rather, as the new company motto put it, the BCD would become "The *Finest* City Center in the
Middle East."

Shifts in the master plan, too, reflected this eclipse of city and nation by
the tourism enclave. While the 1994 plan had included a large marina on the
eastern flank of the Normandy Remblaise, the company is now developing a
second on the St. Georges Bay on the western. In keeping with the drive to
develop a new Monaco in the Middle East, the company also reorganized
the road layout to accommodate Grand Prix automobile racing in the BCD
as a further tourist attraction (Solidere 2005: 38). These shifts confirmed critics' fears that the reconstruction of the BCD would produce a playground for
the local, regional, and global super-rich (Corm 1996).

During an interview in 1998, the head of a much smaller town planning
department struggled to maintain the reconciliation of economic realities
and the local particularities of place. He no longer likened the city center to
the heart of the cosmopolitan nation. Rather, he compared it to a Club

Med: "You go to Turkey and the country is in deep shit but the club is doing well. You know what I am saying? The BCD could be like that (not [that we want] to make it into a Club Med.) . . . It has its own components [such as] the hotels on the waterfront, the marina etc., that are interesting for a certain sector of the society, locally and regionally." As an afterthought, he added, "But we will still make it urban."[10] Those charged with the marketing of the city center, however, have been less equivocal about Solidere's new direction. "Solidere's main objective," one marketing official asserted, "is to encourage tourism to come to Lebanon."[11]

As Harirism enriched bankers and impoverished the average Lebanese, the Souks development entered the pre-marketing phase, during which Tabet's plan collided with economic realities. "Pre-marketing" involves, according to one Solidere official, the adaptation of the urban design and architecture of a development to the needs and desires of the end user. In this case, the international retail consultants and the company's real estate and marketing managers began to redirect the design process toward "shopping tourism" centered upon international brand-name retailers.[12]

These specialists scorned the urbanists and architects who had dominated the planning from 1992 to 1995, to say nothing of Tabet's team. Both, in their opinion, naively put the ethereality of culture before the concrete reality of market considerations and cash flow. When asked about the role of heritage preservation, they acknowledge that it has been very useful as a marketing tool, but there are limits: "Let no one tell me that we haven't done our job in preservation," snapped one marketing official. "We preserved 240 buildings," he said and added, with an exasperated tone, "we are the biggest archaeological site in the world!"[13]

When it comes to leasing the Souks and surroundings, managers argue, the social dimensions of the project and the importance of the city center to the reintegration of the nation were the dreams of architects. Reality for these professionals meant the dictates of the global tourism and retail markets. The nearly exclusive focus on high-end, foreign-brand retailers reflects this effort to entice the global business class and tourists from the oil-rich Gulf states. The company's upscale pricing strategy, they are well aware, means that most prewar sūq traders simply cannot afford it.

The potential returns to the company are enormous. Solidere officials refused to provide concrete figures, but suggested that the base rate for each of the more than 100,000 square meters of leasable space was set at $500. Management fees for the Souks, charged on top of the rent, are estimated at roughly $6 million annually. In addition to these profits, Solidere will also earn substantial "overage fees" from tenants.[14] Such earnings potential, the economic realists argued, cannot be sacrificed for "dreams," especially if those dreams sacrifice gross leasable area, or worse still, risk the injection of disorder in the form of the "traditional Lebanese shopkeeper" into a pristine enclave of wealth. "Look, you don't want those guys coming out and putting their stuff on hangers hanging everywhere around the doors of their shops and them yelling to buy this or that. It is chaos. No. We cannot go back to that. . . . We have no room for that. We want the professionals."[15] Beyond a number of prominent gold and diamond dealers, there was little room for the Lebanese in the company's conception of "retailing for the 21st century." In their place would be global retailers providing "everything the tourist wants to acquire" in an architectural format geared toward inducing, and indeed maximizing, consumption.[16] Tabet's scheme to return prewar tenants to the new Souks was doomed in the face of a failing, yet unfalsifiable, market discourse.

According to the Souks leasing manager, the design of the project, ranging from shop sizes to the tenant mix and distribution throughout the space, had to be reworked in order to "maximize the length of stay and the amount of money spent there."[17] The Beirut Souks would resemble less the traditional sūqs of the nineteenth century and more a "shoppertainment" district of the twenty-first. The dumbbell plan was sound, but shop sizes had to increase well beyond what prewar sūq merchants could afford in order to meet the requirements of "the internationals" such as U.S.-based Timberland, the Spanish Zara, and Sweden's H&M. The number of screens at the cineplex, now the center of a "mega entertainment destination" featuring fast food and a gaming arcade, increased from eight to fourteen (Solidere 2008: 73). The "Ajami Square," imagined by the Tabet team as an outdoor concentration of bistros catering to Lebanon's famous café culture, became a "food court" for Starbucks, McDonald's, and Burger King. "It is only natural that the internationals will want to come here," one marketing official assured me. "We have done our homework. We have a great product."

Landscape of Competition?

Economic realists' arguments against those who would return prewar owners and tenants to the city center in general and to the Beirut Souks project in particular stressed the logic of competition. For the Solidere Souks to be successful, the project had to compete with other retail areas in Beirut, as well as with those in other Arab capital cities. Competition, then, dictated that the design of the Souks accommodate the spatial needs of western multinational retailers, rather than those of those "traditional Lebanese who just want to be their own boss." International brand names were the key to "The *Finest* City Center in the Middle East."[18] As one such specialist put it, "If we don't plan for them they will not come. And if they don't come here, they will go somewhere else. This is the logic of the thing."[19]

A brief survey of the tenants that have opened shops in the Beirut Souks, however, reveals a different story; one that undermines the ontological distinction between the economic and its exterior. Of the 103 shops that participated in the grand opening in late 2009, at least 41 are owned by just five business groups, each of which is distinguished by extensive shop holdings in the BCD. Fifteen are owned by just one such business network: the Azadea Group. The Hamra Shopping and Trading Company (HSTC) owns three, in addition to several shops in the surrounding areas, and is constructing a mini-mall just across the street to the west of the Souks to house its own multibrand "Grand Stores." Another network, the Tony Salameh Group, while owning only five of the shops in the new Beirut Souks, owns several more luxury boutiques on the restored Rue Moutran in the Foch Allenby district just to the east.

The concentration of retail in the hands of a few large business groups suggests that the nature of city making as practiced by Solidere is a network affair. In moments of candor, the Solidere "realists" admit to coordination both "directly and indirectly" with competing developments to ensure complementarity of offer, rather than competition.[20] Indeed, when the origins and operations of such groups are examined, they are but a smaller part of larger, vertically integrated networks through which politics produce the "realities of the market." The case of the HSTC and its relation to one of Solidere's major competitors, the Holiday Inn Dunes Center in the upscale Verdun district of Beirut, is instructive.

The Dunes Center is the largest purpose-built retail venue in Verdun. The shopping mall, the Holiday Inn, and the luxury apartment tower that dwarfs both of them arose on property that, prior to the war, was owned by the French government. The plot was either purchased by or donated to the municipality of Beirut, and ended up in 1988 being owned by a company called Société Les Dunes Immobilieres, SAL, with shareholders from the

Al-Rayess and Tabbara families, with close ties to the Hariri government. According to several sources, Hariri himself, until his assassination in 2005, was a silent partner in the development of the Dunes Center. A subsidiary of this company owns the Dunes Hospitality Company, which, in turn, owns and operates the Holiday Inn.

The networked nature of the development extends to tenanting as well. The Rayess brothers, Fadi and Jamil, own HSTC, which their father began prior to the civil war. HSTC owns a multibrand store known as Grand Stores (GS), which deals in brands HSTC controls through either franchise agreements or exclusive agencies. The brands, over which they have monopoly rights in Lebanon, include Hugo Boss, Bossini, Riverboat, No Fear, Puma, Timberland, Sebago, and Ralph Lauren Polo, among others. GS occupies the largest nonfood retail space in the Dunes Center, operating as a magnet for the multistory mall. Its presence is complemented by two related shops—GS Espace Femme and GS Kids. Other HSTC holdings in the mall are brand-name boutiques, including Polo Jeans, Springfield, and Timberland (www.gs.com.lb and www.hst-lb.com). Indeed, in 2000, approximately a quarter of the retail space provided by the mall was rented to retail shops owned and operated by the mall's owners.

The vertical integration of the companies that produce and derive rents from these shopping spaces reflects the networked nature of property development in Lebanon and the inseparability of political and economic dimensions. Indeed, as one developer put it, the relationship is "incestuous."[21] The "competition" that the Solidere "realists" cited as requiring the company's exclusive focus on upmarket retailers was not competition at all, but rather part of the very network that brought Solidere into being. This cooperation, too, explains why HSTC was allowed to purchase property adjacent to the Beirut Souks for the purpose of building a mini-mall featuring brands they themselves control. Where, within these networks of individuals, families, companies, and political offices, is the demarcation line between the political and the economic in the production of the retail market?

Similar questions can be asked of other retail groups and their deployment of politico-economic power in the production of space. The production of Verdun 730 and 732 also brought together property developers and retail groups linked through the political powerful Amal Movement, headed by the long-time speaker of Parliament Nabih Berri. Out of this complex network of politico-economic power emerged the Azadea Group, holder of the largest number of shop spaces in Solidere's Beirut Souks.[22] Indeed, it is a testament to the networked and highly political nature of the production of space that one of the Al-Hariri network's most potent rivals was invited into the Beirut Souks, by way of an informal agreement, early on in the development process.[23] It is this dynamic of competition, cooperation, and co-optation between politico-economic networks, each made up of individuals, families, and corporations working within and alongside state institutions, that the conventional ontological distinction between the economic sphere and its noneconomic exterior hides from view.

Conclusion

To be sure, the reconstruction of Beirut's city center *is* the creation of an enclave for the super-wealthy of the region. It *does* rely upon imported urbanism in the creation of what *is* a symbolic space within which thin representation and spectacle predominate. Further, it *is* a space of consumption oriented toward not the Lebanese but the expatriate and the tourist, centered upon the paradigmatic urban form of postmodernity: the heritage-themed shoppertainment center. For critics such as Harvey and Jameson, the rapid proliferation of urban images and the emptying out of meaning from once (relatively) stable urban embodiments of history, class, or culture produces alienated urban space within which, at its extreme, streets "become so many aisles of a department store" (Jameson 1991: 98). Is not the Beirut Souks project—an entire city quarter located between the hotel district, the new financial center, and the heritage preservation zones of the Place d'Étoile and Foch-Allenby—the deterritorialized product of a disembodied, all-powerful logic of capitalist globalization?

The narrative of deepening commodification of culture and space is compelling. Like the neoliberal ideology of the market, it shapes what both neoliberals and their critics take to be the realm of reality and the realm of dreamers. In so doing, it discursively produces the city-political and the city-cultural, but privileges the city-economic. Similarly, it imposes significant limits upon those seeking to resist power, and on the imagination of resistance itself.

The "realists" present the Beirut Souks project as the catalyst for and embodiment of the BCD's integration with progressive economic processes of capitalist globalization. From within that neoliberal discourse, only strict adherence to the dictates of the market would allow Beirut to capture its place atop the emerging hierarchy of Arab cities. The "realists" celebrate the new city center and the Beirut Souks as the triumph of precisely such a rationality. At the other end, the Tabet team, which once hoped for the return of middle-class, Lebanese traders to central Beirut, now lament the transformation of the project into a hollowed-out home for international franchises. Yet the solution they proposed, selective de-commodification through the introduction of *nonmarket* regulatory practices, reinforced the image of an essentialized market—a realm of universal economic rationality.

Having granted the existence of this realm of universal reality and confirmed the principles of its operation, Tabet and his allies within the company could only argue for the return of prewar merchants along two lines. The first was to show that despite selective de-commodification, profitability would still be attainable, an argument that still privileges appeals to economic rationality of the market. The second was the moral argument that social diversity and national reintegration are public goods, and as such should trump market rationality. While the former strengthened the hand of market backers directly, the latter presented itself as outside of market logic and so failed to question principles of its operation. On both counts, the efforts to resist the hegemony of the market discourse were easily co-opted or dismissed as "sentimental." Stripped of the actual people and the social relations between them, the Beirut Souks has become, in Tabet's words, little more than "a folkloric tragedy" ("Roundtable Discussion" 1998).

The confinement of the debate to the poles of the economic and its non-economic others discursively hides from view more complex dynamics that reveal the production of space to be anything but the operation of abstract economic principles. Rather, as the development of retail space both within Solidere and Verdun suggests, it is the product and producer of constellations of power within which the political, cultural, and economic are increasingly inseparable. In this sense, then, the tragedy of Solidere is not merely the production of heritage-themed spectacle. It is in the ability of decidedly illiberal and anticosmopolitan forces to turn reconstruction to the reproduction of their own nation-fragmenting power, and so set the stage for Lebanon's next civil war.

7

When the Film Festival Comes to (Down)Town: Transnational Circuits, Tourism, and the Urban Economy of Images

William Cunningham Bissell

Urban sites have long served as concentrated nodes where cultural life, communications, capital, and communities all come together to attain a certain density and power, exercising influence far beyond city limits. The image of downtown certainly testifies to the iconic reach and centralizing force that cities possess, attracting people to the core even as images of downtown radiate outward, broadcasting its allure into a far-flung sphere. Over a century ago, Georg Simmel (1950 [1903]: 419) argued, "It is in the decisive nature of the metropolis that its inner life overflows by waves into a far-flung national or international arena," and this combination of material power and media projection has taken on heightened intensity of late. Within the global economy, as Arjun Appadurai (1996) notes, financescapes and mediascapes coincide with other cultural flows. Anthropologists and urban analysts have emphasized the heightened role of media images and the imagination in contemporary cultural production of late, linking these domains to cities as centers of communication and technology as well as sites of symbolic and cultural capital (Hannerz 1996; Larkin 2008; Malaquais 2006; B. Weiss 2009; Zukin 1995). Others, of course, have focused on urban visual cultures and the mediated metropolis (Wong and McDonogh 2001), noting, "the city is constructed as much by images and representations as by the built environment, demographic shifts, land speculation, and patterns of capital flight and investment" (Fitzmaurice 2001: 20). But while cities get staged and marketed through media images, film plays a role well beyond image making or representation, as mass tourism, heritage and leisure industries, and cultural spectacles powerfully intersect in processes of urban restructuring.

Initial efforts to map global cities often emphasized the importance of capital flows and finance rather than other aspects of urban existence, based on the assumption that the "world economy" plays a central role in shaping the "life of cities" (Sassen 1991: 3). Global cities, it seemed, were global only in certain ways (and many sites were simply left out of the picture). As Jennifer Robinson notes, "there are a large number of cities around the world which do not register on intellectual maps that chart the rise and fall of global and world cities" (2002: 531). John Rennie Short and his colleagues take this point further, arguing, "There is a first-world elitist bias to the globalization literature. Globalization is written from the metropolitan centre" (Short et al. 2000: 317). Cities located beyond the dominant frame were overlooked, while cultural dynamics were consistently downplayed. In this chapter, I address this imbalance, foregrounding the nexus between urban restructuring, cultural heritage, and economic development in the western Indian Ocean. Focusing on the ethnography of a film festival in Zanzibar city, I explore how the transformation of local urban worlds is intrinsically linked with transnational processes of place making and political economy. For more than a decade now, the Zanzibar International Film Festival (ZIFF) has played a key role in refashioning the local urban economy even as it works to resituate Zanzibar city within a broader map of transnational cultural circuits. In tandem with other events and development efforts, ZIFF has sought to foster a cultural renaissance even as it feeds off the restoration of the built environment. Initiatives to rehabilitate the city from its socialist past have entailed using history and heritage to demarcate a renewed center, splitting it off from surrounding neighborhoods and rapidly expanding periurban zones. The remaking of downtown is always an exercise in the spatial expression of social inequality, as investment capital, value, and commerce become concentrated in central districts. Rising demand and desirability in a renewed core produce dislocation as buildings are converted and poorer or more vulnerable city residents get pushed to the outskirts, trying to find viable space in sprawling informal settlements on the urban margins.

Figure 6. Zanzibar International Film Festival sign, Old Fort. Photo by author.

    As restoration of the colonial core of the city has progressed in Zanzibar, neoliberal privatization and the production of cultural patrimony have gone hand in hand, attended by a whole series of paradoxes. First, to be viable, cultural heritage must always be tied to an authentic indigenous identity, connected to roots and the native soil that allegedly nourished it (ideally this process occurs over time, which adds patina). And yet in contemporary Africa, as elsewhere, heritage is rarely produced for locals even though it is made by them, being linked instead to global tourism and mass-mediated forms of display, spectacle, and performance. Second, as this suggests, this domain, which depends on the local and authentic for its very existence, is intimately linked with transnational circuits of capital and mass consumption. Access to global circuits of people, images, and money depends on strategic deployments of the local. And third, while heritage making hinges on the ability to authentically evoke the presence of the past, its success intimately depends on the manipulation of quite contemporary skills—sophisticated marketing, entrepreneurship, and other forms of economic savoir faire. In what follows, I seek to unfold these paradoxes in an ethnographic analysis of the social and spatial complexities that are provoked when the film festival comes to (down)town.

Mediated Centers: Cities, Cultural Spectacle,
and the Global Festival Circuit

In the last quarter of the twentieth century, film festivals rapidly became a global growth industry; so many were founded in quick succession that it was challenging for even industry guides to keep reliable track of them. Estimates fluctuate anywhere from around 500 events to more than 1,000 annually. While many of the earliest film festivals were associated with the nation-state and national culture, of late they are much more closely tied to the urban sites that sponsor them—and the network of cities globally that compete for space, time, and attention on the festival circuit. "Festivals are associated not with their host countries but with the cities in which they take place," writes Tony Fitzmaurice (2001: 24). "The business of the festival is primarily that of spectacularizing those cities, identifying them as prestigious cultural centers, promoting them as glamorous tourist destinations, flagging them as potential sites for investment and development, and only secondarily of encouraging local or national film production."

The urban scene is more than a mere backdrop where festival events just happen to take place. The cultural imagery surrounding particular cities, as well as specific architectural spaces within them, play a critical role in establishing a successful festival. As Kenneth Turan observes, "given that there are so many of them, the key thing these multiple festivals share is a need to differentiate themselves from each other" (2002: 5). There are many ways that festivals (and the cities that sponsor them) can seek to distinguish themselves, but emblems of culture and identity figure very prominently on the list. Julian Stringer (2001) has written about the "aura of exclusivity" that was associated with festivals in an earlier era, when events like Cannes were few and far between. But as the number of festivals grew exponentially in the 1980s and 1990s, this aura disappeared: "With over five hundred events now being held in all four corners of the world, is there really anything special about any of them? Consequently, cities have sought to establish a distinct sense of identity and community—an aura of specialness and uniqueness—through promoting their film festivals within the terms of a highly competitive global economy. Cities and towns all over the world have found it necessary to set up their own events so as not to be left out of the game" (2001: 137).

The first Zanzibar film festival was held in 1998 on the edge of Stone Town in the Bwawani ("In the Swamps") Hotel, a 1970s middling modernist structure indistinguishable from concrete chain motels the world over. A diverse group of local cultural activists and expatriates put the festival together, with an array of aims from cultural development to boosting tourism. From these modest beginnings, the festival grew significantly, shifting to a central location and making use of the landmark structures and settings along the seafront. The tenth anniversary version stretched over ten days, screening over eighty films, and included a festival of music and performance, a conference on "Memories and Visual Cultures," literary forums, a TV talk show on slavery, cultural day trips such as the "Slave Route Day," a women's panorama, and numerous workshops, including sessions on film marketing and distribution. In this burgeoning sprawl of events, ZIFF has come to rival the best-known festival of African cinema, FESPACO, which began modestly in Ouagadougou in 1969 and has grown into an "extravaganza with few peers, a massive cultural happening that shreds preconceived notions of festivals as merely places where tickets are taken and movies are shown" (Turan 2002: 65).

Festival organizers in Zanzibar have emphasized specific aspects of heritage and culture as a means of promoting the event. ZIFF was founded as a nonprofit NGO in 1998, seeking to deploy culture as a tool for economic and social development. The charter document stated that ZIFF was intended to be part of a "continuing process" focusing on decolonization and development. And in that text, the first festival jury highlighted a principal theme for all future festivals: "Simply stated, by remembering our past, we can build our future" ("The First Jury Report" 2007: 21). One of the founders, Fatma Alloo, argues that ZIFF, "in its quest to put together the culture of the dhow countries, is trying to revive some aspect of media images which portrays our own realities" (2007: 16). In this sense, ZIFF is portrayed as part of a cultural project—one that reflects Zanzibar's past and is grounded in local realities. Media reports during the tenth anniversary captured this vision quite well. A review in a Tanzanian newspaper described ZIFF as Zanzibar's "most famous event," emphasizing how it draws on "the magic of the historic Stone Town—said to be the only functioning ancient town in East Africa" (Illah 2007: 35).

What these statements gloss over is the fact that "remembering the past" or "portraying our own realities" might not be quite so simple or straightforward as they suggest. Take the "historic" Stone Town, for example, which is routinely described as "ancient" in mass media accounts. While archaeological evidence indicates that some sites within the current downtown were occupied as early as the twelfth century, the vast majority of the city's structures date back only to the later nineteenth and twentieth centuries (Sheriff 1995). In other words, while Zanzibar may appear old, it is about as "ancient" as, say, Chicago. Moreover, invocations of the city's "age old" status and cultural value are relatively recent innovations. The festival and related events do not just passively reflect the city's heritage or remember its history; instead, they actively work to produce the city as a site steeped in unique cultural value and historical significance, working in tandem with UNESCO, state ministries, tourism investors, cultural entrepreneurs, urban preservationists, and local NGOs. In urban Zanzibar, "many different worlds collide," one travel journalist wrote. "More than anything else, the capital, Stone Town, makes Zanzibar so different from a thousand other tropical isles. Built from the islands' coral stone, the city is spectacular. It has been declared a world heritage site by UNESCO" (Tinkler 2008: 4).

It is no accident that the rediscovery of Zanzibar's Stone Town as a "historic" space has coincided with processes of urban restructuring that have dramatically transformed everyday life (Bissell 2005, 2007). But the festival's role in urban reconstruction and image making remains somewhat obscured, necessarily located off-stage. The construction of heritage, its actual cultural production in the present, is almost a contradiction in terms. Authentic heritage might be discovered, unearthed, or passed down, but never, ever are we supposed to witness the moment of its making. Like modern nationalism, as Eric Hobsbawm (1990) notes, "genuine" heritage comes cloaked in the mists of time, something age-old, hallowed, encrusted with the patina of authenticity. In this sense, heritage inevitably occludes its recent genesis, adopting a form of appearance that suggests more long-term and continuous temporalities.

In events like the film festival, we begin to catch a glimpse of how globalizing forms and forces, emphasizing spectacular events, intensified consumption, and commodification, come to depend on "tradition," history, and emblems of indigenous culture. As a German spectator enthused at the tenth ZIFF festival,

If ever a prize were to be given for the most magical location for a film festival, the Zanzibar International Film Festival ought to get it, winning out over the glamour and the red carpets of Cannes or Venice. Just a few metres from the glittery green sea, with dhows setting out for a fishing trip, not far from the evening confusion of the portable kitchens with their tempting smells of octopus, shrimp, and kebabs, stands the old brick-coloured fort, once built by the Ottoman sultans. It has been used since then by the British colonialists as tennis courts, but now is an open-air cinema and amphitheatre. During the festival, as soon as darkness falls, stories and moving pictures appear as if by magic against the night sky, close to the dark and lively alleys of the historic Stonetown. (Langer 2007)

No matter that the Omanis rather than the Ottomans built the fort: evocative description rather than accuracy of detail is the order of the day. Langer's description foregrounds key elements of the local scene, conveying the aura of ethnographic authority: he has been there, surveyed the landscape, and distilled its essential elements for us. This scene setting resembles the way that indigenous culture is staged in other contexts. Jane Desmond (1999) has explored how the display of the ethnic or gendered body in cultural performance underwrites the authenticity of tourist transactions, opening up "nature" (and exoticized "others") for consumption. Elsewhere, Edward Bruner and Barbara Kirshenblatt-Gimblett (1994) have analyzed how "tourist realism" in East Africa hinges on locating the signs and commercial ephemera of contemporary life—Maasai cell phones, for example—behind the scenes or offstage. In Zanzibar's Stone Town, the built environment serves as a kind of suture bringing very different domains together, facilitating the commodified saturation of culture while explicitly downplaying or denying the commercial interests involved. What the festival reveals is the way that historic architecture serves to undergird the selling of cultural heritage, creating the impression of temporal continuity and crafting an aura "of the really real" (Gable and Handler 1996: 568).

Moving Images (of Urban Heritage): A Cityscape without Integrity or Virtually Intact?

To prove their historic worth, cities (like other material objects of value) need to demonstrate their provenance, suggesting some sort of a connection to an unbroken chain stretching far back into the past. Walter Benjamin writes, "The uniqueness of a work of art is inseparable from its being imbedded in the fabric of tradition" (1969: 223). It is precisely this sense of being culturally embedded and unique that is inscribed in official heritage designations, which come with significant financial implications in terms of increased tourism, donor funding, and sources of investment—as well as bolstering the city's image and placing it on a prestigious global map.

In 2000, Zanzibar's Stone Town was added to UNESCO's World Heritage List. The campaign to achieve this status had been a long time in developing. One scholar described the inclusion as an "outstanding achievement," noting that Zanzibar was one of only two African sites to make the grade that year (while Europe had thirty-two selections); he noted that "developing countries, whatever the merits of their heritage, face an uphill struggle to gain admittance to UNESCO's prestigious list" (Hitchcock 2002: 154). The downtown of Zanzibar city was recognized precisely because it had "evolved through several millennia of maritime mercantile interaction. The surviving town is a physical reflection of . . . this long-term interchange. . . . It gives an authentic impression of the living Swahili culture and it is the best preserved example of its kind." The ICOMOS mission sent out to evaluate the Tanzanian state application agreed, reporting that Stone Town was an "outstanding example of a Swahili trading town. . . . It retains its urban fabric and townscape virtually intact."[1]

What is most striking about these findings is precisely their novelty. Absent from these official reports—altogether submerged and forgotten—was the fact that Tanzania had applied for heritage designation for Stone Town just twenty years previously (in 1981) and was summarily rejected. In the 1970s, Zanzibar was an isolated and insular place. It was emerging slowly from the repression of the 1964 revolution, and outside visitors were few and far between. State officials possessed few contacts in the West and had precious little bureaucratic experience with donors. By the late 1970s, economic crisis and ideological shifts led the Serikali ya Mapinduzi (Revolutionary Government) in Zanzibar to seek out external assistance in order to arrest economic and urban decline. In 1979, a UNESCO consultant was solicited to conduct a brief architectural survey, evaluating the integrity of the urban fabric. He identified seventeen architectural landmarks, most of which dated from the colonial period (including the Old Fort and the Beit el Ajaib, among other landmarks on the seafront); these were photographed, mapped, and otherwise documented. These texts and images were subsequently used to support the state's application for world heritage status for Stone Town in 1981. But in June 1982 in Paris, the Bureau of the World Heritage Committee flatly rejected Zanzibar's proposal, stating, "The character of this City is no longer of sufficient integrity or authenticity to authorize its inscription on the World Heritage List." Zanzibar, UNESCO found, had only preserved the "recent vestiges of its long history" (Issa and Juma 1983: 16), and hence was utterly unworthy of designation.

It is no surprise that this history has been conveniently forgotten. Over the short span of twenty years, ICOMOS teams, the official UNESCO panels in Paris, and other urban experts had produced two starkly opposed assessments of the city, its architecture, and its history. These judgments were supposed to be authoritative, based on compelling criteria—but instead were utterly contradictory. Amid these conflicting depictions of the city and the relationship of its architecture to the past, how might we manage to locate the more "authentic" or even "accurate" account? Was Stone Town "virtually intact" as UNESCO stipulated in 2000—a unique reflection of a transnational culture that emerged over several millennia? Or was the city instead cut off from its past, so broken down and fragmentary that it could only be described as a poor shadow of what it once was, spurious and inauthentic? In the short duration of a couple of decades, what had changed in the space of the city? If the city's architectural heritage was fragmentary and incomplete in 1982, it could not be somehow magically reconstituted by 2000 and invoked as if it represented an unbroken tradition. Or could it?

These dramatically shifting interpretations of the city have very little to do with the formal features of the cityscape or its architectural fabric per se. Instead, what we can glimpse in these opposed accounts is a profound discursive shift in the entire framework by which the city was interpreted and understood. Clearly, in 2000 the city could be imaged and represented to the World Heritage Committee in ways that were not possible in 1982. The different responses to the two applications for Stone Town over time reveal some of the central ambiguities and tensions inherent in heritage production itself. Heritage is never a self-evident category, something that objectively exists "out there" in the world, waiting to be recognized. To make heritage happen, it has to be documented, framed, and presented in an effective way. With regard to Stone Town and other world heritage sites, this means demonstrating both spatial integrity (the landscape is intact, part of a culturally meaningful complex) and long-term temporal continuity with the past. The city must open up a spatial window on history, connected (in terms of its layout or architecture) with a moment in time that has vanished. Without these necessary preconditions, heritage becomes inauthentic or even kitsch, unmoored from culture and tradition. Copies lack presence in time and space, the "aura" of the real thing, as Walter Benjamin recognized long ago: "The presence of the original is the prerequisite to the concept of authenticity," he observed. "The authenticity of a thing is the essence of all that is transmissible from its beginning, ranging from its substantive duration to its testimony to the history which it has experienced" (1969: 220–21).

In lending its imprimatur to Stone Town in 2000, UNESCO could ill afford to acknowledge its earlier judgment. To do so might risk destabilizing the enterprise of heritage designation altogether. If selective forgetting was intrinsic to the operations of the World Heritage Committee, so too with the film festival itself: one cinema scholar who has been active in ZIFF describes Stone Town as "the most atmospheric city south of the Sahara," depicting the "open-air amphitheater inside the 19th-century seaside fort" as "surely one of the most glorious film screening sites in the world" (Slocum 2003). But while the walls of the fort are older, this evocative portrait makes little allowance for the fact that the amphitheater itself was entirely novel rather than "historic"—built in the 1990s to promote cultural tourism following the recommendation of external heritage consultants. A crucial part of the film festival's success lies in its capacity to frame its relationship to its urban setting—suggesting in convincing fashion that its cultural performances unfold against the backdrop of historic architecture (and a city center) that stretches seamlessly back in time.[2] This task is made all the easier insofar as important segments of the audience (critics, filmmakers, cultural tourists, media) are transient visitors who do not speak Kiswahili or know the area. The central irony here, of course, is that this contemporary packaging of the city's historicity involves mostly screening out its actual history. Dynamism, transformation, and mutability are defining features of the modern city, but here they are nowhere to be seen. Shifting social uses of space, breaks or ruptures, historical variability, changes in taste, cultural practice, and senses of identity: these are all elements that cannot be easily combined or coexist with notions of heritage—the making of which often hinges precisely on their active erasure or suppression.

Global Roots of Tradition: Indigenous and Imperial Juxtapositions

The history of urban heritage in Zanzibar reveals surprising reversals and disjunctures, not to mention unexpected juxtapositions of local and non-local forces. In urban Zanzibar, an artist could be well occupied for years, a

European traveler once wrote, but "your matter-of-fact thorough British tourist would vote the place slow, of course, see nothing in it, and sigh for a future of broad streets and civilization, broad-cloth, bottled beer, and black-ing." Tourism was not yet even a glimmer on the horizon, but its eventual prospects seemed to rest on a future of material comforts and modern conveniences. The year was 1879, long before much of the present-day city (or what is now valued as heritage within it) had yet been built. At the time, evocations of the "picturesque" in what J. Frederic Elton (1968 [1879]: 47) called the "quaint, queer, rambling, dirty old Arab town of Zanzibar" were altogether exceptional. Throughout the second half of the nineteenth century, as European traders, travelers, and officials increasingly moved into the western Indian Ocean and Britain tightened its imperial hold over the Zanzibar sultanate, it was far more common for Western visitors to the city to complain about the unsightly, unsavory, and unsanitary state of urban affairs (Christie 2008 [1876], Livingstone 1875; Robb 1879).

Proponents of British overrule sought to draw explicit connections between social order and spatial form, claiming that the alleged "Oriental despotism" of the sultan's rule had created an urban milieu marked only by pervasive disorder and disarray. After imposing a protectorate in 1890, colonial officials vowed to modernize the city, promising, in the words of Sir Gerald Portal, the first British consul general, to "hammer some sort of cosmos out of the chaos previously existing in this country."[3] In the early decades of British colonial rule, the idea of preserving Zanzibar's cultural "heritage" was anathema to officials. Maintaining the city in its existing state was out of the question, as British colonial authorities repeatedly vowed to deliver a whole series of modernizing improvements—broader streets, better buildings, a city that was cleared out and cleaned up. But rationalizing and regularizing urban space was a far more complicated and expensive task than the British ever imagined, and they repeatedly failed to deliver on their vows of modernization, as extensive master plans and programs of reform were framed in the 1920s (and yet again repeatedly between the mid-1930s and the late 1950s) but never managed to get much beyond the drawing board (Bissell 2010).

By the mid-1930s, with the financial collapse and abandonment of the first master plan for urban Zanzibar, colonial officials on the ground began to reverse course on the question of the need for modernization in the colonial heart of the city—the "historic" downtown now recognized as Stone Town. And far from seeking to protect indigenous structures as architectural heritage, Zanzibari intellectuals and elites wanted to see the urban sphere remade in modern guise, sharply lamenting the lack of urban progress under British colonialism. Provoked by a dearth of municipal services and severe housing shortages, they demanded to know in the local press why urban planning had been seemingly abandoned. In one pointed critique published in *Al-Falaq* (The Dawn), the authors noted that the authorities had paid large sums for the development of a plan, "but the whole scheme was shelved, and it may still be rotting in the official musty pigeon-holes!"

> Though Zanzibar is the oldest country in East Africa with a glorious past, . . . [it] is unfortunately being neglected so far as modernisation of the city is concerned. . . .
>
> We have often heard it said that Zanzibar has been able to retain its fame because it is at present the only city in the world which owing to its narrow lanes and other characteristics possess [*sic*] the vista of the Arabian Nights legend, and any attempt to modernise it, according to officialdom, will decurtate [*sic*] all its splendour that haloed the ancient cities of Baghdad and Palestine, but the authorities there thought differently and consequently they have been thoroughly modernized to meet the requirements of the rapid progress the present world is making.
>
> Those that talk about leaving the face of Zanzibar unchanged are only birds of passage, but those that have made this country their home think differently, and they cannot help looking with envy at the rapid modernisation of Mombasa and Dar es Salaam that is taking place now, whilst we have not a single road within the town area worth the name.[4]

By this time, an indigenous intelligentsia had fully taken over and embraced the modernizing rhetoric offered by earlier waves of British colonial officials. Westerners with no roots in the region ("birds of passage") might wish to preserve the status quo, but this position seemed antiquated to those at "home" in the islands. From a local perspective, the way to resurrect Zanzibar's "glorious past" was not to preserve it as an "Arabian Nights" relic, but instead to "meet the requirements of the rapid progress the present world is making." If British authorities chose to ignore this imperative—and failed to deliver on promises they had continually made—locals would be increasingly left behind, gazing with envy at the rapid improvements in other cities in the empire that were laying the groundwork for future development. By this stage, British colonialism had adopted a much more conservative cultural posture in many of its African colonies. Colonial officials increasingly worried about the fast pace of changes unleashed by industrial capitalism and European imperialism, seeking to reduce the risks of destabilization and social disruptions. But authorities also were disciplined by sharp budgetary constraints, and cutting back on ambitious programs of social engineering certainly accorded with the straightened financial conditions of the 1930s.

Heritage preservation and conservation campaigns have deep colonial roots. The ideology of indirect rule was imbued with a deep sense of paternalism, representing the British as stewards of tradition, charged with the task of identifying and preserving what was best and brightest in the cultures they ruled. Seeking to bolster and expand the Archaeological Survey of India, Viceroy Curzon phrased it succinctly in 1900: "It is . . . equally our duty to dig and discover, to classify, reproduce and describe, to copy and decipher, and to cherish and conserve" (quoted in Groslier 1966: 157). In the Zanzibari context, the protection of "ancient monuments" started in 1909 under the auspices of British consul Edward Clarke. Colonial officials sought to identify and document worthy sites over many decades, debating numerous competing lists of historical monuments and trying to decide what criteria should be used to determine significance.

None of the architectural spaces deemed worthy of heritage status today by UNESCO or other conservation groups were ever included in these colonial campaigns, which were almost exclusively focused on ruins or remains that could be linked to prior civilizations. Even after decades of back-and-forth debate, precisely which monuments or ruins to preserve (and why) remained entirely open to question. As late as the 1950s, colonial officials continued to lament the neglect of ruins, calling for "more positive measures to avert the rapid destruction to which ruins are subject if they are left alone save for occasional lopping of the bush." The curator of the Peace Memorial museum at the time agreed that more should be done, but observed, "in the first place, it should be decided definitively which ruins or sites are worthy of preservation." As he further confided, "the ruins in and around Zanzibar are mostly of very recent date, have little historical value and no archaeological interest, but they probably do have quite an interest and value from the tourist traffic angle."[5]

The invocation of tourism in this instance—as opposed to inherent aesthetic worth or indigenous interpretations of value—was by no means incidental. Beliefs about the usefulness of heritage as a kind of tourist attraction have a very long history in Zanzibar, as it turns out. In 1945, when Lionel Bintley, the government architect, proposed yet another scheme to widen Zanzibar's streets, the British resident, Guy Pilling, flatly rejected the proposal, stating, "Zanzibar has few real assets and one of these is undoubtedly its romantic past, which is largely kept alive by the picturesqueness of the stone town. Do away with that and you will kill the goose that lays the golden egg!"[6] This is precisely how heritage gets translated into a "real asset"— through its capacity to evoke a "romantic past," stimulating the imaginaries of visitors quite distanced from the local scene. In the early 1960s, as colonial authorities worked to establish areas of "special control" that would allow them to exercise power over the external appearance of buildings, another official warned about any attempts to interfere with "tourist assets" along the seafront. "The town should not lose its special Zanzibar look," he wrote. "You are aware that the name Zanzibar has a great appeal overseas, and it is very important from a tourist point of view that this name should not lose its appeal because the character of the town has changed and lost its individuality because buildings are put up to an entirely different architectural conception."[7] Just two years later, shortly after independence, a revolutionary uprising surrounded and took over the city, radically altering the "character of the town" and ending its "great appeal overseas." Chou En-lai and Che Guevara came to visit, among other leftist luminaries, but the tourist trade was effectively terminated in the ensuing decades—a hiatus that set the stage for restoration to start up in the neoliberal 1980s.

Cultural Capital: Remaking Downtown

At the end of the twentieth century, from Chinese socialist planners to UN agencies and the Aga Khan foundation, transnational plans to "save" the city's downtown all returned to the same strategy: Stone Town represented a cultural heritage that must be restored, and the best way to fund rehabilitation would be to promote a vigorous tourist economy. In the early 1990s, as urban conservation got underway, tourism consultants lamented the existing state of affairs: quite clearly the global brand of Zanzibar's name had considerably faded. They were dismayed above all that there was a "general lack of awareness of Zanzibar's heritage at home and abroad," and recommended a series of measures to rectify the situation. The Revolutionary

Government should create a new ministry of national heritage; convert landmark structures into five new museums; make efforts to identify a new class of national monuments; initiate a collecting program abroad to repatriate Zanzibari artifacts; clean up historic sites; and actively engage in "overseas publicity to promote Zanzibar's rich heritage." They left little doubt as to what all this activity was about: "Zanzibar's national heritage is an essential part of the tourist package, and it must be seen by the government to be as important to the needs of tourists as clean beaches and good communications" (Walls and Crispe 1991). Four years on, a Western correspondent noted that restoration efforts were underway in Zanzibar, with mixed results:

> The Indian Ocean island off Tanzania is trying to reclaim the mystery and romantic allure normally associated with its storybook name. Eager for the foreign currency that tourists bring, authorities are cleaning up Stone Town, the picturesque heart of Zanzibar where most of its monuments lie. . . . But although it lies just one hour by boat off the coast of Tanzania, many tourists omit it as they pursue the East African safari trail of game parks and nature preserves. Mainly budget travelers and backpackers have followed in the footsteps of Livingstone, exploring Zanzibar's coconut-lined empty white beaches, Arab ruins, and savory Swahili curries. These travelers have had to themselves the forts, bazaars, baths, mazelike narrow streets, dhows (ships), and plantations of cloves and perfumes, all of which are largely unchanged from their past centuries of glory. (Matloff 1995)

The journalist neglects to cite any evidence to support the notion that structures had remained "unchanged from their past centuries of glory," but these fanciful assertions provided valuable marketing assistance to Stone Town hotel developers, investors, and entrepreneurs. At the time, Zanzibari officials had decided to pursue what they called "high class" tourism, believing that luxury travelers would produce higher margins with a lower cultural impact. But exclusive travelers also demand superior amenities and services, which entails larger resort projects, far higher levels of infrastructure and investment, and a more intrusive expatriate presence. High-gloss culture and high-end hotels began to coincide in Stone Town, as tourism rapidly expanded and the face of the city changed in ways great and small. Blurring the lines between "restoration" and wholesale "reconstruction" served broader ends. The Aga Khan Trust for Culture funded a conservation plan for Stone Town in the early 1990s, as well as a landmark renovation of the Old Dispensary. Concurrently, they gained access to several key sites in Zanzibar to develop for high-end tourism using their Serena brand. "The Serena Inn is the Aga Khan's second venture on the island, a project aimed not only at firmly establishing the island as a luxury tourist destination, but also reviving its great cultural legacy," write the authors of *Safari Style*. The building used to be a public library accessible to all, but after being renovated into an upscale hotel, its rooms run anywhere from $310 to $850 a night (2011 rates). But, as *Safari Style* breathlessly informs us, "the finished effect of the restoration is magical, combining Arab exoticism and colonial grandeur with the natural beauty of frangipani trees, a white sand beach, and the clear waters of the Indian Ocean" (Beddow and Burns 1998: 171, 175).

Nor is this just a question of a single hotel development; more than three dozen local residences have been converted to hotels, and whole stretches of the city from Vuga to Shangani and all along the seafront have been taken over for tourists, with museums, cafés, dive shops, boutiques, restaurants, tour operators, and all the rest. No doubt, those who promoted Zanzibar's application for World Heritage status were not simply motivated by visions of spurring capital accumulation. Some may have hoped for increased tourism revenues and economic renewal. Others might have envisioned heritage status as a way to access donor funds, technical assistance, and other means of support. Still others could have endorsed it as the best way to use global leverage to achieve local ends—in effect, deploying UNESCO rules to make the state get serious about implementing and enforcing conservation guidelines on property owners. But whatever the intentions behind the application, the ongoing rehabilitation of Stone Town as "historic" has produced wholly unintended consequences. And no matter how pure or genuine their motives, heritage proponents and preservation experts utterly failed to anticipate the far-reaching effects of unleashing a sprawling tourist economy in the space of the city. As Michael Hitchcock notes, most of the commissioned reports on heritage never accounted for the impact of the "influx of foreign capital and the attendant ills of globalization" in Zanzibar (2002: 165). In the aftermath, commercialization has often been treated as an unexpected by-product or excess, rather than an integral part of the heritage and tourism industries.

Concerns about the commodification of culture were not restricted to the city itself. In Kiswahili, the film festival is known as Tamasha la Nchi za

Jahazi (Festival of the Dhow Countries), and from the outset it has been marked by debates over its motives and mission. The current CEO of the festival writes that ZIFF was founded by cultural activists motivated by "the desire to celebrate the vibrant heritage of the people of the Dhow Countries—Africa, the Middle East, the Indian sub-continent and the Indian Ocean islands." But, as he elaborates, "ZIFF's ultimate aim is to promote culture as an asset, and use the Festival of the Dhow Countries as a vehicle to create a flourishing cultural industry in East Africa" (Mhando 2007: 45). One of the jury members in 2008 and a consultant to the festival echoed this theme, when he told me that ZIFF had to extend the influence of its brand, creating marketable products out of the festival's activities and putting them on display: "They need to create new products and then showcase them, becoming active players in the culture industry."[8]

At the ZIFF conference on "Memories and Visual Cultures" in 2008, this issue also sparked debate. In the discussion following a paper given on the film festival's history, a Zanzibari intellectual long resident in Europe rose to say that "dhow culture" was nothing new to him: "When I saw this, I said, 'yes, we are finally getting recognized.'" But a European historian with long research experience in East Africa questioned this notion. "The original film festival idea was embedded in the notion of creating a certain kind of tourism in Zanzibar. Emerson [an American hotel promoter] was centrally involved in this—the 'dhow culture' as a certain branding for that, linked to high class tourism." In response, a Zanzibari activist involved with the festival since its early days stood up to make her position clear: "There were other criteria to the founding of ZIFF than business. One key issue in the world today is globalization. Zanzibar used to have a globalized economy. And if you look at Zanzibar now, it is pathetic to see the position of fishermen in relation to Italian investors, South Africans, and others who are marginalizing them. I agreed to create ZIFF to use film to tell our perspective, our view, and to challenge our position in the globalized economy. Some members of the board may have wanted to get people to come to fill their hotels, but there was also a broader political objective."[9]

But despite the political hopes of at least some organizers, the festival (and the city itself) is lodged within a political economic landscape where the deployment of culture as a tool of development or decolonization is not a priority at all. In the initial years, the festival had received support from just a handful of donors—the Ford Foundation most prominent among them—and the board was facing pressures to demonstrate that ZIFF had broad appeal and could sustain itself over the long run. Becoming a player in the "culture industry" was one way to do this, but attracting higher levels of corporate sponsorship and entering into cooperative ventures with local businesses were among the other options being discussed. Moreover, as Stringer observes, "The planning of spectacle around a city's distinct festival image has a further function: it helps develop initiatives related to real-estate activity within cities, thus helping to rejuvenate the value of urban space through the mobilization of global interests" (2001: 142). Raising the city's global profile, highlighting its "unique" historic character, and enhancing its cultural desirability all have an impact on the urban real estate market—bringing in new buyers, making investment more attractive, and raising prices and rents, as well as changing the uses of many buildings or even neighborhoods. By the 2006 festival, the Zanzibari cultural activist quoted above had already begun to criticize recent developments in the city. At a roundtable held (ironically) at the Serena Inn focusing on the question of whether cinema can represent slavery, she lamented the increasing loss of historical buildings in Zanzibar: "In this new tourist economy, foreign hotel owners are buying up the old buildings and ruins and converting them into four star tourist resorts, destroying old slave cells with the actual chains still present, building swimming pools over marble Omani baths. It is a tragedy" (quoted in Deckard 2006a).[10]

The Architecture of the Festival:
An (Almost) Opening Night Scene

It is the second night of the tenth anniversary of ZIFF. A large crowd is gathered under the open sky in the amphitheater inside the Ngome Kongwe, or Old Fort—one of the series of landmark structures that makes up the impressive architectural façade along Zanzibar's seafront. Evening has descended, and the moon is rising full and heavy just to the right of the Beit el Ajaib, or House of Wonders, next door (which houses the Museum of the History and Culture of Zanzibar and is used for the festival's daytime screenings). The tableau is visually striking: the rough-hewn walls of the Old Fort supply a backdrop for the stage isolated by dramatic spotlights and festooned with colorful cloth billowing in the breeze. On either side of a big projection screen are decorative *jahazi* (dhow) sails rising above the fort's walls, as if the amphitheater were a local craft adrift in the Indian Ocean.

This visual theme picks up on the festival's signature prize (the golden dhow), as well as echoing this year's theme: "Celebration of Waters and Dreams." Looming above the fort's walls, just beyond the sail on the left, the crowd can see the balconies of the upper floors of the House of Wonders, hanging with large banners advertising festival sponsors: the Ford Foundation, Holiday Inn, Vodacom, and so forth—the museum as huge billboard.

There's a buzz in the air as spectators circulate, exchange greetings, and settle into their seats—an atmosphere of expectation. The opening night's showing was a U.K.-U.S. production, Michael Apted's *Amazing Grace*, but tonight promises a documentary much closer to home: Jord den Hollander's *Many Words for Modern* (2007). The film explores the impact of architectural modernism in Dar es Salaam, Tanzania's capital, focusing on the career of Anthony B. Almeida—an architect of Goan descent who introduced a tropical modernist vocabulary to Dar during the late colonial period and following independence. Almeida himself is in attendance for the showing along with other luminaries from the mainland capital; most of the seats in the front row are reserved for the entourage of special guests. After being introduced, Hollander, the Dutch director of the film, mounts the stage to applause and offers a brief speech introducing the film and his crew, thanking sponsors, and then he descends into the audience, escorting Almeida, the guest of honor, back with him on stage. The architect is an old man, frail, slight, and dapper. He starts his speech on a somewhat grand note, referring to himself in the third person: he never just did his work for Anthony Almeida, he proclaims, but for Tanzania as a whole.

And then he stepped away from the microphone, took out a sheet of paper from his coat pocket, and was ushered by the director back to center stage again. He had some trouble reading in the light, but was assisted by Hollander, who looked on over his shoulder, shining a flashlight. It appeared Almeida had a formal declaration to make. He announced that it was time to open a school of architecture right here in Zanzibar, one that would focus on the tropical styles of Africa—East Africa and West Africa especially—with the aim of supporting an architecture sensitive to local conditions and the environment. "I was glad to see a headline in the local paper recently, 'Why Can't an Architecture of Local Materials Still Be Modern?'" he observed. He said the school would revitalize traditional architecture and protect the rich heritage of Zanzibar's built environment. To be successful, he argued, the venture should take pride of place in one of Zanzibar's central heritage buildings. And it could draw architects from around the world to come to the island, to enjoy a different scene, and to teach or supervise for a time—drawing on the exotic allure of Zanzibar to attract transnational architects and designers. For donor support, he continued, they should turn to organizations like the Aga Khan foundation and other global patrons (including those involved in the making of the film and sponsors of the film festival)—the model here being something like the Dhow Countries Music Academy, which had been founded as an outgrowth of the film festival in its early years. His proposal received enthusiastic applause from the audience, a kind of murmur of delight and agreement that the time for such a venture had indeed come.

"This is the definitive ZIFF experience and dream—to be in the audience in the Old Fort," writes the festival's CEO, Martin Mhando (2006: 7). But if the Ngome Kongwe is the place to be, the architect's appearance there that night crystallized a number of perhaps unintended ironies that the festival represents. There is an intriguing nexus here between the festival as spectacle and the festival as staging ground. Events serve to promote projects, as external NGOs, sponsors, media, and transnational spectators come together to showcase "local" and "traditional" culture—just as Tanzanians draw on the venue to link local initiatives to wider circuits (pan-African film, Indian Ocean dhow culture, and UNESCO initiatives such as the Slave Routes Project). The film festival presents itself as a showcase of culture: a space to celebrate, to circulate, and to consume images and related artistic achievements, including music and books. But the festival also serves as a platform to make cultural production possible, acting to facilitate promotion, networking, and the whole entrepreneurial business of mass-mediated culture in the early twenty-first century.

This tension is amply apparent in the festival's relationship to the city itself—especially with regard to the built environment and questions of historic architecture. Almeida had issued a proposal with an appealing gloss, advocating the creation of a school dedicated to traditional African architecture, grounded in local conditions, materials, and forms.[11] What he was calling for was a center that could conserve the architectural heritage of the coast while collecting local knowledge and transmitting it to a new generation. But he was issuing the call before a transnational audience, in the context of a European-directed film about the importation of modernism into a colonial and postcolonial context. This embrace of "traditional" architecture, moreover, was being voiced in a context where what constituted heritage or tradition was never clear.

Consider, for example, the two historic structures that stage the film festival itself. The Beit el Ajaib was constructed for an Omani sultan drawing on
the latest English engineering innovations. Finished in 1883, it was intended
as a ceremonial palace highlighting the "modernity of the sultanate" (Aga
Khan Trust for Culture 1996: 50). The Beit later housed the offices of the British colonial government, became an "Ideological College of Politics" after the
1964 revolution, and had recently been converted into a history and culture
museum (Myers 2003). Similarly, the Old Fort was built out of the remains
of a Portuguese chapel and merchant house. The conquering Omanis, after
having driven out the Europeans, partially demolished the structures and
turned them into fortifications. The interior of the fort has seen many uses: a
barracks for the sultan's mercenaries and later a prison; storehouse for the
colonial Public Works Department and terminus of the Bububu railway. In
the 1940s, the fort was partly converted into the social center of the Ladies
Purdah Club. Sometime after the 1964 revolution, a pick-up basketball court
was laid inside the crumbling walls, karate practice was held there, and it
used to be rented out for weddings too large to be contained by any of the
city's public squares. More recently, the fort was thoroughly reconstructed as
an open-air cultural performance space with two stages and tourist shops
lining its walls. Like these two landmark structures, most architecture in Dar
and Zanzibar was never "traditional" in any direct or clear sense.

Moreover, Almeida's relationship to the local was anything but simple or
straightforward. (In one of the more disturbing moments in *Many Words
for Modern*, the elderly architect dismisses an African youth with colonial
hauteur, waving the "boy" out of the way as he seeks to show off the façade he
designed of the Goan sports club in Dar for the cameras.) In this sense, his
work shares a great deal with both the film and the festival in which it was
being shown. The architectural modernism Almeida drew on originated in
Europe and moved out into the colonial world, ultimately becoming global
in expression. The local reception of *Many Words for Modern* also revealed
underlying tensions surrounding Almeida's work. In the film, a young architect in Dar es Salaam, Nuru Inyangete, spoke of the challenges of creating
contemporary structures in a distinctively African idiom. Many of her clients wanted modern and sleek designs, the steel and glass towers that fill the
transnational corporate landscape in downtowns across the globe. Almeida
and others had brought a kind of tropical modernism to Dar, but she was
concerned that this work had led to the devaluation of African forms, under-
cutting efforts to create indigenous styles. For local architects, she stated,

"there's certainly a need to find our own style, which mirrors our African heritage" (Stacey 2007: 7). Following the official screening of *Many Words for Modern* in Dar, others seemed to echo these doubts. Lussuga Kironde, a professor at the university's College of Lands and Architectural Studies, asserted, "there were no local architectural values in the documentary which could give a view of national architectural models" (Lukumbo 2007: 2).

"Traditional" Culture and Transnational Chic:
Making Spectacles for Sale

If we examine the recent restructuring of Zanzibar city with a historical eye, it is startling to see just how much of its architectural "heritage" has been dramatically refashioned for tourist consumption. Entire buildings have been given over to cultural troupes, NGOs, and performance spaces, from the Old Dispensary to the Customs House and the Old Fort. In this context, the staging of culture and its commercialization are intimately intertwined. The branding of local heritage has precisely occurred in a context where Zanzibar is being reinserted within transnational circuits of style and spectacle in entirely novel ways. If one goes to the Beit el Ajaib for a film screening, one might eventually wander out through the exhibits of the Museum of the History and Culture of Zanzibar. In 2006, for example, there was a show highlighting the potential risks of tourism for local culture. Afterward, one might browse in the gift shop filled with local crafts, artfully displayed. There you might pick up lavishly illustrated tomes such as *Zanzibar Heritage* or *Zanzibar Style* or *Safari Living* or *Safari Elegance* or even *Swahili Kitchen*—but it is certainly not locals who are snapping these volumes up for $40 to tastefully adorn their coffee tables. In the streets of the city, one can suddenly find all the "goods" (and services) of leisure class consumption— spa treatments, interior design, Swedish massage, sports bars, espresso, even sushi. Cell phones are de rigueur, and if you are looking for all the hotspots and happening places, you can always consult *Swahili Coast*—a glossy monthly where a thin veneer of cultural content provides cover for lush tourism industry advertising and promotion.

Heritage seems hottest when the festival circuit comes to town—indeed, the discovery of Zanzibar's inherent worth is never so apparent as when it is on display for global others and outsiders: the tourists and groupies, press and performers who come for the Sauti za Busara (Voices of Wisdom) music festival or ZIFF. Hipsters can hang at the Dharma Lounge, waiting for word as to where the next full moon rave will be held. The restaurants are packed at night, and hardly a cappuccino or croissant can be found in the cafés in the morning. All the tourist shops that fill the length of Gizenga and Hurumzi streets do a booming business in African carvings and crafts that bear no cultural relation whatsoever to Zanzibar itself. Sprawling boutiques like Zanzibar Gallery, Real Art, Memories of Zanzibar, and Zanzibar Heritage sell more upmarket and vaguely ethnic goods, a pan-tribal mélange that stretches from Morocco to South Asia. In this milieu, even critical observers could find themselves getting drawn in by the atmospherics. On leaving a screening, a British Ph.D. student in postcolonial studies and film critic wrote, "Afterwards, I went to Mercury's for a drink (a Safari) and a perusal of their photos of Freddie Mercury, Queen, and the Bulsara family. It's spuriously named, a tourist joint, since the real Bulsara family home where Freddie grew up is on Kenyatta Street and has since been converted into another Gallery bookstore, and was full of Dutch tourists in vest tops, but the atmosphere was lovely all the same" (Deckard 2006b). Even when recognized as spurious or unreal, the "atmosphere" somehow remains *lovely all the same*.

Preservation professionals might treat all this buying and selling and promoting as a sideshow—cultural happenings, consumerism, and coffee-table compendiums of style, they often claim, have little to do with the "genuine" conservation of authentic heritage. But this is a profoundly idealizing view—one that ignores the power of global branding and the synergies involved with bringing an urban entertainment economy to downtown (Hannigan 1998). It also overlooks the myriad ways that indigenous signs of identity are being recast in commodified form, shaping a global phenomenon that Jean and John Comaroff have dubbed "Ethnicity, Inc." (2009). Indeed, in Zanzibar, it is precisely through the shrewd deployment of sophisticated modes of media and spectacle that the authentic is being produced and performed. To grasp this, we only have to return for a moment to reflect on the short history of Zanzibar's heritage status. In 1982, Zanzibar's world heritage application was not rejected by UNESCO because its architecture was unworthy—far from it. The application was cobbled together out of bits and pieces, consisting largely of images and documents on seventeen prominent architectural landmarks. The materials reinforced the impression that the urban fabric had not survived intact, leading to the World Heritage committee's negative finding. The application failed because local bureaucrats in socialist Zanzibar lacked experience and familiarity with the mechanisms of global grant making, presenting the city in such a way that their bid was quite likely to fail. Urban consultants were not yet locally available to lend their support and advice, nor could officials point to the local activities of NGOs like the Aga Khan Trust for Culture to support their appeal. And much of the material apparatus of marketing and promotion that could be used to support and sustain their claims for heritage status did not yet exist. Few locally or on a global stage recognized Zanzibar for its history or heritage at the time. Nor were there cultural spectacles yet that could be used to put the local on display for wider audiences.

When these elements all began to come together in the later 1990s, they started to interact and reinforce each other—UNESCO's World Heritage designation being supported by (and in turn spurring) the other components of the emerging culture industry in the islands. Local cultural entrepreneurs and officials display a kind of cosmopolitan competence by creating a niche for Zanzibar on the transnational festival circuit, bringing off those performances and generating the requisite buzz and energy to continue year after year. They open up new cultural spaces and possibilities, while demonstrating the sort of savvy and skills that make it possible to attract donors, promote projects, generate grants, and create currency for conservation. These events also serve to put Zanzibar very much on the global map, capitalizing on culture and history to distinguish it from other places in the sun. "What many festivals actually now market and project are not just 'narrative images,' but a city's own 'festival image,' its own self-perceptions of the place it occupies within the global space economy, especially in relation to other cities and festivals" (Stringer 2001: 140). Festivals draw journalists and travel writers, whose work in turn stimulates tourism promotion efforts; heritage is not separate from the entire apparatus of branding, marketing, and display—indeed, it is packaged and made present through beautifully laid out and photographed tomes on architecture, design, and décor. This image making becomes all the more powerful and pervasive when re-creations of "Oriental" style can be readily sampled locally now at a host of deluxe ("authentic, original, and distinctively Zanzibari") hotels and resorts.

In this heady mix, architecture serves as an index of the new spatial and social forms of inequality shaped by tourism. In 2000, one travel writer found that tourism was relatively new in the islands. In her view, Zanzibar had not "yet been scarred by a large infrastructure boom," but even so, at the time she noted her discomfort: "While I was there, though, a kind of unease kept niggling at me. Most of the restaurants, bars and hotels are staffed by Africans but owned by European expats. I don't know about you, but I feel distinctly weird about sitting on a nice veranda with other Europeans while being served G&Ts by black Africans. It gives me the post-colonial heebee-jeebees. The people who ought to be benefiting from Zanzibar's beauty and resources, it seems, aren't" (O'Farrell 2000). In 2008, a young British traveler found himself "overwhelmed" by touts and hustlers (*papasi*), and "couldn't find time alone to appreciate Stone Town's overt charm. The high walls and jumble of alleyways became an oppressive and frustrating maze." Even so, he asserted that tourists have no right to complain. Touts, after all, were just trying to make a living, and "in reality the reason they bug us is they have very little. . . . The rich and poor divide in Zanzibar was verging on the disgraceful. It was such a contrast to see the thriving tourist complexes built on utopian beaches, situated metres from basic mud huts and underprivileged farmlands" (Wilkinson 2008).

But if architecture materializes inequalities, it can also serve as a means of making them possible in the first place. In "African Living, I Presume," an article appearing in the *Sunday Times* of London, we read of an exclusive new gated complex developed on the outskirts of Pingwe, a fishing village on the east coast of the island. More than anything else, this development stands as a potent sign of the times. A three-bedroom, three-bath timber house in "Monsoon Gardens" with a media room and plunge pool runs £395,000, while the higher-end model goes for £695,000. Says the London-based developer: "The philosophy is to have a house in a beautiful place that still retains a local identity. Zanzibar is a special place." The properties, she insists, should be called "houses not villas. 'Villas' sounds like something encroaching from the West" (Davies 2008: 24). Following in the footsteps of Marx—Groucho, not Karl—it seems as if Westerners ironically might not want to buy into a "special place" where the West itself was "encroaching." In this cultural economy of images, without the "local," the authentic, or the historic, globalization simply loses its purchase on space; difference and distinction fall away. In Zanzibar, it is no accident that cultural spectacles linking reified forms of heritage with commodification take place within "historic" structures. This is the essential glue that holds the entire ensemble together, endowing it with value and legitimacy for at least some Zanzibaris and many outsiders. Architecture in this sense is uniquely positioned to supply cultural happenings with a dramatic setting or stage. Layered with patina, built of stone or stucco, the walls seem to signify something solid and enduring; they convey or communicate a process of cultural transmission through time, precisely as Walter Benjamin suggested long ago. Buildings are long-lasting and complex commodities in and of themselves; as such, they often serve as tokens of continuity and tradition, markers of history, the material medium that binds and holds rhetorics of inheritance, identity, and heritage together. The architectural fabric radiates precisely the aura of the work of art that Benjamin feared was so threatened in the age of mechanical reproduction. But these spheres—of culture and commerce—are no longer quite as distinct as he once believed. Indeed, in an era of mass media and new modes of reproduction—one saturated by commodified values and relations—the capacity to create aura and sustain the necessary illusion of authenticity has become all the more precious, potent, and (at least to a select few) entirely profitable.

8

The Future of the Past: World Heritage, National
Identity, and Urban Centrality in Late Socialist Cuba

Matthew J. Hill

The conversion of chance into destiny displaces intimacy in favor
of form. . . . Materially, this reduction is enshrined in that
triumph of place over time . . . [of] monuments over social
experience.

—Michael Herzfeld, *A Place in History:*
Social and Monumental Time in a Cretan Town

As group pasts become increasingly parts of museums, exhibits
and collections, both in national and transnational spectacles,
culture becomes less what Pierre Bourdieu would have called a
habitus (a tacit realm of reproducible practices and dispositions)
and more an arena for conscious choice, justification, and
representation, the latter often to multiple and spatially
dislocated audiences.

—Arjun Appadurai, *Modernity at Large:*
Cultural Dimensions of Globalization

In the summer of 1996, demolition crews arrived in the Plaza Vieja—a
500-year-old plaza in Havana's historic center, Habana Vieja—equipped with
explosive charges. Carrying out orders issued by the city historian, they
planned to eliminate every trace of a republican-era park and an underground

parking structure, which was built to accommodate the "bulky American autos" that blocked the sidewalks of Habana Vieja's narrow streets and entrances to residential courtyards (Scarpaci 2000: 733). In addition to the parking structure, which raised the original height of the square a meter off the ground, the "modernist" Havana Park (constructed in 1952) consisted of an open-air amphitheater with benches, grass, and shade trees. For residents, it was also a public space, where people gathered to listen to music, children rode bikes and played games of pick-up baseball, and the elderly paused to sit and enjoy the breeze from the harbor.

The plan to "implode" the parking structure with explosives engendered what one plaza resident, an architect, referred to as a "tremendous scandal." Late-breaking news of the plan sent "residents *en masse* to the Communist Party and in every direction" to protest an action that they feared would bring not only the park but also its dilapidated tenements to the ground. "Sure," the architect noted, "their strategy was, 'We're going to evacuate everyone ahead of time.' Given the disturbances this would create, the attitude of the authorities was, 'You have to leave here for 3 or 4 days,' who knows where. And if your house collapses, the only thing they have to say is, 'Sorry, you're screwed.'" Chastised by resident appeals to the national leadership, conservation authorities regrouped and decided to eliminate the park with jackhammers, a noisy, dusty process that residents would have to endure for two years. In the end, demolition teams removed 235 tons of concrete from the center of the square, leaving a gaping hole that was subsequently filled with hundreds of truckloads of topsoil. To give the plaza a "colonial" feel, conservationists restored the plaza to street level, and covered it with polished paving stones. Moreover, in the center of the square, where fountains of various sizes and shapes had existed in colonial times, they imported a massive Italian marble and set it in place using a large crane. They subsequently ringed the fountain with a ten-foot-high black iron fence to keep neighborhood children from bathing in its waters. Finally, they barricaded the entrances to the plaza with heavy metal chains and surrounded the periphery with cannonball-shaped iron bollards to keep vehicular traffic from entering the square and spoiling the view.

These processes of remaking and enclosure were complemented by further panoptical transformations which made the plaza further available for the visual gaze. First, conservationists mounted a camera obscura on the roof of the plaza's tallest building, through which tourists are afforded a panorama of the plaza. Next, they opened the restored balconies of former

palaces transformed from tenements into hotels, museums, and shops, offering the tourist another set of viewing points from which to gaze down
upon the square. Further, they mounted a large placard at the main entrance
to the square, depicting enlarged reproductions of various eighteenth-
century engravings of the square by different European traveler artists, and
set in place life-sized cutouts of Spanish colonial troops dressed in signature
red-and-white uniforms, playing fife and drums. Finally, viewers to this
space are instructed in how to see it as part of a "disciplined order of things"
(Boyer 1994: 253) by tour guides who circumambulate through the square,
instructing viewers what to see and how to see it.

  This vignette crystallizes some of the dynamic processes and forces that
are transforming colonial city centers and cultural landscapes throughout
Cuba today. These include at times conflicting agendas of international and
local preservation efforts; marketization, privatization, and the insertion of
global capital combined with the persistence of socialist institutions; the
opening to tourism as a means of "capturing" hard currency; and the turn
to cultural heritage in the search for new symbols from which to construct a
socialist identity in a post-socialist world. This article examines Habana
Vieja, a United Nations Educational, Scientific, and Cultural Organisation
(UNESCO) World Heritage site in Havana, Cuba, and arguably one of the
largest and most significant colonial city centers in Latin America today. It
begins with an analysis of the concept of urban centrality, followed by a discussion of the loss of centrality in Habana Vieja in the aftermath of colonialism. Finally, an analysis of the situation in Habana Vieja reveals how the
recycling of traditional architectural forms in keeping with the demands
of the global economy gives rise to a new centrality in Habana Vieja. It also
demonstrates how this centrality is achieved through a process of modernization which reframes the site through practices of enclosing, selective
highlighting, and forms of social exclusion that create a coherent view of
Habana Vieja as a cosmopolitan, European city.

Urban Centrality in the Spanish American Town

When it comes to the colonial Spanish American town, there are two forms
of social centrality that are critical for understanding the politics of urban
transformation in the contemporary period. These include both the plaza
as an urban form and the grid-shaped Spanish American town which was

defined according to established rules set forth in the *Ordinances for the Discovery, Settlement and Pacification of the Indies* (1573), a set of royal instructions for the urban planning of towns in the empire from 1513 onward (Lefebvre 1991: 151; Kinsbruner 2005: 23).

The first of these forms, the Spanish American plaza, was an urban form whose design was rigorously specified by royal decree. The core main plaza, or Plaza Mayor, was to be rectangular in shape, twice as long as wide to accommodate official celebrations, and located either near the port or, for inland cities, at the center of town. The administrative hierarchy of church and state was to be inscribed and monumentalized on this main plaza, with church and government buildings, respectively, being placed on whole blocks. On the religious side, the institutions of the Catholic Church, the cathedral, parish church, and monastery, were to receive the first lots, followed by the government palace, town hall, customs house, and arsenal, assigned in that order. From the main plaza, the grid was to extend outward in every direction, with remaining lots assigned to settlers by socioeconomic status so that the most prominent families received lots closest to the main plaza (Kinsbruner 2005: 24). On a ritual level, the plaza was intended to accommodate assertions of royal authority that were enacted on the main plaza, including royal births, or the arrival of royal officials, as well as secular and religious celebrations and events such as parades, festivals, bullfights, and public hangings (ibid.: 122). A new Baroque culture underwrote the authority inscribed in this idealized space. It applied the rigid principles of "abstraction, rationalization, and systemization" in an attempt to erase all local expressions of individuality and imagination (Rama 1996: 10). In sum, the architectural design, institutional organization, and officially sanctioned use of the main plaza "embodies an idea of centrality" that represents and instantiates a hierarchical and entrenched regime of urban citizenship that segregates those of lower status to the peripheries (Holston 2009: 246).

The second form of centrality was the Spanish American town itself. Opening out from the main plaza, the Spanish American town possessed an important degree of social centrality that emerged from its role as a civilizing node in the context of the Spanish conquest. This is evinced in the fact that the Spanish American colonial town became "the residences of viceroys, governors, and archbishops, the seats of universities, high courts, and inquisitional tribunals" before it even housed the legislatures of independent republics (Rama 1996: 13). The resilience of this civilizing ideal, which survived three centuries after the conquest, is exemplified by the writings of early republican authors such as Domingo Faustino Sarmiento's *Facundo: Civilización y Barbarie*, published in 1845. Sarmiento emphasized the centrality of the city as a civilizing agent whose civic virtues were capable of overcoming barbarism of the residents of the untamed *pampa* (plains or countryside) through schools and a strong seat of government. He saw the city as a pedagogical instrument for the formation of "citizen-workers" (granting citizenship only after literacy had been first achieved) and supported the immigration of Europeans to offset the crude ways of the gaucho in the countryside (Sarlo 2008: 38). In sum, the social centrality of Spanish American cities was defined by their role as receptacles of imported European culture, and as launching pads from which an educated elite could impose social norms such as literacy on the "savage surroundings" (Rama 1996: 13).

With the advent of twentieth-century mass culture, urban renewal, and elite flight from the city to the suburbs, the lost centrality of the cosmopolitan Spanish American city center engendered elite nostalgia for the cultivated, imperial city or *ciudad letrado*, with its writers, newspapers, government agencies, libraries, universities, concert halls, cafés, theaters, law offices, brothels, churches, and shops located within a quadrangle of ten or so blocks (Rama 1996: 114). To contemporary elites, like Rama's *letrados*, the city appears as if under siege, threatened by the "spatial mutations" and occupation of the uncivilized rural masses accused of destroying its cosmopolitan character (Prakash 2008: 182). The "slumification" of the city further transports images of the city being taken over by internal migrants, returning the city back to nature (Sarlo 2000: 119). Of course this vision, as Prakash notes, is predicated on the lettered intellectual's vision of the cosmopolitan city as an organism, a bounded city defined by an "internally coherent civic life" (2008: 182). In the case of the Habana Vieja, it is this elite vision of the city as a totality that urban conservationists seek to restore—the ordered city that existed only in the lettered intellectual's mind. Yet ultimately, this project of restoration is complemented by the transformation of the city center into a tourist and museum space, which lies side by side with the squalor of slums, crumbling houses, and compromised urban services (Sarlo 2000: 122).

Habana Vieja: The Future of the Past

The construction of anonymous suburbs, the proliferation of insipid commercial buildings, the empty gaps and peripheral areas occupied

by spontaneous settlements of unemployed and impoverished migrants, dispel the image of the city of its primitive coherence and
formal and spatial unity which it preserved ... during the colonial
period. (Segre 1989: 159)

Ironically, the origins of the nostalgic impulse for the conservationist's
recuperación of the "old" Spanish American Havana arose in the aftermath of
its definitive decline. The signal events that inspired this renaissance were the
U.S. intervention in Cuba's second war of independence with Spain (1895–
1898), which brought an end to the colonial era (if not full independence), and
the establishment of a new, North American–inspired center of power just
outside the city wall, in an area known as the Prado, and subsequently in the
garden city suburb of Vedado. It was only with the urbanization of the area
created by the gradual demolition of the city walls beginning in the late nineteenth century and the urbanization of the area left in their wake that a gradual awareness emerged of the difference between the "new" and the "old" city
(Venegas Fornias 1990). It was in this context that the past of old Havana began to be conceived of as belonging to a different realm, one which "validated
and exalted" the present and deserved to be preserved as an emblem "of community identity, continuity and aspiration" (Lowenthal 1988: xvi).

Founded in 1519 on the shores of a large, well-protected harbor, the early
settlement of San Cristobal de la Habana initially developed as a gathering
point for transatlantic shipments between Europe and the New World. For
the first two and half centuries of its existence, it remained a compact, fortified enclave focused on maritime trade rather than on the development of its
hinterlands.[1] Given this form of dependent urbanization, the city developed
at a gradual pace with an irregular pattern of growth along streets and plazas
that failed to conform to the Laws of the Indies (Salinas et al. 1971: 13). As in
other Spanish American colonial cities, the hierarchy of church and state in
Havana was encoded in this spatial arrangement through the insertion of
government buildings, churches, and convents in plazas as public spaces that
exercised ideological and political control over its inhabitants.

Beginning in the late eighteenth century, a new pattern of urbanization
was fueled by the development of vast sugar and coffee plantations in the
rural hinterlands, transforming the city into a major commercial and symbolic center. During this formative period, the streets inside the walled city
were laid out in an ordered grid-shaped pattern; public buildings, theaters,
and markets were built; and the new sugar aristocracy began constructing

monumental baroque palaces around the principal plazas and squares with columned archways. In keeping with this new residential form, the nuclear family became socially stratified, with the original family unit now augmented by administrators, servants, and slaves occupying different levels of the colonial household.

As previously noted, the gradual demolition of the city walls after 1863 and the insertion of North American capital gave rise to a new pattern of monumental urbanization in the area left in the wall's wake. This "new" Havana, which eclipsed the "old" one, was characterized by a plethora of architectural styles (neo-Gothic, Baroque, Beaux Arts, Eclectic, Art Nouveau) that created a "style without style" (Carpentier 1970), while portions of the old city were rebuilt from the ground up (Venegas Fornias 1990).

In the twentieth century, the gradual decline of the "old" Havana was hastened by the subdivision of the old colonial aristocracy's residences to house an influx of rural migrants, and the shift of government and administrative functions outside the city center. The dense concentrations of poverty in the center became a source of speculative pressure in the 1950s as the dictator Fulgencio Batista planned to demolish major portions of the "old" Havana to build high-rise apartments, offices, and roadways and to connect the rest of the city to the previously undeveloped lands in *Habana del Este*. These plans were interrupted by the victory of Fidel Castro's 26th of July Movement in 1959 and subsequent flight of Batista to the United States.

The U.S. occupation of Cuba and modernization of areas outside the city walls gave impetus to a new class of intellectuals who felt nostalgia for the old Havana. In the labyrinth of narrow streets and passageways of this "other" Havana, they were able to detect an "ideal" city, in spite of continuous modifications to the area in the twentieth century. Foremost among these was the American-trained architect Joaquín Emilio Weiss y Sánchez, author of the first compendium of colonial architecture in Cuba (1996). Weiss conferred particular status on colonial architecture, believing that a "revolutionary sensibility" could best be achieved by constructing a "univocal linkage" between the architectures of the colonial past, of the present, and of the future (Lizardi n.d.: 6). These views were carried over to the present era by one of Weiss's disciples, Eusebio Leal Spengler, the current city historian, and head of the *Oficina del Historiador de la Ciudad de la Habana* (OHCH), the entrepreneurial state agency charged by the Cuban government with restoring Habana Vieja. In Spengler's view, the colonial architecture of Habana Vieja "reveals the invisible soul of the country" and a process of transculturation that is "imprinted on the character of the people who inhabit it" (Guerra 1999: 5; Rodríguez Alomá and Ochoa Alomá 1999: 20).

*   *   *

What is significant about this history of "old" Havana for thinking about downtowns, then, is that the primacy of Habana Vieja as the symbolic center of the city was eclipsed in the twentieth century first by the zone of neo-republican expansion outside the city walls and later, in the 1950s, by the emergence of two new symbolic centers: one a modernist high-rise, exclusive commercial and hotel district called La Rampa in the northern Vedado district and the other, to the south, a ceremonial administrative center constructed by Batista named the Plaza Civica (renamed the Plaza de la Revolución after 1959).

The neglect of "old" Havana was continued by a future-oriented Revolution for which historic conservation stood in tension with the desire to create a radically new society based on the values of egalitarianism and collective solidarity embodied in Che Guevara's *Hombre Nuevo* (that is, New Socialist Man). The centrality of the old colonial urban core as the center or downtown of the city was lost in the twentieth century, and would be regained, in the new millennium, only through the work of urban conservationists. Urban centrality, then, like the historicity of the built environment, is not something that is given, but has to be produced through differently scaled political actors and discursive practices such as heritage, or patrimony, as it is more commonly referred to in Latin America.

UNESCO and the World Heritage Grid

Given the historic rupture with the colonial past, the sudden shift in temporal horizons from the future orientation of the Revolution to the engagement and identification with the colonial past that characterizes Cuba today requires explanation. Where heritage conservation was a secondary priority in the revolutionary context, it has become one of the defining characteristics of the late socialist period. On an island of 12 million people, there are now nine UNESCO World Heritage sites, five of which are located in urban settings (Habana Vieja, Santiago, Trinidad, Cienfuegos, and Camaguey). Seven of these sites have been nominated since the 1989 collapse of the

Soviet Union, and six of those in the past decade. Over a million heritage tourists now pass through Habana Vieja annually, and the heritage tourism is an important source of hard currency for the national budget. The discourse of patrimony has been taken up across a range of social domains, from daily conversations, to reader's letters (known as *cartas abiertas*, or "open letters") published in the official press, to community development centers (*talleres integrales*) that operate in local barrios. How has this shift in temporalities come about, and what role has it played in apotheosis of the colonial urban core as the symbolic pole of national belonging?

In the case of Habana Vieja, as I have argued elsewhere (Hill 2007), the heritage assemblage is composed of differently scaled actors that articulate with one another in revalorizing the meaning and value of the site as cultural patrimony. These include international heritage organizations like UNESCO and its subsidiary organization ICOMOS, the socialist state, heritage conservationists, transnational tourism developers, and the people who reside and work in the site. In view of this range of social actors in historical perspective, a great deal of work needed to be accomplished to "condition the possibility" for Habana Vieja to become a World Heritage Site. Each of these actors is involved in reterritorializing Habana Vieja as a heritage site. And yet these multiple territorializations do not legitimate one set of interpretations of a site to the exclusion of another. Rather, the heritage assemblage "makes room for them all" (Breglia 2006 50).

Foremost among the actors engaged in the reterritorialization of Habana Vieja is UNESCO and its World Heritage Convention. Through its designation, cataloging, and monitoring of natural, cultural, and "mixed" heritage sites of "outstanding universal value" around the globe, and the addition of those sites to its World Heritage List, UNESCO is engaged in constituting a global imaginary that comprises a "global heritage grid" (Hill 2007). On an international plane, UNESCO's discourse about places like Habana Vieja reterritorializes by disembedding sites from their concrete locations within the boundaries of local, regional, and national meanings and policies, and reattaching them to UNESCO's World Heritage program and its notions of "universal cultural value" (Breglia 2006:50; cf. Turtinen 2000). State parties to the World Heritage Convention (WHC) elect to participate in this reterritorialization project by agreeing to fulfill a number of responsibilities, including the creation of the "appropriate legal, scientific, technical, administrative and financial measures necessary for the identification, protection, conservation, presentation and rehabilitation of this heritage" (UNESCO 1972:3). They must also adopt the transnational grammar of UNESCO, which universalizes and standardizes cultural, natural, and "mixed" heritage sites across the globe through clearly defined rules, procedures, and actors that play specific roles.

UNESCO's Operational Guidelines form the lynchpin of this grammar, designating the criteria that are used to judge what constitutes "outstanding universal value" and is thus worthy of inclusion on UNESCO's World Heritage List. By selecting sites, defining their outstanding universal qualities, and justifying their inclusion on the World Heritage List, state parties participate in the reterritorialization of local, regional, and national sites within a transnational framework. This process of reterritorialization is not a mere semantic process. It adds global recognition that sets up tourism flows, raises visibility, and ultimately adds tourism revenues to state coffers. The heightened cache of World Heritage objects was not lost on the director of one of Old Havana's main conservation institutions. In response to a question about the importance of the World Heritage designation for Havana's historic center, he commented: "[World Heritage] is very prestigious, an honor. It's the possibility to attract more tourism, to sell more books. It's the possibility for the university to say, come to [Old Havana] to study architecture because [Old Havana] is World Heritage. . . . I believe that World Heritage (*patrimonio mundial*) has been turned into a type of small flag of identity, and people have made a kind of business out of it." Old Havana's 1982 nomination as a World Heritage site offered a source of pride and commercial gain for the state and the Cuban conservation community. But it also relocated Habana Vieja as a universal value on a global circuit that included the most important wonders of the world. Invoking this circuit, the previously mentioned director went on to note, "When we say that [Old] Havana is World Heritage (Patrimonio de la Humanidad), we say that Habana Vieja is on a cultural level with the Pyramids of Egypt or Athens."

What gets pulled out and valued vis-à-vis UNESCO's criteria of outstanding universal value in Habana Vieja is a highly aestheticized and bounded image of an elite cosmopolitan colonial city. The justification for inclusion of the site, which is entitled "Habana Vieja and Its Fortifications," focuses on four of the five principal plazas in Old Havana, a nineteenth-century zone of late colonial expansion outside the city walls, and a series of adjacent fortifications (ICOMOS 1982). Even though the heritage site is a geographic space that includes all the land within the former walled city and its immediate environs, the list of monuments included with the designation concentrates on the monumental political, military, ecclesiastical, and residential architecture of what one conservationist called the eighteenth- and nineteenth-century "palace Havana." Excluded from the list are vernacular elements—tenements, warehouses, docks, industry, red light districts—that played an important role in the history of the district. Even though the working-class neighborhoods on the southern part of the Habana Vieja are of great antiquity, their history is not invoked in UNESCO's description of this cultural property as "an interesting mix of baroque and neo-classical monuments, and homogenous ensemble of civilian houses with arcades, balconies, wrought-iron gates, and interior courtyards."[2] Also excluded are the extramural barrios of Colon, Guadalupe, and Jesús María that formed an integral part of the colonial urban fabric. Finally, nonwhite Cubans who constitute the majority of Habana Vieja residents today are largely constructed as "outsiders" to the heritage narrative, negating the heterogeneous character of the actual colonial city.

Building the Heritage Landscape: The OHCH

While UNESCO and its transnational grammar are involved in reterritorializing local sites around the planet within the circuits that constitute the global heritage grid, the heritage practices of states and conservation authorities do the work of bounding, naming, marking, and regulating the urban landscape so that it can be known and recognized as an "authentic" heritage object. This work of bounding and marking what conservationists refer to as immovable heritage, that is, monuments that are too large to be collected, transported, and displayed in museums, enables them to nevertheless be "collected" in the sense of being possessed by a state agency such as the Oficina del Historiador de la Habana (OHCH), which has the power to reframe and enclose them (Errington 1993: 44). As Shelly Errington notes, this power of enclosing does different work for the national government and for the tourists who visit monumental sites. For the national government, such enclosure nationalizes the site, placing itself in charge, while also constructing an image of the nation for external consumption. For the tourist, the process of enclosure makes the monument knowable, transforming it into a "musem and art object simultaneously" (44).

In Old Havana, the OHCH is the powerful conservation agency that was charged by the socialist state in 1994 with the responsibility of conserving and restoring the Centro Histórico and turning it into a profitable tourist destination. To enable the OHCH to carry out this mandate, the state endowed it with extraordinary powers that are highly unusual in socialist Cuba. It transferred control over the heritage zone "in usufruct" for a period of twenty-five years, and effectively transformed the OHCH into "the zoning authority, the planning board, housing authority, parks commissioner, tax collector, comptroller and final arbiter of nearly every public investment decision" in Habana Vieja (Peters 2001). It also gave the OHCH the power to self-finance the restoration, by enabling it to operate hotels, restaurants, museums, real estate, and other for-profit entities, and to sign joint venture contracts independent of the normal channels approved by the Cuban Ministry of Foreign Investment (Scarpaci 2000).

Through these powers, the OHCH is directly involved in reterritorializing Habana Vieja through the production of an essentialized and homogenized landscape that is placed in the service of creating an authentic tourist experience (Silverman 2002: 887). To foreground this activity, I highlight here three interrelated sets of heritage practices that are central to the building or production of the centralized heritage space in Old Havana. First among these are practices of bounding and naming that turn the Historic Center into a distinct space, while cordoning it off from areas that fail to fit into the heritage frame. Second, I show how OHCH planners work to give the heritage zone a historical cast by selectively highlighting architectural features that index the colonial period, while removing others that fail to fit in this frame of reference. And finally, I show how heritage practices seek to grant the heritage zone a kind of coherence as a colonial city, by excluding social elements and memories that do not fit with this view of the past. In analyzing heritage as a space that is produced by practices, I move beyond notions of heritage as a thing or artifact which is given a priori, and merely in need of dusting off. Rather, I show how heritage practices such as laws, zoning regulations, and physical manipulation of the built environment transform not only space, but social relationships and ideals about the meaning of national identity.

Nationalizing Habana Vieja: Bounding and Naming

I illustrate the practices of bounding and naming by describing a zoning map that is taken from the master plan for Old Havana, the Plan de Desarrollo

Integral (the Integral Development Plan, Rodríguez Alomá 1996: 13). The map is an instance of what urban geographer Henri Lefebvre calls a *representation of space*, an abstract or conceptual view of space that exists in the mind of the technocrat (urban planner, scientist, engineer, and so on). Whether signs, maps, or codes, representations of space seek to order space and spatial practice in ways that are tied to a given mode of production such as heritage tourism (1991: 33–39). The intent of the zoning map is to separate residential from tourism areas. The zoning map points to the difficulty that planners face in producing a coherent heritage narrative and image in a "complex, heterogeneous, living city" like Habana Vieja (Silverman 2002: 884). To produce a sense of coherence, the zoning map seeks to "selectively highlight and ideologically structure reality" (892) by confining visitors to "tourist sectors" that possess the most monumental forms of colonial architecture—plazas, cathedrals, monasteries, government buildings, customs houses, defensive fortresses—and routing them through "view" corridors whose building façades have been revitalized to appear as nineteenth-century shops. Tourists who walk away from this official route, even by so much as one block, are greeted by an entirely different reality, the "residential sectors"—overcrowded tenements in need of paint and repair, the remains of collapsed buildings, and manufacturing and auto repair shops.

These zoning categories in turn form a part of the Regulaciones Urbanísticas (Urban Regulations) that establish "norms and principles" that are to "guide construction urbanism and land use decisions in the prioritized conservation zone" (Reg. Art. 1). In the case of tourism sectors, *usos permitidos* (permitted uses) include cultural, culinary, hospitality, recreational, commercial, business, and financial activities (Reg. Art. 281)—all service-based functions that are transacted in dollars and geared toward tourists. *Usos incompatibles* (incompatible uses) include public services stores, bakeries, butcher shops, *puntas de leche* (milk distribution stations), health centers, gymnasiums, laundries, dry cleaners, tailor's shops, daycare centers, handicapped schools, fire stations, and funeral homes (Reg. Art. 282) as well as industrial uses such as warehouses, loading docks, auto garages, and manufacturing that are to be eradicated, transferred to residential sectors, or moved out of the prioritized zone altogether (Reg. Art. 273). As representations of space, maps and zoning codes move from the mind of the planner to the attempt at organizing what Lefebvre calls *spatial practice*, or the way that people move through and use space. For instance, the busloads of tourists that daily arrive on organized tours of the historic center are met by tour guides who lead them on an hour-long journey through the principal squares and restored buildings that dot the interstitial connecting streets of the old historic nucleus. Tour guides point out to tourists what to see, while narrating how they should see it. They also seek to organize *representational space*, or the way that space is lived and experienced by tourists through (folkloric) images and symbolic meanings that "spill into contemporary lived experience" (1991: 38–39; Breglia 2006 32).

Sector maps and zoning categories that divide and differentiate people and uses then take on a life of their own through spatial practices that turn buildings into monuments in tourism zones, or that police the boundary between residential and tourism areas. One such boundary is a virtual checkpoint at the intersection of Obispo and San Ignacio Streets, where the Obispo pedestrian corridor feeds into the old historic nucleus. Two policemen are perennially stationed at this intersection, where they can be found checking the national ID cards of young Afro-Cuban males in a ritualized routine that is intended to discourage access to the zone. The ID checks and plainclothed policemen who circulate through the tourism configure Afro-Cubans as "dangerous backdrops" (Collins 2008: 295) to the folkloricized areas.[3] Such racially coded practices that also restrict access to tourism sectors and hotels reintroduce the separation of tourist and residential areas.

One other form of bounding that is exemplified by the zoning map is the separation of the UNESCO World Heritage district—Habana *intramuros* and a zone of early republican expansion beyond the city walls—from the rest of the colonial city. In this respect, the UNESCO district presents an artificial view of the colonial city, masking the fact that the neighborhoods surrounding the walls (Colon, Guadalupe, Jesús María) have been incrementally built and blended into the walled city area since the late eighteenth century. The continuity between these neighborhoods and the UNESCO district is further reinforced by the fact that the city walls took many years to complete, and decades more to demolish. Further unifying the two areas are the "cemeteries, hospitals, rest homes, markets, leper colonies, parishes, jails and light industry" outside the city walls that serviced the intramural population (Scarpaci, Segre, and Coyula 2002: 317). Universal building codes and land use regulations ensured the continuity of architectural forms between the two areas throughout the eighteenth and nineteenth centuries (317). In this respect, the UNESCO district creates an artificial break between the two halves of colonial Havana, excluding 1,000 to 2,000 hectares of architecture that grew up outside the city walls. It also names the bounded heritage space, that is, the Centro Histórico, giving it a specificity that it previously lacked.

Selectively Highlighting the Colonial Past

A second aspect of producing a heritage space in Habana Vieja involves the selective highlighting of the physical landscape in ways that give it a colonial cast. In Habana Vieja this is exemplified through the "scraping away" of layers such as republican-era features that fail to fit in the heritage frame, and the creation of new layers that create the appearance of continuity with the colonial past. An example of the former practice is exemplified by the removal of the underground parking structure in Old Havana's Plaza Vieja with which I introduced this article. The new enclosed fountain and "the edge-perching transience" (Silverman 2002) of tourists and residents illustrate the transformation of the Plaza Vieja from a space of public use to a ceremonial space constructed for the "tourist gaze" (Urry 1990). Other transformations to the plaza contribute to the processes of interiorization and embourgeoisification aimed at producing a controlled environment and excluding marginal elements—hustlers, prostitutes, street kids, flâneurs—that fail to fit in the frame.[4] For instance, in the redesigned plaza, the former park benches were removed and replaced with new security features that reinforced the colonial image. In their place, forms of defensive architecture such as heavy metal cannons and chains were installed at the four entrances to the plaza, and metal bollards along its perimeter, prohibiting vehicular traffic from entering the frame and disrupting the image. A police station was also set up in the former printing shop of a ground floor apartment building after a rash of purse snatchings threatened the security of tourists in the newly remade colonial square.

Apart from the practices of "creative destruction" that remove unwanted elements from the heritage landscape, conservationists also create new layers that accentuate the image of the colonial past. For instance, after an eighteenth-century merchant's house collapsed while awaiting restoration in 1993, conservationists reconstructed a replica of the original from the ground up (Hill 2007). The imitation of the original is so convincing that it has become one of the most photographed buildings by unsuspecting tourists in the Plaza Vieja. The practice of replacing neoclassical façades with more traditional design elements—fan-shaped windows, Persian blinds, balconies, iron latticework, and tile roofs—is another means through which layers are added to existing buildings to bring them into alignment with the image of a colonial landscape (Capablanca 1983: 27). Color is also strictly regulated throughout the old city, with buildings painted in the ubiquitous yellow with blue and white doors and balconies to create the effect of uniformity.

But the creation of "new layers" is not limited to the practice of building replicas and other simulacra. Other undesirable architectural features are also covered over to make them invisible. An example of the latter practice can be found in a massive modernist structure known as the "Ministry of Education" building, for the government ministry that occupied it until the mid-1990s. The last remains of the Convent of San Juan de Letrán, the site of Havana's first university, were demolished in 1956 to make way for this con-temporary structure, which separates Old Havana's two most visited plazas, the Plaza de las Armas and the Plaza de la Catedral. Covering an entire city block, the green and white building was built according to the modernist codes of the Wiener-Sert plan for Old Havana, and housed the city's first he-licopter terminal on its rooftop. Conservationists frequently lament the loss of the original university, which according to the city historian of the period "was united with the history of the city and Cuban culture" (Roig de Leuch-senring 1963: 175).

Accentuating the university's importance, his successor, the current city historian, has referred to the building as the "cradle of the [Cuban] En-lightenment, and formation of the Cuban intelligentsia." After a debate in which it was decided that it would be too costly to demolish the new Minis-try of Education building, the decision was made to cover it with reflective glass. A descriptive panel on the outside of the structure describes the pur-pose of the reflective glass, which is "to transform the skin of the building, in order to return it to the city with an appearance that is different from the one that to date has generated so much controversy, and as a sign of the in-tense concern (*la vital inquietud*) with activities that have transformed the appearance of the former city." It adds that "contemporary materials will be used to re-create the image of some of the iconographic elements of the for-mer convent-university, such as the original bell tower, the entrance, and the patio and nave of the church." Such modernist practices of creating new layers that are superimposed on the existing built environment play as im-portant a role in the process of selective highlighting as the practices of scraping away modern accretions that are evident in the case of the underground parking structure in the Plaza Vieja. Scraping away and the creation of new layers then are heritage practices that attempt to overcome the "progressive disarticulation of the urban landscape" (Geertz 1989: 293).

Excluding Memories from the Heritage Frame

In order to grant the heritage space a certain type of coherence as a colonial city, conservationists work to exclude social elements and memories that fail to fit within the heritage frame. Obispo Street, the main pedestrian tourism corridor connecting the historic nucleus and the Paseo del Prado, provides a good example of this type of social exclusion. Obispo was historically one of Havana's principal commercial streets. But throughout the 1980s and 1990s, its stores, like those in the rest of the city, were devoid of commerce. Beginning in the late 1990s, though, the OHCH began to restore the street to its former glory, lining it with relatively fancy dollar shops. The stores were given names of nineteenth-century boutiques and shops—La Francia, Le Palais Royal, and El Almendares—that were meant to conjure images of a boulevard in Paris or London. Period signs posted on the outside of the stores reinforced this transnational imagination of "Parisian" Havana, carrying images of European commodities (Baccarat glassware, fine eyewear, imported clothing) that enabled one to experience—"see, smell, feel"—an "imported modernity that is pretheoretical and synaesthetic" (Guano 2002: 193). This was in spite of the fact that the dollar stores actually offered a disorganized jumble of eclectic fare—Chinese refrigerators, Japanese TVs, and Phillips stereo systems crammed together with cheap imitations of brand-name jeans, sport shirts, frying pans, women's lingerie, lipstick, and deodorant. The use of naming practices throughout the principal tourism zones then contributes to the construction of an essentialized and homogenized past that creates the "authenticity" of Old Havana.

Excluded from this frame are signs and symbols that code Cuba as a socialist country, images that might disrupt the heritage frame. For instance, in 2002, only four shops remained on Obispo Street that continued to offer goods and services to ordinary Cubans in pesos, the local currency. These included a bookstore displaying copies of Marx ahora (Marx Today), a vintage tailor's shop, a women's hair salon with cracked ceiling tiles, and a feria, or five-and-dime shop, with an old-fashioned soda fountain, swivel stools, and mostly empty glass display cases. The latter featured a curious assort-ment of cheap domestic goods—spare bike parts, toy lighthouses, place-mats, cleaning solvents, cooking pots, plastic strainers, trays with a gaudy flower motif—illuminated under eerily glowing fluorescent lights. Similarly removed from the tourist zone are revolutionary events, such as a youth march that I observed just outside the tourism zone in Habana Vieja in 2002. The march consisted of a group of schoolchildren known as *Pioneros* (Pioneers), dressed in signature red and white uniforms and blue bandanas. The children carried a banner that read, *La libertad es lo mas grande de pueblos y hombres. Es mejor morir que pederla* ("Liberty is the greatest value of nations and peoples. It's better to die than to lose it"). Such revolutionary enactments are nowhere to be found in the tourist zone, together with propa-ganda billboards plastered with revolutionary slogans—*Aquí no queremos amos* (Here we will have no masters"), *Con Cuba, con Fidel y el socialismo* ("With Cuba, with Fidel, and socialism"), and *Socialismo o muerte* ("Social-ism or death")—that dot the streets of the rest of the city.

A walk along Obispo Street offers a glimpse of another form of social exclusion. As you make your way past period bars with names like Café Paris, Lluvia del Oro, and La Dichosa, you see Cubans peering in through the metal grates that separate these open-air venues from the street. Inside, white male European tourists often accompanied by Cuban women known as *jineteras* listen to Cuban *conjuntos* that play traditional tourist music like "Guantanamara" and the wistful refrains of Comandante Che Guevara. While the lack of access to dollars accounts in large part for this segregation of hosts and guests, except for relationships of convenience, it also invokes differences of culture.

Daniel, a local musician who plays Rumba, a percussive style of Afro-Cuban folkloric music that he dubbed *música del solar* or music of the tenements, offered commentary on this form of social exclusion. During a well-publicized visit of the governor of Illinois, George Ryan, in the fall of 1999, Daniel was playing with his *conjunto* in one of the main plazas when the governor and his entourage passed by. Although the city historian, who was leading the prominent visitors on a tour, encouraged the group to keep going, Ryan requested that they stop and listen. Before departing, members of the entourage showered the group with tips of $20 and $100 bills. Daniel's *conjunto* was subsequently denied permission to play in the plazas or tourist bars of the heritage district, which he interpreted as a form of discrimina-tion based on his style of music and its Afro-Cuban origins. As Daniel put it, "the *jefes* [managers] of these bars don't want this music in their clubs because they don't want them filled with blacks dancing [*sic*], and lots of noise." He went on to suggest that only *música septeto de turismo* or "whitened" forms of Cuban music acceptable to tourists, such as the son, salsa, and guaracha, were encouraged in the tourism sector. This stands in contrast with music like the rumba, which is linked to the lower classes, and the *rumbero*, who "tries to cultivate a happy life in the face of nothing." Rumba, in other words, is a kind of barrio music that cuts across the grain of the heritage space, producing a disjuncture that marks its practitioners as outsiders.

Conclusion

Although I have focused primarily on the reterritorializing practices of UNESCO and the OHCH, other forms of territorialization compete with conservationists' efforts to enforce a centralized and unified colonial history and identity in Old Havana. The constant references by the city historian to the need for residents to "respect" the heritage, and to allow only those who "love the environment" and "would die of sadness if they were forced to leave" to reside in this "overpopulated sector," point to the underlying social tensions involved in creating a heritage space in the midst of a heterogeneous living city (Molina 1993). Related calls for a modern police force that is "known by the people" and "equipped with the latest technology" to prevent future incidents with "pickpockets" (*rateros*) and "thieves" (*rapiñadores*) highlight underlying tensions over the meaning of Habana Vieja as a place.

The difficulty of constructing a coherent heritage landscape in Habana Vieja, unlike carefully controlled, museum-like environments such as Colonial Williamsburg, is that Habana Vieja is situated in a complex, heterogeneous, lived urban space. Yet the ability to manage the colonial image is accentuated by the control that the OHCH, its team of architects and urban planners, and ultimately Eusebio Leal himself are able to exercise over this heritage site. The OHCH's management of the past extends to every facet of the old city, from the design of building façades and the color of paint to decisions about what to restore and what to tear down, to the naming of hotels and restaurants, enterprises, and shops, and ultimately to the name of the city itself, known variously as Centro Histórico, Habana Profunda, Habana *Mística*, Patriomonio Mundial, and Patrimonio de la Nación. An illustrative *chiste* (joke), which circulated in the streets, captures the power of

Eusebio Leal to determine the image of Old Havana. In it, a group of architects and planners trail in the wake of Eusebio Leal's shadow as he walks through the old city, jotting down his every request for a hotel here, a restaurant there, and a museum over there.

The reterritoralization of Habana Vieja, then, involves the "traditionalization" of a densely settled, diverse, and multifaceted urban space, and its reorganization around the diffuse idea of an "authentic" Spanish colonial town. As a heritage landscape, it consists of a simplified set of spatial perspectives, objects, and discourses that taken together are presented as the suprahistorical embodiment of tradition, history, and identity in the context of the built environment. Although presented as "natural," that is, the living instantiation of 500 years of colonial history, what counts as "tradition" has in fact been carefully produced through a set of emergent institutions, particularly the OHCH, and the discourse that surrounds them. The focus, then, of this analysis has been on the process of selecting and organizing itself, rather than the inherited goods (buildings, monuments, people) that are said to comprise the heritage per se, and on the way in which this process of selection and simultaneous erasure emerges in relationship to the OHCH, its range of commercial enterprises, and the discourses that surround them (Dorst 1989: 129). Taken together, these discourses and practices have transformed Habana Vieja into a new colonial center of power, which has symbolically replaced the modernist commercial Americanized downtown constructed around the Havana Hilton and the La Rampa movie theater in the 1950s. Thus the centrality of the city has shifted, setting up a new set of continuities between Cuba and a globalized European colonial past, in lieu of a problematic, "pseudo-republican," North American one.

PART III

Conflict

9

Utopia/Dystopia: Art and Downtown Development in Los Angeles

Marina Peterson

I think you can't find any city in the world today, in world history, that doesn't have a vibrant center. A place where people from all communities can come together and be in one place. If you don't do that you end up with a divided city. I like seeing lots of people speaking different languages. It feels good.

—Eli Broad, *LosAngelesNow*

A Note on Downtown . . .
. . . because that is all downtown Los Angeles deserves
—Reyner Banham, *Los Angeles: The Architecture of Four Ecologies*

The day began and ended with the LAPD. A morning interview with the captain of the Central City Division of the Los Angeles Police Department extended into the afternoon as I was introduced to one and then another police officer, the last the head of the beat patrol for the Skid Row area, on a mission to defend policing tactics against what he described as attacks by "activists." An interview moved into a walk around Skid Row during which, he assured me, I could ask people anything I wanted. On the street, however, he would approach homeless people he knew and ask them, "What did it used to look like down here? There were a lot of people on the sidewalk?

What were they doing? What does it look like now? Have you witnessed any police brutality?" One woman stood in the street close to the sidewalk, seemingly unaware of the flattened dead rat lying in the gutter whose tail she was stepping on; she said yes, there had been more people here before, and then described how the police had been rounding people up, moving them away. To further convey the import of the work of the police on Skid Row, the police officer took me back to the station to show me photos he had taken. Documenting crime, they showed bags of marijuana laid out in rows, a woman with blood caked on the side of her head, a man affiliated with the aforementioned "activist" group selling knives on a blanket on the sidewalk.

Working under the auspices of the Mayor's Safer Cities Initiative, implemented as a Broken Windows (Kelling and Wilson 1982) policing strategy, the police on Skid Row were involved in a project of clearing the sidewalks of homeless people by targeting what they referred to as "quality of life" crimes.[1] As the police captain explained, these included things such as "possession of a coke pipe, drinking in public, littering, walking against the red light, walking in the middle of the road" (Wakefield, personal communication). Later that evening, after interviewing Gronk, artist and longtime resident of downtown Los Angeles, and visiting the Museum of Contemporary Art on Bunker Hill, I made my way back to Fifth and Spring for a presentation organized by Los Angeles Poverty Department (LAPD), a theater group based on Skid Row. *Glimpses of Utopia: 8-15* was the second in a series *UTOPIA/Dystopia,* so titled because, as LAPD's director John Malpede stated, "One person's utopia is another person's dystopia."

The work of both LAPDs marked a moment of transformation in downtown Los Angeles, which at the turn of the twenty-first century was in the midst of extensive redevelopment organized around the arts. Now clearly urban development organized around art rather than an urban process driven by artists, this dynamic taps into a recognizable trend by using art in the service of real estate investment and capital expansion in the city center (Burayidi 2001; Florida 2004; Ford 2003; Frieden and Sagalyn 1989; Jonas and Wilson 1999; Lees, Slater, and Wyly 2008; Logan and Molotch 2007; N. Smith 1996; N. Smith and Williams 1986; Solnit and Schwartzenberg 2000; Whitt 1987; Zukin 1982, 1995). Moreover, it has been a key element in efforts to make downtown Los Angeles a center for the city. With an eye to New York, Chicago, San Francisco, Barcelona, London, or Paris, Angelenos create downtown in the image of other idealized cities. Neighborhoods like Soho, public space such as the Ramblas, cosmopolitanism experienced in

European metropoles—experiences of walking in cities, shopping, and being a tourist all play into desires for the future of downtown Los Angeles. With downtown figured as a synecdoche for the city, such transformations, it is argued, will make it a center for the city and make Los Angeles a "real" city. To be a "real" city—a pedestrian-friendly, 24/7 city with a centralizing downtown—would mean Los Angeles was more like other cities.

Renowned as the home of globalized media production, Los Angeles has also been called the "capital of the Third World" (Rieff 1991; see also Davis 1992; Soja 1996; Wolch and Dear 1993). Also exemplary of neoliberal global-ization, in 2000 the income gap and poverty rate in Los Angeles exceeded those of the nation as a whole (Institute for the Study of Homelessness and Poverty 2003a, 2003b). This inequality has long been made visible by the pres-ence of the largest homeless population of any city in the United States, long concentrated in the downtown area designated as Skid Row, directly adjacent to the new lofts and galleries.[2] The convergence of the particular processes at play in downtown Los Angeles is unique to the city at the same time that it reflects an emergent dynamic that is part of what positions downtowns as sig-nificant sites in global city formation. Informed by what are now international trends, the particularities of their instantiation in downtown Los Angeles are part of a story that is enacted on a daily basis by politicians, planners, develop-ers, residents, and visitors. Contributing, thus, to globalization, these everyday practices are at once specific to a locale and informed by, part of, and produc-tive of global processes (Keil 1998; Short and Kim 1999; M. Smith 2001).[3]

Generalizing tendencies of globalization make it such that practices and negotiations over the nature of downtown often appear as specifically local. Neoliberal capital investment with a thrust toward profit and privatization, an increasing class divide with homeless and immigrants as the disenfran-chised, and large-scale gentrification are construed as specific to the present and future of downtown Los Angeles. In downtown Los Angeles, art does much of this work of globalization by providing a basis for global compari-sons as well as masking social relations and power dynamics. With art as the border marking inclusion and exclusion, efforts around housing, ameni-ties, and galleries have fixated on a divide between new residents and the homeless, granting authority, rights, and membership to some and not others. Displacement of existing, poor residents has ensued through the redevelop-ment of residential hotels into loft buildings, policing tactics directed to-ward homeless people, and general efforts made to remove poor people and their lifestyle markers from downtown Los Angeles. Hence a symbolic art economy that situates the downtown redevelopment of Los Angeles on the scale of the global has supported urban development projects structured around political struggles over bodies in space (Keil 1998; Lefebvre 1996; Marcuse and van Kempen 2000; Sassen 2000; M. Smith 2001). Art and performance projects by Skid Row residents mark a space of critical engagement with these terms and conditions.

Downtown as Center

Los Angeles is famously decentralized, renowned for sprawl and freeways, for public life lived in cars and shopping malls rather than on sidewalks or in parks. Urban theorists, planners, and boosters have emphasized the form and image of a decentralized Los Angeles for the latter part of the twentieth century (Banham 1971; Dear 1986, 2000, 2002b; Dear, Schockman, and Hise 1996; Fogelson 1993; Garreau 1991; Soja 1996). For many Angelenos, downtown is just another neighborhood in a city of neighborhoods, described alternately as meaning nothing in particular and as exciting. Yet from within the area bounded by the freeways on the north, west, and south and by the river on the east, downtown takes on immense importance. For those politicians, business owners, developers, and residents invested in its present and future, discussions tinged with an air of urgency and import suggest that downtown Los Angeles is a world unto itself, singular in its significance for the city.

In an article that helped launch the Los Angeles School of urbanists at the end of the 1980s, Edward W. Soja and Allen J. Scott (1986) noted the nascent downtown revitalization of Los Angeles, suggesting that "the development of downtown Los Angeles provides a magnified model of similar experiences in other cities around the country" caused by the "gap between the low actual levels of downtown development and the potentially high profits to be realized from investment in central city property and land" (252–53), and that "the historical geography of downtown development in Los Angeles is likely to be a major focus for urban research for many years to come" (253). Shortly after publication, a global economic recession resulted in a decline in downtown real estate investment. Interest in stirrings in the vacated downtown fell to the wayside as Los Angeles as a model of urban sprawl and decentralization made it and its scholars famous (Davis 1992; Dear, Schockman, and Hise 1996; Scott 2000; Soja 1996). Few since have taken up their charge of considering downtown as a subject of research. Yet recent redevelopment projects are part of an active effort to make downtown a center for the region, complicating the now dominant model of Los Angeles as "sprawling, decentered, polymorphic, and centrifugal" (Soja 1996: 296–97).

Defined as prototypical of an urban form of sprawl and decentralization, Los Angeles is also paradigmatic of national and international trends of downtown decline and redevelopment over the course of the twentieth century. Until the mid-1920s, Los Angeles had a bustling downtown where "nearly half its residents went . . . every day" (Fogelson 2001: 2). Don, a resident of an artists' colony north of downtown, recalled going downtown in the 1940s to visit his father's clothing factories, shop at department stores, and attend first-run movies and variety shows. "There were a lot of good restaurants, all the movie theaters were open and had typically first run. They would have an hour, hour and a half performance, a variety show, dancing, singing, some stand up comedy, whatever. And then they would have the main feature, and typically it was a double bill and it was a first run. Complete with cartoons and newsreels." Downtown was then what current development aspires to create anew. Don continued, "I remember when it had a lot of foot traffic. A lot of people on foot. Pedestrian traffic. In downtown. My mom and I would go to Clifton's for lunch, which as a kid was my favorite place. It was like being in downtown Manhattan or downtown San Francisco in terms of foot traffic." In those days, he said, "It was a very vital place. Everyone came downtown" (personal communication). Similarly, in his piece *Lay of the Land*, performance artist Tim Miller describes going downtown for movie premiers as a young child.

A range of well-documented forces that included suburbanization, the popularity of the automobile, and a tire company buyout of the rail lines contributed to downtown's decline (Bottles 1987; Longstreth 1997; Wachs 1996). As Don recalled, "And of course the trolleys ran. We didn't usually take the trolley but we could, it was very easy transportation. Worst thing they ever did to this city was rip the trolley lines up. But it was very vital. And then after the war everyone got the bright idea they had to have a car, and they ripped out the trolley lines, and for awhile it became very inconvenient to be downtown, and then it became really rough and abandoned."

*   *   *

The City of Los Angeles hired its first urban planner around the time when downtown's significance began to wane. Gordon Whitnall, the first director of the City Planning Commission, called for a city that was "a co-ordination of many units" (qtd. in Fogelson 1993: 135), creating a vision of Los Angeles that reflected an emergent decentralization already apparent on the ground.

As those satellite communities gained the resources previously only available downtown, it was no longer necessary to go to Broadway or Seventh Street for shopping or movies. A new "downtown" of gleaming highrises was built on the West Side. The old downtown remained as the site for government and corporate activity, wholesale trades, and Skid Row. Yet even as the city sprawled, becoming a prototype for new theories of urban form such as "Edge City" (Garreau 1991) and "100-mile city" (Sudjic 1992), those invested in downtown redevelopment maintained that a centralized city is necessary to inspire proper urban civility.

Urban civility prescribes a normative person through associations with the aesthetic of the built environment, neighborhood structure, relative density, and living arrangements. Though related to class and habitus, I use civility to capture; organized around an understanding that a healthy social fabric is produced by individual and familial comportment that in turn is supported by urban structures. It is a mutually constituting dynamic integrating urban form with social identification, comportment, and membership. Inherently normative, it allows for social relations to be structured around any of its easily correlating elements, from neighborhood to housing to habitus (Bourdieu 1984; Boyer 1986; Elias 1994; Foucault 1990). As a normative ascription, urban civility is essentially bourgeois, with ideology and property interests bound up in each other. Hence, creating downtown as a center has entailed remaking it as a space hospitable for business and the middle class. Eliminating what the Community Redevelopment Agency/Los Angeles called "nefarious uses" from Main Street and introducing "stable, economically and socially sound commercial and other activities" would presumably support downtown's status as "the most significant area for positive change for the benefit of the entire metropolitan region of Greater Los Angeles" (1986: 12). At the same time, Robert Fogelson explains how downtown redevelopment projects have largely been motivated by business interests (2001). Beginning in the 1960s, plan after plan crafted by the City of Los Angeles and the Community Redevelopment Agency/Los Angeles argued for the revitalization of downtown on the basis of its vital role for both the symbolic and economic health of the region (Davis 2002; see also Department of City Planning 1972; Scott 1998, 2001).

For much of the twentieth century, a suburban model of urban form was presented as the basis for urban civility. The small units espoused by Whitnall, spread across the area yet connected to downtown by rail and later freeway, were understood to foster normative modes of subjectivity, family life, and community, "within each of which there shall be the most ideal living conditions, the most ideal conditions for business or industry, and yet with all of the individuality, with all of the characteristics and all of the ambitions that, after all, are the things that constitute real community spirit, real community pride, those things which can only be found, we discover, in the small unit that a person can intelligently comprehend" (qtd. in Fogelson 1993: 135).

Mel Scott's *Metropolitan Los Angeles: One Community* (1949) posits a suburban model of positive and proper modes of living as part of an argument for urban renewal in downtown Los Angeles. According to Scott, number of people per bedroom, size of rooms and housing lot, and neighborhood density all contribute to a person's relative morals and mental fitness. Prescribing homes with sufficient space and light, including bedrooms with fifty-five square feet of floor space per person and shared by no more than two people, Scott ultimately correlates democracy with neighborhood planning organized around an urban form of decentralization and suburbanization (1949: 100–105).

For those supporting the downtown development of Los Angeles, civility is ascribed to a centralized city, a city with a strong downtown. The desired appearance of this downtown evokes a combination of urban forms that resonate most clearly as a combination of Jane Jacobs's vision and New Urbanism, asserting that positive urban social relations are best fostered by density, diversity of use, and a vibrant street life. At the same time, suburbanization has imbued expectations for residential life, and new downtown residents expect the amenities Scott prescribed: nearby shopping facilities, schools, and parks. This model of neighborhood form is adjusted to include the aesthetic features of downtown and the caché of loft living which fetishize heritage in the built environment; historic façades are left as is, and loft buildings are named after their former use, whether bank, subway terminal, or theater. The creation of a neighborhood form that promotes urban civility, or "proper" social practice in domestic and public spaces, is understood to support downtown as a center, in turn making Los Angeles a "city" insofar as it is structured around a normative urban form. Other urban planners argue that the presence of a park downtown where people would gather, or the reconnection of the north-south axis linking City Hall with the historic Plaza, would support Angelenos' identification of downtown as the center of the city, helping them feel a greater sense of civic identification, with both the city and their fellow Angelenos.

An urban ideology purporting that proper civility is found in a centralized city has supported the development of mixed-use zoning, pedestrian-friendly streets, and increased public transportation. Believing in these markers of urbanism, new residents arrive ready to fight for an image of a city that is these things and more. Large-scale development put into play by projects such as condominium towers in South Park, L.A. Live, and the Grand Avenue plan[4] tower over loft developments, restaurants, and boutiques from the Arts District to Little Tokyo and the Fashion District.[5] The lofting of the Historic Core made possible by the 1999 Adaptive Reuse Ordinance is a key effort in the formulation and implementation of these ideals. Setting the tenor for downtown development, this trend has also distilled and revealed modalities and consequences of making downtown global.

Arts of Distinction

Lofts, galleries, and amenities (restaurants, coffee shops, and gourmet markets) are now *symbols* of art in urban life, granting symbolic membership that does not require an actual relationship to or involvement with artistic practice. Facilitating and marking membership in terms of economic and social normativity, those on the side of art, who are allowed to "be an artist," or exist in the domestic domain of a lifestyle created by urban development around the arts, function as legitimate urban subjects whose interests are privileged. In marking inclusion, art excludes (Zukin 1995). In downtown Los Angeles, each element of the "creative economy" (Florida 2004)[6] presumes and produces a class divide. New York's Soho neighborhood continues to reign as the exemplary case of urban loft development. However, downtown Los Angeles differs from its model insofar as it has an existing population, most of whom live on Skid Row or in SROs located throughout the area, while the gentrification of Soho primarily displaced light manufacturing (Zukin 1982).[7] The history of Skid Row in Los Angeles is intertwined with that of downtown. The first mission opened in downtown Los Angeles at the end of the nineteenth century in an area of dense rail lines and train stations. During the downtown's declining years, Skid Row was out of sight to the majority of Angelenos, and by the turn of the twenty-first century, most of the homeless service providers of Los Angeles were located in and around Skid Row. The presence of Skid Row has been the source of intense anxiety in the face of urban development, with the homeless the most visible population against whom redevelopment processes have taken place.

Lofts

A model set by artists provides the basis for real estate investment in the form of loft development. As Gronk explained, in the 1970s and 1980s, downtown Los Angeles was home to artists living illegally in former financial and industrial spaces then empty above the ground floor. As many as thirty-five galleries provided spaces for these and other artists to show their work and gather. Initially drawn to downtown because of rising rents in Venice and other parts of the city, most of these residents eventually moved away, and galleries closed or dispersed to other parts of the city, leaving the historic part of downtown without a thriving arts scene. Barbara Smith, an artist who lived on Broadway between Second and Third Streets in the 1970s, explained that she and other artists chose to live downtown because there was raw space and it was cheap. However, it was "rough" downtown, their cars were broken into, and they were not "near things." She explained that they were familiar with their East Coast counterparts, and downtown Los Angeles was in this respect not like Soho. People moved elsewhere for various reasons; she got a place in the Hollywood Hills. Many artists were quite invested in creating a stable downtown live/work art scene and organized neighborhood groups that made lists of artists living downtown by building and held meetings to discuss zoning regulations (LAICA archives, Smithsonian Archives for American Art). Lobbying efforts paid off, and in 1979 the State of California passed live/work legislation (California Senate 1979) that two years later, with the support of Councilmember Joel Wachs, was implemented by the City of Los Angeles as an Artist in Residence ordinance.

As downtown Los Angeles faced the effects of a decade-long recession during which many of the artists had moved away, in 1997 an Adaptive Reuse, Live/Work task force was organized by a group of public and private-sector players who hoped to find ways to revitalize the area. Taking Denver, San Francisco, and Lower Manhattan as models of urban development that had been organized around the lofting of historic warehouse buildings, the members of the task force identified a form that satisfied their desire for economic stimulus in downtown and provided a use for empty buildings. Though the Mills Act, which gave tax relief for developers of historic buildings, had been adopted by the city in 1996, without the possibility to adapt buildings for uses other than their original functions as banks and warehouses, there was little incentive to do so. In 1999 the Adaptive Reuse Ordinance was passed by the City Planning Commission to "create incentives to reuse pre July 1, 1974 historic downtown buildings for residential and work facilities." The ordinance allowed smaller units to be created within existing structures, reduced off-street parking and safety requirements, and limited the amount of interior common space. It succeeded as a residential development program. As Hamid Behdad, former director of the city's Adaptive Reuse projects, proclaimed in 2006, "The program has since realized the completion of 4,252 loft units, and promises 4,100 units that are currently under construction, followed by an additional 3,200 units in the development pipeline. The program is responsible for an estimated $6 billion in stimulated economic investments" (Westwater 2006).

Tom Gilmore's conversion of the San Fernando Building on the corner of Fourth Street and Main Street was the first under the ordinance. For Gilmore, like others before, New York provided a model of urbanism for his recognition of the opportunity for loft development downtown. With the San Fernando Building followed shortly thereafter by other developments in the surrounding blocks, Gilmore's lofting of buildings on Main Street that began in the late 1990s has provided a model and anchor for subsequent projects at the same time that it has been instrumental in drawing new residents to downtown Los Angeles. According to Behdad, Gilmore is the "poster child" for Adaptive Reuse. Obscuring his active role in the transformation of downtown, Gilmore said, "A certain level of gentrification is healthy because it's the nature of change. That's the fundamental thing about cities, is that they're constantly changing" (Tom Gilmore, personal communication). Yet Gilmore has worked hard to garner political and economic support. In 1999, two months before the Adaptive Reuse Ordinance was passed, Gilmore's company was granted a loan of $3.8 million by the City Council for the Old Bank District Project at Spring and Fourth Streets, followed two years later by a $1.5 million bridge loan when the project was stalled by cost overruns. The loans were justified by the fact that the project was found to meet the "National Objective of the Housing and Community Development Act and is necessary and appropriate to accomplish the city's economic development objectives" (L.A. City Clerk 1999). Lobbying for the policy that would facilitate his vision, Gilmore attended a city council hearing in which the Adaptive Reuse Ordinance was discussed, marking on his speaker's card that he was in favor of it.

Expanding the definition of "artist" was a key means by which the Adaptive Reuse Ordinance facilitated downtown development. The Central City Association, which represents downtown business interests, lobbied for and supported this. While previously live/work spaces could be inhabited only by "artists and artisans, including individual architects and designers," now "accountants; attorneys; computer software and multimedia related professionals; consultants; engineers; insurance, real estate, and travel agents; photographers; and other similar occupations as determined by the Zoning Administrator" were all eligible. Artists, to the extent there were any in the Historic Core lofts, were soon to be displaced by residents involved in some way with the creative economy of Los Angeles, who became neighbors to if not supplanted by professionals granted creative credibility by the symbolic designation of their domestic arrangements. Six years after the ordinance was passed, the buildings were occupied by predominantly high-income tenants.[8]

"Lofts" maintain a symbolic association with art, but increasingly the new housing in downtown Los Angeles is upscale, market rate and above. As Hamid Behdad told me, the Adaptive Reuse Ordinance is "not about art. It was initiated by artists but is completely transformed to a different thing." Moreover, housing was only one element in a development model that also included retail and services in an effort to foster an "urban" lifestyle. Articulating a relation between urban form and social life while naturalizing the work that went into creating the ordinance as an economic stimulus, he said, "the urban lifestyle was there, dampened by suburbanization. It was just a natural thing; some people had suppressed it for awhile but it's coming back."

Amenities

Loft residents were drawn in part by the urban grit of downtown Los Angeles, recognizing from their knowledge of similar urban spaces around the world that the grimy sidewalks and presence of homeless signified the potential for affordable and spacious studios and housing. As Behdad noted, living downtown went beyond housing to include a "lifestyle." Once there, however, new residents soon began to complain about the lack of a grocery store and the few restaurant options beyond the taco stand, expressing their desire for a place to buy a bottle of wine and rent a movie. The everyday reality of the aesthetic of the street was suddenly less appealing, and residents invoked rights granted under the sign of property to make claims on space. Until a chain grocery store opened downtown in 2007, residents would complain, "maybe you have to go to the grocery store and you have to drive all the way on the freeway to the grocery store and you just think jeez, I wish I lived somewhere where I could just go across the street. And other things. There's no coffee shop open at night." As businesses opened, class lines were drawn around taste and consumption practices related to food and drink, making it clear how an association with the symbolic art economy grants some and not others membership and legitimacy as consumers and enables exclusions to be made on the basis of practices that are clearly codes for social actors.

Amenities have been a dominant element of the economic development of downtown Los Angeles and its emergence as an "urban center." One of the roles of the Downtown Los Angeles Neighborhood Council (DLANC) has been to vet applications for conditional use permits (CUBs) that allow the sale of alcoholic beverages in new restaurants and bars. As part of its role in this process, DLANC formulated an official position that maintains, "The Downtown Los Angeles Neighborhood Council (DLANC) has joined with many stakeholders in effectively making Downtown Los Angeles a vital and thriving 24-hour urban center. One key component of the Downtown revitalization is the addition of appropriate retail and entertainment uses; including but not limited to: restaurants, cafes, markets and nightlife venues." Moreover, it continues, "DLANC acknowledges that the success of these venues, in part, involves the lawful sale and dispensing of alcoholic beverages."

In a moment of intense downtown transformation, DLANC meetings often gravitated toward negotiations about relative inclusions and exclusions in relation to housing, amenities, and the arts, discursively authorizing membership along lines of class as marked by taste and habitus. While DLANC included representatives of the various constituencies of downtown, it was dominated by those who began their statements by saying, "I represent the interests of business." Hence DLANC meetings and documents became a space in which downtown development and its relation to class and race were negotiated discursively in expansive and telling ways. In regulating the axes of alcohol consumption in downtown Los Angeles, poor and homeless people with alcohol addiction were pitted against loft residents wanting wine with their dinner. The "DLANC Position on CUB Applications in Downtown Los Angeles" articulates and inscribes this divide in blatantly discriminatory language that conflates race and class in its conditions for alcohol sale, designating, among other things, that "No self-service of alcoholic beverages will be permitted" and "No pay phone will be maintained on the exterior of the premise." Moreover, in Gourmet Markets, "Malt beverages shall not be sold in single-serving containers larger than 16 ounces capacity. . . . No fortified wines shall be sold. The sale of alcoholic beverage miniature bottles (2 ounces or less), and pint or half pint containers will not be permitted." The criminalization of practices of undesirable populations is a key mode of "cleaning" downtown. In the language of this document, the habitus of those included by merit of their association with an arts economy is validated in its unspokenness; the rules are made around exclusion, associating practices with people such that eliminating the possibility for the presence of a particular habitus removes those people whose practices it reflects. Loft residents, it can be assumed, do not drink "malt beverages."[9]

Gallery Row

Gallery Row is a loose affiliate of artists and gallery owners that draws visitors for a monthly Art Walk. With twenty-three galleries mostly concentrated in an area that runs eight blocks north to south and one block east to west, Gallery Row is a key element in the creation of a 24/7 city, a "pedestrian city," a "real city." Emphasizing the use of art for financial ends, Gallery Row has been conscientiously framed as part of an economic development program supported by a major loft developer entitled "Look What We Can Do." The program provided economic incentives to property owners and "creative business entrepreneurs" who share a vision of downtown Los Angeles as a "pedestrian-friendly, culturally abundant, urban neighborhood" (Gallery Row Organization 2006). Visitors to the monthly Art Walk have come largely from outside downtown. Residents and gallerists thought that most visitors came more for a touristic experience than as art buyers, supporting aspirations of making downtown a "destination" (Frieden and Sagalyn 1989).

Prior to the formation of Gallery Row, the existing urban conditions provided a basis for comparing Los Angeles with other cities, situating it in a national and international context of urban development around the arts. As a gallery owner told me, "In the 1970s and '80s I lived in Soho and the East Village in New York. Back before they were 'the destination.' And I sort of recognized the formula. It was like this is sort of like what that was like back then and there's an opportunity here I definitely want to be a part of." For others, it might be the "feel" imparted by the Art Walk that can invoke an imagining of downtown Los Angeles as making the city feel like a city, and a city that is global. As a downtown resident explained, "Downtown is one of those places where you really feel the energy of a city. It's one of the few places where you get that megacity feeling." He recognized the presence of global capital moving through the high-rise office buildings, affecting the suburbs of Los Angeles and beyond. For him, the Art Walk was a way of localizing the global economy, facilitating social interactions between the agents of global capital who work in the skyscrapers and artists on the streets of downtown Los Angeles. That residents recognized tenets of a global city in the Art Walk indicates the pervasiveness of an understanding of neoliberal globalization and its markers. Its expression "on the ground" suggests how globalization is lived, produced, and recognized by its actors in their everyday environment. The "recognizable formula" provides a framework for economic development in which it is now known that the arts can be used to clean the city, to make the city safe for capital.

Gallery Row lends a credibility of art to the area, staking out a terrain for other modes of social control that support a normative urban civility. A gallerist described how three years earlier the neighborhood had looked, "ugly, bad, filthy, filled with unsavory characters." The presence of galleries helped make it "cleaner, safer and more diverse." A summer 2007 Art Walk saw galleries with people spilling out their open doors, moving from one to the next, crossing Fifth Street to see the paintings in Pharmaka after looking at sculptures in Bert Green Fine Art, going west to Spring Street and south to G727 between Seventh and Eighth, and walking north again to end the evening at Pete's on Fourth and Main, a restaurant on the ground floor of the San Fernando Building. The geographic spread of the galleries kept there from being a critical mass on the street at any given point, but inside the galleries there were clusters of people, sometimes a crowd, drinking wine in plastic cups and looking at what hung on the walls. These people—along with a visible police presence—provided Jane Jacobs's "eyes on the street" and, as a gallerist said, made "drug dealers trying to do business on the corner leave because it would freak them out." With Gallery Row, an art public replaced the previous downtown denizens; whereas "it was just homeless before," now "you come down here and there are all kinds of people walking on the streets." However, he continued, the galleries were not enough. "We were still having occasional problems when during Downtown Art Walks there would be beggars and junkies swarming the crowd and just being crazy or being rude or trying to get money off of them. It was never actually a really dangerous situation, but it was always a tense situation." What really made a difference, he said, was the Safer Cities Initiative, "the police department's decision to make a concentrated effort to crack down on drug dealing and stop it, drive it out of the neighborhood." Yet, while the change has "been remarkable," the neighborhood "is not completely cleaned up, there's a lot more work to do."

Used to encourage and support the removal of the homeless, art brings together a functional program of economic development, policing, and social exclusions worked out in everyday interactions and broader policies. This is reflected in the ways in which Gallery Row and its desired clientele organize the geography of the Safer Cities Initiative. When I interviewed the police captain in her office, where a metal bookcase held a bobble-head doll of Rosie the Riveter, she told me that the downtown Safer Cities Initiative had started on Main Street between Third and Seventh Streets not because it was the most dangerous place, but because of the perception of crime by new residents. "New businesses opening, people walking their dogs at night, restaurants open 'til 2 in the morning, art galleries, the art walk. You had people all over doing drugs, selling drugs, committing crimes. It wasn't a place where you wanted to walk out of your loft now at Sixth and Main and be amongst this. You stayed inside." Continuing, she said, "It was their uncomfortableness with the volume of people on the street, the parolees, the homeless, the gang members. They probably thought crime was out of control. It wasn't. It is probably one of the safest places to be, but it doesn't feel like it sometimes."

Perception of crime was sufficient reason to target particular areas, clearing people from sidewalks who may or may not actually be participating in illegal activity but whose habitus made loft residents fear for their personal safety. A resident knew "it's just the perception, the idea that it's unsafe," but said, when "people just walk up to you and bug you on the street for whatever, I try to be friendly to people, and I get yelled at, and that just shakes you up when you're a girl walking around by yourself." Another newcomer organized a presentation for a DLANC committee meeting on surveillance cameras that could be placed around downtown and connected to police computers. The surveillance cameras were purportedly intended to protect against potential terrorist attacks, but comments made during the presentation about "what goes on on the streets down here" betrayed their likely everyday use. Though Main Street is the western border of Skid Row, the LAPD targeted that area first because new residents were complaining. Using paramilitary tactics, they "went from the western border and brought it in. Dealt with the issues. Held it." The police captain, satisfied with the results, concluded, it "makes you feel you really did something nice, something that changed the quality of life for that resident. Because it's not cheap to buy those lofts."

Artist/Homeless

Just as a DLANC Arts Committee meeting was beginning, a man walked into the gallery in which it was held and announced loudly, "I'm an artist." Articulating a mode through which he might gain access and membership, he continued, "people think people down here are all into drugs and alcohol. We're artists too! I'm one of those." He paused, looked at his audience, and said, "I apologize for barging in. Thank you for letting me in." He was escorted to the door, and the meeting began. A presentation about the Skid Row Housing Trust's potential donation of space to the LAMP Art Project (an art organization for homeless and mentally ill people on Skid Row) in a storefront across the street from the gallery in which we were sitting was met with enthusiasm; one gallery owner expressed his hope that this would be a place they could send "some of the people" who came through their doors, the reference to the man who had opened the meeting left unspoken. Though such attitudes imply a purported inclusiveness of art, the distinctions drawn between the spaces and their respective clientele reflect the exclusions inscribed by the art presented in most downtown galleries.

Arts projects by Skid Row residents are sites of critical analysis that mark the divide between included and excluded. Not the same art as that used by and for development, these art projects—some by homeless, some by low-income downtown residents—reveal the potential for art to enable or restrict membership and access. During the August 2007 Art Walk, the Los Angeles Community Action Network (LACAN), the advocacy group vilified by the police, staged an intervention that looked much more like the work of an

Figure 7. LACAN street intervention. Photo by author.

avant garde of the contemporary art world than anything else seen on Gallery Row, where abstract and representational paintings, sculptures, and other objects crafted with an expressive sensibility dominate. Tents and boxes were stationed on the sidewalk across the street from LACAN's offices. A sign on one read "Save Our Homes," while another on a cardboard box said, "Mayor! Be Our Neighbor."[10] Critiquing current policies and calling politicians to task, the installation and accompanying flyer that was passed out highlighted the inequalities that were being produced and maintained. Tents, boxes, and figures about the numbers of SRO rooms lost and "residents arrested" turned the lens onto the existence of those being removed from downtown Los Angeles. By making the poor visible through art, LACAN drew into focus the presumed position of art in downtown Los Angeles, with the membership granted by art tied to, or serving to mask, economic membership.

Subsequent to the DLANC committee meeting, the LAMP Art Project was given a space on Main Street across from two of Gallery Row's fixtures. It began to use this space during the Art Walk, and felt gratified at being able to participate in the current art scene downtown. There, oil paintings featured street scenes of Skid Row, still lives, and the downtown skyline. Made by the same people who otherwise might be asked to move off the sidewalk during the Art Walk, as artists they are granted inclusion, if only for a night. Allowing LAMP Art's inclusion helped DLANC members feel better about their position in the neighborhood, insofar as charity maintains a social divide while absolving guilt about other punitive tactics enacted by those in power.

Los Angeles Poverty Department, or LAPD, whose performance *Glimpses of Utopia* I attended at the end of a day that began with interviews with police, sustains the use of the arts as a critical tool for addressing the dynamics of exclusion in downtown Los Angeles (Jackson and Malpede 2009). A theater group composed of residents of Skid Row, LAPD's performances are shaped by the pain of people who are not artists, who are without privilege, who are in actual risk of danger, who are excluded. Formed in 1985 by performance artist John Malpede, LAPD came into being when homelessness, having reached record levels and crisis proportion, became a fixture of social concern. Using performance as a mode of civic engagement, LAPD gives men and women living on Skid Row a voice to express their stake in issues affecting their lives. Emerging from a milieu of politically engaged art of the 1980s, LAPD has sustained a performance practice that continues to respond to conditions of homelessness as they are affected by economic globalization, political change, urban development, policing, and public policy. Not art in the service of economic development, but rather a use of art for addressing and engaging with social and human issues, LAPD provides a critical engagement with the issues facing downtown Los Angeles.

Glimpses of Utopia: 8-15 was held in the Red Dot Gallery, a recent addition to Gallery Row and the monthly Art Walk. Half hot dog stand, half gallery, Red Dot was organized with the intention to create a business with financial stability that could provide support for artists. Unique only in its combination of amenities, Red Dot reflects the opportunities presented for businesses in downtown Los Angeles. *Glimpses of Utopia: 8-15*—part of a longer project entitled *UTOPIA/dystopia*—was the second of what would be three similarly framed events, in which eight "selectors" had each chosen a "presenter" to describe his or her vision for the future of downtown Los Angeles. The director of Economic Development and Community Outreach in the office of the Los Angeles city attorney, formerly with the Downtown Center Business Improvement District and Central City Association, was selected by a self-described resident of Skid Row and former addict to whom she had stood out as generous and humane; in speaking that night, she revealed—saying, "I've never told this to anyone"—that she had been homeless as a child. Other presenters included the deputy chief of Operations and Policy for the Community Redevelopment Agency, who narrated a history of downtown Los Angeles beginning with the Spanish settlement; a woman who had lost the space for her beauty parlor in an SRO building that had been converted to lofts; and a performance by a new age cellist. The evening closed with a presentation by the co-director of LACAN, who countered the neutral history of suburbanization told by the Community Redevelopment Agency official, giving it the name "white flight" and asserting that she did not want to have to look back on the current transformations and find she had done nothing to mitigate the impact on those excluded from the benefits of the process.

The range of interests brought together through this event was striking. Each person spoke from his or her own position and experience working or living in downtown Los Angeles. Space was provided to question, contradict, argue with and against, or explain something of one's background that others might not know. The organization of the performance—a simple structure within which individuals had a set amount of time to tell their own stories—was in keeping with other LAPD works. *La Llorona, Weeping Women of Skid Row,* first performed in 2003, used the Mexican folk tale of the weeping woman to frame narratives about people's experiences on Skid Row. Intensely powerful, the untrained actors, some mentally ill, some not, walked around the room with choreographed movements, stopping to tell their personal stories, then moving on to sing in unison, in a performance that both represented and conveyed the pain of life on Skid Row. Similarly, the impact of *Glimpses of Utopia* came from the stories that were told, invoking a longer history and context of policies related to urban development, housing, and public space through the words of those who enact them and those affected by them.

In December 2007, LAPD performed the final part of *UTOPIA/dystopia* at REDCAT, a gallery and performance space affiliated with CalArts located at the back of Disney Hall. With its entrance just off Grand Avenue, it is part of the cluster of art spaces in downtown Los Angeles that are understood as requisite civic institutions, and include the Music Center, the Mark Taper Forum, the Museum of Contemporary Art, and Disney Hall. Entering REDCAT on the evening of the performance, audience members were greeted by a man playing piano and a woman lying in bed wearing a silk robe and holding a red rose while reading *The Downtown News.* Inside the theater, an image of this pair was projected onto a cardboard screen, raised on a cardboard edifice that resembled the base of a skyscraper. When the performance began, the image changed to a projection of a street of Skid Row. Two musicians sat at the back of the stage, holding acoustic guitars.

LAPD's work reveals the relationship between experiences of residents of Skid Row and structural issues, showing the effects of policies on people living on Skid Row. The performance conveyed how abstract policies are enacted by and have consequences for people, with business interests pitted against the everyday lives of residents. The scenarios performed were drawn from research conducted by LAPD members that included attendance at city council meetings, interviews with residents, and applications for downtown lofts. The performance included public speeches, a city council meeting, and statements made by developers, which were shown to affect the lives of individuals in particular ways. LAPD members channeled downtown power brokers, saying the words of, among others, Mayor Antonio Villaraigosa, Councilperson Jan Perry, Chief of Police Bratton, loft developer Tom Gilmore (renamed Ted Biltmore), and George Kelling, co-author of the "broken windows" theory that served as the basis and legitimation for current policing tactics on Skid Row. It turned on a trope of "addiction," with drug and alcohol addiction shifting to developers' addiction to money. John Malpede performed George Kelling. Drawing on the language of the "broken windows" essay, he said:

> Disorder and crime are linked in a kind of developmental sequence. Police officers and social psychologists agree that if a window is broken and left unrepaired, soon all of the windows will be broken because a broken window is a signal that no one cares. Now citizens are primarily frightened by crime, especially the thought of a sudden violent attack by a stranger. But we tend to forget another source of fear. The fear of being bothered by disorderly people. Not violent people or necessarily criminals. Disreputable people, unpredictable people, panhandlers, addicts, the mentally disturbed. Now, by putting more police on the street we can raise the level of public order. (*UTOPIA/dystopia* 2010)

A woman found a loft space for her yoga studio. Later she was threatened with losing it after speaking at the city council meeting, taking a position against that of developers, including her landlord. In another scene a woman was accused of stealing a bottle of water from a local market. A performer discussed addiction and recovery on Skid Row. He addressed the audience at the end of his monologue, blurring the line between art and life as he said, "My name is Kevin Michael and I am an addict. Thank *you* for participating in my recovery." A man wearing a beret performed a community activist, reading the rights citizens have to the sidewalk.

At the center of the performance was a reenactment of a city council meeting in which area stakeholders discussed the enforcement of municipal code 41.18(d). Municipal code 41.18(d) was originally enacted to remove hippies from the Sunset Strip in 1968 (Newsom 1968). At the time of the performance it used predominantly in Skid Row, the placement of the signs marking an informal geography of the area. Enforcement of 41.18(d) has been at the heart of legal and social struggles over the right to space in downtown Los Angeles. With the code's enforcement a main target for police under the Safer Cities Initiative, the ACLU challenged the constitutionality of 41.18(d) and the Ninth Circuit Court of Appeals ruled that people could not be forced to move from the sidewalk as long as there was insufficient shelter. The compromise reached between the city council and ACLU allowed people to be on the sidewalk between 9 PM and 6 AM, after which point police could enforce the code. While breaking this law is purportedly a misdemeanor, people were being routinely arrested, brought into the police department in handcuffs—as I witnessed while waiting to interview the police captain. Signs posted on the exterior walls of Skid Row businesses read:

<u>WARNING</u>

**No person shall sit,
lie or sleep in or upon
any street, sidewalk
or other public way.**

LAMC Sec. 41.18(d)
Violators are subject to prosecution

POSTED BY PROPERTY OWNER

With these signs, the property owner asserts her right to control bodies in public space, with the state legitimating the authority of private property over the use of the sidewalk.

Figure 8. 41.18(d) sign. Photo by author.

One 41.18(d) sign that I photographed a few years prior hung beneath the sign for a perfume company. Stains on the sidewalk below the sign suggest the code had been poorly enforced, and that the space had been inhabited by bodies, food, excrement, and other things that might leave their mark on the concrete surface. That this particular business was a perfume company is ironic on a superficial level, while conveying on a deeper level an urban civility crafted out of a distinction between good and bad smells that define proper and improper subjects correlated with desirable and undesirable urban spaces. The relative citizenship of the immigrant fades into the cityscape, "mayoreo" invoking the lingua franca of L.A. street commerce, with "Baba" of indeterminate linguistic origin.

On stage, the musicians played a song that drew on the language of the measure to express its inherent inequality (*UTOPIA/dystopia* 2010, lyrics courtesy of Ralph Gorodetsky).

Adopted as the law of Southern California, 41.18(d)
You can sit on any street, sidewalk or public way
If you're watching a parade
But on any other day
Just a regular sunny day
When there ain't no parade
You can't sit
You can't sleep
You can't lie
On any street
Sidewalk
Or public way
When there ain't no parade
41.18(d)
don't take your chances
with city ordinances
41.18(d).

The performance indicated some of the ways in which urban development is supported by a neoliberal city and global capital, affecting the social fabric of our cities as a divide between included and excluded is demarcated with increasing force. At the same time, the global is equally made through resistance to these pressures. A response to the criminalization of homelessness, the elimination of existing affordable housing, and the displacement of downtown's poor was to frame the issue in terms of human rights. This tactic was invoked in *UTOPIA/dystopia*, as protests of the enforcement of municipal code 41.18(d) were linked to civil and human rights. Drawing on legal frameworks that posit universal rights on the basis of the human, issues that appear as ostensibly local to Skid Row are scaled to a global legal and moral context.

Conclusion

Downtown Los Angeles distills many of the dynamics of contemporary urbanism marking "global downtowns." Los Angeles boasts a downtown that has followed a national trend of significance and decline as well as an urban form that became paradigmatic for postindustrial cities. Efforts to "revitalize" downtown Los Angeles have been taking place in a moment when downtowns around the world are undergoing remarkably similar processes. The multiscalar nature of downtown development is apparent in the imbrication of issues seemingly specific to Los Angeles with recognizably "global" processes. Globalization is crafted through the city council adopting a housing ordinance, one man having the impetus to develop lofts when few were willing to finance them, and decisions that resulted in the largest concentration of homeless people in any metropolitan area.

Aspirations of being a "real" city with a strong center are enacted in everyday life, using art to organize social inclusion. Positioned on the side of the new residents, the bourgeois subject, and the economically enfranchised, art as deployed in development processes grants membership to some while excluding others. Gallerists and residents assert the privilege designated by art, inscribing the lines between included and excluded in order to make the city in a particular image. The economic and political work supporting these processes is naturalized as the creative economy is linked to habitus and class position, ascribing rights to particular interests over others. At the same time, another art enables those excluded to expose the social dynamics that are otherwise facilitated by the creative economy. With these projects, an alternative model of urban civility is presented, one that asks for the right for presence and participation in the city.

UTOPIA/dystopia performed this distribution and enactment of power in downtown Los Angeles. Speaking the words of power brokers allowed

LAPD members to own the narrative and to ultimately transform it. Turning ethnography into fantasy, the performance ended with the group performing a utopia in which, after the city council passed measures that support developers, all the housing became "market rate" and above. Yet there are not enough people who can afford the rents, and after a "bail out" by the city, 10,000 luxury lofts are given to homeless people.

10

"Slum-Free Mumbai" and Other Entrepreneurial Strategies in the Making of Mumbai's Global Downtown

Liza Weinstein

In late 2004, the municipal government of Mumbai,[1] carrying out orders from the state's chief minister, undertook a massive demolition campaign to clear the city's unregulated slums and squatter settlements. During the four-month campaign, government bulldozers dismantled hutments built along roads and railways and on "open" plots of land throughout the city. In the process, they demolished an estimated 90,000 homes and displaced upward of 400,000 people (Mahadevia and Narayanan 2008b; Weinstein and Ren 2009). Responding to criticism, state officials defended the campaign as necessary to improve the city's quality of life and bolster its competitive position. "The proliferation of slums through the city," the state's chief minister explained at the height of the campaign, had "created obstacles for development." Their clearance, he elaborated, would enable Mumbai's transformation and make it more attractive to global investors (Mahadevia and Naraynan 2008a: 114).

Justifying these actions, state officials cited a series of recommendations made by the international consulting firm McKinsey & Company that promised to make Mumbai a "world class city" within a decade (Katakam 2005; Sharma 2005). Released a few months earlier by the civic association Bombay First, the McKinsey Report warned that Mumbai's economic competitiveness was slipping. "Slums have proliferated and congestion, pollution and

water problems have skyrocketed," the report noted, all of which were leading to "a slippage in rankings" (McKinsey & Company 2003: 3). Among its
recommendations for bolstering Mumbai's standing in the rankings, the report declared that the government should halt the proliferation of slums and
re-house a majority of the city's current slum residents. Although the report
did not explicitly advocate the use of bulldozers to achieve these objectives,
representatives of Bombay First, the organization that commissioned the
report, affirmed their support for the government's actions. "If Mumbai has
to be a World Class city, then the slums have to go and . . . strong and urgent
steps need to be taken" (quoted in Mahadevia and Narayanan 2008b, 551).
Although it is likely that the chief minister's strategy was formulated inde-
pendently and the demolitions would have been carried out in the absence of
the McKinsey Report, the association with the international firm helped deflect some of the negative response and legitimate the state's actions. Meanwhile, as news outlets around the world reported on the demolition campaign,
the action succeeded in bringing international visibility to the state's new
entrepreneurial urban agenda.

As reflected in the demolition campaign, Mumbai's new urban agenda
is grounded in efforts to both beautify the city and replace slum settlements
with glossy downtown developments that obscure the unsightly living conditions of most Mumbai residents. Civic groups like Bombay First assert the
need to remove the eyesores of slums, which they claim hinder Mumbai's
ability to attract businesses and global elites. At the same time, the shortage
of developable land in Mumbai—an island-city with limited transit linkages
to the mainland—has led to an inward turn in search of land. The city's spatial politics have long been shaped by this land shortage, but politicians and
developers have only recently turned to slums and squatter settlements. Estimates suggest that Mumbai's slums, which house upward of 60 percent of
the population, occupy as little as 8 percent of the city's total land area (Appadurai 2000).Yet slums have been identified as the next best hope for solv-
ing central Mumbai's intractable land shortage and constructing the office
parks, high-end residential developments, and consumption spaces that
many believe will help Mumbai become a "world class city."

The demolition campaign also highlights the important new role global
consultants have assumed within this agenda. Leveraging externally conferred expertise, consultants like McKinsey & Company have helped frame
the city's development agenda and legitimated its implementation. Although
consultants and advisors have helped shape Mumbai's development policies

and contributed to land use plans since well before independence, the greater authority they have assumed since the late1990s reflects a shift in the local politics of urban development. A number of scholars have identified the growing influence of consultants in various contexts, but few have looked at this phenomenon in the field of urban development (McCann 2001; Sam and Scherer 2006; Evers and Menkhoff 2004). And while researchers and urban theorists have discussed the formulation of entrepreneurial urban governance agendas in cities throughout the world, this literature has remained largely silent on the role of planning consultants. But highlighting the recent adoption of a downtown development agenda in Mumbai, this chapter identifies a significant new role for globally recognized planning consultants like McKinsey & Company.

The chapter begins with a discussion of downtown development in colonial and postcolonial Bombay. It argues that throughout much of this period, the city's spatial politics have been shaped by a tension between centrality and dispersal. With the city's traditional downtown in South Bombay bursting at its seams, various efforts were undertaken throughout the twentieth century to disperse development activity. It further argues that attempts to de-concentrate the central city were also shaped by an anti-urban bent in state politics. Given the structure of urban governance in India, most urban development activities are formulated at the state level. In the case of Mumbai, this means that downtown development has been overseen by Maharashtra's predominantly rural politicians and bureaucrats. The emergence of a Mumbai-based political movement in the 1990s, however, recentered urban policy and facilitated a return to downtown. Tracing these political shifts, the chapter's first half discusses the emergence of these new spatial politics and the formulation of Mumbai's downtown agenda in the late 1990s.

The chapter then goes on to discuss the place of two consultant-led development plans within this agenda. The next section discusses the creation of the McKinsey Report, highlighting the manner in which McKinsey & Company helped frame the city's urban agenda around the goal of becoming a "world class city." The second case is the Dharavi Redevelopment Project, an effort by a private architect and consultant to redevelop Mumbai's notorious slum of Dharavi and "make Mumbai slum free." Describing the plan's promotion of commercial development in Dharavi—an area far removed, both socially and spatially, from the city's traditional downtown—this section explores the ways slum redevelopment is reconfiguring Mumbai's spatial politics. The chapter concludes by considering the role planning consultants have played in the making of Mumbai's global downtown and the implications of the city's emerging development "consultocracy."

Spatial Politics in Twentieth-Century Bombay

It has been suggested that "the history of Bombay is the history of an acute housing shortage" (Dossal 2010: 183).More than any other factor, the city's geographic layout was shaped by an insatiable demand for space. Over the past two centuries, economic opportunities and an entrepreneurial ethos drew migrants to Bombay, but the small island city could not adequately house all of these workers and their enterprises. The development strategies and proposed solutions to Bombay's spatial deficits fell along two lines. On one side were groups advocating centrality and promoting downtown development in South Bombay. On the other side were those lamenting the city's congestion and pushing for the development of satellite business districts outside the city center. With the two factions working at cross-purposes, this debate ultimately undermined both efforts and hindered attempts at comprehensive planning. Weak municipal governance further undermined efforts to construct adequate housing and provide basic services to residents in the city center.

Until the late nineteenth century, most of Bombay's residents—with the exception of the indigenous residents of the small fishing villages dotting the island's perimeter—were concentrated at the island's southern end, in and around the central business district of the walled-in Fort area (Dossal 2010). As the city grew and emerged as a major manufacturing and trading center in the mid-1800s, its population spread northward, but Fort remained the city's commercial center. The area's monumental Victorian buildings, constructed primarily in the 1870s and 1880s, showcased Fort's wealth and signaled Bombay's presence as a major commercial capital. But by the time Fort's walls were removed in the 1860s, it was clear that South Bombay was facing a severe land shortage and development had to expand outward (Kosambi 1986).

Beginning in the mid-1860s, an effort was undertaken to bolster the land supply around Fort.Called the Back Bay Reclamation Scheme, the plan proposed the dredging of mud and other materials from the sea and using them to build out into the Back Bay. The plan was abandoned during a recession in the early 1870s, but a solution had been identified to South Bombay's spatial shortage (Banerjee-Guha 1995). Over the next hundred years, the scheme was periodically revived by town planners and civic groups advocating particular development plans or the need for open space in South Bombay (Dossal 2010). In the late 1950s, the scheme was revived once again to enable to construction of the business districts of Nariman Point and Cuffe Parade on reclaimed land south of Fort. In the early 1960s, large companies, including Air India, the Express Group of newspapers, and the Mittal Corporation, bought land at Nariman Point (Banerjee-Guha 1995). New development regulations enacted in 1964 reduced existing height restrictions and allowed this area to develop the cluster of downtown high-rises that signaled Bombay's commercial prominence (Panagariya 2007).

Yet around the same time, plans for deconcentration were also being promoted. In the early 1960s, a state advisory committee recommended that the government undertake a series of development projects aimed at pulling commercial development out of South Bombay. The state was persuaded by the committee's suggestion that the development of alternative commercial districts would reduce congestion in South Bombay and improve the city's business climate and quality of life, and the state government undertook two of the committee's main recommendations (Banerjee-Guha 1995; Shaw 2004). One of these projects was a business complex to be built on marshy land on the north shore of the Mahim Creek between the inner-ring sub-urbs of Bandra and Kurla. The second project was the development of a new city on the east side of Bombay's harbor that would be connected to South Bombay by a causeway. This satellite city, called New Bombay (or Navi Mum-bai), was developed in the 1970s and 1980s to house many of the commercial enterprises located in South Bombay, as well as new state government office buildings. Yet with these new projects pursued at the same time as the Back Bay Reclamation and development of Nariman Point, the three develop-ment efforts ultimately undermined one another. Although the state gov-ernment had promised to move many of its administrative offices to Navi Mumbai, it ended up building new offices at Nariman Point instead (Shaw 2004). The Bandra-Kurla Complex competed for commercial tenants with both Navi Mumbai and Nariman Point, pulling the city's commercial activ-ity in three different directions (Banerjee-Guha 1995). Meanwhile, the bridge that was to link Navi Mumbai to South Bombay was never built and the two areas remained physically distant.

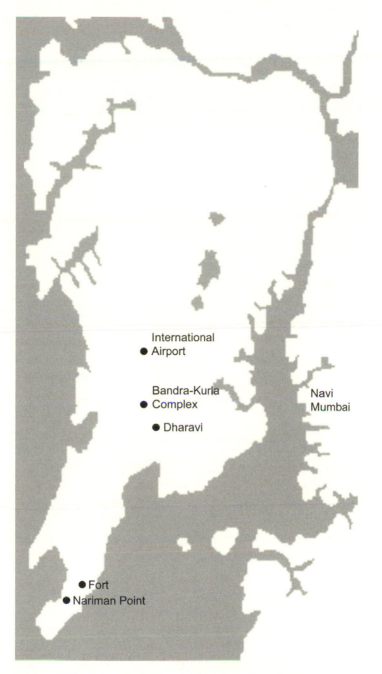

International
● Airport

Bandra-Kurla
● Complex

● Dharavi

Navi
Mumbai

● Fort
● Nariman Point

Figure 9. Map of Mumbai metropolitan region. Photo by author.

As the state's development agencies focused on these large-scale development projects in the 1970s and 1980s, few investments were made in housing or the upkeep of Bombay's civil infrastructures. The promise of opportunity continued to attract workers from all over India, but the existing housing stock proved woefully inadequate to handle the new migrants. Although the developments underway in Navi Mumbai promised to bolster the region's supply of housing, this project moved more slowly than expected and did little to ease the city's housing burden (Shaw 2004). Meanwhile, the new housing that was constructed in Navi Mumbai remained physically inaccessible and unaffordable for the majority of Bombay's residents. With few private-sector investments in residential development and minimal state support for housing in this period, demands for housing continued to outstrip supply and slums proliferated throughout Central Bombay.

The State's Urban Turn

Another explanation for the urban neglect and slum proliferation discernible in this period rests on the weakness of Bombay's municipal governance and the anti-urban bias of the state government. According to the Indian Constitution, housing and urban development are state-level subjects, and decision-making power in these areas, in the case of Mumbai, rests with the Government of Maharashtra. The primary responsibilities of Mumbai's municipal corporation are maintenance and social service activities—including the management of municipal schools, hospitals, parks, fire brigades, sanitation, sewage, and roads. Although an amendment to the Indian Constitution, enacted in the mid-1990s, aimed to devolve greater resources and responsibilities to the municipal level—including the responsibility to plan and implement development schemes—Maharashtra has left the policy largely unimplemented. The state has cited the prohibitive costs of institutional reform, but most observers interpret the state's reticence to implement the amendment as an unwillingness to surrender substantive authority.

As Maharashtra's government has tended to be dominated by rural interests, urban affairs have not received significant attention from the state government (Vora 1996). Changes underway in Maharashtra politics in the mid-1990s, however, created the political conditions for the types of entrepreneurial urban strategies reflected in Bombay First's McKinsey Report and the Dharavi Redevelopment Project. These shifts became apparent after the electoral victory of the right-wing coalition of the Shiv Sena Party and Bharatiya Janata Party (BJP) in 1995. Although the significance of the coalition's five-year rule has generally been understood in the context of anti-Muslim violence and ethnic conflict, the coalition's tenure was also a period of transformation in Mumbai's mode of governance and a greater concern for the conditions of the city. Up to this point, the state's Congress Party—whose leadership hails primarily from rural districts in central and eastern Maharashtra—had maintained almost continuous power in the state. In particular, members of the rural Maratha caste have played a significant role in Maharashtra politics, given the caste members' dominance in local village councils and their control over agricultural cooperatives (Vora 1996). This rural bias in Maharashtra's political leadership helps explain the limited support garnered for housing and urban development efforts throughout much of Bombay's recent history.

In contrast, the government assembled in 1995 was predominantly Mumbai-based, with both its base of support and political leadership hailing from the city (Appadurai 2000; Hansen 2001; Vora 1996). The state's new political geography was reflected in the composition of the government it assembled. The new chief minister, Manohar Joshi, was the first representative of a Mumbai district to hold the chief ministership since the state of Maharashtra was formed in 1960. (In fact, with Dharavi located in Joshi's constituency, Joshi's leadership would help explain the government's support for the Dharavi Redevelopment Project in the coming years.) Eleven out of Joshi's twenty-two cabinet ministers came from urban constituencies and six out of Maharashtra's state ministers came from urban areas (Vora 1996). Key party officials assumed leadership positions in the housing and urban development ministries, and Chief Minister Joshi took control of the urban development portfolio. For the first time in the state's history, development activities in Bombay were overseen largely by Bombayites. This also meant that government officials now had closer ties to the city's business leaders, property developers, and builders—many of whom had open connections to organized crime groups (Hansen 2001; Weinstein 2008). Much of the BJP's leadership was integrated in the city's Gujarati commercial communities and had strong ties to members of the Bombay Chamber of Commerce and Industry (BCCI) (Vora 1996). These ties helped shape a pro-business urban agenda and ensure a strong role for real estate and property interests.

The policies pursued during the government's five-year tenure also reflect its urban composition and base of support. Soon after assuming office, the government sought financing from the World Bank to bolster the city's transportation infrastructure. Under this infrastructure program, some improvements were made along the city's railway lines and more than fifty "flyovers" (overpasses) were built to reduce traffic congestion on the city's overtaxed roads. The government also left a lasting mark on the city's housing landscape. After making the campaign promise of providing free homes to 4 million slum dwellers, the government dramatically expanded the state's slum housing program in the late 1990s—even if the number of units constructed fell far short of its promise (Mukhija 2003). Financed with minimal public expenditure, the new scheme gave private developers access to developable land in exchange for constructing midrise apartment buildings for current slum residents. Although other slum housing programs had been attempted, with varying levels of government commitment, since the early 1970s, this scheme represented the first effort to use inducements to private developers to construct housing (Mukhija 2003; Risbud 2003). The program was seen as particularly attractive to developers because of the high cost of Mumbai's real estate in the mid-1990s. And while local activists initially resisted it, characterizing it as a "give-away to builders," broad-based support eventually emerged. This support reflected the growing belief that the private sector could now play a more visible role in development initiatives (Risbud 2003). Even after the coalition lost power in 1999 and the Congress Party resumed control at the state level, many of these new urban initiatives, including the now popular Slum Housing Scheme, were continued by the new government.

The greater willingness of Maharashtra's government to work with the private sector to pursue these new urban initiatives also reflects a broader ideological shift underway in the mid-1990s. This shift can be explained, in part, as a by-product of the national-level economic reforms undertaken at the time. In 1991, the newly elected national government acquiesced to pressure from the International Monetary Fund to adopt a reform package designed to reduce government regulation and open the economy to foreign investment. Although motions had been made to deregulate certain sectors since the early 1980s, state controls had remained largely intact throughout this period (Denoon 1998; Rudolph and Hoeber Rudolph 1987). Support for economic liberalization had been emerging from certain segments of civil society throughout the 1980s, but India's large and politically powerful industrial houses—most based in Bombay—had maintained resistance to reforms. These firms feared that greater competition would challenge their privileged position, which had been shaped by decades of government subsidies and monopoly protections (Pedersen 2000). For this reason, and because of resistance from influential groups on the left, India moved hesitantly toward liberalization and global integration, even after reforms were adopted in the early 1990s. It has been suggested, then, that the most profound implications of liberalization were more ideological than structural (Corbridge and Harriss 2000; Das 2002). After 1991, there was greater support for the private sector among government officials and the general public; and public-private initiatives became not only feasible but also politically popular.

Meanwhile, the new economic policy also created the perception, both within and outside the country, that India was now open for business. This perception likely explains the sharp rise in Mumbai's real estate prices in the mid-1990s.Land prices rose throughout the city in the 1990s, but commercial real estate in Nariman Point surpassed prices in London's and Tokyo's business districts to become the most expensive property in the world. While the growing distance between this new demand and the dramatically constrained supply helps explain this spike, it has also been suggested that land speculation or "casino capitalism" also drove prices up (Bertaud 2002; Nijman 2000). After liberalization, it was assumed that foreign investors would rush into India's unleashed markets and buy property in the country's commercial capital. And while there was some foreign investment in this period—primarily from nonresident Indians (NRIs), who were allowed to purchase property despite remaining restrictions on foreign direct investment in real estate—the predicted rush never materialized and property prices fell accordingly in the late 1990s (Nijman 2000).

Transforming Mumbai into a World-Class City

Lower-than-expected investments in the 1990s heightened the anxieties of Mumbai's business community that the city's economic position was slipping. Although Mumbai remained India's commercial and financial capital into this period, the deteriorating infrastructures, the proliferating slums, and the prohibitively high cost of real estate—as well as the rise of extremist politics and anti-Muslim violence—were threatening the position the city had held since the early 1800s. Pinpointing the start of this decline, Arjun Appadurai writes: "Sometime in the 1970s all this began to change and a malignant city began to emerge from beneath the surface of the cosmopolitan ethos of the prior period. The change was not sudden, and it was not equally visible in all spheres. But it was unmistakable. Jobs became harder to get. More rural arrivals in the city found themselves economic refugees. Slums and shacks began to proliferate. The wealthy began to get nervous" (2000: 629). These concerns were exacerbated by reductions in industrial employment and relatively slow economic growth in the 1980s (Harris 1995). Meanwhile, South India's high technology centers of Bangalore and Hyderabad were beginning to attract a growing share of foreign and domestic investment. Members of Mumbai's civic leadership grew more vocal about what they perceived as the city's increasingly precarious position.

In the mid-1990s, members of the Bombay Chamber of Commerce and Industry (BCCI) recommended that an organization be formed to advocate for economic development and improvements in the city's quality of life. Modeling itself on a similar organization created by London's business community, the BCCI created Bombay First in 1996. As the former director of Bombay First explained:

> People felt the business was going away, out of Bombay. There was not much business coming into the city. It was moving to Hyderabad, to Bangalore. . . . It was learned that Bombay was going down in two major ways. One was that economic growth in the city was going down. And secondly, economic growth was reducing the quality of life in the city. So in order to bring Bombay back onto the business map of the country, several models were looked into. The New York model was looked into. And London was looked at too. London was going down twenty years ago, when the organization London First had emerged. And we picked up the London First model and we became Bombay First.[2]

Representatives of most of the large foreign and domestic companies with headquarters or offices in Bombay joined these efforts and signed on as members of Bombay First. Bombay First immediately began lobbying the newly elected Shiv Sena–BJP government to make investments and undertake reforms oriented toward improving the conditions of the built environment. With a state government in place that appeared amenable to dedicating resources to urban development and willing to partner with the private sector to secure financing, Bombay First found government generally supportive of its efforts. Meanwhile, its lobbying efforts were helped by the personal and professional ties the new government had to the city's business community.

What was novel about Bombay First were not the specific recommendations its civic leaders made; it was the government's receptivity to those recommendations. The city's civic elite had been demanding investments in housing and land and redevelopment of the city's aging and overtaxed infrastructure since long before independence (Dossal 2010). On a periodic basis, Mumbai's business community and local boosters had formed committees and study groups, together with municipal administrators, to advise the state on urban development priorities. And while the government had adopted some of their recommendations—including the recommendations to develop Navi Mumbai and the Bandra-Kurla Complex in the early 1960s—government priorities and business interests often did not align. Yet with the new government's apparent support of urban development and housing construction and willingness to help private investors secure financing, Bombay First pressed for further investments in these areas.

Even after a Congress Party–led coalition recaptured control of the state in 1999, Bombay First continued to organize seminars and produce reports on issues of concern to its members. The new Congress administration retained a focus on urban development and a willingness to work with the private sector. It continued to work with the World Bank on the Mumbai Urban Transportation Project, continued the private-sector-financed slum housing scheme, and oversaw the sale and development of the city's large plots of defunct textile mill lands. The civic association continued to press the government on what it perceived as its slow pace on these projects and on the absence of comprehensive planning. Consequently, Bombay First hired the global management consulting firm McKinsey & Company to compile a set of recommendations to improve the city's competitive position. Civic leaders recognized that the recommendations of international consultants may carry more weight and bring more attention to their agenda. Over a period of five months, McKinsey & Company analyzed the city's economic conditions and governance arrangements, conducting approximately thirty interviews and holding focus groups with government officials and representatives from business and civil society. They also conducted brief case studies of several cities—including Bangalore, Hyderabad, Shanghai, and Cleveland—that had apparently improved their economic standing in recent years. In September 2003, amidst considerable fanfare, Bombay First released *Vision Mumbai: A Summary of Recommendations for Transforming Mumbai into a World Class City*.

Drawing familiar conclusions, the McKinsey Report attributed the city's precarious position to low levels of job growth and a declining quality of life. It optimistically proclaimed that, with investments of approximately $40 million from the private and public sectors, Mumbai could make "jumps toward achieving world city status" in ten to fifteen years. It recommended that government use tax incentives and direct subsidies to promote job creation in the high technology, retail, and entertainment sectors. It recommended that further investments be made to improve the city's transportation infrastructure, bolster its housing stock, and increase the supply of developable land. And, in the short term, it recommended that the municipal corporation revamp Mumbai's sanitation and waste management systems and renovate the international airport. Although it also made recommendations for improving municipal governance and facilitating job growth, much of the report focused on the city's physical construction. In order to become a world-class city, it suggested, government would have to make a commitment to urban development through investments in housing and infrastructure. In contrast to many of the earlier study groups and advisory committees, the McKinsey Report's development recommendations were centered in the city itself, rather than on developing outlying regions. This signaled a revived push to the city center and a revival of downtown development.

Although the report was a surprisingly thin thirty-page document, repeating recommendations made by civic leaders and municipal administrators for decades, it immediately generated debate and criticism. It also appeared to elicit government action, including the slum demolition campaign of 2004–2005. In early December 2003, the city's academics and activists held a seminar at the Tata Institute of Social Science to express concerns about the McKinsey Report. The seminar yielded over a dozen papers critiquing the report's recommendations on social, political, and environmental grounds. Housing advocates and social service organizations criticized its recommendations as anti-poor and identified the negligible role for community groups, while environmental groups expressed concern about the potential impacts of its recommended development on the city's fragile ecosystem. Meanwhile, the chief minister created a government taskforce to issue its own plan for "transforming Mumbai into a world class city" within a decade (State of Maharashtra 2004). The taskforce plan adopted many of the McKinsey Report's recommendations verbatim and created an administrative structure to carry them out. In an effort to hold itself accountable and bring greater legitimacy to this new development agenda, the government hired McKinsey & Company to oversee implementation of the taskforce plan. Over the next three years, McKinsey & Company was paid roughly $200,000 to conduct an audit of the government bureaucracy and document the implementation activities (Marpakwar 2006). Meanwhile, many of the government's actions undertaken over the next year, including its massive slum demolition campaign, were justified as means necessary to transform Mumbai into a "world class city."

"Slum-Free Mumbai"

The same month that it released the taskforce plan, the State of Maharashtra adopted a second consultant-devised development scheme to address the city's housing problem and bolster its competitive position. This scheme proposed the redevelopment of the one-square-mile slum settlement of Dharavi—popularly referred to as "Asia's largest slum"—by replacing its housing stock, making infrastructure improvements, and promoting commercial development in the area. Approved at a state cabinet meeting with significant media attention, bold proclamations were made that Dharavi would be transformed into a cultural, business, and knowledge center and that Mumbai would be "slum free by 2020." In doing so, the state made slum redevelopment a key component of Mumbai's transformation to a "world class city" by preparing to remove the eyesore that Dharavi had been for decades and facilitating the clearance of land for commercial development. As the government affirmed its commitment to these objectives, it approved the plan developed by the private developer and architect Mukesh Mehta and hired his company MM Consultants to oversee its implementation.

Mehta's plan for Dharavi's redevelopment has gone through many incarnations since it garnered state approval in February 2004, and it will likely change further before it is implemented in the coming years. The current version proposes Dharavi's division into five sectors of roughly equal size. Each sector will continue to house most of the current residents and much of the commerce and industry currently located in the area, in addition to significant new commercial developments. New schools, parks, hospitals, and other civic amenities are proposed for each sector, along with improved transportation and utility infrastructures across all of Dharavi. Each household deemed eligible for "rehabilitation"[3] will receive an apartment in a mid- or high-rise building. Consistent with the Slum Housing Scheme launched by the Shiv Sena government in the mid-1990s, the project will be financed by consortia of private developers, who will be compensated with additional land and increased height allowances to develop commercial properties. Project delays, administrative problems, and the current global financial crisis have reduced the attractiveness of the project in recent years, leading to the withdrawal of many of the development firms that initially applied to bid on the project in June 2007. Yet the remaining developers have been assured that they will easily recoup their expenses and make considerable profits on the proposed commercial developments given Mumbai's high land prices and the desirability of Dharavi's location.

The project also reflects the new objectives of Mumbai's slum housing program, namely, the conversion of land to facilitate commercial and residential development. Earlier programs—notably the "sites and services" programs of the 1970s and 1980s—provided residents the opportunity and resources to make improvements on their homes and construct sanitation and utility infrastructures (Risbud 2003).The current housing scheme created in the 1990s, meanwhile, is based on the demolition of low-lying hutments and construction of midrise apartment blocks. In the process, hundreds of acres of developable land have been freed up. While the shift from slum improvement to slum rehabilitation has had significant implications for the residents, it has also led to a new context of urban development and new opportunities for development in the central city. Amid this shift, the improved housing for residents has gone from being the program's primary objective to becoming simply the means to meeting the new ends of clearing centrally located and potentially valuable land for development.

Although this plan was not explicitly mentioned in either the McKinsey Report or the taskforce document, these objectives are consistent with the government's new development agenda. Furthermore, the taskforce did include certain development activities in Dharavi among its immediate and longer-term goals. Specifically, the document recommended the development of "at least three sectors of Dharavi for commercial or office use, and [the extension of] the Bandra-Kurla Complex to Dharavi" (State of Maharashtra 2004: 14). The Bandra-Kurla Complex, whose construction was initially proposed by the state government advisory committee in the early 1960s, has been identified as one of the major successes of the government's urban development efforts of the past few decades. Although the project faced significant political and technical hurdles and took almost four decades to complete, it has yielded hundreds of acres of highly coveted office space a short distance from Mumbai's international airport. In a series of auctions in the mid-2000s, land prices in the complex surpassed those in Nariman Point to become Mumbai's most expensive real estate. With Dharavi located directly adjacent to the Bandra-Kurla Complex, separated by a short causeway across the Mahim River, the government has linked slum improvement in Dharavi to the complex's commercial development. And given that a major route from both the international airport and Bandra-Kurla Complex to South Mumbai's central business district now passes through Dharavi's narrow and congested roads, improvements in Dharavi's transportation infrastructure would better link developments across Greater Mumbai.

In addition to the plan's congruence with the McKinsey Report, the state's endorsement of Mehta's plan must also be attributed simply to his perseverance. Government approval of the Dharavi Redevelopment Project in February 2004 was the culmination of seven years Mehta spent designing the plan and soliciting support from the government. Originally from Mumbai, Mehta had settled in the United States, earning a degree in architecture and eventually working on the development of high-end residential properties on Long Island. He returned to India in 1997 to explore the possibility of participating in the government's new slum redevelopment scheme and constructing housing in Dharavi. Mehta was one of the many developers interested in participating in the new slum scheme in the mid-1990s, recognizing it as a way to acquire developable land in Mumbai's lucrative real estate market. Although he was a U.S. citizen, Mehta had the opportunity to invest in the scheme given his status as an NRI. He then spent more than five years selling his plan to officials in the state and central governments. As he began to elicit government support for the project, his role shifted from developer to consultant and housing advisor. By the time the state approved the Dharavi Redevelopment Project in 2004, Mehta would no longer be a developer on the scheme, but had assumed the more powerful and likely more lucrative position of Project Management Consultant.[4] Before construction on the project had even begun in Dharavi, Mehta had established himself as a consultant on slum and housing issues. In recent years, his consulting firm, MM Consultants, has been providing technical assistance on slum redevelopment to several cities in India, including Hyderabad,

Bangalore, and Nagpur, and making presentations to government officials throughout the world.

Mumbai's Development "Consultocracy"?

Mukesh Mehta and McKinsey & Company are not the first international consultants to contribute to land use planning and urban development in Mumbai. In the early twentieth century, Scottish planner and sociologist Patrick Geddes proposed coordinated land use plans for the city, while American Albert Mayer helped design the city's first master plan in the late1940s. The construction of the satellite city of Navi Mumbai in the 1970s and 1980s was based largely on the designs of private architects and planners (Shaw 2004). The Mumbai Urban Transportation Project and other World Bank–financed initiatives have, meanwhile, employed World Bank economists and advisors to provide guidance and oversight. Yet what differentiates the current role McKinsey and Mehta have assumed is the visibility of their consulting activities. While consultants on earlier schemes had advised Indian bureaucrats in the background, today Mehta and McKinsey consult in the foreground, in public announcements and amid considerable media attention.

The publicity these consultants have received has given visibility and legitimacy to the state's development agenda. The state's willingness to back Mehta's plan and support the recommendations of the McKinsey Report can be attributed less to the content of their recommendations and more to the premium placed on the consultants' global recognition. As a Mumbai-based economist and former advisor to Bombay First explained:"What happens is there's a lot of pressure—pressure from big business, pressure from multilateral aid agencies, pressure to make reforms. . . . If I were a politician, and I was told, look you're doing nothing for Bombay, what would I do? I'd say look I've appointed the best consulting firm in the world. Look, I've appointed McKinsey. So, I could say we're doing something."[5]

The local prominence Mehta and McKinsey have achieved is not unique to Mumbai, but it is reflective of the growth of consultancy across all economic sectors. With greater uncertainty arising from the integration of the global economy, consultants have been employed to advise firms and governments on external conditions and help them mitigate risk (Clark and Dear 1984; Evers and Menkhoff 2004; Giddens 1999). Meanwhile, it has been recognized that as globalization brings greater uniformity to state structures and local policy instruments, consultants act as the diffusers of globally accepted norms and practices (Fourcade 2006; Meyer et al. 1997). As global recognition becomes a precondition for acquiring local legitimacy, governments have grown dependent on consultants to legitimate a variety of policy initiatives. This has created the condition some scholars have referred to as a "consultocracy" (McCann 2001; Sam and Scherer 2006). Under this condition, the experience of local actors is less valued than the expertise of external consultants. A premium is placed on their knowledge of external conditions, their global standards, and their notoriety. Although this condition has been recognized in other contexts, it appears to have particular resonance in India, where local and national governments have approached global integration with greater hesitancy.

The greater mobility of capital and the growing perception that the work of capitalism can be done from anywhere in the world led cities to adopt entrepreneurial strategies to attract economic activity like those recommended by McKinsey & Company. While economists debate how much control local policy makers have over the location of firms and whether the strategies they employ actually improve the competitiveness of particular places, it is apparent that urban governance has been recast in a competitive frame (Gordon 1999; Lever and Turok 1999). And as local governments increasingly adopt entrepreneurial strategies to court "customers"—that is, investors, transnational firms, residents, tourists, and others who will support cities' economic activity—consultants are believed to provide the information necessary to bolster cities' competitive positions.

These dynamics help explain the visibility of planning consultants within the formulation of Mumbai's current downtown development agenda. Even though the recommendations of the McKinsey Report were similar to those made by Mumbai's civic leadership and municipal bureaucrats for decades, the state's efforts to implement them were legitimated by their association with McKinsey & Company. Similarly, the value placed on external knowledge helps explain why the government chose to support Mehta's plan for redeveloping Dharavi when similar, locally conceived plans had failed to elicit state action. The global recognition Mehta bestowed on the project gave the government the confidence to pursue the Dharavi project. By associating with these external planning consultants, the Government of Maharashtra has been able to deflect some of the political fallout resulting from its adoption of an entrepreneurial urban agenda. The urban poor, who remain politically engaged and vote en masse, tend to punish politicians for undertaking slum clearance and pursuing a pro-business agenda. And because the majority of state-level politicians continue to represent rural constituents, the use of state resources to finance urban development activities remains largely untenable. Yet with the city's civic leadership and national government placing pressure on the state to prioritize urban development, Maharashtra's politicians have faced a difficult political calculus. By forming strategic partnerships with private consultants, the state can more legitimately carry out a downtown development agenda it feels both obliged and constrained to pursue.

Noting these conditions and highlighting two recent consultant-led development plans, this chapter has revealed the value placed on the authority and legitimacy of private consultants in Mumbai's recent pursuit of a downtown development agenda. Although further research is required to more fully reveal the implications and discover its relevance in other contexts, it is likely that this phenomenon is not unique to Mumbai. Although it is likely more prevalent in Indian cities, given the particular politics of economic liberalization and globalization, cities in other regions are likely employing externally recognized consultants to help in the construction of global downtowns.

11

Downtown as Brand, Downtown as Land: Urban Elites and Neoliberal Development in Contemporary New York City

Julian Brash

On Monday, July 6, 2005, the New York Public Authority Control Board (PACB) took a fateful vote. This obscure governmental body, its members appointed by the governor and the leaders of the two houses of the state legislature, held the power to approve—or deny—the public borrowing necessary to fund the New York Sports and Convention Center, or as it was better known in the city, the west side stadium. The stadium, to be built over rail yards owned by a public authority, the Metropolitan Transportation Authority (MTA), would occupy three large blocks on Manhattan's Hudson River waterfront. It would serve as the central facility of the 2012 Summer Olympic Games, for which New York City was a candidate, as well as the home of the New York Jets football team, currently located in New Jersey. It was also a key element of a massive and complex development scheme put forward by the mayoral administration of ex-CEO billionaire Michael Bloomberg in partnership with NYC2012, the private organization organizing the city's bid for the games. The Hudson Yards plan, as it was known, would push Manhattan's Midtown central business district westward from Times Square to the Hudson River by extending the city's subway system, stimulating commercial and residential development, expanding the Jacob Javits convention center (also on the Hudson), and developing acres of new park land. The stadium served as the political lynch-pin of the plan: by linking it to the Olympic bid, the stadium would neutralize the community opposition that had helped scuttle a decades-long series of plans for the makeover of the west side. Or so it was hoped by the plan's proponents, anyway.

As of that Monday in July 2006, the stadium had one significant hurdle left to overcome: the PACB. But after a frantic weekend of lobbying by stadium proponents, the board rejected the funding for the stadium. The community, it seemed, had won the battle.

A Model of Urban Neoliberalism?

Jeff Maskovsky has written that "neoliberal [urban] governance has been conceptualized to help make the crucial link between the broad economic changes known as 'globalization' and the actual ideological and political practice of governance at the municipal level in the wake of those changes" (2006: 77). Neoliberal urban governance constitutes an effort on the part of the local state to restructure economic, cultural, social, and political relations and processes within cities according to the perceived realities of globalization. This has typically entailed an interrelated set of tactics aimed to attract mobile capital and populations deemed crucial to the new global/ postindustrial economy, as well as the reconstruction of urban environments in line with these goals (Hackworth 2007; Peck 2005; Peck and Tickell 2002). But such broad consistencies across space do not mean that neoliberal governance is monolithic, self-contained, or all-powerful (Kingfisher and Maskovsky 2008; Wilson 2004). Instead, it is highly contingent on local conditions, articulated with other processes and projects, and subject to political contestation. Neoliberal urban governance reflects the very sort of scalar and theoretical tensions encapsulated in the notion of the "global downtown."

This chapter focuses on the implications of this formulation of neoliberalism for urban politics. Many analyses of the politics of urban neoliberalism have reflected the broader tendency within urban studies to paint the constitution of and relationships between elites and non-elites in broad and oversimplified strokes: as structured around conflicts between those dedicated to the commodification of the city (real estate developers, most politicians, representatives of global capital, and so on) and those ("the community") attempting to resist such efforts and preserve the use-values derived from place. However, a number of scholars have sought to complicate this picture, arguing that we need to see "contestation as more than just resistance to neoliberalism" (Leitner et al. 2007: 2), bringing into view the complex political relationships between communities and neoliberalizers. These relationships involve not just straightforward opposition but negotiation, mutual co-optation, and even alliance (Larner and Butler 2007; Morgen and Gonzales 2008; Wilson 2008).

Crucial to this work has been the insight that communities are not "static, place-based social collective[s] but . . . power-laden field[s] of social relations whose meanings, structures, and frontiers are continually produced, contested, and reworked in relation to a complex range of sociopolitical attachments and antagonisms" (Gregory 1998: 11).[1] Communities are internally differentiated by gender, class, race, ideology, sexuality, ethnicity, tenure, age, and so forth. As their members pursue their various agendas, interests, and projects, communities are linked in complex, changing, and even constitutive ways to processes, people, and institutions beyond their borders. These connections can compound the complexities of community, often in ways that make allegiances ambiguous and that exacerbate power differentials within communities. All this has important implications for the analysis of the political dynamics of neoliberalization, as it renders nonsensical the simple couplet of neoliberal power and community resistance.

As much as urbanists have done to explore the political dynamics of urban neoliberalism *within* communities and to sketch out the ways in which members of communities engage as well as oppose neoliberal development strategies, they have paid relatively little attention to *elite* agents of neoliberalization.[2] When urban elites involved in neoliberal urban development are discussed, they tend to be portrayed as static, undifferentiated, and motivated directly (as in the case of developers and corporate executives) or indirectly (as in the case of neoliberalizing politicians) by the enhancement of the exchange value extracted from urban space, that is, as avatars of neoliberal policies, rather than as individuals and groups with complex identities, interests, motivations, and relationships. The view up seems a lot simpler than the view down.

Moreover, there is little exploration of the ways in which neoliberalization might produce intra-elite conflict. This is a noteworthy oversight given the fact that the neoliberal development of cities in the United States has gone hand in hand with the ascension of a new postindustrial elite composed of both upper professionals and corporate executives (Brash 2006; Ley 1996). While this new elite group has generally avoided direct involvement in the political process, it has nevertheless been a direct beneficiary and core constituency of neoliberal urban development. It seems reasonable to expect that the relations between this emergent elite, with its very particular cultural, political, and economic makeup, and more established elite groups will be as complex and ambiguous as those within communities.

Drawing on this uneven theoretical terrain, it is possible to view the story of the west side stadium as familiar and straightforward, albeit with a relatively rare outcome. The Hudson Yards plan seems a paradigmatic neoliberal development scheme, yet another effort to restructure a section of an American downtown as a space hospitable to corporate investment, real estate development, and elite consumption and leisure. The tenements, industrial buildings, and transportation infrastructure currently characterizing the west side would give way to eighty-story office buildings housing finance and media companies, upscale residences, outlets for leisure and waterfront activities, and a lavishly subsidized, architecturally cutting-edge (and ostensibly "green") stadium—a playground for postindustrial professionals and corporate executives. All this would be governed by nominally public authorities and public-private partnerships essentially outside the realm of democratic accountability, and financed by risky and labyrinthine financing arrangements predicated on a lack of federal funding and an aversion to traditional (that is, legislatively approved) methods. Finally, the Hudson Yards plan was subsumed in a broader development agenda animated by the marketing and management techniques that Mayor Bloomberg and many of his top aides had imported from the private sector, aiming to enhance New York City's "brand" as a postindustrial powerhouse hospitable to media, finance, business services, and information technology firms and as a space of cosmopolitanism, consumption, and culture appropriate to their elite employees in the name of competitive advantage, economic development, and growth.

Against this neoliberal juggernaut stood a diverse and often unstable coalition of poor people, artists, disaffected professionals, and affordable housing advocates who aimed to defend their neighborhood against what they saw as an onslaught of commodification, hyper-gentrification, cultural deracination, corporatization, and spiraling costs. Despite its internal differences, the community struggled, unsuccessfully, to articulate an alternative vision of the city and of development that reflected its own priorities. But it was able to muster enough influence to halt what was, in its members' eyes, the most egregious element of the Hudson Yards plan, the west side stadium.

While in keeping with the evolving consensus of the critical scholarship of urban neoliberalism, this framing of the Hudson Yards plan and the west side stadium also reflects its shortcomings: all the tension, contingency, and specificity remain on the side of the community. Little attention is paid to the social makeup, interests, imaginaries, or internal divisions of the project's elite proponents. This is a problem. For what might seem at first glance like a straightforward victory of the community over a paradigmatic neoliberal development project was enabled by intra-elite conflict. In the pages that follow I will draw on fieldwork focusing on the Hudson Yards plan conducted in New York City from 2000 to 2006 to explore this conflict and its impacts on the outcome of the controversy over the west side stadium.

Downtown as Brand

As enhancing competitiveness has become a central goal of urban policy in the United States, cities have sought to distinguish themselves via shifts in urban policy and concrete interventions into urban space (Harvey 2001; Peck and Tickell 2002). They have also attempted interventions in imaginative space, through the use of branding and marketing techniques. In fact, these two strategies have been tightly linked, as "the 'real' material city [has been] altered as much as possible to conform to the idealized image of the brand" (Greenberg 2008: 34).

Broader political-economic shifts no doubt set the stage for branding's new importance in the production of urban space, but they cannot account for the emergence of branding campaigns in particular cities. Explaining why such strategies emerge when they do and how they do or how they relate to other neoliberal (and non-neoliberal) policies requires close attention to the agents behind particular branding strategies, the urban imaginaries branding campaigns draw upon and propagate, and the details of their implementation and relationship with other policy areas. The Hudson Yards plan was part of a larger branding strategy developed by the administration of Mayor Michael Bloomberg; the provenance of this branding strategy and the plan's place in it were crucial to the outcome of the conflict over the

Hudson Yards plan. With that in mind, let us explore the social origins and development of this unmistakably neoliberal but nevertheless unique branding strategy.

The Postindustrial Elite Enters City Hall

The neoliberalizing regime of fiscal austerity and business friendliness imposed after New York City's fiscal crisis of the 1970s supercharged the postindustrialization of its economy. It weakened support for working and middle-class consumption and undercut industrial diversity while lavishing government largesse on the financial, media, business services, and information industries and on the real estate developers who built the shiny new Manhattan office buildings that housed these industries (Brash 2004; Sites 2003). The result was a transformation of not just New York City's economy and landscape, but its class structure, as this period saw the development of an economically ascendant postindustrial elite consisting of executives and high-level professionals. From the 1970s through the 1990s, this postindustrial elite generally shaped urban policy in indirect ways. Most notable were attempts on the part of city government to cater to its members' tastes, desires, and needs through the rollback of crime and disorder and the production of desirable consumption, leisure, and residential spaces. It was with the 2001 election of Michael Bloomberg as mayor that this group directly engaged the city's governance. Bloomberg's managerial and entrepreneurial experience, pithily summarized by one journalist as "I'm a good manager; therefore, I should run the city" (Wolff 2001), served as the core of his campaign appeal.

Once the Bloomberg administration was ensconced in City Hall, its class character quickly became apparent. Bloomberg made a number of important hires from the private sector, especially from the financial and management consulting industries, to aid in the development of a new competitive strategy for the city. The first was that of Daniel Doctoroff, a successful investment banker who first entered public life in 1994, when he began the campaign to bring the 2012 Summer Olympic Games to New York City by founding NYC2012. A second was Andrew Alper, a former COO of Goldman Sachs and political neophyte, who was appointed head of the city's chief economic development agency, the Economic Development Corporation (EDC). Other members of the city's postindustrial elite accompanied these two into city government. While their service in the administration was in part induced by a sense of obligation to the city in its post-9/11 time of need, it was also motivated by a sense of collective identity founded upon social and personal connections, professional networks, and a shared ideology of globality and managerialism. No longer just encountering each other on the streets of the Upper East Side or in the conference rooms of midtown skyscrapers, members of New York City's postindustrial elite now brushed shoulders in the grand chambers and back rooms of City Hall.

Rebranding New York City

Whereas other mayors, in New York City and elsewhere, have viewed the fierce interurban competition that is central to contemporary urban policy as a necessary evil, a political reality in globalizing times, Mayor Bloomberg enthusiastically placed increasing competitiveness at the center of city development policy. Along with many of the key staffers he pulled from the private sector, the mayor brought to municipal government a deep-seated belief in the beneficence of competition, not just for consumers, but for competitors as well. Under the rubric of competitiveness, urban development policy melded with issues of identity and meaning (Brash 2006).

Accordingly, Mayor Bloomberg, Deputy Mayor Doctoroff, and EDC President Alper placed enhancing the city's competitiveness at the center of economic and urban development strategy. "New York is in a fierce, worldwide competition," Bloomberg said in his 2003 State of the City address: "we must offer the best product—and sell it, forcefully" (2003). Early in Bloomberg's first term, EDC President Andrew Alper, testifying before the City Council, said:

> We are . . . trying to make sure that we do a better job of marketing and positioning New York City *as a brand*. McKinsey & Co. [has] interviewed companies . . . to help us think about . . . our competitive advantages and disadvantages. . . . . We are thinking about what companies we should target. . . . In the past, I think, we relied on the fact that New York is the crossroads of the world, it is the business capital of the world. We sort of let people come to us. Well, you know what? We need to go to them now. It is time for us to get on the road and tell

our story. It is a very compelling story. Yes, it is expensive. Yes, it is
crowded, but there is a reason it is crowded. It is a great place to live
and to work . . . we have to get that story out. (2002; emphasis added)

Throughout 2002, Alper and his staff conducted an intensive campaign of
market research, supplementing the McKinsey study with meetings with
the city's leading business group and consultation with economic development experts. Meanwhile, Deputy Mayor Doctoroff reorganized city development agencies, consolidating them under his command and implementing
a number of private-sector managerial techniques. The result was a streamlined and powerful development apparatus focused intently on enhancing
the city's competitiveness.

The results of this year of reorganization and research were unveiled at a
major economic development summit hosted by Mayor Bloomberg in January 2003. During the conference, Bloomberg made it clear that the city's
competitive strength was not its costs but the value it offered. "If New York
City is a business, it isn't Wal-Mart—it isn't trying to be the lowest-priced
product in the market," said Bloomberg. "It's a high-end product, maybe
even a luxury product. New York offers tremendous value, but only for those
companies able to capitalize on it" (Cardwell 2003). The particular market
that this "product" would be geared toward was the very high-end corporate
sector that Bloomberg, and others, had emerged from. "When you start to
get to the higher value-added businesses," the summit's chair, the financier
and former Treasury Secretary Robert Rubin, said after the summit, "the
advantage of being here is so enormous that it seems to me [the city's] going
to continue to hold and attract businesses" (Cardwell 2003).

This "luxury city" strategy soon had concrete effects. The administration
curtailed the indiscriminate granting of business retention tax incentives
prevalent in the past, labeling them "corporate welfare" and promising that
incentives would be used only to attract jobs and investment. When faced
with budget gaps early in his first term, Mayor Bloomberg pushed to raise
property taxes rather than slashing services, in direct contrast to the tax-
cutting orthodoxy embraced by his predecessor and fellow Republican
mayor, Rudy Giuliani. For the Bloomberg administration, value trumped
cost: high-quality public services were more important than low taxes for
the kinds of businesses and employees likely to be attracted to New York City.

In pursuing this strategy, the administration was replicating state-of-
the-art competitive strategy. David Aaker, a prominent expert in this field,

has written, "brand power ... is the only alternative to destructive price competition. The customer's loyalty needs to be based not on prices, but on points of differentiation, including brand personality, intangibles, emotional benefits and self-expressive benefits" (2002: xi). Management superguru Tom Peters puts it even more starkly when he writes, "in an increasingly crowded marketplace, fools will compete on price. Winners will find a way to create lasting value in the customer's mind" (Aaker and Joachimsthaler 2000: 16). Mayor Bloomberg, Deputy Mayor Doctoroff, and EDC President Alper had certainly been winners in their private-sector careers: now, in Bloomberg's words, they were "preparing all of New York to compete—and win" (2004).

Urban Development as Product Development

The task now was to develop the "product" and to sell it. EDC President Alper would be in charge of marketing the city through direct media, road shows, corporate outreach, and advertising: practices typical of urban marketing campaigns in New York and elsewhere. More pertinent to this discussion, and more remarkable, was the approach Deputy Mayor Doctoroff, as the official charged with guiding planning and urban development policy, would take. Doctoroff explicitly conceptualized urban development as product development, particularly in the arena of office development, speaking repeatedly of the need to "offer different products for different corporate customers" (DeDapper 2004).

In his 2003 State of the City address, Mayor Bloomberg indicated that the notion of urban development as product development went well beyond the development of diversified office districts. He argued that exploiting the city's competitive advantages required nothing less than an aggressive transformation of its physical form in order to produce an environment appropriate to the needs and desires of the well-educated professionals and their employers in the city's postindustrial sectors: "To capitalize on [our] strengths, we'll continue to transform New York physically ... to make it even more attractive to the world's most talented people. New York is the city where the world's best and brightest want to live and work. That gives us an unmatched competitive edge, one we'll sharpen with investments in neighborhoods, parks and housing[,] neighborhood livability, cultural organizations, education, research and medicine. . . . That [also] means starting today to expand and develop business districts in all five boroughs" (2003). Bloomberg outlined an aggressive and comprehensive program of urban development. Each element of this program was clearly related to the enhancement of the city's competitive strengths. Waterfront development, new parks, housing development, and steps toward neighborhood "livability" would create a high-quality residential and recreation environment attractive to well-educated professionals. The development of new office districts in Manhattan's west side, downtown Brooklyn, Long Island City and Flushing in Queens, and the Hub in the Bronx would provide space for both high-level and back-office functions. Over the rest of its first term, the administration aggressively pursued this agenda, as Deputy Mayor Doctoroff's efficient and centralized development apparatus successfully moved a series of major rezonings and development projects through the approval process.

The Hudson Yards Plan

This agenda of urban development as product development represented the most aggressive of its type since the days of Robert Moses. While all the elements of this strategy were important, one project was first among equals: the Hudson Yards plan. The plan served as both capstone and microcosm of the Bloomberg administration's development strategy. It would create the city's next great office district, where eighty-story office buildings would provide "prestigious addresses" for the high-margin companies that administration officials had indicated were best suited to capitalize on a New York City location. Its proposals for luxury housing, waterfront development, and new open spaces would appeal to the postindustrial elite. Its convention center expansion would bolster the marketing of the city as a magnet for visitors from the world over. Finally, the Hudson Yards plan was the most important element of NYC2012's plan for the Olympics, an event that dovetailed with the ideas of competition, ambition, cosmopolitanism, and diversity so crucial to the administration's efforts to market the city, as well as to the vision of the city held by its ex-corporate executive leaders.

So, while the Hudson Yards plan can be viewed as a typical neoliberal downtown development megaproject, it emerged from a particular social, economic, and political context. The Hudson Yards plan was part of a citywide development strategy animated by a particular corporatized imagining of the city as a product to be branded and marketed. In turn, this neoliberal urban imaginary and development strategy were themselves rooted in processes of class transformation in the city, as an ascendant postindustrial elite sought to put its stamp on the city and, in the process of doing so, solidified its own collective identity. But this only goes so far in explaining the political trajectory of the Hudson Yards plan in general, and the west side stadium in particular. To complete our analysis, we need to now turn to the role of intra-elite conflict. For crucial opposition to the stadium came not only from the community, but from another segment of the city's elite, its real estate interests.

Downtown as Land

Despite the historical importance of the city's financial industry and the recent growth of other postindustrial sectors, "New York's main business is and always has been real estate development" (Zukin 2002: 16). Accordingly, New York City's politics have long been dominated by real estate interests (Angotti 2008; Fainstein 2001; Fitch 1993), particularly the city's great real estate dynasties, families that own and have developed countless residential commercial buildings throughout the city. The economic and political dominance of these families has eroded somewhat in recent years because of familial conflict and the resulting liquidation of real estate holdings (Shachtman 2000), as well as the increasing investment in city real estate by foreign real estate investors and national real estate investment trusts (Angotti 2008: 52–58). Nevertheless, the scions of these families, men (and they are almost entirely male) such as Douglas Durst, Larry Silverstein, Joseph Rose, Richard Ravitch, and William Rudin, have been the most prominent and powerful figures in city development politics (Angotti 2008: 41–42; Fainstein 2001: 74, 133; Moody 2007: 206). For these families, urban development has intense familial, social, and cultural connotations shaped by both a deep commitment to the city and a sense of insularity and exclusivity.

This commitment to the city is embodied by the fact that, for a number of reasons, the city's great real estate fortunes have been built on buying and holding, rather than short-term speculation (Shachtman 2000). Real estate development, especially in New York's complex political, regulatory, and economic context, is heavily dependent on local knowledge: particular real estate projects can take decades to develop and implement, and require constant supervision (Fainstein 2001: 69–73). In addition, the dynastic aspect of the city's real estate elite imbues projects with a level of meaning that transcends the economic alone—as one prominent real estate lawyer said in an interview, as he gestured out the window of his midtown office at the surrounding skyscrapers: "Look around . . . I've had a hand in almost everything; most of them are my babies" (Real Deal 2004). This leads to an unwillingness to sell property unless absolutely necessary (Shachtman 2000: 12).

This sense of commitment leads to the intense involvement of members of the city's real estate dynasties in efforts aiming to safeguard the city's prosperity. Many have served in powerful positions within the various bureaucracies that shape urban development in New York City, or have led or participated in particular redevelopment efforts. They head civic organizations, sit on the boards of major cultural, medical, and educational institutions, and pour vast amounts of money into philanthropic causes, often without public acknowledgment (Shachtman 2000: 9), in stark contrast to much corporate philanthropy, which often serves as a form of public relations.

Of course, these economic and philanthropic commitments, and even philanthropic anonymity, are not completely selfless. Even as it benefits the city at large, philanthropy supports the social, medical, and cultural infrastructure that undergirds its economy, which in turn helps prop up the value of real estate. Such commitments also bind together the city's real estate dynasties into a self-conscious, coherent, and highly exclusive social group.

Indeed, the city's prominent real estate families often display a deep insularity and a deep suspicion of outsiders and of competing interests. Social interaction and intermarriage are quite common, and are reinforced by common history and cultural heritage (Shachtman 2000: passim). Many of these real estate families came to New York at the end of the nineteenth century, driven by a series of Russian anti-Jewish pogroms. For a variety of historical, political, and economic reasons, they moved into the city's real estate and building trades industries, and began "to a degree far exceeding any other small group of people, to shape the city's skyline" (Shachtman 2000: 56; see 54–76 for more on this history).

This history, along with the structural position of real estate capital, has much to do with the high degree of insularity displayed by the members of these families. As one former official in the city's Real Estate Board, which represents the industry, told me, they "live in great terror—of tenants, of zoning, of politicians." Real estate development in New York City is heavily dependent upon and regulated by the local government, with which it has a symbiotic, if at times tense, relationship. On the one hand, there is mutual benefit: politicians draw much of their campaign funding from the real estate industry and the local government derives much of its revenue from real estate taxes of various sorts, while real estate projects depend on the local government for tax incentives, favorable zoning changes, and supportive infrastructure investments. On the other hand, local government is often pressured by tenants to keep a lid on rents and by neighborhood residents and groups to limit the scale of real estate development, making politicians at times unreliable partners. Moreover, real estate's immobility makes it an attractive target for taxation in times of budgetary crisis, giving large property owners a sense, often overstated, of being treated as municipal piggybanks (see Shachtman 2000: 20).

These various social, economic, and cultural currents have generated an imagining of the city and its downtown as *land*: land as a valuable and deeply emplaced source of not just wealth but familial heritage, local commitment, and in-group status. A quote and an anecdote from my fieldwork capture this. The quote is from Joseph Rose, a scion of a major New York real estate family, who at the time—December 2000—was Mayor Rudy Giuliani's city planning commissioner. Rose concluded his remarks at a conference focused on the redevelopment of the west side by saying: "This is our future, our growth potential. . . . This is clearly our birthright" (2000). Conceptualizing the redevelopment of the west side as crucial to the city's future economic growth is not particularly remarkable. But the notion of the development of the west side as "birthright" clearly indicates that far more than money is at stake.

However, money *is* at stake for real estate elites, though it too is inextricably bound to the land; or rather *in* the land, as the anecdote I want to relate will make clear. In November 2004, Henry Wollman, a former developer with deep roots in the city's real estate elite who at the time headed a local real estate policy institute, presented an alternative plan for the redevelopment of the west side to the local community board. It entailed razing the Jacob Javits Convention Center, which occupied several blocks along the Hudson, and reconstructing it perpendicular to the river. Wollman excitedly described the result: "Once the flip is done, look [at] what it gives you: a blank slate from 34th to 41st Street along the waterfront. The unlocked value of those blocks is $3 billion . . . [value] that with the Javits Center cannot be accessed. . . . By removing the Javits Center, we will be unleashing $3 billion worth of the real estate value of the city" (2004). Here we see an imagining of land as a storehouse of value, just waiting to be unlocked.

Real estate elites and their allies understand themselves as charged with protecting and exploiting this source of multifaceted value in the face of shortsighted politicians, knee-jerk opponents of development, parochial neighborhood groups, and others who would undermine the city's prosperity by placing curbs on real estate development. Thus, implicitly paired with this urban imaginary is a development strategy premised on the idea that the role of public action is to facilitate the private development of particular parcels of land to the highest intensity that political and economic conditions allow (Angotti 2008: 37–79; Fitch 1993: 49). Given the complexities of the development process, this requires a good deal of coordination among public, private, and hybrid institutions. But however difficult this process might be, the enhancement of real estate value is its ultimate end, an outcome that generally is viewed not just as a private good but in the interest of the city as a whole.

This narrow focus typically has led to a consistent avoidance of large-scale or citywide urban planning or economic development strategies in favor of a piecemeal approach (Garvin 2000), in clear contrast with the citywide approach to development embraced by the Bloomberg administration, which embraced a multidimensional sense of urbanism that incorporated not just the profitable construction of office towers or luxury housing, but the construction of open and recreational space and the cultivation of culture, leisure, consumption, and neighborhood quality of life. The outcome of the Hudson Yards planning process—and in particular the fate of the west side stadium—hinged on this contrast in development strategies, which itself was linked to clashing elite interests and imaginaries.

Who Killed the Stadium?

We are now in a position to explain why the conflict and controversy over the Hudson Yards plan developed the way it did, and why the stadium proposal met its demise on that Monday morning in July 2006. The Bloomberg administration and its allied supporters of the Hudson Yards plan faced potential opposition not just from the west side community, but also from the city's real estate elite. These two elite groupings embraced specific urban imaginaries and development strategies that, while not necessarily irreconcilable, were not identical. Let us see how this potential tension played out.

The killing of the stadium's funding by the PACB was the culmination of a complex five-year-long process that began in the early days of the Bloomberg administration, at which point real estate elites viewed the new mayor and his administration with a mix of suspicion and optimism. On one hand, the mayor had financed his own campaign and thus was not in the political debt of the real estate industry. Unconstrained by the usual forms of political control wielded by the real estate industry, he was something of a wild card. On the other hand, Bloomberg was well known to many real estate elites in his roles as a philanthropist, socialite, and past benefactor of NYC2012, and as a successful businessman he was considered unlikely to pursue policies inimical to real estate interests.

Early actions by the administration alarmed real estate elites. While previous administrations had drawn heavily on the real estate industry to fill development-related positions, Bloomberg's instead turned to the corporate and nonprofit sectors. One executive of a business newspaper with significant ties to the real estate industry said to me in 2003: "Many real estate people think [the administration is] anti-development. Doctoroff and [Department of City Planning head] Amanda Burden are the only economic development officials in my 20 years in New York to win the praise of the Municipal Arts Society [a civic group dedicated to urban beautification], which is, in anybody's legitimate view, like the worst anti-development group around. So, what kind of businessman mayor is this?" When Mayor Michael Bloomberg pushed through his property tax increase to close fiscal shortfalls in late 2002, real estate elites were stunned. Previous efforts to raise property taxes in the face of fiscal crisis had been stymied by real estate power. But this time was different. "He's not seeking our counsel," complained one developer to a *New York Times* reporter. "He didn't talk to us. He just [did] it" (Bagli 2002). In the same report, the head of the Real Estate Board ruefully complained that under Bloomberg "we never get everything we want," demonstrating how accustomed real estate elites were to having their interests catered to by city government. Real estate elites did soon get some relief, as it became apparent that the Bloomberg administration's development agenda would give real estate elites a lot, if not all of what they wanted. Nevertheless, if it was clear that the Bloomberg administration was hardly "anti-development," its development strategy did have potential points of tension with the profit-centered development strategy endorsed by the city's real estate elite.

The controversy over the Hudson Yards plan typified this mix of tension and confluence. The idea that the Midtown Manhattan central business district should eventually stretch to the Hudson had been gospel to real estate elites since the late 1920s (Fitch 1993), so they cheered the administration's efforts to implement the rezoning that would permit the transformation of the area into a new, high-end, mixed-use district—and a bonanza of real estate profits. In contrast, they gave the west side stadium a far cooler reception. This was not the first stadium proposed for the area: previous efforts to build a stadium there had failed, and many real estate elites felt that a political fight over the stadium might endanger the rest of the plan. Moreover, a number of prominent real estate developers had long coveted the rights to develop the Hudson rail yards, where the stadium would be located. Given the MTA's general sympathy toward the industry (its chairmanship had often been occupied by members of prominent real estate families), many developers had long hoped that the development rights for the yards, owned by the organization, could be obtained for a relative pittance. As the Hudson Yards planning process ramped up, these rights became even more desirable, as the area between the Hudson River and the existing high-rent agglomeration of midtown was now slated for development, which would fill a physical gap that had long made development of the yards problematic.

The rezoning portion of the plan easily passed the City Council in early 2005. At this point the stadium plan began to dominate debate, and the conflict between real estate elites and the Bloomberg administration reached a head in early 2006, when the disposition of the rights to develop the rail yards emerged as an issue. The administration had always expected the MTA to sell these rights to the New York Jets (who would be the formal developer and owner of the stadium) for a mutually agreeable price. However, public pressure forced an open bidding process for the right to develop the yards.

Remarkably, none of the real estate developers who coveted the right to develop the yards bid on them. Why was this the case? To put it simply, they were afraid to incur the wrath of the administration, given the control over economic and urban development agencies, and thus over the fate of many development and building projects, now held by Deputy Mayor Doctoroff, perhaps the most devoted proponent of the stadium. The rail yard is "clearly valuable," one major residential developer anonymously told the *New York Times*. "But can anyone in my position say so on the record? Everyone, including me, is scared to cross [Bloomberg and Doctoroff] on this. I've got too many things cooking in this town" (Bagli 2005).[3]

Developers had good reason to fear. The administration had not reacted well when other elites had openly opposed the stadium. Most notable in this regard was the Cablevision corporation, owner of the Madison Square Garden arena, which would have been in direct competition with the domed west side stadium for indoor events. While Cablevision was not as vulnerable to administration retribution as real estate developers, its direct opposition to the stadium, as well as its community opponents, earned threats of punitive action via the revocation of subsidies as well as sustained and vituperative public condemnation from the administration (Brash 2006).

So it is understandable that when real estate developers actively worked against the stadium, they did so only surreptitiously. Along with Cablevision, some developers provided financial support to community groups opposing the stadium, but this support was never made public and its recipients were sworn to secrecy. New York's real estate elite, as the one major developer, Richard Ravitch, who spoke publicly against the stadium at this time, put it, were "in the witness protection program" (Lehrer 2005). Shrewd and aggressive real estate developers, some of the richest and most powerful men and families in the country, if not the world, were not only afraid to bid on one of the most profitable development sites the city had ever seen but were afraid to be seen as actively working against the wishes of the mayor.

The administration would soon get its comeuppance, when the PACB rejected the funding of the stadium. The process leading up to this was complex, but here I want to focus on the role played by Sheldon Silver, whose position as State Assembly speaker gave him a seat on the PACB. Silver had tight links to the city's real estate elite, and particularly to downtown interests. He had represented Lower Manhattan for decades, and was a fierce advocate for the area, especially after the terrorist attacks of September 11, 2001 accelerated its long-term decline as a home for high-end commercial real estate relative to Midtown Manhattan (Boyer 2002: 112–14). Silver had long criticized the Bloomberg administration's prioritization of the Hudson Yards plan over the reconstruction of the site of the former World Trade Center, and had repeatedly raised concerns about competition between commercial development on the west side and downtown. Administration officials had repeatedly dismissed these concerns by arguing that Lower and Midtown Manhattan were different "products" appealing to different market niches. This seemed to be a dismissal of Lower Manhattan's viability as a first-class central business district, a notion only reinforced by the administration's plans to encourage mixed-use rather than high-end office development downtown.

Silver had long made clear his unwillingness to approve the stadium's funding if the administration did not accede to his demands for a "Marshall Plan" for Lower Manhattan. The administration finally did so in April 2006, just two months before the International Olympic Committee would choose the location of the 2012 Summer Games, a decision that was expected to hinge upon whether or not the west side stadium had received the necessary approvals. But for Silver, this was too little, too late. Despite further entreaties and offers from the administration, Silver still refused to commit to approving the stadium's funding, citing many of the critiques west side community members had made of the project. And when the administration, in league with Governor George Pataki, called Silver's bluff by forcing the stadium onto the agenda of the PACB in early June 2006, Silver responded by vetoing the stadium's funding, effectively killing the project.

It is notable that Silver rejected the stadium's funding even *after* he received promises of city government aid and attention to Lower Manhattan development. For Silver's rejection of the stadium was not just about whose interests would be privileged by development policy, but about how development linked up with issues of identity, meaning, and emotional investment in the city. In public comments, Silver made clear that the problem was only partially the prioritization of Midtown over Lower Manhattan. Also crucial was a potent mix of personal and political resentment aimed at the Bloomberg administration and its efforts to restructure development policy in accordance with its own vision of the city. Speaking after he voted against the stadium, Silver said of the Bloomberg administration, "I just think that nobody's opinion counted until it counted. . . . They just proceeded ahead" (Steinhauer 2005). This comment was echoed in the press as well as in my fieldwork: what was at stake in the debate over the Hudson Yards plan was not just economic interests, though they were important, but the interrelated legitimacy of the postindustrial elite's political ascendancy and the urban imaginary it promulgated.

Intra-elite conflict was crucial to the outcome of the debate over the west side stadium. The political ascension of a postindustrial elite had challenged the hegemonic position of the city's real estate elite. The Bloomberg administration attempted to impose a development strategy that, while not inimical to development per se, was not always in keeping with the strict logic of real estate profitability. Deputy Mayor Doctoroff captured this when, speaking of the desire of the administration to substitute luxury housing for office space at the World Trade Center redevelopment site over the wishes of the site's owner, Larry Silverstein, said: "There is an inherent conflict between someone who is market-driven and the city's interests, which should be rationally discussed" (Magnet 2005). For decades, the interest of the city and the interest of "market-driven" real estate investment were conflated: what was good for real estate was good for New York. But no longer. As my ex–Real Estate Board informant put it, "for the first time in years, somebody bigger than real estate is on the block."

Even the very community members so often seen as the primary antagonists of neoliberal development schemes like the Hudson Yards plan acknowledged the importance of intra-elite conflict to their successful opposition to the west side stadium. After the stadium was rejected by the PACB, one of the leaders of the community opposition to the west side stadium told a reporter: "The stuff you heard coming out of [Sheldon Silver's] mouth [were] arguments we helped develop that went up through the food chain . . . and in the end won the day. . . . We've learned how to take our own parochial interests and connect them up with the broader interests that other New Yorkers might have because we knew we weren't going to kill this if it was just a 'not in my backyard' argument" (Murphy 2005). In some ways, this echoes what scholars of urban neoliberalism have argued: that the successful opposition of neoliberal projects needs to articulate local concerns with broader ones (Hackworth 2007: 131–33; Sites 2003: 203). But whereas these scholars typically have in mind the alliance of grassroots or community groups across space, something different was happening here: the crucial links made by the west side community were not to grassroots groups elsewhere in the city, but to elites such as real estate developers and the owners of Cablevision. The community opposition to the stadium attempted to exploit intra-elite conflict; anti-stadium elites attempted to exploit community opposition to the project. Intra-elite struggle shaped the fate of the stadium as much as the struggle between a neoliberalizing Bloomberg administration and a resistant community.

Conclusion

The case of the west side stadium indicates that explaining the trajectory of neoliberal downtown development in contemporary cities requires a focus on the dynamics of elite constitution, cooperation, and conflict. Patterns of conflict and accommodation among elites are as crucial to the outcome of particular neoliberal downtown development projects as those between community members and neoliberalizing elites. Indeed, as this case indicates, intra-elite competition, compromise, and accommodation can establish the material and ideological arena of political contestation that less powerful groups have to negotiate. Thus, this is not only an academic matter; it has political ramifications as well. For the foreseeable future, it is likely that those who also struggle against neoliberal projects and strategies will be facing a difficult political environment, in which tough tactical decisions must be made and allies have to be taken as they come. Those attempting to oppose, roll back, or ameliorate the effects of neoliberal development strategies will have to understand and exploit intra-elite conflicts, an effort to which critical urban scholarship can make a real contribution. The community activists and residents who successfully opposed the west side stadium understood the importance of intra-elite conflict to their struggle against a neoliberal mega-project. A theoretically robust and politically useful analysis of the production of neoliberal downtowns requires that urban scholars follow their lead.

12

Beside Downtown: Global Chinatowns

Gary W. McDonogh and Cindy Hing-Yuk Wong

For much of the nineteenth and twentieth century, in Barcelona's *barrio chino/barri xino*, decaying tenements and crowded streets housed thousands of immigrant workers slaving in aging factories or seeking day-to-day opportunities at the nearby port. Only the broad, tree-lined Rambles, a promenade beloved of flâneurs, separated the middling classes and elites of the historic city center from this "Chinatown" (this boulevard, in fact, had replaced an earlier urban wall). After dark, however, exotic nocturnal amusements including prostitution, drugs, and gambling lured adventurous bourgeois men, bohemian artists, journalists, and even transnational revolutionaries into the barrio chino. In the twenty-first century, nonetheless, as Barcelona's post-Olympic urban revitalization has spread from the port and historical core outward, this "Chinatown," rechristened as the historic Raval, has been demolished in favor of neoliberal development of sanitized public spaces, new hotel and tourist services, gentrified residences, and cultural facilities including museums, foundations, and the Universitat de Barcelona. The Raval has displaced the chino, its older inhabitants, its bars, social centers and memories (McDonogh 1987, 2002; McNeill 1999; Magrinyà and Maza, this volume).

While this may seem to be a stereotypical Chinatown in location, function, and imagery, it differs from others where we have worked in a fundamental demographic element—the absence of Chinese. Barcelona had few Chinese until the 1990s. Instead, many inhabitants of this dense central zone had arrived from poorer Spanish regions of Andalusia and Aragon.

Journalist Paco Madrid borrowed the sobriquet "Chinatown" in 1927 from his reading of San Francisco, using *barrio chino* as an urban metaphor to evoke an ambience of cosmopolitan mystery and Barcelona's status as a world city (McDonogh 1987). When the first waves of Chinese arrived in Spain in the late 1990s, in fact, they settled elsewhere, including an important cluster next to the downtown area of a suburban Barcelona satellite city, Santa Coloma. Nonetheless, Barcelonans' metaphorization of the early twentieth-century location and imagery of Chinatowns, like the demands and pressures of center city development that continue to change the area, are familiar and even suggestive phenomena for global downtowns.

For more than a decade we have lived, worked, and studied in Chinatowns worldwide, including Chinese enclaves in and around Chicago, New York, Sydney, Lima, Los Angeles, Bangkok, Havana, Paris, San José, Panama City, and São Paulo, in addition to our anchorage in Wong's native Hong Kong and our home in Greater Philadelphia. These Chinatowns sometimes have been backgrounds for other projects in urban studies, mass media, architecture, and visual culture (for example, Wong 1991, 1999); they also have become interwoven with lives of our family and friends. Our experiences and investigations underpin the complexities of multisite downtown ethnography through which we have examined shared characteristics of place, function, ideology, and evolution (McDonogh and Wong 2005). These social, special, and cultural features embody both Chinese agency and evolving Chinese globalization, although we do not develop such a phenomenological exploration here. Instead, we argue that Chinatowns are deeply enmeshed with the structure and nature of central districts that such Chinatowns often border, a relationship mapped decades ago by Burgess and the Chicago School (Burgess 1925: 56). Chinatowns provide a multivalent vantage from which to illuminate critical features of global downtowns, including the evolution of central spaces and functions, the competitive markets for people and capital they embody, and the play of locality, region, nation-state, and transnational articulation shaping downtowns as well as Chinatowns.

To analyze the dialectic of Chinatowns and global downtowns, we consider five specific themes: (1) the emergence and movement of Chinatowns in relation to urban cores; (2) the imagery of Chinatowns as cultural spaces that illuminates race, immigration, gender, and morality in downtowns; (3) competing contemporary demands for land, development, and movement, both Chinese and non-Chinese; (4) the meaning of Chinatowns in relation to suburban and global networks; and (5) new Chinatowns as a counterpoint to future downtowns. Together, these themes underscore the fact that Chinatowns are not exotic alternative spaces but offer fundamental insights on downtowns as urban/regional places of political economic power, social structure, and cultural meaning constituted by multilayered and contested global flows of goods, people, knowledge, and imagery.

Coevolution: Global Downtowns and Chinatowns

As Ernest Burgess generalized from Chicago's experience, the space occupied by many Chinatowns falls into a transitional light or early postindustrial mixed zone located near downtown areas: "In the zone of deterioration encircling the central business section are always found the so-called 'slums' and 'bad lands,' with their submerged regions of poverty, degradation and disease and their underworlds of crime and vice. . . . The area of deterioration, while essentially one of decay, of stationary or declining population, is also one of regeneration, as witness the mission, the settlement, the artists' colony, radical centers—all obsessed with the vision of a new and better world" (1925: 54–56; Rotenberg, this volume). These transitional areas offer mixed residential, commercial, and industrial structures to accommodate the needs of downtown institutions for storage, labor, or services. Deterioration marks these zones as areas of unplanned expansion, residential areas abandoned in an outward movement of elites, or older centers in cities where more complex industrial/financial developments have recast power and centrality (for example, older port zones in financial/industrial cities like Hong Kong or New York; see Magrinyà and Maza, this volume). Chinatowns thus have become spatialized as global enclaves whose proximity to urban centers has not entailed high rents, or cherished values, or careful control. Instead, location has allowed the possibility of creative reuse. As the WPA guide for San Francisco noted, "Destroyed by the successive conflagrations of the 1850s and 1860s, Chinatown rose repeatedly on old foundations that no sufficient majority of San Franciscans cared to reclaim" (Writers Program of the Works Progress Administration of Northern California 1940: 224).

It might seem self-evident why entrepreneurial immigrants would settle in such areas, but Chinese immigrants did not necessarily seek out these zones specifically. Instead, Chinese communities near downtowns have coalesced around many different pressures of social definition and exclusion. Chinatowns in the Americas and Australia, for example, came to embody a multigenerational Chinese definition of near-downtowns as global destinations over time. Most nineteenth-century Chinese emigrants traveled from South China through colonial Hong Kong and Macau to these new worlds as male contract laborers who only passed through port cities briefly en route to isolated work sites. The social separation of Chinese often was established by pre-urban labor relations where Chinese became plantation coolies (Peru, Cuba, Sarawak) or miners and laborers (Australia, the United States, Canada). Host societies or states eventually created immigration laws that restricted the reproduction of community through limits on immigration, denial of citizenship, or exclusion of Chinese women. Debates over the nature of the host society spilled over into riots and destruction of Chinese communities. Chinese bachelors, meanwhile, found support and solace in the shared housing, food, amusements, and cultural ties of mining camps and railroad tents (McWaters 2002).

Many modern urban Chinatowns in these nations emerged as Chinese laborers and coolies escaped rural isolation and moved to cities. These immigrants faced constraints of race, citizenship, and class but together created opportunity amid constraints. In both Lima and Melbourne, for example, Chinese established strong ties with the city's central markets, constructing enclaves near these central service areas. Chinese formed clusters in cheap commercial properties, offering food, cleaning, and housing to each other and, over time, to a wider mixed clientele. That is, Chinese learned the Chicago School model from the ground up (Balbi 1999). Such nascent clusters, in turn, attracted middle-class merchants and entrepreneurs from Hong Kong and South China as well as agents of the Qing government and its opponents, who added further layers of transnational connections and hierarchy to overseas Chinese enclaves (Hsu 2000; McDonogh and Wong 2005; McKeown 2001). These elites centralized stores, temples, associations, cemeteries, and connections to China while creating links to both downtown leaders and Chinese or Hong Kong resources.

Chinatowns and downtowns have moved around cities in intricate pas de deux. In New York, Chinese sailors settled in the most southerly part of the island, the "down" of downtown, where they lived alongside Irish immigrants and global sailors (see Lui 2004; Tchen 1999). Only in the mid-nineteenth century did Chinese businesses coalesce as an enclave farther uptown around Chatham Square, amid an emergent array of ethnic and racial groups and zones (Hell's Kitchen, Little Italy, the Lower East Side) *near but not in* the somewhat mobile financial-commercial center. All were isolated from the northward march of middle and upper classes along Broadway and Fifth Avenue (Page 1999). Similarly, in Sydney, the first Chinese settled in the Rocks—a polyglot portside slum of dangerous reputation and mixed population. The Chinese moved later to an area north of the current central business district that constitutes the core of the contemporary Chinatown (Lydon 2002). By the late nineteenth century, the self-made Guangdong-born millionaire, Quong Tart, had traded the gold fields for a fashionable tea room in central Sydney and offices in the elite downtown Queen Victoria Building. He lived with his Irish-Australian wife in suburban Ashfield and acted as overseer and intermediary for working-class Chinese in the Chinatown near—but separate from—his own downtown base (Travers 2004).

In the twentieth century, Chinatown in Los Angeles illustrates this continuing co-evolution (Peterson, this volume). The national transportation hub of Union Station displaced an earlier Chinatown in the 1930s; 3,000 Chinese settled in a contiguous "China City" built, in part, with leftover Hollywood sets, Orientalizing a century-old community into a globally recognizable Hollywood landscape. This urban transformation intersected with the growth of the business center and the romantic reconstruction of Olvera Street as a sanitized mummification of the city's Latino heritage in a "former" downtown. For both sites, proximity to the primary Los Angeles CBD remained important: "Tourists and locals could now escape the congestion of downtown to explore the ancient mysteries of *Canton* or the romance of *Jalisco*, all within convenient walking distance of City Hall in a safe, clean and orderly setting" (Estrada 1999: 122; emphasis in original).

Indeed, proximity also incorporated spatial strategies that distinguished public interactions from nearby private worlds. That is, the first floors of Chinatown buildings offer public, street-level interactions in shops and restaurants that negotiate global identities with outsiders. Yet, they must be understood in the context of vertical Chinese choices to situate family and regional associations, gambling clubs, factories, temples, and even housing on the less visible floors above. Nayan Shah observed of San Francisco that "the creation of knowledge of Chinatown relied on three spatial elements: the dens, density and labyrinths" (2001: 18). Spatialization involves complex choices over time, intertwined with the power, functions, and images of downtown districts.

Figure 10. L.A. downtown seen through Chinatown gate. Photo by authors.

What constitutes the frontier of Chinatown and global downtowns? Walking "into" many Chinatowns today, whether in Philadelphia, Sydney, Los Angeles, Havana, or Lima, one finds a self-conscious gateway/boundary marking the interface of downtown and Chinatown with a colorful ceremonial arch (Mandarin *paifang*; see Figure 10). While these evoke history and a distant China, many such arches were constructed in the 1970s at the intersections of local Chinese citizenship and global Chinese power. Havana's arch, for example, was a donation from Beijing to a socialist ally. The arch in Philadelphia, by contrast, was built for the Bicentennial in 1976. Lima's arch was built in the 1970s by Taiwan but refurbished in the 1990s by Beijing, making concrete the shift of the Peruvian state government in recognizing the "real" global China. Chinese in Barcelona are now arguing for their right to an arch—against the wishes of city authorities—while a new Chinatown for San José, Costa Rica, was defined as a global goal by the attribute "con los arcos y todo" (with the arches and everything).

In practice, the fluid borders of urban Chinatowns generally have incorporated the existing patterns of major streets (for example, Canal Street in Manhattan, St. George in Sydney), nuanced by transportation arteries or barriers necessary to downtown—train tracks or highways—and by sprawling facilities such as central markets that break up urban fabrics. Chinese immigrants, too, have claimed and demarcated their spaces by signage, lights, businesses, and sheer human presence, ebbing and flowing around shop fronts, tea houses, and tenements over decades. Such a public and private flow remains visible block by block in Manhattan's Little Italy or the intermeshing Chinese and Jewish businesses in Belleville, Paris. Language, residence, kin and clan ties, and cultural celebrations have reinforced architectural hallmarks of space in such intimate differentiation.

Competition and fear have strengthened boundaries, as well as they did in rural areas. In Honolulu, for example, an important Chinatown developed in the era of an independent Hawai'ian kingdom, as merchants from China joined families who had arrived as rural laborers in the canefields but came to control half the city's retail activity in the 1880s. Here, Chinese in prime downtown locations faced contests of sovereignty between native Hawai'ians and insurgent Whites from the Mainland. Chinatown was torched in 1900, ostensibly to control bubonic plague, but this action incidentally dispersed a global challenge to North American merchants colonizing yet another downtown (McKeown 2001; Mohr 2005).

The evolving location, embodiment, and functions of Chinatowns repeated across so many cities worldwide meant that immigrant entrepreneurs built communities in available *and* central locations while dealing with difference and concepts of danger imposed and exploited by people in their "host" societies. Chinatowns became highly visible loci of alternative downtown development that resonated with the construction of centrality in other "ethnic" mini-CBDs that we might associate with Hispanic centers swallowed by North American expansion, "Little Italies," Japantowns, or Koreatowns. Separate centers were especially evident in the pre–Civil Rights segregation of parallel Black and White downtowns across the United States (McDonogh 1993), and the role of Harlem as a global "Black Metropolis" (see Fogelson 2001; Isenberg 2005 on desegregation). Exclusion by law, behavior, and economics has been as much a part of downtown as attraction and desire—and continues to factor into the intense negotiations of contemporary global downtowns and contiguous Chinatowns. Nonetheless, outsiders and Chinese have crossed borders frequently, confirming Chinatowns as centers for Chinese and destinations for others who are especially attracted by images and mysteries of difference.

Imagery, Gender, Morality, and Space

Chinatowns across the world have meshed cultural formations of Chinese as others and Chinese images of foreign societies to which they immigrate. Many Chinese, for example, have seen migration as temporary. They have formed centers of communication, relying on Cantonese, Toisanese and Fujianese dialects, and have created spaces for familiar food, recreation and religion as global havens in hostile, strange new worlds. These communities also have been reinforced by Chinese attitudes—disdainful, distant, or curious—about the people among whom they settled (see Botan 2002 [1969] and Skinner 1957 on Chinese in Thailand; Arkush and Lee 1993 on North America).

These transnational choices and images form part of our larger ethnography of global Chinatowns, but for the examination of downtowns themselves, the images projected onto Chinese prove more compelling. As Tchen (1999) has pointed out, urban images of Chinese evoke an Orientalization that justified limiting the flows or presence of Chinese nationals and their descendants in metropolitan areas even before Chinatowns took shape. Whether Chinese were seen as competitors for scarce work or wages, dubious intermediaries in commerce or colonial administration, or dangerous racial others, these images became part of the moral spatialization of the Chinese and, as such, elements in the cultural construction of "good" downtowns (see Lui 2004; Mayne 1993).

Nor were race, language, and culture the only themes of difference, which also encompassed mappings of gender, virtue, and even disease (Mayne 1993; Shah 2001). Consider, for example, the important European and American gendering of downtowns by the nineteenth century, which divided the world of production and administration from nearby temples of consumption. City Hall, banks, halls of justice, religious edifices, and other monuments defined a downtown of male global connections (as they still do in many central business districts). The markets, the shops, and above all, the department stores and their overpowering displays of goods, by contrast, emphasized powerful attractions for the middle-class female. Consumption defined a proper bourgeois female downtown role as homemaker and shopper increasingly attuned to cosmopolitan goods that had traveled some distance by rail or ship, globalizing and modernizing downtown. These emporia of desire also invited transgressions by those who could not licitly achieve this level of expense and display (Abelson 1989; Fogelson 2001; Isenberg 2005; Schivelbusch 1977).

Chinatown, however, challenged these associations of place, power, and gender in sometimes contradictory fashion. Almost all Chinatowns prior to the late twentieth century began with young males as labor migrants. Some nation-states further excluded Chinese women unless they formed part of middle-class families (merchants, religious leaders, or dignitaries; McDonogh and Wong 2005; McKeown 2001). Despite subsequent scholarly reevaluation, Chinatowns in North America, Australia, and even Latin American were *seen* by many as bachelor cities populated by men, at once decadent and threatening. Chinese women were either invisible in a private middle-class realm or identified with illegality and prostitution—because of where they lived and whom they lived with.

Race and gender relations were actually more complex: Mary Ting Yi Lui (2004) has underscored the presence of stable, mixed (Chinese-Irish) working-class families in New York, echoing patterns of intermarriage in Latin America. Sucheng Chan and others (2005) also have shown that there were more Chinese women in such areas than previously thought, although their public presence might not have been acknowledged by Chinese or others. Meanwhile, Ivan Light showed that Irishmen ran various institutions in New York's Chinatowns for other Whites, especially those attracted to Chinatown brothels by anonymity, security, and low prices (1974: 372, 374). Still, myths powerfully reinforced spatial divisions and temptations: non-Chinese women targeted as consumers for downtown were warned of special risks *near* such districts, a warning reinforced by lurid images of young girls lured into white slavery by drugs. D. W. Griffith's film *Broken Blossoms: The Yellow Man and the Girl* (1919), set in London's original Chinatown, became one of the first commercial films to try to tackle interracial romance. Its Buddhist missionary hero, played by a White actor, appears to be sensitive but weak and addicted to opium (a drug whose dangers for English women are introduced early on). His care and love for the Cockney waif (Lillian Gish) is nevertheless smashed by her brutal boxer father, leading to the deaths of all involved. Griffith made *Broken Blossoms* to show his sensitivity to racial issues after the furor surrounding *Birth of a Nation* (1915), but its stereotypes of space, race, class, gender, and morality resonate with generations of global media imagery that have followed.

Chinese transnational male leisure activities such as gambling and opium reinforced frontiers of morality and temptation. Still, although particular forms of gambling (for example, mahjong) were clearly Chinese, gambling as an urban practice was not so socially limited, ethnically marked, or even policed as it is today. Opium and opiates also drew a cosmopolitan crowd into Chinatown, before such drugs—spread by British imperialism—were increasingly condemned by global activists in late Victorian society. Moreover, mythic geographies of Chinatown as an evil place full of dangerous men distilled the ethnic and social complexity surrounding vibrant downtowns into erroneous reductions. Historian Adam McKeown, for example, shows that Chicago's nineteenth-century visible Chinese clustering of businesses and sleeping quarters on Clark Street took shape in a polyglot area already well-known for its dissolute Irish ways: "the bulk of Clark Street's fame, and the attraction that brought visitors from around the Midwest arose from its position as a main thoroughfare of the 'Levee,' the largest vice district in one of the most 'wide open towns' in the United States" (2001: 193). Bars, gambling, brothels, and crime were rife before and after Chinese arrived. In fact, by 1912, internecine battles between rival Chinese networks, conflicts with local politicians, and pressures from the growth of Chicago's central business district forced Chinatown's leaders to move Chinatown two miles farther south (McKeown 2001: 211–12).

Thus, nineteenth- and early twentieth-century media and popular associations of Chinatowns with prostitution, gambling, and drugs attached gender roles and moral values to ethnic space—and reaffirmed the gendered images and power that shaped Barcelona's barrio chino (and the experiences of its inhabitants; McDonogh 1987, 2002). Yet, these images betray ambiguous visions of exotic temptation that would underpin a shifting touristic gaze that swept from downtown to Chinatown in the twentieth century. As Light noted, "By the 1890s, middle-class whites had begun to tour Chinatowns to get a first-hand glimpse of the filth and depravity they expected to find. These sensation hungry tourists arrived at a juncture when the American Chinese driven out of the general labor force for discrimination were casting about for an alternative means of livelihood" (1974: 368). Chinese, of course, could manipulate this gaze. Hence, chop suey replaced opium and mahjong—or moved them upstairs.

The idea of Chinatown as an exotic downtown destination remains strong worldwide as Chinese immigrants, their hybrid or assimilated descendants, and non-Chinese manipulate established imagery, albeit with different commitments, motivations, and contradictions. Hence, hyphenated Chinese today may be idealized as the model minority rather than the sinister Oriental, while many cities celebrate Chinese New Year as a downtown multicultural event. Nevertheless, Chinatowns worldwide still face

criticism for gang activities, local and global organized crime (Triads), unfair working conditions, and illegal immigration (Yun and Poisson 2004).
While all these social phenomena are present in Chinatowns, the image
of Chinatown as an absolutely distinctive place divorced from "legitimate"
global downtown finances and regeneration artificially separates Chinatown issues from wider urban contexts where unfair working conditions,
crime, and illegal immigration may well reflect the same global forces.

These themes of difference in Chinatown images thus underscore cultural limits on downtown as a central public space that permeate many essays in this volume. Chinatown lights, firecrackers, and dragon dances, just
like New Year's Eve in Times Square, artistic events in Zanzibar and Los
Angeles, and the celebrations at the recreational port of Barcelona, evoke
images of vibrant mixture and democracy. Yet as work by Mike Davis (1992),
Michael Sorkin (1992), and many others reminds us, downtown always has
entailed structured exclusions as well as inclusions; its myths affirm social
and political economic distinction even as it proclaims centrality. These
contradictions have become even more intense with post-1990s revitalization of downtowns worldwide, involving global investment, global branding, and global consumers who compete with Chinatowns.

Chinatowns Today: The Pressures of Global
Downtown Development

Contemporary changes in local-global functions of many downtowns have
put special pressures on their neighbors, mediated through immigration,
tourism, real estate development, and competitive urban branding. Here,
the "walling in" of Philadelphia's Chinatown exemplifies an important
convergence of urban issues. These "walls"—by highways and massive construction projects—have not been racially motivated but arise from publicly
funded projects that embody the quest for modern global downtown identities while overlooking the claims, histories, and needs of near neighbors.
The position of Chinatown as victimized or reactive space, in turn, reveals a
critical struggle for rights in the city and its downtowns (McDonogh and
Wong 2005).

To the east of Philadelphia's Chinatown, U.S. national history has been
enshrined at Independence Hall, its greensward Mall, and the adjacent Constitution Center. This global attraction, continually reworked, began to take

its present shape in the 1940s when planners eliminated a warren of older homes and rooming houses to create a park. These buildings had shared the original decrepit urban fabric in which Chinatown had taken root near a newer central business district, but Philadelphia authorities found such a slum inappropriate for national memory and iconic vistas. Today, walking from Chinatown to the Mall, one meets tailored landscapes, public buildings, and acres of parking: spaces that sacrifice residential and commercial growth to the city as a national and international pilgrimage site. Here, Chinatown met its first wall.

Highways provide another ubiquitous pressure in downtown development, especially in the United States. The Vine Street Connector in Philadelphia (I-676), another wall for Chinatown, was projected in the 1930s as a key to modernization and urban competitiveness, but it was not built until the 1980s. Its original route would have destroyed Holy Redeemer Catholic Church and School, one of Chinatown's central institutions; Chinese protests forced a rerouting of the highway, which was built below ground level. Still, few pedestrians cross this unfriendly multilane canyon, although Chinese businesses and public housing have taken root in the area beyond the highway. Similar urban transportation reforms have reinforced boundaries in other cities: highways have vivisected Chinatowns in Boston, Los Angeles, Honolulu, and Oakland.

A third wall came from conversion of isolated downtown stores into an enclosed mall, the Galleria, as a bulwark against midcentury downtown decline (Fogelson 2001). As we have seen, downtown malls were more regional than global attractions, attempting to bring consumers back to downtown through spaces and amenities resembling the suburbs. Their ubiquity nonetheless underscores global competition among cities and the position of Chinatowns as local settings to be sacrificed to a common urban good.

Competition in the form of the Pennsylvania Convention Center, built in 1992, completed the enclosure of Philadelphia's Chinatown on its western edge. Convention centers represent a common downtown development project that has faced Chinatowns elsewhere (for example, Washington, D.C.). These buildings embody a neoliberal paradigm in which the city has become involved in constructing private attractions for the public good, and in the process has defined which publics are less integral to the city (or less likely to protest or vote). In fact, additions to this gigantic space have continued to redefine space and connections in downtown Philadelphia in the twenty-first century.

By the early 1990s, the downtown streets of Philadelphia's Chinatown had been enclosed by projects that served the region or a wider global population of tourists and conventioneers. This made Chinatown a convenient lunchtime or tourist space, but new developments have come at the cost of possible expansion or access. Chinatown businesses must compete for parking with the clientele of the regional auto show and the Philadelphia International Flower Show at the convention center. The drive to make downtown more attractive for visitors competes with the labor and residential functions of Chinatown, and complicates connections with Chinese suburbanites who use its services.

The conflictive interests of downtown Philadelphia, Chinatown, and Chinese residents outside Chinatown intensified as the city government mounted campaigns in the 1990s to put a prison and then a baseball stadium in areas bordering Chinatown, seeing those areas as underutilized spaces of opportunity (as in the Chicago School). In yet another layer of downtown strategies, urban leaders proposed to establish casino gambling in the fading Galleria in 2008, replacing one revitalization strategy with another. All these projects have been intended to serve particular downtown functions. The prison would have provided secure and connected holding for a justice center that embodies downtown as a governing center. The stadium, a clearly neoliberal attraction, sought to imitate the success of downtown stadia in Baltimore and Cleveland. The casino campaign has read downtown as a neutral site after other residential neighborhoods agitated against the localized impact of such development. In both early cases, Asian American organizations fought against development and, for once, beat City Hall: downtown, in this sense, forced new social cohesion on nearby residents. Casino gambling, though, remains a volatile issue at this writing.

In the twenty-first century, proximity to downtown also has meant growing pressures from the more amorphous processes of center city development that have raised property values in condos located in Chinatown but not belonging to it in demographic or cultural terms. Gentrification of space inverts a multigenerational Chinese trajectory of moving from the center to the suburbs as a marker of social responsibility and family and class mobility. While Chinese Americans leave Chinatowns behind, downtown gentrification revalues older buildings in terms of location rather than place memory or cultural cohesion. While an address in Chinatown may add exotic cachet, new residents in Philadelphia's Chinatown have complained about neon and noise, and in one case fought a lengthy court battle against the hanging sign of a contiguous Chinese business (www.blackbottom.org/ chinatown). Threats of gentrification also have spurred alternative visions of community through negotiations for affordable housing with developers (http://www.chinatown-pcdc.org) and a new Chinese charter school to promote sociocultural reproduction of Chinese community (Macabasco 2005). So far, this area has not seen the phenomenon reported for Manhattan's Chinatown of a gentrification *by* suburbanized Chinese Americans moving back to the center.

Chinatown gentrification is not merely local, however, as the markets surrounding transnational Asian suburban enclaves remind us (Chen 1992; Li 2006). While many middle-class Chinese immigrants have moved directly from Asia to North American suburbs, Mainland immigrants have been buying into Philadelphia Chinatown housing as they have in New York and Paris, grinding the Chinatown housing market between local and global pressures. Nor have Chinatowns been exclusively Chinese in their globalization. Japanese businesses expanded San Francisco's Chinatown prior to World War II internment (Varzally 2008: 122–38). James Mohr (2005) notes Vietnamese businesses in Honolulu's Chinatown (although these may well include Vietnamese Chinese like those who dominate one of Paris's Chinatowns). Chinese in Sydney, meanwhile, complained in 2007 about new Korean investments in properties in and around downtown Chinatown, an area ripe for gentrification. While ethnic labeling read from a more powerful center may overlook such diversity, the presence of many Latinos working in kitchens and stores in Chinatowns in Philadelphia and other North American cities underscores issues of class and global migration interwoven with historical ethnicity: Chinatowns can be as dualized as any of Saskia Sassen's global downtowns.

Again, the processes afflicting Chinatowns as near neighbors to revitalizing downtowns illuminate the general structure and globalization of such business districts, where the idea of the city as a whole and the rights of its wider citizenry become distilled in a central iconic place. Other global encroachments through the contiguity of downtowns have been unexpected yet have had devastating impacts on particular Chinatowns. Events of 9/11 at the World Trade Center, for example, meant the loss of power, access, and clientele to businesses in Manhattan's Chinatown who not only suffered isolation for months but may carry effects into subsequent generations (Lederman et al. 2004). Changes at the national level are important as well. North American Chinese left for Cuba in the nineteenth century to escape discrimination, but Havana's Chinatown, which once rivaled Lima as the largest Chinese enclave in the Americas outside San Francisco, was devastated by the 1959 triumph of the Cuban revolution. Many Cuban Chinese fled to the United States, leaving an architectural shell behind that has been revived as a tourist attraction for a global city. Ironically, while Chinatowns and Chinese had been depicted as people and places of urban danger in the nineteenth century, Chinese in the twenty-first century have been endangered by downtowns themselves.

Articulating Alternative Downtowns: Neighborhoods, Regions, and Worlds

As we see across this volume, global downtowns connect and compete with other parts of the metropolis and at the same time with other centers around the world. Downtowns as loci for regional and state services—finance, entertainment, governance, religion—dominate "neighborhoods" and suburbs. Central cities embody historical depth, monumentality of forms, and density of connections and services that attract and bind suburbs. Urban and regional leaders continue to assert this strategy in touting downtowns as centers for capital, arts, education, regional and global sports, and metropolitan tourism. In fact, the sheer goal of attracting and serving suburbanites as well as tourists and investors sets the downtown apart from other residential or industrial sections of large cities.

The rise of multiple suburban Chinatowns worldwide replicates and complicates this question of articulation. Chinatowns *near* downtowns have provided centers for consumption, services, and even social exchange for Chinese dispersed throughout cities and regions. A reductive spatialization of race, namely, "All Chinese live in Chinatown," is simply untrue. Instead, the reification of Chinese space made their residence elsewhere seem more assimilated, more flexible, more upwardly mobile, and perhaps less threatening to neighbors (see Cheng 2006; Li 2009). At the same time, downtown Chinatowns compete with other Chinese nuclei inside and outside the city, whether Taiwanese in Flushing, New York; in Monterey Park and other suburban communities around Los Angeles (Fong 1994; Li 2009); in Scarborough near Toronto; or in the suburban Chinese enclave at Lorgnes outside Paris.

The complicated Chinese nuclei of Paris exemplify spatial articulations of multiple global connections, including France's colonial heritage in Asia and the presence, interpretation, and suppression of other immigrant populations in the city. Unlike the Cantonese labor migrants who crossed the Pacific to create Chinatowns in the Americas, the first major Chinese cohorts arrived in France to build trenches in World War I (Xu 2011). Most of those who survived returned to China, but some remained and were joined by merchants and students from Northern China; perhaps 2,000 lived in the nation by the 1920s (Costa-Lascoux and Live 2002). A proto-Parisian Chinese enclave took shape around the Gare de Lyon, a not atypical near-central hub for Chinatowns, but Sino-Chinese remained few for the decades that followed.

In the aftermath of the French defeat in Indochina, however, emigration from Southeast Asia created new Chinese concentrations in the rather nondescript towers of the 13th Arrondissement (the "Triangle de Choisy"). Many of these Chinese had become acclimated to French colonial values, including urban segregation, and had occupied middleman roles in Vietnam, Laos, and Cambodia (Costa-Lascoux and Live 2002). In Paris, these multilingual refugees found residences in housing opened by the replacement of fading industrial plants near the urban periphery. While Franco-Asians account for less than 25 percent of residents on Boulevards de Choisy and Ivry, the visibility of stores, restaurants, and Chinese institutions there underpins public perceptions of a Chinatown (Banassat 2002; Zheng 1995).

Another Chinese enclave to the north, in Belleville, has been dominated by 1980s and 1990s migration from the Mainland, especially Wenzhou. Here, Chinese migration fits into a longer history of social and spatial polarization. As nineteenth-century elites claimed extensive and redesigned Hausmannian urban spaces for the bourgeoisie, they had pushed the working class to the margins (Harvey 2003). Belleville, until the late nineteenth century a suburb of Paris, became a heartland of the 1870 communards and has long been a center for working-class populations and activities. Today, Chinese storefronts there are interspersed among the businesses and lives of other migrants, including Turks, Maghrebi Jews, Arabs and various Africans. Ethnic and class negotiations reminiscent of the *ville* and *banlieue* occur every day in streets and markets, within the city but not at its core.

Between these two outlying urban Chinatowns lie other central but less visible enclaves. One, near the cultural node of Beaubourg/Centre Pompidou, occupies only a few streets and focuses on wholesale leather goods and jewelry, part of a network of Chinese wholesalers that stretches to Place République. Another nearby cluster, on Rues Sedaine-Popincourt, encompasses three to four blocks of modest apartment buildings whose first floors have been crammed with Chinese clothing wholesalers. This area has become a center for global commerce, packed each day with local Franco-Chinese and Franco-Français buyers as well as customers from Africa and Eastern Europe. Older (French) neighbors, meanwhile, have protested the loss of a "neighborhood" character in an area devoted solely to business: a new global center. Interestingly, this controversy seems to be less about a competing economic downtown near other central locations than about the fabric of neighborhood life, when bakeries and bars that used to dominate the streetscape have been turned into wholesalers for nonresidents. These Eastern European and African buyers are also clearly not French according to some conservative conceptions of Frenchness (Pribetich 2005).

All these quartiers chinois raise important questions about what constitutes the "downtown" of Paris. Clearly, Chinese are urbanites; informants scoff at the prospect of moving even a few blocks away to outlying metropolitan centers like Vitry-sur-Seine (which nonetheless now hosts Chinese industrial enterprises). Neither Choisy nor Belleville borders the historical core of Notre-Dame and the Ile de la Cité or other global centers of government, culture, and consumption. Nonetheless, Choisy, République, Sedaine-Popincourt, and Belleville articulate a central spine of variable visibility across Paris, connected via metro and boulevards into a chain of residence and business, wholesale and retail. Thus, these communities as a network seem to centralize Chinese within Paris in counterpoint to the multiple centralities of the French capital. This network, in turn, has extended through public transportation to reach new suburban Chinese residential enclaves such as Lorgnes.

These connections allow for articulation of services across Chinese centers: Choisy, for example, hosts temples, banks, doctors, a Catholic center, and Chinese media as well as major Chinese businesses such as Tang Frères/ Chénshì Xiōngdì Gōngsī, founded by the Cantonese Thai Rattanavan Brothers (Banassat 2002; Costa-Lascaux and Live 2002). In fact, Tang Frères now has its headquarters outside the city (Vitry-sur-Seine), but has established branches in many Parisian Chinese enclaves, including Lorgnes. The business further supplies myriad smaller markets, restaurants, and *traiteurs asiatiques* (vendors of prepared Asian food) found in seemingly every Parisian neighborhood. It also has expanded into the cable distribution of Chinese television, bioengineering, and transnational investment, jockeying for further local, regional, and national centrality as Paris seemingly becomes the capital—or downtown—of Chinese in the European Union (www.tang freres.com).

In many cities, the central Chinatown remains a locus of intensive global and local articulation for widely dispersed Chinese enclaves, isolated widespread businesses (restaurateurs and small retailers), and families who have established their more private Chinese immigrant lives elsewhere. In Philadelphia, for example, most Chinese churches and family associations are located in the downtown Chinatown, although some churches are now establishing suburban branches. Chinese-speaking lawyers, tax accountants, travel agents, doctors, and dentists who can serve monolingual clients or act as intermediaries maintain offices in Chinatown. Global media—newspapers and videos—are also centrally produced and distributed but are increasingly available directly to the home through computers and satellite transmission. Centrality becomes especially evident at points of public ritual celebration such as the Mid-Autumn festival or Chinese New Year. Still, suburban Chinese will celebrate these events at home or with friends before meeting for collective parties; in 2009, central Philadelphia charged so much for security for public events that dragon dances for the New Year cropped up in outlying areas. Chinatowns thus articulate public and semi-private roles that resonate with other global downtowns.

Meanwhile, suburban Chinese make choices about how they relate to polycentric Chinese downtowns. While Philadelphia's central Chinatown serves a diffuse Asian population, Vietnamese Chinese strip malls in North and South Philadelphia are easier destinations for bulk purchases packed into the suburban minivans that fill their parking lot on weekends. Such trajectories may involve ethnic histories and choices as well; both areas are dominated by Southeast Asian Chinese rather than mainlanders and offer a wider range of Vietnamese, Cambodian, Laotian, and Indonesian stores and services than the older Chinatown in Center City.

Chinatown schools, Catholic and public, offer core programs in Cantonese and Mandarin (Macabasco 2005). Yet, the old elite Main Line acts as a node for suburban Chinese, with three Saturday schools in Cantonese and Mandarin occupying inner-suburb private school campuses that are themselves regional hubs for mixed populations during the week. This concentration suggests that suburbs can link to other suburbs to compete with downtowns, depending on functions, access, and needs. We have found similar patterns in Lima, where newspapers, major associations, and wholesale businesses remain downtown but Chinese restaurants have recognized the peculiar anticentralism of limeños and have opened suburban branches in Miraflores, San Isidro, and other expensive suburbs to which newspapers and producers now make direct deliveries. Meanwhile, Chinese schools are found in middle-class inner-suburban areas accessible to other suburban Peruvian Chinese (and to some non-Chinese Peruvians who see them as portals to globalization).

Polycentric Chinatowns reflect wider regional competition among cities and outlying areas or suburbs and challenge our conceptions of global suburbanization as much as global downtowns. Los Angeles Chinese Americans, for example, had already formed suburban clusters by the 1920s, although the downtown Chinatown only became fixed in its location in the late 1930s. As Li Wei notes, "their suburbanization was not accompanied by complete assimilation, nor did only the more affluent segments of Chinese communities move to the suburbs. Instead, there was a spatial transformation of the Chinese community. While Chinatown persisted, a new suburban area emerged. It was characterized by a high concentration of Chinese-owned businesses and industrial districts, and high levels of Chinese participation in local politics and community" (2006a: 79; see Fong 1994; Li 2009). In fact, the suburbanization of Chinese became a badge of both successful assimilation and global connections (Cheng 2006).

These cases remind us that globalization in downtowns can never be treated as an isolate and that urban and suburban populations demonstrate a range of relations to downtowns. Movements of people and capital may involve decisions that favor centrality. Yet families, institutions, and corporations also find values in other locations articulated with new centers—whether in establishing a business in a suburb or forming ethnic clusters that allow for isolation as well as metropolitan interactions. Chinese Americans (Chinese French, Chinese Peruvians), like other metropolitan citizens, balance residence and business, private space and public roles, moving between multiple suburban and urban locales. Such flexibility illustrates the dangers of planning around simplistic divisions of "global" downtowns and "local" suburbs.

The articulation of Chinatowns raises further questions for global networks across downtowns as well. The movement of people and goods through Hong Kong, for example, created Golden Mountain firms there that maintained networks of people, goods, capital, and information among Chinese and Chinatowns across Australia and the Americas in the nineteenth and twentieth centuries. Through their base in Hong Kong, overseas

Chinese had access to food, opium, and newspapers; could send news and money home to villages in China; or could intervene with massive capital donations after natural disasters or in times of political crises (Hsu 2000). Both the Qing Court in Beijing and revolutionary parties in exile saw China-towns worldwide as fields of competitive activity and fundraising—political economic globalizations continued by both the Mainland and Taiwan today (McKeown 2001). These Chinatown connections challenge the ways in which models of globalization have emphasized the experience of a few key cities—New York, London, and Tokyo—and a Western-dominated vision rather than alternative Chinese or grassroots imaginations (McDonogh and Wong 2005).

Moreover, these historical articulations guide us toward wider contemporary connections. Parisian Chinatowns, for example, are not only centers for a city, region, and nation-state, but also serve as centers for an entire body of European Chinese moving among growing centers and opportunities in Milan, Barcelona, and Eastern Europe. While many Europeans still grapple with definition capitals for a united Europe, Euro-Chinese, apparently, already have chosen one. And concomitant global pathways continue to take shape. For example, the fruits and vegetables of Chinatowns in France now rely on producers in Southeast Asia and Africa specialized in a Euro-Chinese market, just as foods for North American Chinese have created producer networks across Latin America. Hence, foodways map out global connections through global farmers, "Chinese" downtowns, restaurants, and homes.

Conclusions: New Chinatowns, New Downtowns, New Futures

While global Chinatowns allow us to reread the past and present of global downtowns, they also pose questions for the future. We have suggested some of these in talking about Chinese articulations regionally and globally as alternatives to downtowns. The widespread emergence of newly planned Chinatowns worldwide raises even more intriguing questions for the future of downtowns as spaces of connection and imagination, with which we close.

Some of these projects fall within the framework of regional development: malled Chinatowns, for example, have appeared in Manila and have been added to the fantastic landscape of Las Vegas (and serve the latter's global Chinese tourist base as a downtown away from downtown; Tsui 2009). Meanwhile, the Chinagora of Paris, a less-than-successful Chinese government overseas investment of the 1960s, plopped stodgy Chinese architecture and curios into the old suburbs of Paris (Alfort). This effort seems to have had little, if any, local impact beyond its generally deserted hotel-restaurant complex (www.chinagora.fr).

In other cities and nation-states, where a global imbalance of goods and capital is more evident, newly powerful Chinese are building downtowns without necessarily Sinicizing them. Africa, for example, has become one of the most important foci for Chinese investment and the creation of a new Chinese presence that may include some sort of Chinatown. Some entrepreneurs are creating retail clusters that recall those established by merchants in nineteenth-century cities in Australia and the Americas (although without any large existing Chinese clientele). In other cities, however, a Chinese presence expresses different relations of global power. Luanda, Angola, for example, has been infused by up to $412 billion in loans from a China that wants to ensure a steady flow of oil to its growing industries. China has contributed new skyscrapers and banks in center cities across the country (Lafraniere 2007). Here, a new Chinatown means a neocolonial enclave where Asian managers may live in safety and comfort in separated worlds (Beuret, Serge, and Woods 2008). Again, this globalization entails multiple trajectories: there are now roughly 10,000 Africans in Guangzhou as well as daily flights to this global hub from many African capitals, linking downtown to downtown in ways that raise questions for Chinese cities as well.

At the same time, in cities as far-flung as Guayaquil (Ecuador), Santiago (Chile), Manila (Philippines), and San José (Costa Rica), the construction of entirely new Chinatowns has been promoted to attract and articulate global capital, tourism, and other connections. In Guayaquil, for example, a new Chinatown proposed in 2005 was a joint project of the municipality and Mainland Chinese investors, planned as part of ongoing revitalization of the harbor area and reconstitution of Guayaquil as a world port of exchange. In fact, this is a much more complicated case. Guayaquil had a flourishing Chinatown near the port and central business district from the turn of the century through the 1950s (Marmalejo 2003). A successful and highly assimilated suburban Chinese Ecuadorian population still bemoaned the loss of this center, its school, and its conviviality during our fieldwork there in 2005. These Sino-Ecuadorians nonetheless seemed to overlook the presence of Fujianese family businesses that have moved into this same central area. Ignoring both past and present Chinese globalization, the plan for a new Chinatown offered commodified Chineseness—pavilions, red tile roofs, restaurants, hotels, and curios—that strip the local from the global. It offered no residence, everyday services, or social connections through children or the elderly. Yet, it underscored China's keen awareness of Ecuador as a trading partner, especially with regard to oil that China needs. This Chinatown was not a symbol of global Chinese people or of Guayaquil as a global city but, as in Barcelona's metaphoric *barrio chino*, an icon of globalization itself. Similarly ambitious—but perhaps more tenuous—are projects that have been announced in Santiago, Chile, and San José, Costa Rica, to build new Chinatowns as commercial spaces to *attract* Chinese investors and global tourists.

Certainly, these ideas of building global spaces speak anew to the challenges of global downtowns in the future, including those of China. In the last decade, Mainland Chinese, buoyed by new wealth and power evident in their expansion worldwide, have undertaken massive physical reconstruction from Beijing and Shanghai to Guangzhou and Chengdu. Some areas have planned for completely new downtowns on greenfields outside existing cities (McDonogh and Wong 2005; Wu 2006). But the idea of building a new Chinatown also evokes more widespread visions of creating modern urban and national central places, icons in a global political economy of place epitomized in the history and symbolism of capitals such as Canberra, Brasilia, Puttrajaya, and Washington, D.C. (and their "downtowns") or discussions of multiple capitals for a united Europe (Hein 2004). "New" Chinatowns, like new capitals, ask us if the symbolic registers of the center, of inclusion and exclusion, monumentality and connection, are actually transferable to projects that seek to insert central spaces on a world map.

At the same time, the commodification and movements of Chinatown within different eras and meanings of globalization force us to question less extensive downtown "renewal" that appears through so many articles in this volume. As downtowns have been read by governments, developers, and planners as attractions for concrete particular audiences, including investors, tourists, DINKs (dual income, no kids), and suburban consumers, do they risk becoming artificial spaces detached from the everyday history and fabric of urban life? The global city of Saskia Sassen (2001), for example, is one of growing polarization: tensions we read not only within downtowns and cities but also in competition among global downtowns. If downtown becomes a homogenized space targeting global tourism markets with McDonald's, Sofitels, and H&M or builds to emphasize global fashions (film festivals, ludic waterfronts, or convention centers) instead of incorporating social services and local needs, is it so different from a new Chinatown with its own global crimson-and-golden arches?

The complexity and changes of global Chinatowns remind us that all downtowns have been areas of global movement, negotiation, and conflict. Chinatowns speak to what people value in downtowns in motion. They also show how immigrants, citizens, governments, developers, and mobile visitors grapple with exclusion, competition, and identity. Indeed, all lessons need not be so ominous. Chinatowns, after all, can be read in many cities as truly successful examples of urban renewal, producing flourishing communities in deteriorated built environments near downtowns.

Moreover, in teasing apart these many global cases, we have suggested the importance of balancing Chinatown as a visible, shared public space with private and semiprivate spaces, whether upstairs spaces, homes, nearby neighborhoods, or suburban networks. Privacy involves differences of language, ethnicity, gender, age, immigration status, and assimilation that may be present but not determinant in collective public spaces like Chinatown. Similarly, in a time of new residential patterns, global downtowns incorporate wider meanings of public and private framed by inherited monumentality and attractions as well as places for families, individuals, and private choices—parks, bars, apartment buildings, churches. The sense of downtown as a vital, democratic, visible, and global space is not opposed to the home or to zones of diverse sociability. Yet, the intersections of public and private cannot be reduced to easy dichotomies: we must recognize the complexity that links them to local and global, visibility and invisibility, city and suburb, and heritage and future reproduction. All of these themes are parts of the practice and the myths of downtown as centers for cities, regions, and nation-states across the world. And citizens and elites of these downtowns prove keenly aware of their competition, old and new.

Finally, all these ideas from and about Chinatowns around the world underscore the value of the comparative anthropological study of downtowns as global sites, through multisite ethnography as well as comparative projects. Both the global Chinese agency and the widely shared non-Chinese imagery we have examined here resonate in other chapters in this volume with processes that emerge from careful analysis of local history, social forces, and cultural debates. Comparisons clarify shared structures of space, people, capital, and conflict in modern cities as well as connections among them. Somewhere beside downtown, then, we need a place to sit, to sip a cup of tea, and to reflect on flows of power and people that have created and re-create these central places in our cities and our lives.

NOTES

Chapter 1. Toward a Genealogy of Downtowns

1. See http://www.essential-architecture.com/ARCHITECT/ARCH-Burnham.htm for images of these plans.

Chapter 2. From Peking to Beijing

I would like to thank the editors and the reviewers for commenting on earlier drafts of this chapter.

1. "Great Olympics, New Beijing" is the official English slogan for the 2008 Beijing Olympics.

2. One USD is about 7 RMB. In Chinese, 1 billion is counted as 1,000 million.

3. The three CBDs are in the Chaoyang, Xicheng, and Haidian districts.

4. Other major examples of revived historical places for tourism promotion include the Shishahai area, Yongding Gate, and Ming City Wall Park.

5. Most designations of cultural districts occurred after the success of the 798 art district around 2005.

6. The five imperial dynasties are the Liao (938–1122), Jin (1122–1215), Yuan (1267–1367), Ming (1368–1643), and Qing (1644–1911). From 1949 to the present, Beijing has been the capital of the People's Republic of China.

7. I follow historians such as Susan Naquin and define the early modern period of the Ming and Qing dynasties as the imperial period. In 1403, the Emperor Yongle of the Ming dynasty relocated the capital from Nanking to Peking. The fall of the Qing dynasty in 1911 is widely agreed upon as the beginning year of the Republican era. 1978 is the year of Reform and Opening, and it is usually taken as the turning point of China's transition from a socialist to a market economy.

8. Beijing has been called by different names in Chinese. It was first called Ji as the small center of the Warring States Kingdom of Yan, and then Youzhou in the medieval period, Dadu during the Yuan dynasty, and Jingshi in the Ming and Qing periods. It was renamed Beijing in 1912 by the Nationalist Party, changed to Beiping later in 1928, and back to Beijing again in 1949 by the socialist regime. Although Beijing is used as the official name after 1949, the name *Peking* was widely used in the Western

media until the 1980s. Beijing and Peking are different romanizations of the same Chinese word, 北京. See details on the name changes in Naquin 2000.

9. Ming emperor Yongle rebuilt Yuan Dadu as Peking in the 1500s. Structures and shapes from Yongle's Peking have remained for five centuries and are still visible today.

10. Although not explicitly recognized in most historical accounts in Chinese, the Manchu rule during the Qing dynasty can be seen as an instance of globalism as the Manchu elites in the Inner City distinguished themselves by superiority to the mercantile Chinese culture of Qianmen. I would like to thank Gary McDonogh for pointing out this connection.

11. Such subcenters include, for example, the area of Drum and Bell towers, Xisi, Dongsi, Xidan, Dongdan, Di'an Gate, Chongwen Gate, and Dashilar.

12. The name Wangfujing means "Well of Princely Mansion." The presence of Manchu nobility within the Inner City during the Qing period was physically marked by their conspicuously grand mansions (*wangfu*). By the middle of the eighteenth century, more than thirty such princely mansions occupied substantial portions of the urban real estate in the Inner City (Broudehoux 2004). Wangfujing was the residence of the highest-ranking princes and nobles, with a history dating back to the Ming emperor Yongle (1403–1424).

13. Xidan was another commercial center that emerged in the republican period, characterized by new styles of specialty shops. It was smaller in scale, compared with Wangfujing.

14. See Beijing City Government (1993).

15. See Beijing City Government (1998).

16. From the CBD Administration Committee; see http://www.bjcbd.gov.cn.

17. The eight firms are Skidmore, Owing & Merrill; Johnson Fain & Partners; NBBJ from USA; GMP from Germany; Urban Environment and Research Institute from Japan; Kuipercom & Pangnons from Holland; and two Chinese firms—Beijing Planning and Design Institute and Shanghai Urban Planning and Design Institute.

18. All interview quotes in this section are from the author's fieldwork in Beijing, 2004 and 2005.

19. http://www.bjcbd.gov.cn

20. There are a number of publications specifically addressing the issues of displacement, housing rights, and urban renewal in Chinese cities. For example, see Ren (2008); Weinstein and Ren (2009); Zhang (2004, 2006); Zhang and Fang (2004).

21. Most recent publications on Chinese cities focus only on the contemporary period; see Wu, Xu, and Yeh (2007); Logan (2002, 2008).

Chapter 3. Simulations of Barcelona

Epigraph: Subirós 1996. This chapter was translated by Gary W. McDonogh.

Chapter 4. Urbanist Ideology and the Production of Space
in the United Arab Emirates

These ideas are further developed in my book, *Dubai, The City as Corporation* (Kanna 2011). I am indebted to Gary McDonogh and Marina Peterson for inviting me to participate in this volume, and for close, critical readings of drafts of this chapter. Thanks also to Hassan-Uddin Khan, Suha Özkan, and Marc Treib for engagement with and critique of a version of this chapter presented at the Roger Williams University International Fellows conference in July 2008.

Epigraphs: Lefebvre 2003: 109; Khater Masaad, assistant to the ruler of Ras al-Khaimah, UAE (Wide Angle Transcript 2007: 5).

1. The GCC countries are Bahrain, Kuwait, Oman, Qatar, Saudi Arabia, and the UAE. Excellent interactive maps and websites summarizing major Dubai projects can be accessed at http://www.emaar.com/index.aspx?pagehome, http://www.dubailand .ae/, http://www.nakheel.com/en. These are the websites of EMAAR, Nakheel, and Tatweer, giant parastatal members of the private company owned by the Dubai ruler Muhammad bin Rashid Al Maktoum. Images of and information about Snøhetta's Ras al-Khaimah Gateway, part of the proposed Ras al-Khaimah downtown, can be viewed at http://www.snoarc.no/#/projects/21/false/all/. Snøhetta is also designing a major museum project in Abu Dhabi: http://www.snoarc.no/#/projects/24/false/all/. Koolhaas 2009 is an excellent summary of OMA's adventures in the UAE.

2. At the time this chapter was being written, the world economic crisis had not yet fully impacted the UAE. The aftermath of the crisis is now well documented in both the Arabic local press and the Western press: a massive slowdown of construction in Dubai (if not in oil-rich Abu Dhabi), mass layoffs of construction workers, suspension or cancellation of major starchitectural projects in Dubai (such as Koolhaas-OMA's Waterfront City and Hadid's Dubai Opera House). The crisis has also altered relations between the individual emirates, with Abu Dhabi asserting its centralizing interests over the more federalist tendencies of Dubai. This is reflected in the built environment. See, for example, the case of the building formerly known as Burj Dubai, flagship project of the EMAAR firm owned by Dubai ruler Muhammad bin Rashid Al Maktoum, now rebranded "Burj Khalifa," the Khalifa Tower, in honor of Abu Dhabi's Khalifa bin Zayed Al Nahyan, UAE president. This followed a US $25 billion bailout of Dubai by Abu Dhabi. See Tomlinson and Robertson 2010.

3. My thanks to Gary McDonogh for pointing this out.

4. Lloyd and Christens, in this volume, suggest that urban entrepreneurs in Nashville valorize Dubai's spirit of seemingly unrestrained urban entrepreneurialism and commodification of urban space. Nashville's municipal authorities and real estate developers might have images such as EMAAR's Downtown Dubai project in mind. See http://www.emaar.com/index.aspx?pageemaaruae-downtownburj.

5. Defining the term *elite* and avoiding reifications of it are more complicated than they appear, as both Najib Hourani on Beirut and Julian Brash on New York point out

in this volume. Emirati elites are no exception. They constitute a diverse social formation, the contours of which shift depending upon perspective. For example, the UAE
is a majority expatriate country. In Dubai, expatriates make up around 80 percent of
all residents. So, in the broadest sense, Emirati citizens form an elite in relation to
most expatriates: Emiratis usually enjoy generous welfare state benefits, sinecures in
the public sector, and an average per capita income that is among the highest in the
world. From another, narrower perspective, it is the owners of large holding companies, beneficiaries of exclusive, state-distributed trade concessions at the time of UAE
independence (1971), that, along with the ruling families of the federation, make up
the elite (see Abdulla 1980, 1984; Davidson 2005, 2008; and Kanna 2010, 2011, for a
more detailed discussion). Moreover, elites, as Brash argues, are not homogeneous.
They can have very different agendas. This is also true for the UAE. For example, one
of the structural tensions in the Dubai merchant/corporate–ruling family bloc relates
to the disproportionate amount of land owned by the ruling family. Merchants often see the ruler as a monopolist restricting their, the merchants', economic opportunities. My aim in this chapter, however, is to show the influence of a certain style of
imagining urban centrality and the role of experts in how powerful actors in local
contexts give shape to such images, images shared by members of the merchant–
ruling family elite. Emirati political theorist Abdul Khaleq Abdulla summarizes the
political structure of the UAE thus: at the apex is the Supreme Council, composed of
the seven rulers of the emirates (with the Abu Dhabi and Dubai rulers, respectively,
holding the presidency and the vice presidency); the Council of Ministers or Executive Council, composed both of royals and appointed nonroyal technocrats; and the
National Council, the most participatory of the three bodies, consisting of forty appointed members, some of whom are "not totally beholden to the regime" (Abdulla
1980: 20). Even so, says Abdulla, the National Council is strongly tribal in character.
Ultimately, "there are some 7 or 8 families who dominate the whole UAE" (Abdulla
1980: 20).

    6. See, for example, the planned urban renewal of Satwa, a poor and working-class
neighborhood in Dubai, where a large real estate firm is in the process of razing
homes and evicting thousands of residents to put up a large resort (*Istabsir* n.d.).

    7. The UAE is a majority expatriate country. In Dubai, a majority of the popula-
tion (perhaps 80 percent) is expatriate, and a majority of the citizenship is ethnically
Persian, not Arab. The ruling families of each emirate, however, are ethnically Arab.
Since independence, the UAE state began inventing an Arab identity, creating an
"Arab" national costume among other things. The ethnically Arab ruling families
have become identified with the authentic culture of the UAE. I discuss the intersection of ethnicity, national identity, and Arabization in detail elsewhere (Kanna 2011;
see also Onley 2007).

    8. The original 1960 plan, it seems, is in the private collection of John Harris's
family. Thanks to Yasser Elsheshtawy for bringing the 1960 document to my attention

and for contextualizing the 1971 document. Research based on Elsheshtawy's access to the 1960 plan and interviews with Harris's family appears in Elsheshtawy 2009. The 1971 document is not originally paginated. The paginations here are my own and begin with the page preceding the table of contents.

9. Personal communication, June 17, 2009.

10. Indeed, one should, as well, avoid the temptation to homogenize the ruling Maktoum family. Rashid's vision for Dubai and his intentions, while perhaps broadly similar to those of his successor Muhammad, were far more aesthetically modest than those of his son. Rashid seems to have been more concerned with modern infrastructures, Muhammad with global imagery and urban entrepreneurialism.

11. In the interests of full disclosure, I was interviewed by the film's producers for contextual background and one of my articles is listed as a resource on the film's website.

12. The speed of the realization of projects and the extremely short timeframes that local developers demand of architects are often noted and positively evaluated in urbanist accounts or UAE architecture, but rarely is the social context mentioned: a deregulated labor market consisting of cheap foreign labor drawn from the immense surplus labor pools of the Middle East and South Asia (see Ali 2010; Human Rights Watch 2006; Kanna 2007).

13. Gehry's talk about the local context being a "clean slate" resonates in striking and unappealing ways with another project in which he was simultaneously involved: a Jerusalem project of the U.S.-based Simon Wiesenthal Center carrying the Orwellian name "Museum of Tolerance," for which Gehry was until recently the chief architect. The land on which the museum is planned is an ancient Muslim cemetery called Ma'man Allah. Construction has already begun, unearthing scores of bones, according to Saree Makdisi (2010). Many Palestinians and Jews, along with people from across the world, have understandably recoiled at this project, which even the head archaeologist at the site, an Israeli, has sharply protested. Gehry recently announced that he was withdrawing from the project, ostensibly to focus on other, more urgent commitments.

14. To be fair, Giesen's theory is not uncontested by architects working in the UAE. Another colleague of his, to whom I spoke, gave an opposite theorization of UAE architecture: it is a triumph of impermanence and consumer space. This architect argued that Dubai was an example of the Generic Cities theory (Koolhaas 1978). This architect, who saw Dubai as an example of successful urbanism within the frame of Generic Cities, attributed this success to the city's rejection of permanence, continuity, and vernacular and emphasis on what he called "spontaneity" and "the psychology of attraction and enjoyment."

15. See the following website for images and plans of the Intelligent Tower: http://ardalanassociates.com/projects/tower/

16. This is to say nothing about the fact that the majority foreign population of the UAE is excluded from the Arab-tribal framing of the identity of the nation-state.

17. Donald McNeill's reflections on the "architect as anthropologist" are fascinating in this connection, especially since McNeill too questions the cultural claims about the Other that Koolhaas often makes. See McNeill 2009: 106–11.

18. Nationalism lives on in various manifestations in today's UAE. The most visible form is what the political scientist Anh Nga Longva has called "ethnocracy," a sense of national belonging based on shared ethnicity (to be contrasted from both democracy and autocracy, in Longva's argument. See Longva 2005). Ethnocracy is the official UAE construction of national identity and maintained partly to keep in place a generous welfare state for the minority who count as citizens. It is a result, I argue, of the defeat of alternative constructions of nationalism (Kanna 2011). For example, ethnocracy is related, but not identical, to notions of Emiratiness based in ideas of *patrie*, a feeling of attachment to the national project of the UAE, rather than feelings of shared ethnicity. This sense of Emiratiness as a national project is summarized by Abdul Khaleq Abdulla (2009b) in the following way: "I am Emirati because I am proud to be Emirati (*ana Imarati wa aftakhir*)." This formula, for Abdulla, is the only relevant criterion for determining who is a real Emirati. In other words, Abdulla connects Emiratiness not with shared ethnicity but with identification with the project of Emirati sovereignty. This is in turn reflected in debates over "localism" or "federalism" (*al-mahalliyya*), on the one side, and "national unity" (*al-ittihad*), on the other. These debates contain faint but recognizable traces of the older struggles between pro-Western (federalist) tendencies and anticolonial, pro-independence (national) tendencies (see Abdulla 2009a).

Chapter 5. Reaching for Dubai

Epigraph: Tony Giarratana (Chamberlain 2006).

1. Dubai, however, with its hyper-exclusivity and nouveau riche extravagances, evokes Vegas ice bars and high-roller pits, while Nashville, with the gaudy Opryland resort and scale replica of the Parthenon, is more like the midmarket Luxor and Excaliber hotels.

2. The phantasmagoria, as analyzed by Benjamin, signals the dreamscapes of capitalist modernity, exemplified in nineteenth-century Paris by the electric-lit Arcades. As we trace the implications of Benjamin's analysis, each epoch is characterized by its own mode of urban fantasy, and its own modes of obfuscation—the phantasmagoria always conceals its own origins in alienated labor—commodity fetishism impressed upon the city landscape (see Benjamin 1999; Jameson 1991).

3. Examples are the credit default swap and the "synthetic" market in mortgage bonds (Lewis 2010).

4. Two venerable European cities sought to efface staid older traditions in favor of a wholehearted embrace of deregulated capitalism and intense real estate speculation, Dublin and Reykjavik, the Celtic and Nordic tigers, respectively. Given their current

economic states, Nashville should be grateful that it never could match the extravagance of their apparent if short-lived success prying their way into the global economy. Dublin in particular was leveraged to prove the manifest excellence of both the Creative City model and deregulated financial markets in the mid-2000s.

5. For a catalogue of these incongruous structures in the mid-South city, see Kreyling et al. 1996.

6. "Everyone wants a warehouse district [to turn into lofts and nightclubs]," an official in the MDHA told us. "We don't have the building stock," he added, shrugging. "They want it anyway."

7. The demolition handily won the "I wish they hadn't torn it down" nod that year in the *Nashville Scene* Reader's Poll.

8. These investments were partly aided by preferential treatment from the federal government, as Nashville, unlike other large southern cities, peacefully complied with desegregation. This was reminiscent of the role Nashville played during Reconstruction, when it was a preferred destination for northern attempts at redevelopment and charity (Carey 2005).

9. These sorts of sanitized, themed environments have been soundly condemned by urban scholars as bland, derivative, and disintegrated from the fabric of the larger city (Judd 1999; Sorkin 1992).

10. Referred to as the "Mother Church of Country Music," the Ryman housed the Grand Ole Opry until it was moved to the suburbs in the 1970s. The structure narrowly escaped demolition, and has today once again become a premier destination for live music performances.

11. One official laughed when asked in his MDHA office (the windows protected by steel mesh) if developers felt comfortable coming there. "If they want the money, they come," he said.

12. Downtown developers largely declined to pursue claims against buyers abandoning presale contracts in 2008, though there are indications that this stance may be shifting. In 2009, Bristol (the developer of ICON) began exploring seeking damages from welchers on its Midtown condominium project, Bristol West End (Sisk 2009a: Tony Giarratana).

13. District 6 encompasses downtown and the gentrifying East Nashville.

14. On the relationship between the Real World, diversity, and the hip urban imaginary, see Lloyd 2010: 147–53.

Chapter 6. From National Utopia to Elite Enclave

1. For Solidere's current approach to reconstruction, including images, interactive maps, and highly informative, downloadable publications, see the company website at www.solidere.com. "Souks" is Solidere's spelling of the word, and I will utilize this spelling when referring to the Solidere project of the same name. The

roper transliteration of the Arabic, *sūq* (pl. *aswaq*), shall be used in all other instances.

2. A 1977 General Directorate of Urban Planning study found that the nearly 2,000 plots in the BCD hosted more than 7,000 shops; 5,000 residential units; nearly 5,600 offices; 1,360 small factories and workshops; 700 warehouses; more than 340 hotels of varying classes; nearly 400 restaurants and cafes; and 45 drinking establishments (Marqos 1990).

3. Interview with Oussama Kabbani, Town Planning Department, Solidere, June 16, 1998.

4. Interview with Nabil Rashed, Solidere Public Relations Department, Solidere, October 10, 2000.

5. Kabbani interview.

6. Interview with Jade Tabet, June 23, 1998.

7. Interview with M., Solidere Board of Directors, August 4, 2000.

8. These indicators provide only crude estimates of the extent of the real estate explosion. Statistics kept by the Directorate of Real Estate Affairs at the Ministry of Finance are highly unreliable. According to a ministry official who requested anonymity, the figures are based on the values declared by the parties to the transaction. In the absence of oversight, they undervalue the deals to avoid taxes and fees.

9. Kabbani interview.

10. Kabbani interview.

11. Interview with Anonymous, Sales and Marketing Department, Solidere, February 2001.

12. Interviews with N., Souks Project, Solidere, July 1, 1997 and October 19, 2000.

13. Interview with Anonymous, Sales and Marketing Department, Solidere, May 2001.

14. Overage is calculated as a percentage of sales after a specified target has been reached, generally ranging from 2 to 4 percent.

15. N. interview, July 1, 1997.

16. N. interview, October 19, 2000.

17. N. interview, July 1, 1997. This fundamental principle of shopping mall design has been perfected in the United States, where length of stay increased from twenty minutes in 1960 to more than three hours by 1992 (Crawford 1992: 14).

18. N. interview, July 1, 1997.

19. Interview with M., Marketing, Solidere, May 11, 2001.

20. N. interview, October 19, 2000.

21. Interview with Anonymous, a prominent property developer, September 6, 2000.

22. I examine this rise of this network in greater detail in Hourani 2009.

23. Interview with W., MaxiMa Fashion, September 20, 2001. Later MaxiMa Fashion's brands, along many of its owners and executives, became the core of the regional Azadea Group.

Chapter 7. When the Film Festival Comes to (Down)Town

More information on the Zanzibar International Film Festival can be found at the official website, http://www.ziff.or.tz/. Photographs and other factual details can be found at http://www.filmfestivalworld.com/festival/Ziff_Festival_Zanzibar/. A range of festival videos can be found at www.youtube.com/, including some of the promotional films put together by ZGFilms (for example, see http://www.zgfilms.com/events .html#ziff).

1. UNESCO World Heritage List, http://whc.unesco.org/en/list/173/documents, accessed 12 March 2010.

2. While trumpeting history, local promoters seem quite willing to play fast and loose with the historical record. A press release for the twelfth festival in 2009 in *Africa Travel Magazine* is typical in this regard. In it, the Tanzania Tourist Board describes Stone Town as "a place of festivals, from music to movies to dance." Performances take place outdoors, we are told, in the "city's Old Fort, featuring an ancient amphitheatre"; later, we are informed that the city retains "much of its 16th century architecture"—an assertion that misses the mark by only three centuries or so.

3. Gerald Portal to Lord Salisbury, August 19, 1892, Rhodes House Library (RHL): Mss.Afr.s.106.

4. "Town Planning," *Al-Falaq*, November 13, 1937, Zanzibar National Archives (ZNA): AB 39/207.

5. Senior Commissioner A. P. Cumming Bruce to Chief Secretary, September 10, 1952, and Curator J. D. Robertson to Chief Secretary, November 26, 1952, ZNA: AB 31/10.

6. Resident Guy Pilling to Acting Chief Secretary, August 5, 1945, ZNA: AB 39/166.

7. Permanent Secretary (C. M.) M. V. Smithyman to Permanent Secretary (W. C. L.), January 27, 1962, ZNA: AE 5/4.

8. Fieldnotes, interview with Gregory Baptiste, July 4, 2007.

9. Fieldnotes, discussion session at ZIFF Conference on Memories and Visual Cultures, July 3, 2007.

10. Controversy about property speculation and suspicious deals has surfaced most recently with regard to a significant piece of open land and a historic building (Mambo Msiige) in Shangani—one of the last areas potentially available for large-scale tourist redevelopment along the seafront. The Aga Khan Development Network was well advanced in negotiations over the site when the area was suddenly fenced off and the Starehe Club, a run-down bar on the site of the old colonial sailing club, was summarily demolished. Just days before leaving office in 2010, high officials in the outgoing CCM government had signed a last-minute deal with the Kempinski hotel group, granting a ninety-nine-year lease to the prestige site for a mere US$1.5 million. Other officials, residents, and civic NGOs questioned the

terms and legality of the deal, protesting in the media about the lack of consultation or transparency; high-level corruption and back-door payments were widely suspected. UNESCO also weighed in on the dispute, threatening to revoke Zanzibar's heritage status if the hotel development went through. Despite the objections, the government seemed likely to push the deal through, unbowed in its efforts to woo investors and attract luxury tourism. As the new president declaimed, "The government has not made a mistake . . . it can make any decision, especially regarding its properties, and no one can question it." See, for example, Mike Mande, "Zanzibar May Be Axed from World Heritage Site," *The Citizen*, January 22, 2011. Electronic document, http://www.thecitizen.co.tz/sunday-citizen/40-sunday-citizen-news/7549-zanzibar-may-be-axed-from-world-heritage-site.html, accessed February 2, 2011, and "Dr Shein Justifies Leasing of Stone Town Buildings," *The Guardian*, May 4, 2011. Electronic document, http://www.ippmedia.com/frontend/index.php?l28751, accessed May 25, 2011.

    11. As of 2011, no real progress has been made to fulfill Almeida's vision of a school of traditional architecture in Zanzibar—either by donors or the government. But efforts to use the festival to promote historic architecture (and conversely to have restored buildings then serve as a platform for the festival itself) very much continue. In conjunction with the 2011 festival, for example, the ZIFF board launched an international campaign to raise funds to rehabilitate the art deco Majestic Cinema. Zanzibar's three public cinemas have all long been shuttered, and there were hopes of remaking the structure into a 200-seat multipurpose space for "corporate events, seminars and workshops along with a café." Press reports highlighted claims that a small group of elderly men continued to show films in the roofless cinema, even in the rain, holding onto the vestiges of a fading culture of public cinema spectatorship that needed to be rejuvenated. Drawing on film images certain to feed this nostalgia in European circles, the festival's CEO described the Majestic as "the Cinema Paradiso of Zanzibar." See David Smith, "Tanzania's Art Deco Ruin, the Majestic Cinema, Inspires Restoration Campaign," *The Guardian* (UK), June 3, 2011. Electronic document, http://www.guardian.co.uk/world/2011/jun/02/zanzibar-mjaestic-cinema-restoration-campaign, accessed June 5, 2011.

Chapter 8. The Future of the Past

    Epigraphs: Herzfeld 1991: 11; Appadurai 1996: 44.
    1. As Marikay McCabe notes, lacking any industry of its own, colonial Havana provided infrastructural support for the movement of goods from the interior of the island to the Spanish metropole, and served as a seat of colonial administration (2004: 10).
    2. http://whc.unesco.org/en/list/204.
    3. On Rastafarians in Cuba, see Hansing (2006).

4. The notion of interiorization and embourgeoisification is taken from Walter Benjamin's theorization of the Paris Arcades. For a further discussion, see Gilloch 1997.

Chapter 9. Utopia/Dystopia

Support for research for this chapter was provided by a Creative Research Award from the College of Fine Arts at Ohio University and an HSSC/Haynes Research Stipend.

Some websites reflecting the interests of the various stakeholders in downtown Los Angeles include those of the Downtown Los Angeles Neighborhood Council (www.dlanc.com), the Downtown Center Business Improvement District (www.downtownla.com), the Los Angeles Downtown News (www.ladowntownnews.com), Gallery Row (www.galleryrow.org), the Los Angeles Poverty Department (www.lapovertydept.org), and the Los Angeles Community Action Network (www.cangress.org).

Epigraphs: *LosAngelesNow*, 2004; Banham, 1971: 183.

1. In their article "Broken Windows," George L. Kelling and James Q. Wilson (1982) maintain that disrepair and disorder in the urban environment—such as broken windows—will result in further disorder and, more importantly, serious crime. Conversely, maintaining, repairing, and cleaning will deter crime. "Disorder" includes material and social conditions, such as the visible presence of homeless and mentally ill. Kelling was hired as a consultant for the chief of police's 2006 Safer Cities Initiative, a program aimed at reducing crime in and around Skid Row. Prior to the Safer Cities Initiative, an estimated 6,000 to 8,000 people slept on the street every night in a fifty-square-block area (Rivera 2004).

2. The rise of homelessness in the 1980s in American cities was in part an effect of global economic restructuring that played out on the local level in the form of changes in the job market, the decline of the welfare state, and a loss of affordable housing (Wolch and Dear 1993).

3. Michael Peter Smith uses "transnational urbanism" to describe "the cross-cutting local, translocal, and transnational social practices that 'come together' in particular places at particular times and enter into the contested politics of place-making, the social construction of power differentials, and the making of individual, group, national, and transnational identities, and their corresponding fields of difference" (2001: 5).

4. The Grand Avenue plan, supported by the city, county, and local boosters and developers, and subsequently funded by the royal family of Dubai, is intended to make Grand Avenue a destination for the arts, a pedestrian street anchored by a large public park where events will be presented and Angelenos will gather downtown. It has been subject to turns in the economy, but as of the beginning of 2011 seemed to be moving forward.

5. There is also an ongoing effort to restore the historic theaters on Broadway. This plan would entail removing a lively gray market economy dominated by Mexican immigrants.

6. Florida's term *creative class* is probably more apt as a descriptor for the new residents of downtown Los Angeles, especially with its associated economic justification, as housing, galleries, and amenities are all discussed and framed in relation to economic development; ultimately it is the drive for economic development that provides the conditions for and supports class exclusions. Nevertheless, a specificity of art is still persistent in the development processes seen in downtown Los Angeles today, exemplified by the number of small galleries in which area artists show their work.

7. An SRO, or single-room occupancy, is a low-rent building that offers tenants a single, private room usually with a shared bathroom.

8. The *Los Angeles Downtown News* sent a "Breaking News" report when figures were released from a survey that found that the median income of those who had moved downtown in the last three years was $90,000 per year, higher, it was noted, than the median income of Beverly Hills, renowned as a high-income neighborhood (*Los Angeles Downtown News*, email, January 31, 2005).

9. In William Pope.L's performance of *Thunderbird Immolation* (1978), the artist sat on the sidewalk outside a gallery with, among other things, a Coke can, a bottle each of Thunderbird and Wild Irish Rose, and a mug with a mixture of Coke and Thunderbird. He remained sitting on a square of yellow fabric inside a circle made of matchsticks and drank his cocktail until a gallery employee asked him to leave. Darby English explains, "it was arguably the bottle of Thunderbird, a drink of choice for many street dwellers that is also known as 'bum wine,' that most effectively asserted the 'clear-cut' distinction between these constituencies and called for Pope.L's ejection" (2007: 293).

10. A similar tent was later installed as part of LAPD's 2008 exhibit "Skid Row History Museum" at the Box Gallery in Chinatown.

Chapter 10. "Slum-Free Mumbai" and other Entrepreneurial Strategies in the Making of Mumbai's Global Downtown

1. This chapter refers to the city both as Mumbai and by its former name, Bombay. When discussing the city pre-1995, when its name was changed from Bombay, this chapter uses the former name.

2. Author interview, November 18, 2005.

3. "Rehabilitation" refers to onsite resettlement of slum-dwellers in tenement buildings as specified by the Slum Rehabilitation Scheme in a 1995 amendment to the Slum Areas Act of 1971.

4. Mehta's consultancy fee is 1 percent of total project expenditures, which are estimated at $2 billion, making Mehta's share approximately $20 million.

5. Author interview, November 8, 2005.

Chapter 11. Downtown as Brand, Downtown as Land

1. See also, inter alia, Dávila 2004; Maskovsky 2006; G. Pérez 2004; Susser 1982; B. Williams 1988.

2. For some exceptions, see Chesluk 2008; Greenberg 2008; Nevarez 2003; Rutheiser 1996.

3. In the end, the Jets were awarded the rights to develop the rail yards, though for hundreds of millions of dollars more than they had initially expected to pay.

Chapter 12. Beside Downtown

This project is part of a longer ongoing study of global Chinatowns that has been supported by our home institutions and the Fulbright Fellowship program, among other resources. A larger contextual framing of the project can be found in McDonogh and Wong 2005. Chinatowns are by their nature as tourist sites highly visible; hence, as in other articles, it is easy for readers to find commercial, private, and public interest websites that provide multiple illustrations as well as additional perspectives. Among websites we recommend for individual cities and Chinatowns are those for Philadelphia (http://www.chinatown-pcdc.org [Philadelphia Chinatown Development Corporation] and http://www2.hsp.org/exhibits/Balch%20exhibits/chinatown/chinatown .html [an exhibit at the Balch Institute]); San Francisco (http://www.sanfranciscochi natown.com); New York (http://www.chinatown-online.com); Singapore (mappery. com/Singapore-Chinatown-Map); Honolulu (http://www.chinatownhi.com); Chicago (www.chicagochinatown.org); Lima (www.barrio-chino.com); Los Angeles (http:// www.chinatownla.com); and Paris (www.aujourdhuilachine.com).

BIBLIOGRAPHY

Aaker, David A. 2002. Foreword. In S. Davis, *Brand Asset Management: Driving Profitable Growth Through Your Brands*, vii–x. San Francisco: Jossey-Bass.

Aaker, David A., and Erich Joachimsthaler. 2000. *Brand Leadership*. New York: Free Press.

Abbott, Carl. 1993. "Five Strategies for Downtown." *Journal of Policy History* 5: 5–27.

Abdulla, Abdul Khaliq. 1980. "The Revolution in Iran Stimulated the Existing Contradictions in the United Arab Emirates." *MERIP (Middle Eastern Research and Information) Reports* 85: 19–22, 25.

———. 1984. "Political Dependency: The Case of the United Arab Emirates." Ph.D. dissertation, Georgetown University.

———. 2006. "Dubai: rihlat madina 'arabiyya min al-mahalliyya ila l-'alamiyya" (Dubai: The Journey of an Arab City from Localism to Cosmopolitanism). *Al-Mustaqbal al-Arabi* 323: 1–28.

———. 2009a. "Al-Imarat ma ba'd al-azma al-maliyya al-'alamiyya" (The UAE after the World Financial Crisis). *Al-Khaleej*, September 29. www.alkhaleej.ae/portal/feac9f81-0a50-49f2-a443-564b457c7a43.aspx, accessed February 12, 2010.

———. 2009b. "Man huwa al-Imarati?" (Who Is the Emirati?). *Al Khaleej*, October 27. www.alkhaleej.ae/portal/bf15e4de-5772-4aec-bc52-7aa60a1350a6.aspx, accessed February 12, 2010.

Abelson, Elaine. 1989. *When Ladies Go a-Thieving: Middle-Class Shoplifters in the Victorian Department Store*. Oxford: Oxford University Press.

Abrahamson, Mark. 2004. *Global Cities*. Oxford: Oxford University Press.

Abu-Lughod, Janet L. 1999. *New York, Chicago, Los Angeles: America's Global Cities*. Minneapolis: University of Minnesota Press.

Acebillo, Josep. 1992. "Places dures, rondes verdes: la lógica urbanística del projecte olímpic." In *El vol de la fletxa: Barcelona '92: Crònica de la reivenció de la ciutat*, ed. Marina Palà and Pep Subirós. Barcelona: Electa.

Aden, Gareth. 1967. "The Loops: When and Where." *Nashville Magazine* January.

Adorno, Theodor. 2005 [1952]. *In Search of Wagner*. Trans. Rodney Livingstone. New York: Verso.

Aga Khan Trust for Culture. 1996. *Zanzibar: A Plan for the Historic Stone Town*. Geneva: Aga Khan Trust for Culture.

Ajuntament de Barcelona (City Hall, Barcelona). 1991. *Àrees de Nova Centralitat: New Downtowns in Barcelona*. 2nd ed. Barcelona: Ajuntament de Barcelona.

———. 1996. *La segona renovació*. Barcelona: Ajuntament de Barcelona.

———. 1998. *Anuario estadístico de la ciudad de Barcelona, 1987–1997*. Barcelona: Ajuntament de Barcelona.

Alegre, Pau. 1995. *Atlas del Port de Barcelona*. Barcelona: Port de Barcelona.

Alemany, Joan. 1998. *El Port de Barcelona*. Barcelona: Lunwerg.

Ali, Syed. 2010. *Dubai: Gilded Cage*. New Haven, Conn.: Yale University Press.

Alloo, Fatma. 2007. "Introduction and Acknowledgment." In *Ten Years of ZIFF*, ed. Fatma Alloo. Zanzibar: Gallery Publications.

Alonso, William. 1964. *Location and Land Use: Toward a General Theory of Land Rent*. Cambridge, Mass.: Harvard University Press.

Alper, Andrew. 2002. Testimony. Hearing on Corporate Subsidies, Committee on Economic Development, New York City Council, New York, June 11.

AME Info. 2005. "Facing Up to Our Ecological Footprint." February 14. http://www.ameinfo.com/53883.html, accessed May 27, 2008.

Amen, Michael Mark, Kevin Archer, and M. Martin Bosman, eds. 2006. *Relocating Cities: From the Center to the Margins*. Lanham, Md.: Rowman and Littlefield.

Anderson, Benedict. 1991. *Imagined Communities: Reflections on the Origin and Spread of Nationalism*. New York: Verso.

Angotti, Thomas. 2008. *New York for Sale: Community Planning Confronts Global Real Estate*. Cambridge, Mass.: MIT Press.

Antolín, J. B. 2006. "El nodo español en las diásporas de Asia Oriental." In *Las diásporas de Asia oriental en Europa occidental*, ed. J. B. Antolín. Barcelona: CIDOB November. 101–24.

Appadurai, Arjun. 1996. *Modernity at Large: Cultural Dimensions of Globalization*. Minneapolis: University of Minnesota Press.

———. 2000. "Spectral Housing and Urban Cleansing: Notes on Millennial Mumbai." *Public Culture* 12, 3: 627–51.

Applebome, Peter. 1997. *Dixie Rising: How the South Is Shaping American Values, Politics, and Culture*. New York: Mariner Books.

Arcspace. 2007. "Ando, Gehry, Hadid, and Nouvel, Saadiyat Island." February 7. http://www.arcspace.com/architects/aghn/aghn.html, accessed May 25, 2008.

Arkush, R. David, and Leo Ou-Fan Lee, eds. 1993. *Land without Ghosts: Chinese Impressions of America from the Mid-Nineteenth Century to the Present*. Berkeley: University of California Press.

Arreola, Daniel, and James Curtis. 1992. *Mexican American Border Cities*. Tucson: University of Arizona Press.

Associated Press. 2010. "Southeast Sees Big Influx of Illegal Immigrants: New Federal Report Tracks Flow of Workers During Economic Boom Years." *MSNBC*, February 23. http://www.msnbc.msn.com/id/35546061/ns/us_news-life, accessed March 23, 2010.

Augé, Marc. 1995. *Non-Places: Introduction to an Anthropology of Supermodernity.* Trans. John Howe. New York: Verso.

Ayyash, Imad. 1991. "Edde: Beirutism Will Erase Lebanonism." *Al-Nahar*, September 21.

Azuá, Félix de. 1998. "Barcelona y el Titanic." *La Vanguardia.*

Bagli, Charles. 2002. "Big Real Estate Groups Mobilizing against Proposed Jump in Property Taxes." *New York Times*, November 21.

———. 2005. "Suddenly, Developers Yearn for the Gritty Far West Side." *New York Times*, February 14.

Balbi, Mariell. 1999. *Los Chifas en el Peru: historia e recetas.* Lima: Universidad San Martín de Porres, Escuela de Turismo y Hotelería.

Banassat, Michel. 2002. *Chinatown ou les mystères et les splendeurs d'une cité interdite a Paris.* Paris: You-Feng.

Banerjee, Tridib, and Anastasia Loukaitou-Sideris. 1992. *Private Production of Downtown Public Open Space: Experiences of Los Angeles and San Francisco.* Los Angeles: School of Urban and Regional Planning, University of Southern California.

Banerjee-Guha, Swapna. 1995. "Urban Development Process in Bombay: Planning for Whom?" In *Bombay: Metaphor for Modern India,* ed. Sujata Patel and Alice Thorner, 100–20. Oxford: Oxford University Press.

Banham, Reyner. 1971. *Los Angeles: The Architecture of Four Ecologies.* Berkeley: University of California Press.

Barber, Lynn. 2008. "Zaha Hadid." *Observer*, March 9. http://arts.guardian.co.uk/art/architecture/story/0,,2263977,00.html, accessed June 4.

Bauman, John F. 2008. "The American Downtown: Sagas of Race, Place, and Space." *Journal of Urban History* 34, 3: 520–31.

Baz, Freddie. 1998. "The Macro-Economic Basis of Reconstruction." In *Projecting Beirut: Episodes in the Construction and Reconstruction of a Modern City,* ed. Peter Rowe and Hashim Sarkis, 165-172. Munich: Prestel.

BBC Radio 3. 2004. "Architecture in Dubai." CD, personal collection, George Katodrytis.

Beauregard, Robert. 1996. *When America Became Suburban.* Minneapolis: University of Minnesota Press.

Beddow, Tim, and Natasha Burns. 1998. *Safari Style.* New York: Stewart, Tabori, and Chang.

———. 1996. *Al-'Imar wal-Maslahat al-'Ammat: Fi Ijtima' wal-Thaqafat.* Beirut: Dar al-Jadid with Ford Foundation and Institute for Urban Studies.

Beijing City Government. 1993. *Beijing General City Plan.*

———. 1998. *Specific Controlling Plan of Beijing.*

Benjamin, Walter. 1969. "The Work of Art in the Age of Mechanical Reproduction." In *Illuminations,* 217-251. New York: Schocken Books.

———. 1978. "Paris, Capital of the Nineteenth Century." In *Reflections,* 146–62. New York: Harcourt Brace.

———. 1999. *The Arcades Project*. Cambridge, Mass.: Harvard University Press.

Berry, Brian J. L. 1971. "City Size and Economic Development." In *Urbanization and National Development*, ed. Leo Jakobson and Ved Prakash, 111–56. Beverly Hills, Calif.: Sage.

Bertaud, Alain. 2002. "India—Urban Land Reform Issues." Unpublished White Paper. http://alain-bertaud.com/, accessed June 5, 2011.

Beuret, Michel, Michel Serge, and Paolo Woods. 2008. *La Chinafrique: Pékin à la conquête du continent noir*. Paris: Grasset & Fasquelle.

Beyhum, Nabil. 1992. "The Crisis of Urban Culture: The Three Reconstruction Plans for Beirut." *Beirut Review* 4: 43–62.

Birch, Eugenie. 2002. "Having a Longer View on Downtown Living." *Journal of the American Planning Association* 68, 1: 5–21.

———. 2005. *Who Lives Downtown?* Washington, D.C.: Metropolitan Policy Program, Brookings Institution.

———. 2009. "Downtown in the 'New American City.'" Annals of the American Academy of Political and Social Science 626: 134–53.

Bissell, William Cunningham. 2005. "Engaging Colonial Nostalgia." *Cultural Anthropology* 20, 2: 215–48.

———. 2007. "Casting a Long Shadow: Colonial Categories, Cultural Identities, and Cosmopolitan Spaces in Globalizing Africa." *African Identities* 5, 2: 181–97.

———. 2010. *Urban Design, Chaos and Colonial Power in Zanzibar*. Bloomington: Indiana University Press.

Bloch, Ernst. 1986. *The Principle of Hope*. 3 vols. Trans. Neville Plaice, Stephen Plaice, and Paul Knight. Cambridge, Mass.: MIT Press.

Bloomberg, Michael. 2003. State of the City Address. New York, January 23. http://www.gothamgazette.com/article/searchlight/20030123/203/233, accessed March 22, 2004.

———. 2004. State of the City Address. New York, January 8. http://www.gotham gazette.com/searchlight/2004.state.of.city.bloomberg.shtml, accessed March 22, 2004.

Bohigas, Oriol. 1983. "'Per una altra urbanitat' en Ajuntament de Barcelona." In *Plans i projectes per a Barcelona 1981–1982*, 12–21. Barcelona: Ajuntament de Barcelona, Area de urbanisme.

———. 2000. "Menos urbanismo y más sociología." *El Periódico*, October.

Bohigas, Oriol, Peter Buchanan, and Vittorio Magnago Lampugnani. 1991. *Barcelona, arquitectura y ciudad, 1980–1992*. New York: Rizzoli.

Borja, Jordi, and Manuel Castells. 1999. *Local y global*. Madrid: Ed. Taurus.

Borja, Jordi, Oriol Nello, and Josep M. Valles. 1998. *La ciutat del futur, el futur de les ciutats*. Barcelona: Fundació Rafael Campalans.

Borja, Jordi, and Muxi Zaida. 2001. *L'espai públic: ciutat i ciutadania*. Barcelona: Diputació de Barcelona.

Botan. 2002 [1969]. *Letters from Thailand*. Trans. Susan F. Kepner. Chiang Mai: Silk-worm Books.

Bottles, Scott L. 1987. *Los Angeles and the Automobile: The Making of the Modern City*. Berkeley: University of California Press.

Bourdieu, Pierre. 1984. *Distinction: A Social Critique of the Judgement of Taste*. Trans. Richard Nice. Cambridge, Mass.: Harvard University Press.

Bourdieu, Pierre, and Loïc Wacquant. 2001. "Neoliberal Newspeak: Notes on the New Planetary Vulgate." *Radical Philosophy* 105: 2–5.

Boyce, James K. 2002. *Investing in Peace: Aid and Conditionality After Civil Wars*. Adelphi Papers 351. Oxford: Oxford University Press.

Boyer, M. Christine. 1986. *Dreaming the Rational City: The Myth of American City Planning*. Cambridge, Mass.: MIT Press.

———. 1994. *The City of Collective Memory: Its Historical Imagery and Architectural Entertainments*. Cambridge, Mass.: The MIT Press.

———. 2002. "Meditation on a Wounded Skyline and Its Stratigraphies of Pain." In *After the World Trade Center: Rethinking New York City*, ed. Michael Sorkin and Sharon Zukin, 109–20. New York: Routledge.

Brash, Julian. 2004. "The Work of 9/11: Myth, History and the Contradictions of the Post-Fiscal Crisis Consensus." *Critique of Anthropology* 24, 1: 75–99.

———. 2006. "Re-Scaling Patriotism: Competition and Urban Identity in Michael Bloomberg's New York." *Urban Anthropology and Studies of Cultural Systems and World Economic Development* 35, 4: 387–423.

Breese, Gerald William. 1949. *The Daytime Population of the Central Business District of Chicago*. Chicago: University of Chicago Press.

Breglia, Lisa C. 2006. *Monumental Ambivalence: The Politics of Heritage*. Austin: University of Texas Press.

Brenner, Neil, and Roger Keil, eds. 2006. *The Global Cities Reader*. New York: Routledge.

Brenner, Neil, and Theodore Nik. 2002. "Cities and the Geographies of 'Actually Existing Neoliberalism.'" *Antipode* 34, 3: 349–79.

Bromley, R. J. 1974. *Periodic Markets, Daily Markets and Fairs: A Bibliography*. Monash Publications in Geography 10. Melbourne: Department of Geography, Monash University.

Broudehoux, Anne-Marie. 2004. *The Making and Selling of Post-Mao Beijing*. New York: Routledge.

———. 2007. "Spectacular Beijing: The Conspicuous Construction of an Olympic Metropolis." *Journal of Urban Affairs* 29, 4: 383–99.

Brown, Matthew. 2008. "Hadid Leading Architectural Rush to the Emirates." *International Herald Tribune*, April 3. http://www.iht.com/articles/2008/04/03/properties/dub.php, accessed May 25.

Brumann, Christoph. 1999. "Writing for Culture: Why a Successful Concept Should Not Be Discarded." *Current Anthropology* 40 S1:S1–S27.

Bruner, Edward M., and Barbara Kirshenblatt-Gimblett. 1994. "Maasai on the Lawn: Tourist Realism in East Africa." *Cultural Anthropology* 9, 4: 435–70.

Bullard, Robert D., Glenn S. Johnson, and Angel Torres, eds. 2000. *Sprawl City: Race Politics and Planning in Atlanta*. Washington, D.C.: Island Press.

Burayidi, Michael A., ed. 2001. *Downtowns: Revitalizing the Centers of Small Urban Communities*. New York: Routledge.

Burgess, Ernest W. 1925. "The Growth of the City: An Introduction to a Research Project." In *The City: Suggestions of Human Behavior in the Urban Environment*, ed. Robert E. Park and Ernest W. Burgess, 47–62. Chicago: University of Chicago Press.

Burnett, Ricky, and Dayn Sudjic. 2008. *The Endless City: The Urban Age Project by the London School of Economics and Deutsche Bank's Alfred Herrhausen Society*. London: Phaidon.

Busquets, Joan. 1992. *Barcelona: evolución urbanística de una ciudad compacta*. Barcelona: Ed. Mapfre. English ed. Harvard GSD/Nicolodi, 2005.

Caldeira, Teresa. 2000. *City of Walls: Crime, Segregation and Citizenship in São Paulo*. Berkeley: University of California Press.

California Senate. 1979. An act to amend Sections 1790, 17922, and 17980 of, and to add Sections 17920.3 and 17958.11 to, the Health and Safety Code, relating to housing. Senate Bill 812, Chapter 434.

Calvino, Italo. 1978. *Invisible Cities*. Trans. William Weaver. New York: Harvest/HBJ.

Campany, Maria Aurèlia. 1990. *Fem memòria: el Port de Barcelona*. Barcelona: Port Autònom de Barcelona y Lunwerg Editores.

Capablanaca, Enrique. 1983. *Habana Vieja: anteproyecto de restauración*. Departamento de Monumentos. Dirección de Patrimonio Cultural. Ministerio de Cultura. Republica de Cuba.

Capel Sáez, Horacio. 2005. *El modelo Barcelona: un examen crítico*. Barcelona: Serbal.

Cardwell, Diane. 2003. "Mayor Says New York Is Worth the Cost." *New York Times*, January 8.

Carey, Bill. 2005. Commodores, Chancellors and Co-eds: A History of Vanderbilt University. Nashville: Clearbrook Press.

Carpentier, Alejo. 1970. *La ciudad de las columnas*. Buenos Aires: Editorial Lumen.

Casas, Xavier, 1997. "La transformació del litoral del pla de Barcelona com a motor de la renovació de la ciutat, en 1ª jornades sobre el litoral de la regió metropolitana de Barcelona." *Consorci el Far*, 16–17, April 18, 1–21.

Casselman, Ben. 2007. "Animal House Meets the Empty Nest: Condos Built for Hipsters Draw Folks over 50; Showdown at the Pool." *Wall Street Journal*, May 11.

Castañeda Fraile, Ana Maria. 1988. "La recuperació de la façana marítima." *Barcelona Metròpolis Mediterrània* 12.

Castells, Manuel. 1996. *The Rise of the Network Society*. Cambridge: Blackwell.

Certeau, Michel de. 1984. *The Practice of Everyday Life*. Berkeley: University of California Press.

Chamberlain, Lisa. 2006. "Creating Demand for City Living in Nashville: Developer Bets on Downtown Units, and Takers Line Up." *New York Times*, June 21.

Chan, Sucheng, ed. 2005. *Chinese American Transnationalism*. Philadelphia: Temple University Press.

Chen, Hsiang-Shui. 1992. *Chinatown No More: Taiwanese Immigrants in Contemporary New York*. Ithaca, N.Y.: Cornell University Press.

Chen, Xianming, ed. 2009. *Shanghai Rising: State Power and Local Transformations in a Global Megacity*. Minneapolis: University of Minnesota Press.

Cheng, Cindy I-Fen. 2006. "Out of Chinatown and into the Suburbs: Chinese Americans and the Politics of Cultural Citizenship in Early Cold War America." *American Quarterly* 58, 4: 1067–90.

Chesluk, Benjamin. 2008. *Money Jungle*. New Brunswick, N.J.: Rutgers University Press.

Choi, C. Y. 1975. *Chinese Migration and Settlement in Australia*. Sydney: Sydney University Press.

Christaller, Walter. 1966. *Central Places in Southern Germany*. Trans. Carlisle W. Baskin. Englewood Cliffs, N.J.: Prentice-Hall.

Christie, James. 2008 [1876]. *Cholera Epidemics in East Africa: An Account of the Several Diffusions of the Disease in That Country from 1821 till 1872*. Whitefish, Mont.: Kessinger Publishing.

Clark, Gordon, and Michael Dear. 1984. *State Apparatus: Structures and Language of Legitimacy*. Boston: Allen & Unwin.

CMES. 2007. "Reconceiving the Built Environment in the Gulf." Workshop, Center for Middle East Studies, Harvard University, April 29.

Cobb, James C., and William Stueck. 2005. *Globalization and the American South*. Athens: University of Georgia Press.

Coderque, Isabel. 1988. "Al port de Barcelona hi ha un miler de pescadors: la pesca, una industria singular." *Barcelona Metròpolis Mediterrània* 12: 93–97.

Collins, John. 2008. "'But What if I Should Need to Defecate in Your Neighborhood Madam?': Empire, Redemption, and the 'Tradition of the Oppressed' in a Brazilian Heritage Site." *Cultural Anthropology* 23, 2: 279–328.

Comaroff, John L., and Jean Comaroff. 2009. *Ethnicity, Inc*. Chicago: University of Chicago Press.

Community Redevelopment Agency/City of Los Angeles. 1986. *Central Business District Redevelopment Project: Biennial Report*. Los Angeles: Community Redevelopment Agency.

Constable, Nicole. 1997. *Maid to Order in Hong Kong: Stories of Filipina Workers*. Ithaca, N.Y.: Cornell University Press.

Cooper, Matthew. 1999. "Spatial Discourses and Social Boundaries: Re-Imagining the Toronto Waterfront." In *Theorizing the City: The New Urban Anthropology Reader*, ed. Setha Low, 377–400. New Brunswick, N.J.: Rutgers University Press.

Corbridge, Stuart, and John Harriss. 2000. *Reinventing India: Liberalization, Hindu Nationalism, and Popular Democracy*. Malden, Mass.: Polity Press.

Corm, George. 1996. *Al-'Imar wal-Maslahat al-'Ammat fi Iqtisaad ma-ba'd-al-harb wa siyasatihi*. Beirut: Dar al-Jadid with Ford Foundation and Institute for Urban Studies.

Corporación Metropolitana de Barcelona. 1987. *Pla de costas: proposta d'ordenació de la zona costanera metropolitana de Barcelona*. Barcelona: Corporación Metropolitana de Barcelona.

Costa-Lascaux, Jacqueline, and Live Yu-Sion, 2002. *Paris-XIIIème, lumières d'Asie*. Paris: Autremont.

Crang, Michael. 2010. "Cyberspace as the New Public Domain." In *Urban Diversity: Space, Culture and Inclusive Pluralism in Cities Worldwide*, ed. Caroline Kihato, Mejgan Massoumi, Blair A. Ruble, Pep Subirós, and Allison M. Garland, 99–122. Washington, D.C.: Woodrow Wilson Center.

Crawford, Margaret. 1992. "The World in a Shopping Mall." In *Variations on a Theme Park: The New American City and the End of Public Space*, ed. Michael Sorkin, 3–30. New York: Hill and Wang.

Cronin, Anne M., and Kevin Hetherington, eds. 2008. *Consuming the Entreprenuerial City: Image, Memory, Spectacle*. New York: Routledge.

Cronon, William. 1991. *Nature's Metropolis: Chicago and the Great West*. New York: Norton.

Currid, Elizabeth. 2007. *The Warhol Economy: How Fashion, Art, and Music Drive New York City*. Princeton, N.J.: Princeton University Press.

Dar al-Handasah. 1991. *Beirut Central District: Master Plan*. 3 vols. Trans. from French. Beirut: Dar al-Handasah.

———. 1994. *Beirut Central District Detailed Plan Report*. 2 vols. Beirut: Dar al-Handasah.

Das, Gurcharan. 2002. *India Unbound: The Social and Economic Revolution from Independence to the Global Information Age*. New York: Anchor Press.

Davidson, Christopher M. 2005. *The United Arab Emirates: A Study in Survival*. Boulder, Colo.: Lynne Rienner.

———. 2008. *Dubai: The Vulnerability of Success*. New York: Columbia University Press.

Davies, Helen. 2008. "African Living, I Presume." *Sunday Times*, July 6, 24.

Dávila, Arlene M. 2004. *Barrio Dreams: Puerto Ricans, Latinos, and the Neoliberal City*. Berkeley: University of California Press.

Davis, Mike. 1992. *City of Quartz: Excavating the Future in Los Angeles*. New York: Vintage Books.

———. 2001. *Magical Urbanism: Latinos Reinvent the Big US City*. New York: Verso.

———. 2002. *Dead Cities*. New York: Free Press.

———. 2006. "Fear and Money in Dubai." *New Left Review* 41: 47–68.

Dear, Michael. 1986. "Postmodernism and Planning." *Environment & Planning D Society & Space*: 4: 367–84.

———. 2000. *The Postmodern Urban Condition.* Malden, Mass.: Blackwell.

———, ed. 2002a. *From Chicago to L.A.: Making Sense of Urban Theory.* London: Sage.

———. 2002b. "Los Angeles and the Chicago School: Invitation to a Debate." *City and Community* 1, 1: 5–32.

Dear, Michael, H. Eric Schockman, and Greg Hise, eds. 1996. *Rethinking Los Angeles.* Thousand Oaks, Calif.: Sage.

De Castro, José Maria. 1987. "Entrevista a Manuel de Solà Morales." *La Vanguardia,* April 1.

Deckard, Sharae. 2006a. "Can Cinema Represent Slavery?" In *Zanzibar: A Journey in Film and Art,* entry for July 21. http://blogs.warwick.ac.uk/zanzibar/daily/030706/, accessed March 22, 2010.

———. 2006b. "Raising the Tanga: The Festival Opens." In *Zanzibar: A Journey in Film and Art,* entry for July 16. http://blogs.warwick.ac.uk/zanzibar/daily/030706/, accessed March 18, 2010.

DeDapper, Jay. 2004. "Interview with Daniel Doctoroff." News Forum. *WNBC,* April 11.

De Frantz, Monica. 2005. "From Cultural Regeneration to Discursive Governance: Constructing the Flagship of the 'Museumsquartier Vienna' as a Plural Symbol of Change." *International Journal of Urban and Regional Research* 29, 1: 50–66.

De Frantz, Monica, and Michael Keating. 2004. "Culture-Led Strategies for Urban Regeneration: A Comparative Perspective on Bilbao." *International Journal of Urban and Regional Research* 16, 3: 187–94.

Dennis, Richard. 2008. *Cities in Modernity: Representations and Productions of Metropolitan Space, 1840–1930.* Cambridge: Cambridge University Press.

Denoon, David B. H. 1998. "Cycles in Indian Economic Liberalization, 1966–1996." *Comparative Politics* 31, 1: 43–60.

Department of City Planning. 1972. *Los Angeles Central City Community Plan: A Part of the General Plan of the City of Los Angeles.* Los Angeles: Department of City Planning.

Desmond, Jane. 1999. *Staging Tourism: Bodies on Display from Waikiki to Sea World.* Chicago: University of Chicago Press.

Dong, Madeleine Yue. 2003. *Republican Beijing: The City and Its Histories.* Berkeley: University of California Press.

Dorst, John Darwin. 1989. *The Written Suburb: An American Site, an Ethnographic Dilemma.* Philadelphia: University of Pennsylvania Press.

Dossal, Mariam. 2010. *Theatre of Conflict, City of Hope: Mumbai 1660 to the Present.* New Delhi: Oxford University Press.

Douglas, Mary. 1966. *Purity and Danger: An Analysis of Concepts of Pollution and Taboo.* London: Ark Paperbacks.

Doyle, Don. 1985. *Nashville Since the 1920s.* Knoxville: University of Tennessee Press.

DuCros, Hilary, and Yok-Shiu Lee, eds. 2004. *Cultural Heritage Management in China: Preserving the Cities of the Pearl River Delta.* London: Routledge.

Dupuy, Gabriel. 1996. *Urbanismo de redes, teorías y métodos*. Barcelona: Oikos Tau.

Durrschmidt, Jor. 2001. *Everyday Lives in the Global City: The Delinking of Locale and Milieu*. New York: Routledge.

Eade, John. 1996. *Living the Global City: Globalization as Local Process*. New York: Routledge.

Echegaray, Chris. 2009. "Nashville Draws L.A. Transplants: Nissan, Music, Quality of Life Bring Steady Stream from California." *Tennessean*, January 4.

"Economy Continues to Decline as IMF Urges Tighter Fiscal Policy on Government." 1991. *Lebanon Report* 2, 1: 4.

Elias, Norbert. 1994. *The Civilizing Process: The History of Manners and State Formation and Civilization*. Trans. Edmund Jephcott. Oxford: Blackwell.

Elsheshtawy, Yasser. 2009. *Dubai: Behind an Urban Spectacle*. London: Routledge.

Elton, J. Frederic. 1968 [1879]. *Travels and Researches among the Lakes and Mountains of Eastern and Central Africa from the Journals of J. Frederic Elton*, ed. H. B. Cotterill. London: Frank Cass.

Engels, Friedrich. 1958 [1844]. *The Condition of the Working Class of England*. Trans. and ed. W. O. Henderson and W. H. Chaloner. Oxford: Blackwell.

English, Darby. 2007. *How to See a Work of Art in Total Darkness*. Cambridge, Mass.: MIT Press.

Errington, Shelly. 1993. "Making Progress on Borobudur: An Old Monument in New Order." *Visual Anthropology Review* 9, 2: 32–59.

Esteban, Juli. 1988. "El Pla metropolità de costes." *Barcelona Metropolis Mediterrània* 12.

Estrada, William D. 1999. "Los Angeles' Old Plaza and Olvera Street: Imagined and Contested Space." *Western Folklore* 58, 2: 107–29.

———. 2008. *The Los Angeles Plaza: Sacred and Contested Space*. Austin: University of Texas Press.

Ethington, Philip. 2008. "The Global Spaces of Los Angeles, 1920s–1930s." In *The Spaces of the Modern City*, ed. Gyan Prakash and Kevin M. Kruse, 58–98. Princeton, N.J.: Princeton University Press.

Evans, Graeme. 2003. *Cultural Planning: An Urban Renaissance?* London: Routledge.

Evers, Hans-Dieter, and Thomas Menkhoff. 2004. "Expert Knowledge and the Role of Consultants in an Emerging Knowledge-Based Economy." *Human Systems Management* 23: 123–35.

Fabre, Jaume, and Huertas, Josep Maria. 1997. *Tots els barris de Barcelona*. Vol. 7. Barcelona: Edicions 62.

Fainstein, Susan. 2001. *The City Builders: Property Development in New York and London, 1980–2000*. Lawrence: University of Kansas Press.

———. 2010. *The Just City*. Ithaca, N.Y.: Cornell University Press.

Fattah, Hassan. 2007. Celebrity Architects Reveal a Daring Cultural Xanadu for the Arab World. *New York Times*, February 1. http://www.nytimes.com/2007/02/01/arts/design/01isla.html?_r1&orefslogin, accessed May 25, 2008.

Firey, Walter. 1947. *Land Use in Central Boston*. Cambridge: Harvard University Press.

Fishman, Robert. 1977. *Urban Utopias in the Twentieth Century: Ebenezer Howard, Frank Lloyd Wright, and Le Corbusier*. New York: Basic Books.

Fitch, Robert. 1993. *The Assassination of New York*. New York: Verso.

Fitzmaurice, Tony. 2001. "Film and Urban Societies in a Global Context." In *Cinema and the City*, ed. Mark Shiel and Tony Fitzmaurice, 19–30. Oxford: Blackwell.

Florida, Richard. 2002. *Rise of the Creative Class*. New York: Basic Books.

———. 2004. *Cities and the Creative Class*. New York: Routledge.

Florida, Richard, and Scott Jackson. 2008. "Sonic City: The Evolving Economic Geography of the Music Industry." Working paper, Martin Prosperity Institute.

Fogelson, Robert. 1993 [1967]. *The Fragmented Metropolis: Los Angeles, 1850–1930*. 2nd ed. Berkeley: University of California Press.

———. 2001. *Downtown: Its Rise and Fall, 1880–1950*. New Haven, Conn.: Yale University Press.

Fong, Timothy. 1994. *The First Suburban Chinatown*. Philadelphia: Temple University Press.

Ford, Larry R. 2003. *America's New Downtowns: Revitalization or Reinvention?* Baltimore, Md.: Johns Hopkins University Press.

Foucault, Michel. 1977. "Nietzsche, Genealogy, History." In *Language, Countermemory and Practice*, ed. D. Bouchard, 139–64. Oxford: Blackwell.

———. 1986. "Of Other Spaces." *Diacritics* 16: 22–27.

———. 1990. *History of Sexuality, Vol. 1: An Introduction*. New York: Vintage.

Fourcade, Marion. 2006. "The Construction of a Global Profession: The Transnationalization of Economics." *American Journal of Sociology* 112, 1: 145–94.

Freund, Charles Paul. 2001. "Muerte a Las Vegas." *Reason Online*, January. http://www.reason.com/news/show/27902.html, accessed June 4, 2008.

Frieden, Bernard J., and Lynne B. Sagalyn. 1989. *Downtown, Inc.: How America Rebuilds Cities*. Cambridge, Mass.: MIT Press.

Friedman, Thomas L. 2000. *The Lexus and the Olive Tree: Understanding Globalization*. New York: Farrar, Straus and Giroux.

Fulton, William B., Rolf Pendall, Mai Nguyen, and Alicia Harrison. 2001. *Who Sprawls Most: How Growth Patterns Differ Across the U.S.* Survey Series. Washington, D.C.: Brookings Institution, Center on Urban and Metropolitan Policy, July.

Gable, Eric, and Richard Handler. 1996. "After Authenticity at an American Heritage Site." *American Anthropologist* 98, 3: 568–78.

Gallery Row Organization. 2006. "Look What We Can Do." Programs. Gallery Row. http://galleryrow.org/look.shtml, accessed February 5, 2011.

Garcia Espuche, Albert. 1995. "La creación de una fachada." In Ajuntament de Barcelona and CCCB, *Retrat de Barcelona*. Barcelona: Ajuntament de Barcelona and CCCB.

Garreau, Joel. 1991. *Edge City: Life on the New Urban Frontier*. New York: Anchor.

Garvin, Alexander. 2000. "An Insider's View: How the Planning Game Works in the Big Apple." *Planning* 66, 3: 4–9.

Gates, Carolyn L. 1998. *The Merchant Republic of Lebanon: Rise of an Open Economy.* London: Tauris.

Gaubatz, Piper. 1995. "Urban Transformation in Post-Mao China: Impacts of the Reform Era on China's Urban Form." In *Urban Spaces in Contemporary China: The Potential for Autonomy and Community in Post-Mao China*, ed. R. K. Deborah S. Davis, Barry Naughton, and Elizabeth J. Perry, 28–60. New York: Cambridge University Press.

———. 1999. "China's Urban Transformation: Patterns and Processes of Morphological Change in Beijing, Shanghai and Guangzhou." *Urban Studies* 36, 9: 1495–1521.

———. 2005. "Globalization and the Development of New Central Business Districts in Beijing, Shanghai and Guangzhou." In *Restructuring the Chinese City: Changing Society, Economy and Space*, ed. Laurence J. C. Ma and Fulong Wu, 98–121. New York: Routledge.

Gavin, Angus. 1998. "Heart of Beirut: Making the Master Plan for the Renewal of the Central District." In *Projecting Beirut: Episodes in the Construction and Reconstruction of a Modern City*, ed. Peter Rowe and Hashim Sarkis, 217–35. Munich: Prestel.

Gavin, Angus, and Ramez Malouf. 1996. *Beirut Reborn: The Restoration and Development of the Central District.* London: Academy Editions.

Geertz, Clifford. 1989. "Toutes directions: Reading the Signs in an Urban Sprawl." *International Journal of Middle East Studies* 21, 3: 291–306.

Gibson-Graham, J. K. 1995. "Identity and Economic Plurality: Rethinking Capitalism and 'Capitalist Hegemony.'" *Environment and Planning D: Society and Space* 13, 3: 275–82.

Giddens, Anthony. 1999. "Risk and Responsibility." *Modern Law Review* 62, 1: 1–10.

Gilloch, Graeme. 1997. *Myth and Metropolis: Walter Benjamin and the City.* New York: Polity Press.

Giroir, Guillaume. 2006. "A Globalized Golden Ghetto in a Chinese Garden: The Fountainebleau Villas in Shanghai." In *Globalization and the Chinese City*, ed. Wu Fulong, 208–27. London: Routledge.

Glaeser, Edward L. 1998. "Are Cities Dying?" *Journal of Economic Perspectives* 12, 2: 139–60.

Glancey, Jonathan. 2006. "I Don't Do Nice." *Guardian*, October 9. http://arts.guardian .co.uk/features/story/0, 1890945,00.html, accessed June 4, 2008.

Gordon, Ian. 1999. "Internationalisation and Urban Competition." *Urban Studies* 36, 5–6: 1001–16.

Gotham, Kevin Fox. 2006. "The Secondary Circuit of Capital Reconsidered: Globalization and the U.S. Real Estate Sector." *American Journal of Sociology* 112, 1: 235–71.

———. 2007. *Authentic New Orleans.* New York: New York University Press.

"Government Fights Attacks from Parliament and Media." 1992. *Lebanon Report* 3, 4: 6.

Gqola, Pamla Dine. 2010. "Negotiating Gender and Access to Knowledge Technology in the Urban Context." In *Urban Diversity: Space, Culture and Inclusive Pluralism in Cities Worldwide*, ed. Caroline Kihato, Mejgan Massoumi, Blair A. Ruble, Pep Subirós, and Allison M. Garland, 123–42. Washington, D.C.: Woodrow Wilson Center.

Gratz, Roberta Brandes, with Norman Mintz. 1998. *Cities Back from the Edge: New Life for Downtown*. New York: Wiley.

Greenberg, Miriam. 2008. *Branding New York: How a City in Crisis Was Sold to the World*. New York: Routledge.

Gregory, Steven. 1998. *Black Corona: Race and the Politics of Place in an Urban Community*. Princeton, N.J.: Princeton University Press.

Grosfoguel, Ramón, and Ana-Margarita Cervantes-Rodríguez, eds. 2002. *The Modern/Colonial/Capitalist World System in the Twentieth Century*. Westport, Conn.: Greenwood.

Groslier, Bernard Philippe. 1966. *Indochina*. Geneva: Nagel.

Gruen, Victor. 1964. *Heart of Our Cities*. New York: Simon and Shuster.

Guano, Emanuela. 2002. "Spectacles of Modernity: Transnational Imagination and Local Hegemonies in Neoliberal Buenos Aires." *Cultural Anthropology* 17, 2: 181–209.

Guerra, Charro. 1999. "Eusebio leal: la ciudad es el hombre que la habita." *Gaceta de Cuba*.

Guggenheim, Michael, and Olaf Söderström. 2009. *Reshaping Cities: How Global Mobility Transforms Architecture and Urban Form*. London: Taylor and Francis.

Gunewardena, Nandini, and Mark Schuller, eds. 2008. *Capitalizing on Catastrophe: Neoliberal Strategies in Disaster Reconstruction*. Lanham, Md.: Alta Mira Press.

Hackworth, Jason. 2007. *The Neoliberal City*. Ithaca, N.Y.: Cornell University Press.

Hall, Tim, and Phil Hubbard. 1998. *The Entrepreneurial City: Geographies of Politics, Regime and Representation*. New York: Wiley.

Halle, David, ed. 2003. *New York and Los Angeles: Politics, Society, and Culture: A Comparative View*. Chicago: University of Chicago Press.

Hamill, Pete. 2004. *Downtown: My Manhattan*. New York: Little, Brown and Company.

Hammoud, Hani. 1991. "Interview with Al-Fadl Shallaq." *Al-Hayat*, July 11.

Hannerz, Ulf. 1996. *Transnational Connections*. London: Routledge.

Hannigan, John. 1998. *Fantasy City: Pleasure and Profit in the Postmodern Metropolis*. London: Routledge.

Hansen, Thomas Blom. 2001. *Wages of Violence: Naming and Identity in Postcolonial Bombay*. Princeton, N.J.: Princeton University Press.

Hansing, K. 2006. *Rasta, Race and Revolution: The Emergence and Development of the Rastafari Movement in Socialist Cuba*. Berlin: Lit Verlag.

Harris, John R. 1971. *Dubai Development Plan: Development Plans of the GCC States, 1962–1995*. Amersham, U.K.: Demand Editions.

Harris, Nigel. 1995. "Bombay in the Global Economy." In *Bombay: Metaphor for Modern India*, ed. Sujata Patel and Alice Thorner, 47–63. New Delhi: Oxford University Press.

Harvey, David. 1990. *The Condition of Postmodernity*. Cambridge: Blackwell. Spanish Translation, Buenos Aires: Amorrortu.

———. 1998. "The New Urbanism and the Communitarian Trap: On Social Problems and the False Hope of Design." *Harvard Design Magazine*, Winter/Spring: 68–69.

———. 2001. "From Managerialism to Entrepreneurialism: The Transformation in Urban Governance in Late Capitalism." In *Spaces of Capital: Towards a Critical Geography*, 345–69. New York: Routledge.

———. 2005. *Paris, Capital of Modernity*. New York: Routledge.

———. 2007. *A Brief History of Neoliberalism*. Oxford: Oxford University Press.

Havighurst, Craig. 2007. *Air Castle of the South: WSM and the Making of Music City*. Urbana: University of Illinois Press.

Hawthorne, Christopher. 2008. "Architect Rem Koolhaas Saw What Vegas Didn't Have, Not What It Needed." *Los Angeles Times*, May 13. http://www.latimes.com/entertainment/news/arts/la-et-vegas13-2008may13,0,4985463.story, accessed June 4.

Hein, Carola. 2004. *The Capital of Europe*. New York: Praeger.

Hemphill, Paul. 1970. *The Nashville Sound*. New York: Simon and Schuster.

Heron, Katrina. 1996. "From Bauhaus to Koolhaas." *Wired* 4, 7. http://www.wired.com/wired/archive/4.07/koolhaas.html, accessed June 4, 2008.

Herzfeld, Michael. 1991. *A Place in History: Social and Monumental Time in a Cretan Town*. Princeton, N.J.: Princeton University Press.

Herzog, Lawrence. 2006. *Return to the Center: Culture, Public Space, and City Building in a Global Era*. Austin: University of Texas Press.

Hill, Matthew J. 2007. "Reimagining Old Havana: World Heritage and the Production of Scale in Late Socialist Cuba." In *Deciphering the Global: Its Spaces, Scales and Subjects*, ed. Saskia Sassen, 59–78. New York: Routledge.

Hitchcock, Michael. 2002. "Zanzibar Stone Town Joins the Imagined Community of World Heritage Sites." *International Journal of Heritage Studies* 8, 2: 153–66.

Ho Pui Yin. 2004. *Challenges for an Evolving City: 160 Years of Port and Land Development in Hong Kong*. Hong Kong: Commercial Press.

Hobsbawm, E. J. 1990. *Nations and Nationalism Since 1780*. Cambridge: Cambridge University Press.

Hodos, Jerome. 2007. "Globalization and the Concept of the Second City." *City and Community* 6, 4: 315–33.

Hollander, Jord den. 2007. *Many Words for Modern: A Survey of Modern Architecture in Tanzania*. Tanzania/Netherlands: Jord den Hollander Films.

Holston, James. 1989. *The Modernist City: An Anthropological Critique of Brasilia*. Chicago: University of Chicago Press.

———. 2009. "Insurgent Citizenship in an Era of Global Urban Peripheries." *City & Society* 21, 2: 245–267.

Hopkins, A. H., ed. 2002. *Globalization in World History*. Boston: Norton.

Hourani, Najib. 2009. "War by Other Means: Neo-liberalism and the Reconstruction of Beirut." Paper presented to Health, Cities, and the Post-Conflict Environment Conference, Woodrow Wilson International Center for Scholars, Washington, D.C., April 24.

Hoyt, Homer. 1933. *One Hundred Years of Land Values in Chicago*. Chicago: University of Chicago Press.

Hsu, Madeline. 2000. *Dreaming of Gold, Dreaming of Homei*. Stanford, Calif.: Stanford University Press.

Huertas, Josep M., and Pepe Encinas. 1995. *50 vegades Barcelona*. Barcelona: Ajuntament de Barcelona.

Human Rights Watch. 2006. *Building Towers, Cheating Workers: Exploitation of Migrant Construction Workers in the United Arab Emirates*. Report 18(8) E. New York: Human Rights Watch.

ICOMOS. 1982. *Advisory Body Evaluation*. Paris: International Council on Monuments and Sites.

Ikels, Charlotte. 1996. *Return of the Gods of Wealth: The Transition to a Market Economy in Urban China*. Stanford, Calif.: Stanford University Press.

Illah, Jibril. 2007. "ZIFF 2007." *The Guardian* (Tanzania), July 1, 35.

Inda, Jonathan, and Renato Rosaldo, eds. 2008. *The Anthropology of Globalization*. Malden, Mass.: Blackwell.

Institute for the Study of Homelessness and Poverty. 2003a. *Poverty in Los Angeles Facts*. Los Angeles: Weingart Center.

———. 2003b. *The Puzzle of the Los Angeles Economy: A Look at the Last Thirty Years*. Los Angeles: Weingart Center.

Isenberg, Alison. 2005. *Downtown America: A History of the Place and the People Who Made It*. Chicago: University of Chicago Press.

Issa, A. S., and A. M. Juma. 1983. "Conservation of Historic Towns and Monuments in Zanzibar." Paper presented at Seminar on the Conservation of Historic Towns and Monuments, Bagamoyo, Tanzania, November 14–18.

Istabsir. n.d. "Al Satwa in a Changed World." *The National*, online video. http://multimedia.thenational.ae/istabsir/index.html, accessed February 15, 2010.

Jackson, Maria Rosario, and John Malpede. 2009. *Making the Case for Skid Row Culture: Findings from a Collaborative Inquiry between the Los Angeles Poverty Department and the Urban Institute*. Washington, D.C.: Americans for the Arts.

Jacobs, Jane. 1957. "Downtown Is for People." In Editors of Fortune, *The Exploding Metropolis*. New York: Doubleday.

———. 1961. *The Death and Life of Great American Cities*. New York: Vintage.

Jacoby, Russell. 2005. *Picture Imperfect: Utopian Thought for an Anti-Utopian Age*. New York: Columbia University Press.

Jameson, Fredric. 1974. *Marxism and Form: Twentieth-Century Dialectical Theories of Literature*. Princeton, N.J.: Princeton University Press.

———. 1991. *Postmodernism, or the Cultural Logic of Late Capitalism*. Durham, N.C.: Duke University Press.

———. 1997. "Culture and Finance Capital." *Critical Inquiry* 24, 1: 246–65.

———. 2003. "Future City." *New Left Review* 21: 65–79.

Jonas, Andrew E. G., and David Wilson. 1999. *The Urban Growth Machine: Critical Perspectives, Two Decades Later*. Albany: State University of New York Press.

Judd, Dennis. 1999. "Constructing the Tourist Bubble." In *The Tourist City*, ed. Dennis Judd and Susan Fainstein, 35-54. New Haven, Conn.: Yale University Press.

Judd, Dennis, and Susan S. Fainstein. 1999. *The Tourist City*. New Haven, Conn.: Yale University Press.

Juliana, Enric. 1988. "L'hora del Port Vell." In *Barcelona Metròpolis Mediterrània* 12: 80–83.

Kabbani, Oussama. 1992. *The Reconstruction of Beirut*. Oxford: Centre for Lebanese Studies.

———. 1996. "Postwar Reconstruction of Beirut Central District & the Experience of Solidere." Paper presented at The Construction of the Mediterranean City, University of Venice, April 26-27.

———. 1998. "Public Spaces as Infrastructure: The Case of the Postwar Reconstruction of Beirut." In *Projecting Beirut: Episodes in the Construction and Reconstruction of a Modern City*, ed. Peter Rowe and Hashim Sarkis, 240–59. Munich: Prestel.

Kanna, Ahmed. 2007. "Dubai in a Jagged World." *Middle East Report* 243: 22–29.

———. 2010. "Flexible Citizenship in Dubai: Neoliberal Subjectivity in the Emerging 'City-Corporation.'" *Cultural Anthropology* 25, 1: 100–129.

———. 2011. *Dubai, the City as Corporation*. Minneapolis: University of Minnesota Press.

Karam Group. n.d. "Agora, Beirut: Lebanon's Newest Shopping Experience." Marketing brochure.

Kasarda, John D., and Greg Lindsay. 2011. *Aerotopolis: The Way We'll Live Next*. New York: Farrar, Straus and Giroux.

Katakam, Anupama. 2005. "For a New Mumbai, at a Great Cost." *Frontline Magazine* 22, 2: 15–28.

Keil, Roger. 1998. *Los Angeles: Globalization, Urbanization and Social Struggles*. New York: Wiley.

Kelling, George L., and James Q. Wilson. 1982. "Broken Windows: The Police and Neighborhood Safety." *Atlantic Monthly*, March, 29–37.

Khalaf, Samir. 1991. "Ties That Bind: Sectarian Loyalties and the Restoration of Pluralism in Lebanon." *Beirut Review* 1, 1: 32–61.

———. 1998. "Contested Space and the Forging of New Cultural Identities." In *Projecting Beirut: Episodes in the Construction and Reconstruction of a Modern City*, ed. Peter Rowe and Hashim Sarkis, 140–64. Munich: Prestel.

Khalaf, Suleyman. 1999. "Camel Racing in the Gulf: Notes on the Evolution of a Traditional Cultural Sport." *Anthropos* 94, 1–3: 85–106.

Khoury, Leila. 1996. "Three Billion Dollars of Real Estate Investment in 1995." *Al-Mal wal-Alam*, March, 26.

Kihato, Caroline, Mejgan Massoumi, Blair A. Ruble, Pep Subirós, and Allison M. Garland, eds. 2010. *Urban Diversity: Space, Culture and Inclusive Pluralism in Cities Worldwide*. Washington, D.C.: Woodrow Wilson Center.

Kingfisher, Catherine, and Jeff Maskovsky. 2008. "The Limits of Neoliberalism." *Critique of Anthropology* 28, 2: 115–26.

Kinsbruner, Jay. 2005. *The Colonial Spanish-American City: Urban Life in the Age of Atlantic Capitalism*. Austin: University of Texas Press.

Klingmann, Anna. 2007. *Brandscapes: Architecture in the Experience Economy*. Cambridge, Mass.: MIT Press.

Knowles, Scott Gabriel, ed. 2009. *Imagining Philadelphia: Edmund Bacon and the Future of the City*. Philadelphia: University of Pennsylvania Press.

Knox, Paul L., and Peter J. Taylor, eds. 1995. *World Cities in a World-System*. Cambridge: Cambridge University Press.

Koolhaas, Rem. 1978. *Delirious New York: A Retroactive Manifesto for Manhattan*. New York: Oxford University Press.

———. 2009. "Dubai: From Judgment to Analysis." Lecture, Sharjah UAE Biennial, March 17. http://www.oma.eu/index.php?optioncom_content&taskview&id149&Itemid25, accessed January 28, 2010.

Kosambi, Meera. 1986. *Bombay in Transition: The Growth and Social Ecology of a Colonial City, 1880–1980*. Stockholm: Almqvist & Wiksell.

Kotkin, Joel. 2008. "Suburbia's Not Dead Yet." *Los Angeles Times*, July 6.

Krane, Jim. 2009. *City of Gold: Dubai and the Dream of Capitalism*. New York: St. Martin's Press.

Kreyling, Christine. 2007. "New Analysis: The Marketing of May Town." *Nashville City Paper*, May 17.

Kreyling, Christine, Wesley Paine, Charles Waterfield, Jr., and Susan Ford Wiltshire. 1996. *Classical Nashville: Athens of the South*. Nashville: Vanderbilt University Press.

Kunstler, James Howard. 2003. "Nashville Skyline Revisited." *Metropolis*, February: 92–96. 116–19.

Lacayo, Richard. 2008. "Rem Koolhaas." *Time*, April 29. www.time.com/time/specials/2007/article/0,28804,1733748_17337521735981,00.html, accessed June 4, 2008.

L.A. City Clerk. 1999. "Tom Gilmore." Council File 99-1528. http://cityclerk.lacity.org/lacityclerkconnect/index.cfm?faccfi.viewrecord&cfnumber99-1528, accessed May 29, 2011.

Lafraniere, Sharon. 2007. "As Angola Rebuilds, Most Find Their Poverty Persists." *New York Times*, October 14.

Langer, Detlef. 2007. "Zanzibar Film Festival: Dealing with the Gruesome History of Slavery." *Qantara.de: Dialogue with the Islamic World*. http://www.qantara.de/webcom/show_article.php/_c-310/_nr-445/i.html, accessed March 20, 2010.

Larkin, Brian. 2008. *Signal and Noise: Media, Infrastructure, and Urban Culture in Nigeria*. Durham, N.C.: Duke University Press.

Larner, Wendy. 2003. "Neoliberalism?" *Environment and Planning D: Society and Space* 21: 509–12.

Larner, Wendy, and Maria Butler. 2007. "The Places, People, and Politics of Partnership: After Neoliberalism in Aotearoa New Zealand." In *Contesting Neoliberalism: Urban Frontiers*, ed. Helga Leitner, Eric S. Sheppard, Kristin Sziarto, and Anant Maringianti, 71–90. New York: Guilford.

Lassiter, Matthew D. 2006. *The Silent Majority: Suburban Politics in the Sunbelt South*. Princeton, N.J.: Princeton University Press.

Lebanese Order of Engineers. 1998. "Nadwa Hawla Mashrou' al-Aswaq fi Wasat Beirut al Tijari." *Al-Mouhandess*, 8.

Lederman, Sally Ann, Virginia Rauh, Lisa Weiss, Janet L. Stein, Lori A. Hoepner, Mark Becker, and Frederica P. Perera. 2004. "The Effects of the World Trade Center Event on Birth Outcomes Among Term Deliveries at Three Lower Manhattan Hospitals." *Environmental Health Perspectives* 112, 17: 1772–78.

Leenders, Reinould. 1998. "Lebanon: Disturbing Statistics." *Middle East International* 573, 24: 8–9.

Lees, Loretta, Tom Slater, and Elvin Wyly. 2008. *Gentrification*. New York: Routledge.

Lefebvre, Henri. 1991 [1947]. *Critique of Everyday Life. Introduction*. Vol. 1, Trans. John Moore. New York: Verso.

———. 2003 [1970]. *The Urban Revolution*. Trans. Robert Bononno. Minneapolis: University of Minnesota Press.

———. 1992 [1974]. *The Production of Space*. Trans. Donald Nicolson-Smith. New York: Wiley-Blackwell.

———. 1996. *Writings on Cities*. Trans. and ed. Eleonore Kofman and Elizabeth Lebas. Oxford: Blackwell.

Lehrer, Brian. 2005. Interview with Richard Ravitch. *The Brian Lehrer Show*, WNYC, February 2.

Leinberger, Christopher. 2005. *Turning Around Downtown: Twelve Steps to Revitalization*. Washington, D.C.: Brookings Institution.

———. 2007. *The Option of Urbanism: Investing in a New American Dream*. Washington, D.C.: Island Press.

Leitner, Helga, Eric S. Sheppard, Kristin Sziarto, and Anant Maringianti. 2007. "Contesting Urban Futures: Decentering Neoliberalism." In *Contesting Neoliberalism: Urban Frontiers*, ed. Helga Leitner, Jaime Peck, and Eric. S. Sheppard, 1–25. New York: Guilford.

LeJeune, Jean-François, ed. 2003. *Cruelty and Utopia: Cities and Landscapes of Latin America*. New York: Princeton Architectural Press.

Lever, William F., and Ivan Turok. 1999. "Competitive Cities: Introduction to the Review." *Urban Studies* 36, 5–6: 791–93.

Lewis, Michael. 2010. *The Big Short*. New York: Norton.

Ley, David. 1996. *The New Middle Class and the Remaking of the Central City*. Oxford: Oxford University Press.

Li, Wei. 2006a. "Spatial Transformation of an Urban Ethnic Community: From Chinatown to Ethnoburb in Los Angeles." In *From Urban Enclave to Ethnic Suburb: New Asian Communities in Pacific Rim Countries*, ed. Wei Li, 74–94. Honolulu: University of Hawai'i Press.

———, ed. 2006b. *From Urban Enclave to Ethnic Suburb: New Asian Communities in Pacific Rim Countries*. Honolulu: University of Hawai'i Press.

———. 2009. *Ethnoburb*. Honolulu: University of Hawai'i Press.

Light, Ivan. 1974. "From Vice District to Tourist Attraction: The Moral Career of American Chinatowns, 1880–1940." *Pacific Historical Review* 43, 3: 367–94.

Lin, Jan. 1988. *Reconstructing Chinatown: Ethnic Enclave, Global Change*. Minneapolis: University of Minnesota Press.

Livingstone, David. 1875. *The Last Journals of David Livingstone in Central Africa*. New York: Harper and Brothers.

Lloyd, Richard. 2010. *Neo-Bohemia: Art and Commerce in the Postindustrial City*. 2nd ed. New York: Routledge.

———. 2011. "East Nashville Skyline." *Ethnography* 12, 1: 114–54.

Lloyd, Richard, and Terry Nichols Clark. 2001. "The City as an Entertainment Machine." *Research in Urban Sociology: Critical Perspectives on Urban Redevelopment* 6: 357–78.

Logan, John R. 2002. *The New Chinese City: Globalization and Market Reform*. Oxford: Blackwell.

———. 2008. *Urban China in Transition*. Oxford: Blackwell.

Logan, John R., and Harvey L. Molotch. 2007. *Urban Fortunes: The Political Economy of Place*. 2nd ed. Berkeley: University of California Press.

Longstreth, Richard. 1997. *City Center to Regional Mall: Architecture, the Automobile, and Retailing in Los Angeles, 1920–1950*. Cambridge, Mass.: MIT Press.

Longva, Anh Ng. 2005. "Neither Autocracy nor Democracy but Ethnocracy: Citizens, Expatriates and the Socio-Political System in Kuwait." In *Monarchies and Nations: Globalization and Identity in the Arab States of the Gulf*, ed. Paul Dresch and James Piscatori, 114–35. London: Tauris.

Lopez, Russ, and H. Patricia Hynes. 2003. "Sprawl in the 1990s: Measurement, Distribution, and Trends." *Urban Affairs Review* 38: 325–55.

Lorimer, John Gordon. 1984 [1915]. *Gazetteer of the Persian Gulf, Oman, and Central Arabia*. Vol. 2. Amersham. U.K.: Demand Editions.

LosAngelesNow. 2004. A film by Phillip Rodriguez. Photography by Claudio Rocha. A PBS Documentary. City Project.

Lösch, August. 1954. *The Economics of Location*. Trans. Wolfgang F. Stolper. New Haven, Conn.: Yale University Press.

Loukaitou-Sideris, Anastasia, and Tridib Banerjee. 1998. *Urban Design Downtown: Poetics and Politics of Form.* Berkeley: University of California Press.

Low, Setha. 2000. *On the Plaza.* Austin: University of Texas Press.

Lowenthal, David. 1988. *The Past Is a Foreign Country.* London: Cambridge University Press.

Lubow, Arthur. 2000. "Rem Koolhaas Builds." *New York Times,* July 9. www.nytimes.com/library/magazine/home/20000709mag-koolhaas.html, accessed June 4, 2008.

Lucas, Robert E. 1988. "On the Mechanics of Economic Development." *Journal of Monetary Economics* 22: 19–62.

Lui, Mary Ting Yi. 2004. *The Chinatown Trunk Mystery: Murder, Miscegenation, and Other Dangerous Encounters in Turn-of-the-Century New York City.* Princeton, N.J.: Princeton University Press.

Lukumbo, Lukas. 2007. "Architecture: A Serious Look at Dar's Face." *The Guardian* (Tanzania), July 1, 10.

Lydon, Jane. 2002. "Historical Archaeology, Cultural Exchange and the Chinese in the Rocks, 1890–1930." In *Chinese in Oceania,* ed. Pookong, Kee, Ho Chooi-hon, Paul Macgregor, and Gary Presland, 7–21. Victoria: Association for the Study of the Chinese and Their Descendants in Australasia and the Pacific.

Ma, Eve. 2000. *Hometown Chinatown.* New York: Garland.

Macabasco, Lisa. 2005. "Philly Approves Chinatown Charter School." *Asian Week* 6/5/2005news.asianweek.com/news/view_article.html?article_id44b340e2a12e7d6949dc854b76c4403b, accessed February 6, 2007.

Mackay, David. 2000. *La recuperació del front marítim.* Barcelona: Aula Barcelona.

Madigan, Charles. 2004. *Global Chicago.* Urbana: University of Illinois Press.

"The Magi Opened the New Marine Promenade of the Moll de la Fusta Today." 1987. *El País,* January 2.

Magnet, Alec. 2005. "Doctoroff: Mayor's Support Unwavering for Rebuilding of Ground Zero." *New York Sun,* October 26.

Magrinyà, Francesc. 2003. "Hacia una relectura de los espacios públicos desde la posmodernidad: el ejemplo del Raval en Barcelona." In *Idensitat: proyectos de intervención crítica e interacción social en el espacio público,* 229–39. Madrid: Editorial Injuve.

Magrinyà, Francesc and Eva Gimeno. 1994. "La intervención de cerdà en la construcción del ensanche." In *Cerdà, urbs i territori: una visió de futur,* Catálogo de da exposición Mostra Cerdà. Urbs i Territori, September 1994–January 1995, 167–88. Barcelona: Electa.

Mahadevia, Darshini, and Harini Narayanan. 2008a. "Slumbay to Shanghai: Envisioning Renewal or Takeover." In *Inside the Transforming Urban Asia: Processes, Policies and Public Actions,* ed. Darshini Mahadevia, 94–169. New Delhi: Concept Publishing.

———. 2008b. "Shanghaing Mumbai: Politics of Evictions and Resistance in Slum Settlements." In *Inside the Transforming Urban Asia: Processes, Policies and Public Actions*, ed. Darshini Mahadevia, 549–89. New Delhi: Concept Publishing.

Makdisi, Saree. 2010. "A Museum of Tolerance We Don't Need." *Los Angeles Times*, February 12. http://articles.latimes.com/2010/feb/12/opinion/la-oe-makdisi12 -2010feb12, accessed February 18.

Malaquais, Dominique. 2006. "Douala/Johannesburg/New York: Cityscapes Imagined." In *Cities in Contemporary Africa*, ed. Martin J. Murray and Garth A. Myers. New York: Palgrave Macmillan.

Mamdani, Mahmood. 2004. *Good Muslim, Bad Muslim: America, the Cold War, and the Roots of Terror*. New York: Three Leaves.

Maragall, Pascual. 1991. *Barcelona, la ciutat retrobada*. Barcelona: Edicions 62.

Marcuse, Peter, and Ronald van Kempen, eds. 2000. *Globalizing Cities: A New Spatial Order?* Oxford: Blackwell.

Marmalejo, José. 2003. *De China con honra*. Guayaquil: n.p.

Marpakwar, Prafulla. 2006. "McKinsey Shows Makeover Way." *Times of India*, November 2.

Marqos, Michel. 1990. "The Center of Beirut Ties the Veins." *Al-Nahar*, December 17: 8.

Maskovsky, Jeff. 2006. "Governing the 'New Hometowns': Race, Power and Neighborhood Participation in the New Inner City." *Identities* 13, 1: 73–99.

Matloff, Judith. 1995. "Zanzibar Island, Gem of Arab Décor, Tries to Restore Heyday." *Christian Science Monitor*, August 30: 12.

Mauri, Luis, and Lluis Uria. 1998. *La gota Malaia: una biografía fe Pasqual Maragall*. Barcelona: Edicions 62.

Mayne, Alan. 1993. *The Imagined Slum: Newspaper Representations in Three Cities, 1870–1914*. Leicester: Leicester University Press.

McCabe, Marikay. 2003. "Parameters of the Public: Commercial and Legal Topographies of Nineteenth-Century Havana, Cuba." Ph.D. dissertation, Columbia University.

McCann, Eugene J. 2001. "Collaborative Visioning or Urban Planning as Therapy? The Politics of Public-Private Policy Making." *Professional Geographer* 53, 2: 207–18.

McDonogh, Gary. 1986. *Good Families of Barcelona*. Princeton, N.J.: Princeton University Press. Spanish Edition Omega 1988.

———. 1987. "The Geography of Evil: Barcelona's Barrio Chino." *Anthropological Quarterly* 60, 4: 174–84.

———. 1993. *Black and Catholic in Savannah, Georgia*. Knoxville: University of Tennessee Press.

———. 1999. "Discourses of the City: Policy and Response in Post-Transitional Barcelona." In *Theorizing the City: The New Urban Anthropology Reader*, ed. Setha Low, 342–76. New Brunswick, N.J.: Rutgers University Press.

———. 2002. "Myth, Space and Virtue: Gender, Bars and Change in Barcelona's Barrio Chino." In *The Anthropology of Space and Place*, ed. Setha Low and Denise Lawrence, 264–283. London: Blackwell.

———. 2008. *Iberian Worlds*. London: Routledge.

McDonogh, Gary, and Cindy Wong. 2005. *Global Hong Kong*. London: Routledge.

McGee, Terry G., George C. S. Lin, Andrew M. Marton, Mark Y. L. Wang, and Jiaping Wu. 2007. *China's Urban Space: Development Under Market Socialism*. London: Routledge.

McKeown, Adam. 2001. *Chinese Migrant Networks and Cultural Change: Peru, Chicago, Hawaii, 1900–1930*. Chicago: University of Chicago Press, 2001.

McKinsey & Company. 2003. *Vision Mumbai: Transforming Mumbai into a World-Class City*. Mumbai: Bombay First.

McNeill, Donald. 1999. *Urban Change and the European Left: Tales from the New Barcelona*. London: Routledge.

———. 2009. *The Global Architect: Firms, Fame and Urban Form*. New York: Routledge.

McQuire, Scott. 2008. *The Media City: Media, Architecture and Urban Space*. London: Routledge.

McWaters, Vivienne. 2002. *Beechworth's Little Canton: The History of Spring Creek Chinese Camp and Its Residents*. Beechworth: Author.

Mera, Koichi. 1973. "On the Urban Agglomeration and Economic Efficiency." *Economic Development and Cultural Change* 21, 2: 301–24.

Merleau-Ponty, Maurice. 1966. *Phenomenology of Perception*. Ed. Colin Smith. London: Routledge.

Meyer, John, John Boli, George M. Thomas, and Francisco O. Ramírez. 1997. "World Society and the Nation State." *American Journal of Sociology* 103, 1: 144–81.

Mhando, Martin. 2006. "Review of the Film Festival." *ZIFF Journal* 3: 5–12.

———. 2007. "Zanzibar International Film Festival: A History, A Vision." In *Ten Years of ZIFF*, ed. Fatma Alloo, 45–51. Zanzibar: Gallery Publications.

Mignolo, Walter. 2000. *Local Histories/Global Designs*. Princeton, N.J.: Princeton University Press.

Miller, Michael. 1991. *The Bon Marché: Bourgeois Culture and the Department Store, 1869–1920*. Princeton, N.J.: Princeton University Press.

Mitchell, Jerry. 2001. "Business Improvement Districts and the 'New' Revitalization of Downtowns." *Economic Development Quarterly* 15, 2: 115–23.

Mitchell, Timothy. 2002. *The Rule of Experts: Egypt, Techno-Politics, Modernity*. Berkeley: University of California Press.

Mohr, James. 2005. *Plague and Fire: Battling Black Death and the 1900 Burning of Honolulu's Chinatown*. Oxford: Oxford University Press.

Moix, Llàtzer. 1994. *La ciudad de los arquitectos*. Barcelona: Anagrama.

Molina, Gabriel. 1993. "Old Havana Struggles for Its Glory." *Granma International*, December 22, 16.

Montero, Luis. 1997. "Proyectos de ampliación y estrategias de desarrollo del puerto de Barcelona. En 1ª jornades sobre el litoral de la regió metropolitana de Barcelona." *Consorci El Far*, April 16–17, 18.

Monzó, Quim. 2002. "La cigala de Mariscal: nos vendían el Moll de la Fusta como el no va más de la noche, el lugar que nadie debía perderse." *La Vanguardia*, June 3.

Moody, Kim. 2007. *From Welfare State to Real State: Regime Change in New York City, 1974 to the Present*. New York: New Press.

Moore, Tracy. 2008. "The Seduction: High-rise Condos Are Sprouting Up All over Town, Betting on Nashville's Pursuit of Cool." *Nashville Scene*, August 21.

Morgen, Sandra, and Lisa Gonzales. 2008. "The Neoliberal American Dream as Daydream." *Critique of Anthropology* 28, 2: 219–36.

Morris, Aldon. 1984. *The Origins of the Civil Rights Movement*. New York: Free Press.

Mukhija, Vinit. 2003. *Squatters as Developers? Slum Redevelopment in Mumbai*. Burlington, Vt.: Ashgate.

Murphy, Jarrett. 2005. "Stopping a Stadium." *Village Voice*, June 7.

Mustafa, Amr. 2004. "Make No Little Plans: Dubai's Transformation into a Global City." Panel paper, Seventh Annual Sharjah Urban Planning Symposium, April 4–6, American University of Sharjah, UAE.

Myers, Garth Andrew. 2003. *Verandahs of Power*. Syracuse, N.Y.: Syracuse University Press.

Naquin, Susan. 2000. *Peking: Temples and City Life, 1400–1900*. Berkeley: University of California Press.

Nash, Matt. 2009. "Shopping Malls Spreading in and Around Beirut." http://www.nowlebanon.com/NewsArchiveDetails.aspx?ID121191, accessed June 5, 2011.

Nashashibi, Rami. 2007. "Ghetto Cosmopolitanism: Making Theory at the Margins." In *Deciphering the Global: Its Spaces, Scales and Subjects*, ed. Saskia Sassen, 243–64. New York: Routledge.

Nevarez, Leonard. 2003. *New Money, Nice Town: How Capital Works in the New Urban Economy*. New York: Routledge.

Newman, Peter, and Isabel Jennings. 2008. *Cities as Sustainable Ecosystems*. Washington, D.C.: Island Press.

Newsom, Jim. 1968. "Sidewalk Hippie Law-In." *Citizen News*, June 28, 1–2.

Nijman, Jan. 2000. "Mumbai's Real Estate Market in the 1990s: De-Regulation, Global Money, and Casino Capitalism." *Economic and Political Weekly*, February 12, 575–82.

Oakman, Jonathan, ed. 2006. *The New Downtowns: The Future of Urban Centers*. Princeton, N.J.: Policy Research Institute on the Region.

O'Farrell, Maggie. 2000. "Relax, Paradise Island Is Here to Stay." *The Independent* (London), September 24, Features, 1.

Olds, Kris. 2001. *Globalization and Urban Change: Capital, Culture, and Pacific Rim Mega-Projects*. Oxford: Oxford University Press.

Onley, James. 2005. "Transnational Merchants in the Nineteenth-Century Gulf: The Case of the Safar Family." In *Transnational Connections and the Arab Gulf*, ed. Madawi al-Rasheed, 59–89. New York: Routledge.

———. 2007. "De Perse, d'Inde et d'Afrique." *Qantara* 64 (summer): 36–37.

Ouroussof, Nicolai. 2008. "City on the Gulf: Koolhaas Lays Out a Grand Urban Experiment in Dubai." *New York Times*, March 3.

Page, Max. 1999. *The Creative Destruction of Manhattan, 1900–1945*. Chicago: University of Chicago Press.

Pàmies, Sergi. 2001. "Sopa de Maremàgnum." *El País*, February 4.

Pan, Shiyi. 2000. *SoHo New Town Files*. Tianjin: Tianjin Academy of Social Science.

Panagariya, Arvind. 2007. "Mumbai: Self-Inflicted Wounds." *Economic Times*, August 27.

Park, Robert E., Ernest W. Burgess, and Roderick Duncan McKenzie. 1967. *The City: Suggestions of Human Behavior in the Urban Environment*. Chicago: University of Chicago Press.

Parker, Ian. 2005. "The Mirage: The Architectural Insanity of Dubai." *New Yorker*, October 17, 128–43.

Peck, Jamie. 2005. "Struggling with the Creative Class." *International Journal of Urban and Regional Research* 29, 4: 740–70.

Peck, Jamie, and Adam Tickell. 2002. "Neoliberalizing Space." *Antipode* 34, 3: 380–404.

Pedersen, Jan. 2000. "Explaining Economic Liberalization in India: State and Society Perspectives." *World Development* 28, 2: 265–82.

Pérez, Gina. 2004. *The Near Northwest Side Story: Migration, Displacement, and Puerto Rican Families*. Berkeley: University of California Press.

Pérez, Louis A., Jr. 1992. *Slaves, Sugar, & Colonial Society: Travel Accounts of Cuba, 1801–1899*. Wilmington, Del.: Scholarly Resources.

Peters, Philip. 2001. *Rescuing Old Havana*. Arlington, Va.: Lexington Institute.

Peterson, Marina. 2010. *Sound, Space, and the City: Civic Performance in Downtown Los Angeles*. Philadelphia: University of Pennsylvania Press.

Peterson, Richard A. 1999. *Creating Country Music*. Chicago: University of Chicago Press.

Peterson, Richard A., and Russel B. Davis. 1977. "The Fertile Crescent of Country Music." *Journal of Country Music* 6: 19–27.

Polanyi, Karl. 1975. *The Great Transformation*. New York: Octagon.

Polanyi, Karl, Conrad M. Arensberg, and Harry W. Pearson, eds. 1957. *Trade and Market in the Early Empires: Economies in History and Theory*. Glencoe, Ill.: Free Press.

Pomés, Juliet, and Ricardo Feriche. 2001. *Barcelona Guide Design*. Barcelona: Ed Gustavo Gili.

Port de Barcelona. 1999. *Memoria d'activitats de la gerència urbanistica Port 2000 de l'autoritat portuària de Barcelona 1995–1998*. Barcelona: Port de Barcelona.

Porter, Eduardo. 2007. "Housing Slump Takes a Toll on Illegal Immigrants." *New York Times*, April 17.

Prakash, Gyan. 2008. "Mumbai: The Modern City in Ruins." In *Other Cities, Other Worlds: Urban Imaginaries in a Globalizing Age*, ed. Andreas Huyssen, 181–204. Durham, N.C.: Duke University Press.

Pribetich, Justine. 2005. "La construction identitaire d'un quartier: l'example de Sedaine-Popincourt." *Hommes & migrations: Chinois en France* 1254: 82–90.

Raffestin, Claude. 1980. *Pour une géographie du pouvoir*. Paris: Litec.

Raines, Patrick, and LaTanya Brown. 2006. "The Economic Impact of the Music Industry in the Nashville MSA." Report prepared for Nashville Area Chamber of Commerce.

Rama, Angel. 1996. *The Lettered City*. Durham, N.C.: Duke University Press.

Rannells, John. 1956. *The Core of the City: A Pilot Study of Changing Land Uses in Central Business Districts*. New York: Columbia University Press.

Rapkin, Chester and William G. Grimsby. 1960. *The Demand for Housing in Racially-Mixed Areas: A Study of the Nature of Neighborhood Change*. Philadelphia: Special Report to the Commission on Race and Housing of the Philadelphia Housing Authority.

Real Deal. 2004. "New York's Top Real Estate Lawyers." *The Real Deal*, March.

The Real Estate Agency. 1992. "The Real Estate Agency: Implementation and Economic Reflections." *Al-Iqtisaad wal-'Amaal*, January, 42.

"The Real Estate Market in Lebanon." 1994. *Al-Iqtisaad wal-'Amaal*, April, 42–48.

Ren, Xuefei. 2008. "Forward to the Past: Historical Preservation in Globalizing Shanghai." *City and Community* 7, 1: 23–43.

Republic of Lebanon. 1995. *"Horizon 2000" Main Report*. Beirut: Council for Development and Reconstruction.

Rieff, David. 1991. *Los Angeles: Capital of the Third World*. New York: Simon & Schuster.

Risbud, Neelima. 2003. "The Case of Mumbai, India." In *Understanding Slums: Case Studies for the Global Report on Human Settlements*. London: UN-Habitat.

Rivera, Carla. 2004. "Advocates Rally Homeless to Get Out the Vote." *Los Angeles Times*, October 11. http://www.latimes.com/news/politics/2004/complete/la-me-homeless11oct11,1,1805356.story?collla-elect2004-complete, accessed February 6, 2009.

Robb, John. 1879. *Medico-Topographical Report on Zanzibar*. Calcutta: Office of the Superintendent of Government Printing.

Robertson, Kent A. 1995. "Downtown Redevelopment Strategies in the United States: An End-of-the-Century Assessment." *Journal of the American Planning Association* 61: 429–37.

Robinson, Jennifer. 2002. "Global and World Cities: A View from off the Map." *International Journal of Urban and Regional Research* 26, 3: 531–54.

Rodríguez Alomá, Patricia. 1996. *Viaje en la memoria: apuntes para un acercamiento a La Habana Vieja*. Ciudad/City 2. La Habana Vieja, Cuba: Oficina del Historiador de la Ciudad de La Habana; Navarra: Colegio Oficial de Arquitectos Vasco Navarro.

Rodríguez Alomá, Patricia, and Alina Ochoa Alomá. 1999. *Desafío de una utopía: una estrategia integral para le gestión de salvaguardia de la habana vieja.* Ciudad/City 4. La Habana Vieja: Oficina del Historiador de la Ciudad de La Habana; Navarra: Colegio Oficial de Arquitectos Vasco Navarro.

Roig de Leuchsenring, Emilio. 1963. *La Habana: apuntes históricos.* 3 vols. Vol. 2. Havana: Consejo Nacional de Cultura.

Rose, Joseph. 2000. "Comments." Midtown-West: Options for Mid-Manhattan's Last Frontier, New York, December 8. New York Real Estate Forum.

Rotenberg, Robert. 1979. "Fighting with Time: Intraregional Conflicts in Public Schedules in Austria." *Urban Anthropology* 8, 1: 73–94.

———. 1995. *Landscape and Power in Vienna.* Baltimore, Md.: Johns Hopkins University Press.

Rothfield, Lawrence, Don Coursey, Sarah Lee, Daniel Silver, and Wendy Norris. 2007. "Chicago: Music City." Report for the Chicago Music Commission.

"Roundtable Discussion Concerning the Souks Plan in the Beirut Central Commercial District." 1998. *Al-Mouhandas*, Number 8.

Rowe, Peter, and Hashim Sarkis, eds. 1998. *Projecting Beirut: Episodes in the Construction and Reconstruction of a Modern City.* Munich: Prestel.

Rudolph, Lloyd, and Susanne Hoeber Rudolph. 1987. *In Pursuit of Lakshmi: The Political Economy of the Indian State.* Chicago: University of Chicago Press.

Rutheiser, Charles. 1996. *Imagineering Atlanta: The Politics of Place in the City of Dreams.* New York: Verso.

Saba, Bassam. 1992. "The Ruins of Memory and the Bulldozer of War." *Al-Nahar*, April 17.

Sahlins, Marshall. 1972. *Stone Age Economics.* Chicago: Aldine.

Salinas, Fernando. 1971. "Transformacion Urbana en Cuba: La Habana." *Arquitectura Cuba* 340, 3.

Sam, Michael Patrick, and Jay Scherer. 2006. "The Steering Group as Policy Advice Instrument: A Case of 'Consultocracy' in Stadium Subsidy Deliberations." *Policy Science*, 39: 169–81.

Sarlo, Beatriz. 2008. "Cultural Landscapes: Buenos Aires from Integration to Fracture." In *Other Cities, Other Worlds: Urban Imaginaries in a Globalizing Age*, ed. Andreas Huyssen, 27–50. Durham, N.C.: Duke University Press.

Sassen, Saskia. 1991. "The Informal Economy." In *Dual City: Restructuring New York*, ed. John Mollenkopf and Manuel Castells, 79–102. New York: Russell Sage.

———. 1992. *The Global City: New York, London, Tokyo.* Princeton, N.J.: Princeton University Press.

———. 2000. *Cities in a World Economy.* 2nd ed. Thousand Oaks, Calif.: Pine Forge Press.

———. 2001. *The Global City: New York, London, Tokyo.* 2nd ed. Princeton, N.J.: Princeton University Press.

———. 2007. *Territory, Authority, Rights: From Medieval to Global Assemblages.* Princeton, N.J.: Princeton University Press.

Scarpaci, Joseph L. 2000. "Reshaping Habana Vieja: Revitalization, Historic Preservation, and Restructuring in the Socialist City." *Urban Geography* 21, 8: 659–69.

Scarpaci, Joseph L., Roberto Segre, and Mario Coyula. 2002. *Havana: Two Faces of the Antillean Metropolis.* Chapel Hill: University of North Carolina Press.

Schivelbusch, Wolfgang. 1977. *The Railway Journey.* New York: Urizen.

Schuyler, David. 2002. *A City Transformed: Redevelopment, Race and Suburbanization in Lancaster, Pennsylvania, 1940–1980.* University Park: Pennsylvania State University Press.

Scott, Allen J. 1998. *Regions and the World Economy.* London: Oxford University Press.

———. 2000. *The Cultural Economy of Cities: Essays on the Geography of Image-Producing Industries.* London: Sage.

———. 2001. *Global City-Regions.* New York: Oxford University Press.

Scott, Allen J., and Edward Soja. 1996. *The City: Los Angeles and Urban Theory at the End of the Twentieth Century.* Berkeley: University of California Press.

Scott, James C. 1998. *Seeing Like a State: How Some Schemes to Improve the Human Condition Failed.* New Haven, Conn.: Yale University Press.

Scott, Mel. 1949. *Metropolitan Los Angeles: One Community.* Los Angeles: Haynes Foundation.

Seed, John. 2006. "Limehouse Blues: Looking for 'Chinatown' in the London Docks, 1900–40." *History Workshop Journal* 62: 58–85.

Segre, Roberto. 1989. *Arquitectura y urbanismo de la revolución cubana.* Havana: Editorial Pueblo y Educación.

Shachtman, Tom. 2000. *Skyscraper Dreams: The Great Real Estate Dynasties of New York.* Lincoln, Neb.: iUniverse.com.

Shah, Nayan. 2001. *Contagious Divides: Epidemics and Race in San Francisco's Chinatown.* Berkeley: University of California Press.

Sharma, Kalpana. 2005. "Forget Shanghai, Remember Mumbai." *The Hindu,* February 21.

Shaw, Annapurna. 2004. *The Making of Navi Mumbai.* Hyderabad: Orient Longman.

Sheller, Mimi, and John Urry. 2003. "Mobile Transformations of 'Public' and 'Private' Life." *Theory, Culture and Society* 20, 3: 107–25.

Sheriff, Abdul, ed. 1995. *The History and Conservation of Zanzibar Stone Town.* London: James Currey.

Short, John Rennie. 2004. *Global Metropolitan.* New York: Routledge.

Short, John Rennie, C. Breitbach, S. Buchman, and J. Essex. 2000. "From World Cities to Gateway Cities: Extending the Boundaries of Globalization Theory." *City* 4, 3: 317–40.

Short, John R., and Yeong-Hyun Kim. 1999. *Globalization and the City.* New York: Longman.

Sigler, Jennifer. 2000. "Rem Koolhaas." *Index Magazine.* http://www.indexmagazine
.com/interviews/rem_koolhaas.shtml, accessed June 4, 2008.

Silverman, Helaine. 2002. "Touring Ancient Times: The Present and Presented Past in
Contemporary Peru." *American Anthropologist* 104, 3: 881–902.

Simmel, Georg. 1950 [1903]. "The Metropolis and Mental Life." In *The Sociology of
Georg Simmel,* ed. Kurt H. Wolff. Glencoe, Ill.: Free Press.

Sisk, Chas. 2009a. "Condo Developer May Sue Buyers." *Tennessean,* February
19, B6.

———. 2009b. "Gulch Certified as Green Area: Neighborhood Wins Rare Honor."
Tennessean, February 18, 7B.

Sites, William. 2003. *Remaking New York: Primitive Globalization and the Politics of
Urban Community.* Minneapolis: University of Minnesota Press.

Skinner, G. William. 1957. *Chinese Society in Thailand.* Ithaca, N.Y.: Cornell University Press.

———. 1964. "Marketing and Social Structure in Rural China: Part 1." *Journal of
Asian Studies* 24: 3–43.

———, ed. 1977. *The City in Late Imperial China.* Stanford, Calif.: Stanford University
Press.

Sledge, Coly. 2008. "Politicos, Media to Find More than Music." *Tennessean,* September 28, 1A, 15A.

Slocum, J. David. 2003. "Zanzibar International Film Festival 2003." In *Senses of
Cinema.* http://archive.sensesofcinema.com/contents/festivals/03/28/zanzibar.html,
accessed March 23, 2010.

Smith, Michael Peter. 2001. *Transnational Urbanism: Locating Globalization.* Oxford:
Blackwell.

Smith, Neil. 1996. *The New Urban Frontier: Gentrification and the Revanchist City.*
London: Routledge.

———. 2002. "New Globalism, New Urbanism: Gentrification as Global Urban Strategy." *Antipode* 34, 3: 434-57.

———. 2003. "Gentrification Generalized: From Local Anomaly to Urban 'Regeneration' as Global Urban Strategy." In *Frontiers of Capital: Ethnographic Reflections
on the New Economy,* ed. Melissa S. Fisher and Greg Downey, 191-208. Durham,
N.C.: Duke University Press.

Smith, Neil, and Peter Williams. 1986. *Gentrification of the City.* Boston: Allen &
Unwin.

Smith, Robert. 2005. *Mexican New York.* Berkeley: University of California Press.

Smithsimon, Gregory. 2006. "The Shared City: Using and Controlling Public Space in
New York City." Ph.D. dissertation, Columbia University.

———. 2010. "Inside the Empire: Ethnography of a Global Citadel in New York."
Urban Studies 47, 4: 699–724.

Sobrequés i Callicó, Jaume. 1997. *Historia de Barcelona: el segle XX. Del creixement
desordenat a la ciutat olímpica.* Vol. 8. Barcelona: Ajuntament de Barcelona.

Soja, Edward W. 1989. *Postmodern Geographies*. New York: Verso.

———. 1996. *Thirdspace: Journeys to Los Angeles and Other Real-and-Imagined Places*. Oxford: Blackwell.

Soja, Edward W., and Allen J. Scott. 1986. "Los Angeles: Capital of the Late Twentieth Century." *Environment and Planning D: Society and Space* 4: 249–54.

Soldevila, Carlos. 1957. *Barcelona Vista pels seus artistes*. Barcelona: Aedos.

Solidere. 1994. *The Reconstruction of the Souqs of Beirut: An International Ideas Competition*, 4 vols. Beirut: Solidere.

———. 2005. *Annual Report*. Beirut: Solidere.

———. 2008. *Annual Report*. Beirut: Solidere.

———. 2009. *Solidere Quarterly*, January–March. Beirut: Solidere.

Solnit, Rebecca, and Susan Schwartzenberg. 2000. *Hollow City: The Siege of San Francisco and the Crisis of American Urbanism*. London: Verso.

Sorkin, Michael. 1992. *Variations on a Theme Park*. New York: Hill and Wang.

Stacey, Cynthia. 2007. "Good or Bad . . . Architecture . . . Impacts on Us All." *The Guardian* (Tanzania), June 30: 7.

State of Maharashtra. 2004. *Transforming Mumbai into a World-Class City*. Chief Minister's Taskforce.

Steinhauer, Jennifer. 2005. "Requiem for a Stadium: Overtures Came Too Late." *New York Times*, June 8.

Stine, James H. 1962. "Temporal Aspects of Tertiary Production Elements in Korea." In *Urban Systems and Economic Development*, ed. Forrest R. Pitts, 68–88. Eugene: University of Oregon Press.

Stringer, Julian. 2001. "Global Cities and the International Film Festival Economy." In *Cinema and the City*, ed. Mark Shiel and Tony Fitzmaurice, 134–44. Oxford: Blackwell.

Strom, Elizabeth. 2008. "Rethinking the Politics of Downtown Development." *Journal of Urban Affairs* 30, 1: 37–61.

Subirós, Pep. 1996. "Barcelona, Port 2000. De la metáfora al simulacro." *Quaderns d'arquitectura i urbanisme* 212.

Sudjic, Deyan. 1992. *The 100 Mile City*. London: A. Deutsch.

Susser, Ida. 1982. *Norman Street: Poverty and Politics in an Urban Neighborhood*. New York: Oxford University Press.

Tabet, Jade. 1993. "Towards a Post-War Master Plan for Lebanon." In *Recovering Beirut: Urban Design and Post-War Reconstruction*, ed. Samir Khalaf and Philip Khoury, 81–100. Leiden: Brill.

Tabet, Jade, and Benjamin Thompson & Associates, 1995. *Beirut Souks Project Master Plan: General Report*. Beirut: Solidere.

Tan Chee-Beng. 2004. *Chinese Overseas: Comparative Cultural Issues*. Hong Kong: Hong Kong University Press.

Tatjer, Mercedes. 1996. "La construcción del espacio costero siglos XX–XX: del mundo portuario al mundo del ocio. El caso del puerto de Barcelona 1856–1936." In *Actas del coloquio Internacional "El sistema portuario español."* Madrid: CEHOPU, Ministerio de Fomento, CSIC.

Taylor, Peter, Ben DeRudder, Pieter Saey, and Franck Wilcox, eds. 2007. *Cities in Globalization.* New York: Taylor & Francis.

Tchen, John Kuo Wei. 1999. *New York Before Chinatown: Orientalism and the Shaping of American Culture, 1776–1882.* Baltimore, Md.: Johns Hopkins University Press.

"The First Jury Report." 2007. In *Ten Years of ZIFF*, ed. Fatma Alloo, 21-3. Zanzibar: Gallery Publications.

Thrift, Nigel. 2004. "Driving in the City." *Theory, Culture and Society* 21, 4/5: 41–59.

Thünen, Johan Heinrich. 1966. *Von Thünen's Isolated State.* Ed. Peter Hall, trans. Carla M. Wartenberg. Oxford: Pergamon Press.

Tinkler, Chris. 2008. "Spice Island Melting Pot Boost Dhow Zones Index." *Sunday Herald Sun* (Australia), August 3, Escape section, 4.

Tolosa, Eduardo, and Daniel Romani. 1996. *Barcelona escultura guía.* Barcelona: Gustavo Gili.

Tomlinson, Hugh, and David Robertson. 2010. "Burj Dubai Becomes Burj Khalifa as Emirate Loses Out on Crowning Glory." *Times Online.* http://www.timesonline .co.uk/tol/news/world/middle_east/article6976011.ece, accessed February 15.

Travers, Robert. 2004. *Australian Mandarin.* Kenthurst, Australia: Rosenberg Publishings.

Tsui, Bonnie. 2009. *American Chinatown.* New York: Free Press.

Turan, Kenneth. 2002. *Sundance to Sarajevo: Film Festivals and the World They Made.* Berkeley: University of California Press.

Turtinen, Jan. 2000. *Globalising Heritage: On UNESCO and the Transnational Construction of a World Heritage.* Stockholm: Stockholm Center for Organizational Research.

Tusa, John. 2004. Interview with Frank Gehry. bbc.co.uk/radio3/johntusainterview/ gehry_transcripts.html, accessed June 4, 2008.

UNESCO. 1972. Convention Concerning the Protection of the World Cultural and Natural Heritage. Paris. http://whc.unesco.org/en/conventiontext, accessed June 5, 2011.

Urry, John. 1990. *The Tourist Gaze: Leisure and Travel in Contemporary Societies.* Thousand Oaks, Calif.: Sage Publications.

——. 2007. *Mobilities.* Cambridge: Polity Press.

UTOPIA/dystopia. 2010. Dir. John Malpede. Roy and Edna Disney/CalArts Theater. Los Angeles, CA. December 6–8.

Varzally, Allison. 2008. *Making a Non-White America.* Berkeley: University of California Press.

Vázquez Montalbán, Manuel. 2000. *El hombre de mi vida: vuelve Pepe Carvallo.* Barcelona: Planeta.

Venegas Fornias, Carlos. 1990. *La urbanización de las murallas: dependencia y modernidad.* Havana: Letras Cubanas.

Vidal, John. 2008. "Desert State Channels Oil Wealth into World's First Sustainable City." *Guardian*, January 21. http://www.guardian.co.uk/environment/2008/jan/21/climatechange.energy, accessed May 27.

Vladislavić, Ivan. 2009. *Portrait with Keys: The City of Johannesburg Unlocked*. New York: W. W. Norton & Co.

Vora, Rajendra. 1996. "Shift in Power from Rural to Urban Sector." *Economic and Political Weekly*, January 13–20.

Wachs, Martin. 1996. "The Evolution of Transportation Policy in Los Angeles: Images of Past Policies and Future Prospects." In *The City: Los Angeles and Urban Theory at the End of the Twentieth Century*, ed. Allen J. Scott and Edward W. Soja, 106–59. Berkeley: University of California Press.

Walls, Archie, and Louisa Crispe. 1991. *The National Heritage of Zanzibar: Its Future*. Report to the Government of Zanzibar for the attention of the Minister of State for Special Duties, President's Office (unpaginated). Zanzibar.

Weinstein, Liza. 2008. "Mumbai's Development Mafias: Globalization, Organized Crime and Land Development." *International Journal of Urban and Regional Research* 32, 1: 22–39.

Weinstein, Liza, and Xuefei Ren. 2009. "The Changing Right to the City: Urban Renewal and Housing Rights in Globalizing Shanghai and Mumbai." *City and Community* 8, 4: 407–32.

Weiss, Brad. 2009. *Street Dreams and Hip Hop Barbershops: Global Fantasy in Urban Tanzania*. Bloomington: Indiana University Press.

Weiss y Sanchez, and Joaquín Emilio. 1996. *La Arquitectura Colonial Cubana: siglos XVI al XIX*. Havana: Instituto Cubano del Libro.

Westwater, Brady. 2006. "Hamid Behdad—Adaptive Reuse Czar and Mr. Downtown to Leave Public Service!" *L.A. Cowboy*, December 4. http://lacowboy.blogspot.com/2006/12/hamid-behdad-adaptive-resue-czar-and-mr.html. Accessed August 3, 2008.

"What's in a Name? City Hopes Money." 2007. *Chicago Tribune*, November 24, 24.

Whitt, J. Allen. 1987. "Mozart in the Metropolis: The Arts Coalition and the Urban Growth Machine." *Urban Affairs Quarterly* 23, 1: 15–36.

Whyte, Martin King, and William Parish. 1984. *Urban Life in Contemporary China*. Chicago: University of Chicago Press.

Wide Angle. 2007. *The Sand Castle*. Eirin Gjørv, director. http://www.pbs.org/wnet/wideangle/shows/uae/index.html, accessed May 24, 2008.

Wide Angle Transcript. 2007. Transcript, *The Sand Castle*. http://www-tc.pbs.org/wnet/wideangle/shows/uae/transcript.pdf, accessed May 24, 2008.

Wild, Mark. 2008. *Street Meetings: Multiethnic Neighborhoods in Early Twentieth Century Los Angeles*. Berkeley: University of California Press.

Wilkinson, Ben. 2008. "Zanzibar: The Rich and Poor Culture." *Arusha Times*, May 10–16. http://www.arushatimes.co.tz/2008/18/society_1.htm, accessed March 12, 2010.

Williams, Brett. 1988. *Upscaling Downtown: Stalled Gentrification in Washington, D.C.* Ithaca, N.Y.: Cornell University Press.

Williams, Gwyndaf. 2003. *The Enterprising Citycentre: Manchester's Development Challenge.* London: Spoon Press.

Wilson, David. 2004. "Toward a Contingent Urban Neoliberalism." *Urban Geography* 25, 8: 771–83.

——. 2008. "Neoliberal Redevelopment in Western Cities: Neglected Underpinnings." *Urban Geography* 29, 3: 193–95.

Wolch, Jennifer, and Michael Dear. 1993. *Malign Neglect: Homelessness in an American City.* San Francisco: Jossey-Bass.

Wolff, Michael. 2001. "Bloomberg News." *New York Magazine*, August 27.

Wollman, Henry. 2004. Presentation of Newman Center Plan to Manhattan Community Board Four, New York. November 8.

Wong, Cindy. 1991. "Rituals Revisited." In *Moving the Image: Independent Asian Pacific American Media Arts*, ed. Russell Leong, 197–99. Los Angeles: UCLA Asian American Studies.

——. 1999. "Cities, Culture and Cassettes: Hong Kong Cinema and Transnational Audiences." *Post Script* 19, 1: 87–106.

Wong, Cindy Hing-Yuk and Gary W. McDonough. 2001. "The Mediated Metropolis." *American Anthropologist* 103(1): 96–111.

Wong, Marie Rose. 2004. *Sweet Cakes, Long Journey: The Chinatowns of Portland Oregon.* Seattle: University of Washington Press.

World Bank. 1993. *Lebanon: Stabilization and Reconstruction*, Report 11406-LE, March 1. Washington, D.C.: World Bank.

Writers Program of the Works Progress Administration of Northern California. 1940. *San Francisco: The Bay and Its Cities.* New York: Hastings House.

Wu, Fulong, ed. 2006. *Globalization and the Chinese City.* London: Routledge.

Wu, Fulong, Jiang Xu, and Anthony Gar-On Yeh. 2007. *Urban Development in Post-Reform China: State, Market and Space.* New York: Routledge.

Xu Guoqi. 2011. *Strangers on the Western Front: Chinese Workers in the Great War.* Cambridge: Harvard University Press.

Yun Gao and Véronique Poisson. 2005. *Le trafic et l'exploitation des immigrant chinois en France.* Genève: Bureau International du Travail.

Zakhour, Antoine. 1992. "Brasilia or the New Beirut?" *Al-Bayan*, April, 14.

Zhang, Li. 2004. "Forced from Home: Property Rights, Civic Activism, and the Politics of Relocation in China." *Urban Anthropology* 33: 247–81.

——. 2006. "Contesting Spatial Modernity in Post-Socialist China." *Current Anthropology* 47: 461–84.

Zhang, Yan, and Ke Fang. 2004. "Is History Repeating Itself? From Urban Renewal in the United States to Inner-City Redevelopment in China." *Journal of Planning Education and Research* 23, 3: 286–98.

Zheng, Li-Hua. 1995. *Les chinois de Paris et leurs jeux de face.* Paris: L'Harmattan.

Zukin, Sharon. 1982. *Loft Living: Culture and Capital in Urban Change.* Baltimore, Md.: Johns Hopkins University Press.

———. 1995. *The Cultures of Cities.* Cambridge, Mass.: Blackwell.

———. 2002. "Our World Trade Center." In *After the World Trade Center: Rethinking New York City,* ed. Michael Sorkin and Sharon Zukin, 13–22. New York: Routledge.

CONTRIBUTORS

William Cunningham Bissell is Associate Professor in the Department of Anthropology and Sociology, Lafayette College, Easton, Pennsylvania. His research interests include cities, cinema, and spatial dynamics; globalization and African film; modernity and development; urban planning and power. He is the author, most recently, of a book on the failures of colonial planning, *Urban Design, Chaos, and Colonial Power in Zanzibar* (Indiana University Press, 2010).

Julian Brash is Assistant Professor of Anthropology at Montclair State University. He is the author of *Bloomberg's New York: Class and Governance in the Luxury City* (University of Georgia Press, 2011) and articles in *Social Text*, *Urban Anthropology, Critique of Anthropology,* and *Antipode.* He received a Ph.D. in Anthropology from the Graduate Center of City University of New York in 2006 and a Masters Degree in Urban Planning from Columbia University in 2000.

Brian D. Christens is Assistant Professor of Interdisciplinary Studies in Human Ecology and Community and Environmental Sociology at the University of Wisconsin–Madison. His research is focused on participation and empowerment in community and organizational settings, and has appeared in the *American Journal of Community Psychology, Health Education & Behavior,* the *Journal of Community Psychology,* and *Youth & Society.* He is a member of the editorial board of the *Journal of Youth & Adolescence* and is currently co-editing a volume of *New Directions for Child & Adolescent Development* on youth civic development.

Matthew J. Hill (MA Boston College, Ph.D. University of Chicago) is an urban anthropologist currently writing an ethnography on the politics of heritage in Havana's historic center, Old Havana. He teaches and conducts research on cities and globalization, heritage politics, and comparative urbanism in the Urban Studies Program at the University of Pennsylvania. He has published work on Havana's historic center in Saskia Sassen's *Deciphering the Global*. He is also principal of Civic Futures, a consulting firm which specializes in research and evaluation, strategic planning, and civic engagement processes in the not-for-profit and public sectors. He is a past dissertation fellow at the Lincoln Institute of Land Policy.

Najib Hourani received his Ph.D. in Politics from New York University (2005). Today, he holds a joint appointment in the Department of Anthropology and the Global Urban Studies Program at Michigan State University. He is currently writing a book on neoliberal urbanism in the Arab World, with a focus on Beirut and Amman.

Ahmed Kanna teaches international studies and anthropology at the University of the Pacific. His research focuses on the intersections of culture, politics, and urbanism in the Middle East, especially the Persian/Arab Gulf region. His publications include *Dubai, The City as Corporation* (University of Minnesota Press, 2011).

Richard Lloyd is Associate Professor of Sociology at Vanderbilt University. He is author of *Neo-Bohemia: Art and Commerce in the Postindustrial City*. His current research focuses on globalization and the American South.

Francesc Magrinyà is Professor of Urban Planning at the Politechnic University of Catalonia. He holds a Ph.D. in Urban Planning (University Paris I-ENPC, Paris) and has done research on urban planning and networks, sustainable transport planning, development cooperation and human development and recently is the co-author of *Cerdà: 150 Years of Modernity* (2009).

Gaspar Maza is Professor in the Program in Urban Anthropology at the Universitat Rovira i Virgili in Tarragona. He has worked extensively on issues of immigration and marginality in the Raval neighborhood of Barcelona and on issues of sport and society. He is currently working on a project on soccer and transnational identities in Europe and Morocco.

Gary W. McDonogh, trained as an urban anthropologist, is Professor in the Growth and Structure of Cities Department at Bryn Mawr College and Coordinator of the Program in Latin American, Latin and Iberian Peoples and Cultures there. He has published widely on issues of urban form, imagery and conflict in Europe, the Americas and Asia, including *Good Families of*

Barcelona, Black and Catholic in Savannah, Iberian Worlds and *Global Hong Kong* (with Cindy Wong).

Marina Peterson is Assistant Professor of Performance Studies in the School of Interdisciplinary Arts at Ohio University. She received her Ph.D. in anthropology from the University of Chicago in 2005. Her work focuses on music and performance, urban space, and emergent social formations in late liberalism. She is the author of *Sound, Space, and the City: Civic Performance in Downtown Los Angeles* (University of Pennsylvania Press, 2010).

Xuefei Ren is Assistant Professor of Sociology and Global Urban Studies at Michigan State University and a 2011 fellow at the Woodrow Wilson International Center for Scholars in Washington, D.C. She is the author of *Building Globalization: Transnational Architecture Production in Urban China* (University of Chicago Press, 2011).

Robert Rotenberg holds a doctorate in anthropology from the University of Massachusetts. He is Vincent de Paul Professor of Anthropology and chair of the department at DePaul University in Chicago. His book *Landscape and Power in Vienna* received the Barbara Jelavich Book Prize from the American Association for the Advancement of Slavic Studies and the Prize for the Best Book in English in Austrian Studies in 1995 from the Austrian Cultural Institute of New York.

Liza Weinstein is Assistant Professor of Sociology at Northeastern University. Her research and teaching interests include urban political economy and the politics of residential informality in India and in comparative perspective. She is the author of several articles and chapters and is currently preparing a manuscript on the policies and practices of slum housing in Mumbai. She received her Ph.D. from the University of Chicago in 2009.

Cindy Hing-Yuk Wong is Associate Professor and Chair of the Department of Media Cultures at the College of Staten Island, City University of New York. Trained in anthropology, production, and communications (Ph.D. University of Pennsylvania), she has worked on grassroots media and Chinese transnationalism and has recently published *Global Film Festivals* (Rutgers University Press, 2011).

INDEX

ACKNOWLEDGMENTS

This volume orginated from a panel organized at the Washington AAA in 2005 by Marina Peterson and Sareeta Amrute entitled "Center, Symbol, Site: Reexamining Downtown." McDonogh at that time was a discussant alongside Travis A. Jackson. We would like to thank all the participants who created the path that led to this project in that invigorating session that spurred discussion of space, conflict, centrality, and globalization.

Three years later, McDonogh and Peterson organized a new panel that included most of the contributors here, with Robert Rotenberg and Ted Bestor as discussants. Again we enjoyed a lively session that led to shared ideas and a commitment to move ahead with an edited volume. While Bob turned his comments into the paper we now include here, we want to thank Ted for his insight and support, as well as acknowledge the paper of Laurie Hart on Marseilles that could not be included in this collection.

At that time we recognized our concentration in major cities of North America and Europe and sought to expand our global vision. This brought in important contributions from Weinstein, Kanna, Bissell, Hourani, Lloyd and Christens, and Maza and Magrinyà that have enriched our discussion. Over the past two years, the addition of such new papers and the discussion, revision, and support from these and other ongoing contributors has made this an especially rewarding project.

As we moved forward with the project, we also enjoyed the commentary and support of Peter Agree at the University of Pennsylvania Press, our extremely thorough outside reviewers, and series editor Eugenie Birch, who contributed some especially important ideas on readership and scope to our revisions.

Finally, of course, we recognize that this long term project has drawn on the experience and support of colleagues for all of us, as acknowledged in individual essays. As editors, we recognize the support of our individual

institutions, Ohio University (Peterson) and Bryn Mawr College (Mc-
Donogh). In addition, McDonogh would like to thank his colleagues Juan
Arbona, Jeff Cohen, Gaspar Maza, and Barbara Lane with whom he has
discussed this project, the library staff at Bryn Mawr College, Pam Cohen
and Margaret Kelly who have been invaluable in the mechanics of the process, and his family collaborators Cindy Wong, Larissa McDonogh-Wong
and Graciela McDonogh-Wong. Peterson would like to thank the Center for
International Studies at Ohio University for funding for research that helped
enrich the project, Saskia Sassen for her enthusiasm, John Malpede for ongoing conversation and collaboration that has been crucial for thinking
about downtowns, and Hamza Walker for words (literally) and for the rich-
ness of life.